OSPF

Anatomy of an Internet Routing Protocol

OSPF

Anatomy of an
Internet Routing Protocol

John T. Moy

▲
▼▼

Addison-Wesley

An Imprint of Addison Wesley Longman, Inc.

Reading, Massachusetts ▪ Harlow, England ▪ Menlo Park, California
Berkeley, California ▪ Don Mills, Ontario ▪ Sydney
Bonn ▪ Amsterdam ▪ Tokyo ▪ Mexico City

Many of the designations used by manufacturers and sellers to distinguish their products are claimed as trademarks. Where those designations appear in this book, and Addison-Wesley was aware of a trademark claim, the designations have been printed in initial capital letters or all capital letters.

The author and publisher have taken care in preparation of this book, but make no expressed or implied warranty of any kind and assume no responsibility for errors or omissions. No liability is assumed for incidental or consequential damages in connection with or arising out of the use of the information or programs contained herein.

The publisher offers discounts on this book when ordered in quantity for special sales. For more information please contact:

Corporate & Professional Publishing Group
Addison-Wesley Publishing Company
One Jacob Way
Reading, Massachusetts 01867

Library of Congress Cataloging-in-Publication Data

Moy, John T.
    OSPF : anatomy of an Internet routing protocol / John T. Moy.
      p.   cm.
    Includes bibliographical references and index.
    ISBN 0-201-63472-4
    1. Internet (Computer network)   2. Computer network protocols.
    3. Computer network architectures.   I. Title.
    TK5105.875.I57M69   1998
    004.6' 6—dc2l   97-39463
                                                 CIP

Cover art: Turner & Devries, The Image Bank

ISBN 0-201-63472-4
Text printed on recycled paper
1 2 3 4 5 6 7 8 9—MA—0201009998
First printing, January 1998

Contents

List of Tables

List of Figures

Preface

Introduction

The Internet is a global communications network. With connections in more than 100 countries, tens of millions of people use the Internet for business, education, and recreation. Electronic commerce is beginning on the Internet as businesses connect to sell their products and services. Academics collaborate over the Internet by exchanging electronic mail. People can converse using Internet phones, send faxes, participate in online chats and bulletin boards, play multiuser games, and experiment with virtual environments.

Special-purpose computers called routers connect the Internet together. As data is forwarded from one place in the Internet to another, it is the routers that make the decisions as to where and how the data is forwarded. The protocols that dynamically inform the routers of the paths that the data should take are called routing protocols. It is the job of these protocols to react quickly to changes in the Internet's infrastructure, such as transmission lines going in and out of service, routers crashing, changes in network policies, and so on.

Routing is what makes the Internet tick. Although many users of the Internet and the World Wide Web are unaware of the machinery underlying the network applications, routing is an interesting but complicated subject. Routing protocols are sophisticated distributed algorithms that must also be extremely robust to keep a large, decentralized network like the Internet running smoothly.

Audience

This book is for students of data communications, TCP/IP network administrators, protocol designers, developers of routing protocol software, and other professionals involved in the design, development, and management of TCP/IP networks. The book is a practical, hands-on description of Internet routing rather than a theoretical treatment. Although we describe how the various protocols were intended to work, we also describe how well the design has translated into practice. Internet protocol design is a practical undertaking itself, with efficiency of implementation often dictating design choices. For this reason, this book gives an in-depth treatment of how a router really works. Instead of just describing the algorithms, the book goes beyond to show how the algorithms are implemented.

We often present ideas in a historical context, showing how Internet protocols have evolved. This is done for two reasons. First, you can learn a lot from the mistakes (and successes) of the past. Second, in order to participate in Internet discussion groups, many of which are dominated by old-timers, it is good to have some context.

This book is not an elementary introduction to TCP/IP and its routing. Instead we assume that you have some familiarity with the TCP/IP protocol suite and some exposure to the basic concepts of routing. These assumptions allow us to explore many of the facets of Internet routing in greater detail than possible in an introductory text.

Organization of This Book

This book is organized into five parts. Part I sets the groundwork for a discussion of Internet routing. After a brief description of how routing fits together with the rest of the Internet's protocols, Chapter 1 describes in depth how a router forwards packets. This discussion naturally leads to an explanation of IP addressing and CIDR, as well as of the interaction of hosts and routers. Internet routing protocols are introduced in Chapter 2, beginning with a treatment of the end product of all routing protocols: the router's routing table. Chapter 2 ends with an overview of the Internet's routing architecture and the two main routing technologies in use in today's Internet: Distance Vector and link-state algorithms.

Part II describes the Internet's OSPF routing protocol. We start in Chapter 3 with an explanation of why the OSPF protocol was developed in the first place. Chapter 4 discusses the basics of link-state routing; Chapter 5, how OSPF behaves over various subnet technologies; Chapter 6, its use of hierarchical routing; and Chapter 7, extensions to OSPF. Each chapter not only describes how OSPF works but also explains why it works that way. We explore the reasons behind OSPF's design decisions and how the OSPF protocol has evolved to keep pace with the rapidly changing Internet environment. Part II concludes with an OSPF FAQ (Chapter 8).

Part III (Chapters 9 and 10) describes TCP/IP multicast routing, including broadcast and multicast forwarding, the MBONE, and the two distinct types of multicast routing protocols: source-based trees and shared-tree algorithms. As we did with unicast routing, we go further into the subject of multicast routing through the examination of a particular multicast routing protocol: the Multicast Extensions to OSPF (MOSPF).

Part IV covers the configuration and management of Internet routing. The configuration and management of OSPF is explained in detail in Chapter 11. Chapter 12 describes the tools used to monitor and debug routing in a TCP/IP network. For each tool, we describe its use, how it works, and its advantages and drawbacks.

Part V is a comparison of Internet routing protocols. Chapter 13 compares and contrasts the routing protocols in use in the Internet: RIP, OSPF, BGP, IGRP, and IS-IS. In Chapter 14, we examine the available multicast protocols: DVMRP, MOSPF, PIM Dense and Sparse, and CBT.

Following Chapter 14 is an extensive bibliography arranged and numbered in alphabetical order. Within the text, the citation [85], for example, refers to item 85 in the bibliography.

Companion Book: *OSPF Complete Implementation*

The companion book *OSPF Complete Implementation*, in keeping with the Internet tradition that reveres "working code" over all else, explores even further the mechanics of Internet routing through examination of a real, working OSPF implementation. The book contains a complete implementation of OSPF on CD. Written in C++, the OSPF implementation is intended to be portable to a wide range of environments. Two sample ports are included: an OSPF routing daemon (called **ospfd**) for FreeBSD 2.1 and an OSPF routing simulator that can be run on Windows 95. The OSPF implementation has been developed using publicly available tools.

Acknowledgments

I would like to thank the technical reviewers who improved this book through their thoughtful and timely reviews: Ran Atkinson, Eural Authement, Fred Baker, Howard Berkowitz, Jeffrey Burgan, Joel Halpern, Mukesh Kacker, Robert Minnear, Jim Reid, and W. Richard Stevens. Thanks also to Tim Stoddard and the Arkansas Public School Computer Network (APSCN) for letting me collect OSPF statistics on the APSCN network and use that network as an example of OSPF configuration in Chapter 11, OSPF Management. Thanks to S. Randall McLamb for drawing the figures.

I would also like to acknowledge the help of my editors at Addison Wesley Longman over the long life of this project: Carol Long, Karen Gettman, and Mary Harrington.

And special thanks to my wife, Sonya Keene, who designed the book, edited rough drafts, created the index, and gave encouragement while this book was being written.

J.M.
October, 1997

Part I

Internet Routing Overview

In Part I, we lay the groundwork for an examination of Internet routing. Chapter 1, Role of Routers in the Internet, introduces routing through a detailed examination of the special-purpose computers executing these protocols: the Internet's routers. The interaction between hosts and routers, IP options, the ICMP protocol, and CIDR addressing are covered. The chapter ends with a short synopsis of the next generation of the IP protocol: IPv6.

Chapter 2, Internet Routing Protocols, begins to describe the routing protocols themselves. First, we describe a router's routing table, which is the forwarding database that all routing protocols attempt to build. We explain the Internet's routing architecture. The two basic routing technologies in use in the Internet, link-state and Distance Vector, are then compared and contrasted.

1

Role of Routers in the Internet

The Internet is a packet-switching network that enables its attached computers—the PC on your desk, the high-end workstation that enables you to enroll in your local university over the Web, the mainframe that checks your credit card balance, the supercomputer that you use for simulations in your physics labs—to exchange information. This information is encoded as long strings of bits called *packets*. As these packets travel through the Internet on their way to their destination computers, routing decisions are made: Should the packet be sent this way or that way? The devices making these decisions are themselves computers, called *routers*. The distributed algorithms that the routers run among themselves in order to make the correct routing decisions are called *routing protocols*. These routing protocols, and, in particular, the specific routing protocol called the *Open Shortest Path First* (OSPF) protocol, are the main subject of this book.

A simple example is shown in Figure 1.1. Five routers, A through E, are pictured, interconnected via telephone lines of various speeds. Suppose that workstation S1 sends a packet for delivery to workstation D1. Router A receives the packet and then has to make a decision: Should it forward the packet to router B, C, or D? The routing protocols that are being run among the five routers will give A the answer: Forward the packet to C over the optimal path to the destination consisting of two T1 lines. Later, if router C goes out of service, the routing protocols will come into play again, telling A that the new best path is now via the slower-speed lines through router D.

Of course, the Internet is much, much larger and more complicated than our simple example. Starting with the ARPANET network in 1969 as a network of four

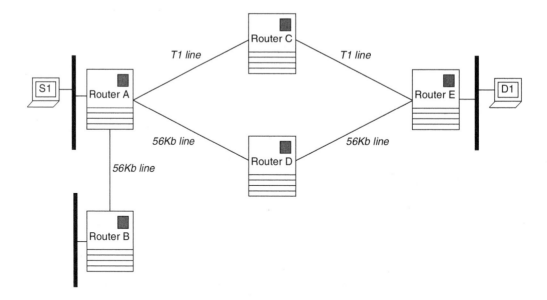

Figure 1.1 Simple routing example. A routing protocol would select the higher-speed path through router C. When routing protocols detect that router C is out of service, the slower-speed path through router D would then be selected.

packet-switching computers, today's Internet has tens of thousands of routers, operated by various Internet Service Providers (ISPs) and various academic, research, government, and commercial organizations. These routers are manufactured by a variety of vendors, using varied hardware and software. In this environment, routing becomes not only a technical problem but also a cooperative management problem.

In this introductory chapter, we concentrate on the role of the routers in the Internet. First, we examine how the protocols used by routers fit in with the rest of the Internet's protocols. Routing protocols enable routers to find paths from Internet sources to Internet destinations. But how does a router use these paths to forward packets? We explain the forwarding process within a router in great detail, including how routers interact with the packets' sources and destinations. We also explain the organization of Internet addresses, which are the instructions carried within the packet to identify the packet's destination.

1.1   The Internet Protocol Suite

In order to achieve the transfer of packets between computers connected to the Internet and between the routers making up the Internet itself, certain rules about packet format and processing must be followed. These rules are called *protocols*. The suite of protocols used by the Internet is called TCP/IP.

Internet protocols have been separated into layers in an attempt to simplify protocol design. Ideally, one could replace the protocol at one layer while leaving the other protocol layers in place. These layers provide a useful reference but should not be taken as hard-and-fast boundaries on protocol design. Internet protocols sometimes blur the layer distinctions or violate them outright for reasons of efficiency. The layering of Internet protocols can be viewed in terms of the ubiquitous seven-layer OSI reference model, as displayed in Figure 1.2.

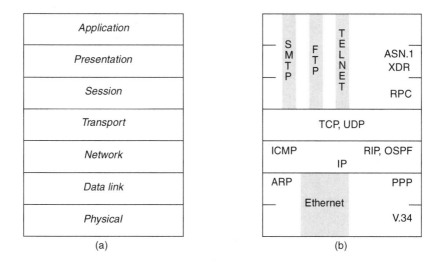

Figure 1.2 The seven-layer OSI reference model (a), together with the TCP/IP equivalents (b).

The computers communicating over the Internet are sometimes also called *hosts,* or *end stations*; these computers and the Internet's routers are interconnected using a wide variety of link technologies. Telephone lines, Ethernet segments, packet radio, and satellite links are some of the traditional Internet link types. Nowadays many other link types can be found, including Frame Relay, ATM, FDDI, IEEE 802.5 Token Ring, SMDS, and AppleTalk segments. Methods for running the TCP/IP protocols over each of these link types have been defined. Indeed, it is a point of pride among Internet protocol designers that TCP will run over everything, including "tin cans connected by string."

When viewing the layers of a protocol, one commonly speaks of a *protocol stack*. In the OSI reference model, the lowest layer of the stack consists of the *physical protocols*; the highest layer, the *application protocols*. You should think of packetized data from a network application being handed down through the layers in the source host, each layer prepending a header of its own. Figure 1.3 shows the headers that would be prepended to the Internet's TELNET application's data before the data is transmitted onto an Ethernet segment. At the destination host, the headers are then stripped before handing the data to the destination's application entity.

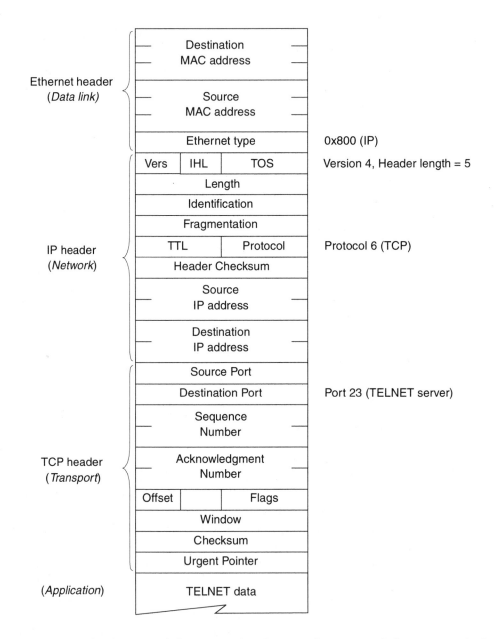

Figure 1.3 Internet headers prepended to TELNET data, from user client to server, before it is transmitted onto an Ethernet segment.

Each layer of the protocol stack usually provides multiplexing services so that multiple instances of the next-higher level can be run simultaneously. For example, a link's data-link protocol will allow packet multiplexing based on packet type so that multiple protocol stacks (for example, both TCP/IP and Novell's IPX protocols) can be supported on a single link.

The OSI reference model is fairly useful in discussing Internet protocols from the physical to the transport layers. However, not all of the Internet's protocols fit into such neat layers. For example, the Internet's Address Resolution Protocol (ARP) [192] straddles the network and data-link layers. ARP is used to map IP addresses into data-link addresses so the correct data-link headers can be built as a packet is forwarded hop by hop from one link to another. Also, some of the higher layers of the OSI reference model, such as the session and presentation layers, have little relevance to the Internet protocol suite.

The discussion in this chapter relates to point-to-point, or *unicast*, communication over the Internet. The Internet and the TCP/IP protocol suite also support *multicast* communication—the ability for a host to send a single packet for delivery to multiple destination hosts. Parts of the unicast TCP/IP stack have multicast equivalents. We defer further discussion of multicast until Chapter 9, Internet Multicast Routing.

Physical Layer

The *physical layer* specifies how the bits of the packet are physically encoded when transmitted and received over a given link technology. Bits are typically encoded as electronic or light pulses, organized so that transmission errors can be detected. For example, the physical layer on telephone lines is defined by various modem standards, such as V.34.

Data-Link Layer

The *data-link layer* specifies how packets are transmitted and received over a given link technology. Services provided at this layer include identification of end stations on the link, specification of maximum packet size supported (the Maximum Transmission Unit, or MTU), and, sometimes, transmission-priority schemes. For example, the Point-to-Point Protocol (PPP) [232] is the data-link protocol commonly used in the Internet over telephone lines. Often the data-link protocols are specified together with physical protocols, as in Ethernet. The 14-byte Ethernet data-link header provides a 6-byte source address (IEEE MAC address), a 6-byte destination address, and a 2-byte Ethernet type for packet multiplexing.

Network Layer

The *network layer* is responsible for forwarding packets across multiple links (that is, through one or more routers) when a packet's source and destination are on different links, or *network segments*. Since this book is about Internet routing, most of the discussion in this book is limited to issues within the Internet's network layer.

Usually a network-layer addressing scheme is provided, enabling the routers to figure out which network segment the destination host belongs to. Sometimes a fragmentation-and-reassembly capability is provided, allowing the network layer to accommodate, transparently, links supporting different maximum packet sizes. Dynamic routing protocols, which allow the routers to automatically find paths to network-layer destinations, are also usually considered part of the network layer, as are protocols controlling the interaction between hosts and routers.

The Internet's network layer is called the *Internet Protocol* (IP) [195]. Network-layer packets are called *IP packets,* or *IP datagrams.* The *IP addresses* contained in IP packets are 32 bits long (see Section 1.2.1). Each network segment is assigned a range of IP addresses, represented as an address prefix. Internet routers route packets to these prefixes instead of to individual hosts (see Section 2.1). When a host is attached to a network segment, or has an *interface* to the segment, it is given a unique IP address in that segment's address range. Hosts with multiple interfaces have multiple IP addresses. IP has many routing protocols, including OSPF, RIP, and BGP, which are discussed later in this book. The *Internet Control Message Protocol* (ICMP) ([57], [165], [194]) allows hosts to find the routers attached to their segments and provides certain diagnostic capabilities to the hosts when the routers are unable to deliver packets to addressed destinations.

Transport Layer

The *transport layer* provides an end-to-end connection between applications running in the source and destination hosts. Services in this layer often include error detection, error correction, and data sequencing. The TCP/IP protocol suite has two transport protocols. The *Transmission Control Protocol* (TCP) [197] provides a reliable byte stream between applications. Major advances in TCP's congestion avoidance and control [115] have allowed the Internet to continue to prosper in recent years. The User Datagram Protocol (UDP) [198] provides connection without reliability guarantees and is normally used by relatively stateless applications, such as Sun's Network File System (NFS) [29].

Higher Layers

The *session layer* provides mechanisms for starting and stopping transport connections. The *presentation layer* provides standard ways for encoding and representing an application's data types. By and large, the Internet does not have explicit session- and presentation-layer protocols; instead these functions are usually built directly into Internet applications. There are, however, some exceptions. The Internet's Remote Procedure Call (RPC) protocol [234] fits into the session layer, and some Internet applications use the ASN.1 [113] or External Data Representation (XDR) [235] protocols, which fit into the presentation layer.

The *application layer* can be thought of as the protocols that implement the kinds of network services that you would expect from any computer's operating system. In the Internet, application protocols include the Simple Mail Transfer Protocol (SMTP) [196]; file-transfer protocols, such as FTP [199] and TFTP [233]; and the protocol for remote login, TELNET [200].

The Internet's Domain Name System (DNS) [163] also probably fits into the application layer. It is the DNS that converts human-friendly host names, such as `www.altavista.com`, into destination IP addresses that can be routed by the Internet's routers at the network layer.

1.2   Forwarding IP Datagrams

The various network segments making up the Internet are interconnected by routers. A router receives an IP packet on one of its interfaces and then *forwards* the packet out another of its interfaces (or possibly more than one, if the packet is a multicast packet), based on the contents of the IP header. As the packet is forwarded hop by hop, the packet's network-layer header (IP header) remains relatively unchanged, containing the complete set of instructions on how to forward the packet. However, the data-link headers and physical-transmission schemes may change radically at each hop in order to match the changing media types. Let's use an example to examine the IP forwarding process in more detail.

Suppose that the router receives a packet from one of its attached Ethernet segments. The router's Ethernet adapter has indicated the size of the packet received; the packet may look like the packet pictured in Figure 1.3. The router first looks at the packet's data-link header, which in this case is Ethernet. If the Ethernet type is set to 0x800, indicating an IP packet, the Ethernet header is stripped from the packet, and the IP header is examined. Before discarding the Ethernet header, the router notes the length of the Ethernet packet and whether the packet had been multicast/broadcast on the Ethernet segment (by checking a particular bit in the Destination MAC address). In some cases, routers will refuse to forward data-link multicasts/broadcasts, as described later.

The router then verifies the contents of the IP header by checking the Version, Internet Header Length (IHL), Length, and Header Checksum fields. The Version must be equal to 4 (in this book, we mean IPv4 when we say IP; a new version of IP, IPv6, is being developed, however, and is discussed in Section 1.3). The Header Length must be greater than or equal to the minimum IP header size (five 32-bit words). The length of the IP packet (Length), expressed in bytes, must also be larger than the minimum header size. In addition, the router should check that the entire packet has been received, by checking the IP length against the size of the received Ethernet packet.

Finally, to verify that none of the fields of the header have been corrupted, the 16-bit ones-complement checksum of the entire IP header is calculated and verified to be equal to 0xffff. If any of these basic checks fail, the packet is deemed so malformed that it is discarded without even sending an error indication back to the packet's originator.

Next, the router verifies that the TTL field is greater than 1. The purpose of the TTL field is to make sure that packets do not circulate forever when there are routing loops. The host sets the packet's TTL field to be greater than or equal to the maximum number of router hops expected on the way to the destination. Each router decrements the TTL field by 1 when forwarding; when the TTL field is decremented to 0, the packet is discarded, and an ICMP TTL Exceeded message is sent back to the host. On decrementing the TTL, the router must adjust the packet's Header Checksum.

The router then looks at the Destination IP address. The address indicates a single destination host (unicast), a group of destination hosts (multicast), or all hosts on a given network segment (broadcast). Multicast and broadcast forwarding are discussed in Chapter 9, Internet Multicast Routing.

Unicast packets are discarded if they were received as data-link broadcasts or as multicasts; otherwise, multiple routers may attempt to forward the packet, possibly contributing to a packet proliferation called a *broadcast storm*. In unicast forwarding, the Destination IP address is used as a key for the routing table lookup (Section 2.1). The best-matching routing table entry is returned, indicating whether to forward the packet and, if so, the interface to forward the packet out of and the IP address of the next IP router (if any) in the packet's path.

If the unicast packet is too large to be sent out the outgoing interface in one piece (that is, Length is greater than the outgoing interface's Maximum Transmission Unit, or MTU), the router attempts to split the packet into smaller pieces, called *fragments*. Fragmentation can affect performance adversely [125]. Hosts may instead wish to prevent fragmentation by setting the Don't Fragment (DF) bit in the Fragmentation field. In this case, the router does not fragment but instead drops the packet and sends an ICMP Destination Unreachable (subtype Fragmentation Needed and DF Set) message back to the host. The host uses this message to calculate the minimum MTU along the packet's path [165], which is in turn used to size future packets.

The router then prepends the appropriate data-link header for the outgoing interface. The IP address of the next hop is converted to a data-link address, usually using ARP [192] or a variant of ARP, such as Inverse ARP [25] for Frame Relay subnets. The router then sends the packet to the next hop, where the process is repeated.

Modification of Forwarding

The basic IP forwarding process described earlier can be modified in a number of ways, resulting in data packets' taking different paths through the network. First, a router may have multiple paths to a destination. These paths can be used to spread out traffic to a destination prefix across alternative links, called *multipath routing,* or *load balancing.* The end result of multipath routing is that more bandwidth is available for traffic to the destination. When there are multiple paths to a destination prefix, the router's routing table lookup will return multiple next hops. Which of these next hops is used for a particular packet depends on the implementation. Routing table entries represent the route to a given address prefix; the same routing table entry may be used by many TCP connections. Routers generally want to guarantee that packets belonging to a given TCP connection always travel over the same path; if they were sent over multiple paths, reordering of the TCP packets is likely leading to reduced TCP performance. For this reason, routers typically use a hash function of some of the TCP connection identifiers (source and destination IP addresses) to choose among the multiple next hops.

The Type of Service (TOS) field in the packet's IP header can also affect the packet's path. Five TOS values have been defined for IP: normal service, minimize monetary cost, maximize reliability, maximize throughput, and minimize delay [3]. A packet's TOS designation would help the router choose an appropriate path for a given packet. For example, packets requesting to maximize throughput might be transmitted over high-bandwidth satellite links, whereas these very same links would be avoided by packets requesting to minimize delay. To implement TOS routing, a router would keep separate routing tables for each TOS value. When forwarding a packet, the router would first choose a routing table, based on the packet's TOS, and would then perform the normal routing table lookup.

The TOS bits in the IP header should not be confused with the IP precedence bits, which are collocated in the same byte of the IP header with the TOS bits. A packet's IP precedence label does not affect the path of a packet but instead specifies transmission priority at each router hop. The precedence bits remain in IPv6 (see Section 1.3), recast as packet priority.

TOS routing has rarely been used in the Internet. Only two Internet routing protocols, OSPF and IS-IS (Section 13.5), have ever supported calculation of separate paths for each TOS value. Because there has been very little deployment of TOS routing, TOS has recently been removed from the OSPF specification [178]. For the same reason, TOS has also been omitted from IPv6.

An application can also modify the handling of its packets by extending the IP headers of its packets with one or more *IP options*. IP options are used infrequently for regular data packets, because most Internet routers are heavily optimized for forwarding packets having no options. It is not uncommon for a router's performance to degrade by an order of magnitude when forwarding packets with IP options. Most IP options (such as the *record-route* and *timestamp* options) are used to aid in statistics collection but do not affect a packet's path. However, the *strict-source route* and the *loose-source route* options can be used by an application to control the path its packets take.

The strict-source route option is used to specify the exact path that the packet will take, router by router. The utility of strict-source route is limited by the maximum size of the IP header (60 bytes), which limits to 9 the number of hops specified by the strict-source route option. The loose-source route is used to specify a set of intermediate routers (again, up to 9) through which the packet must go on the way to its destination. Loose-source routing is used mainly for diagnostic purposes, such as an aid to debugging Internet routing problems (see Sections 12.4 and 12.5). Loose-source routing also has been used in the past as a *tunneling* (see Section 1.2.3) mechanism.

Some network operators consider IP source routing a security hole. If security is being provided through address filtering, the problem with source routing is that the ultimate destination of the packet is buried within the IP options field. For this reason, some network operators configure their routers to drop packets containing the source routing options.

Sending ICMP Errors

TCP/IP hosts get information from routers via the Internet Control Message Protocol (ICMP) [194]. There are ICMP messages to discover routers (ICMP Router Discovery messages), the best router to use for a particular destination (ICMP Redirect messages), and whether a router and/or host is reachable (ICMP Echo and Echo Reply messages). There are also ICMP error messages that a router uses to inform a host that something is wrong with a particular packet the host has sent. The router drops the packet with the error, and the ICMP error message returned contains the beginning of the packet causing the error (at least through the TCP or UDP header), giving the host (or the person behind the host) a chance to fix the problem.

If the IP header of the packet is malformed, the router sends an ICMP Parameter Problem message back to the host. If the packet's IP destination is unreachable, an ICMP Destination Unreachable message is returned. The common cause for this message is that there is no path to the destination host, but Destination Unreachable messages also are used to indicate that the peer application is not available in the destination host (subtype Protocol or Port Unreachable) or that the source host has prevented fragmentation and the packet is too big to be sent over the next link (subtype Fragmentation Needed and DF Set). If the packet has already traveled the maximum number of hops as originally specified by the host in the packet's TTL field, an ICMP TTL Exceeded message is returned.

Routers must be careful that the sending of ICMP errors does not adversely affect the network. For this reason, ICMP errors are never sent in response to IP broadcast or multicast packets or to packets that were received as data-link multicast/broadcasts; in all these cases, to send an error would risk having one packet generate many ICMP errors in response. In order to avoid an unending stream of ICMP errors, routers never send ICMP error messages in response to ICMP messages themselves; the one exception is that ICMP errors are sent in response to ICMP Echo or Echo Reply packets that have problems. Also, routers no longer send ICMP Source Quench messages. These messages were originally intended to indicate network congestion to hosts but were found to do more harm than good by adding more packets to an already congested network.

ICMP errors are intended to be for diagnostic purposes only and are generally not supposed to cause the host to take specific actions. For example, receipt of a Destination Unreachable message should not cause a host to reset TCP connections [22]. However, ICMP error messages sometimes are used to implement network functionality, or diagnostic tools. Hosts can discover the MTU available to a destination via the reception of ICMP Destination Unreachable messages (subtype Fragmentation Needed and DF Set) (see [165]). The network utility most commonly used to track down network routing problems, `traceroute` (Section 12.5), is implemented through clever manipulation of ICMP TTL Exceeded messages. It has even been suggested that ICMP Source Quench messages be reenabled in the Internet's routers to enhance congestion-control algorithms [75].

Add-Ons

Besides dynamically finding the paths for datagrams to take toward their destinations, routers also implement other functions. For example, routers play an important role in TCP/IP congestion-control algorithms. When a TCP/IP network is congested, routers cannot forward all the packets they receive. Simply by discarding some of their received packets, routers provide feedback to TCP congestion algorithms, such as the TCP slow-start algorithm [115], [239]. Early Internet routers simply started discarding excess packets instead of queuing them onto already full transmit queues; these routers were eventually termed *drop-tail gateways*. However, this discard behavior was found to be unfair, favoring applications that send larger and more bursty data streams. Modern Internet routers employ more sophisticated, and fairer, drop algorithms, such as *Random Early Detection* (RED) [77].

Algorithms also have been developed that allow routers to organize their transmit queues so as to give resource guarantees to certain classes of traffic or to specific applications. For example, a router may be configured to dedicate half of its link bandwidth to interactive traffic or to reserve 5 kilobits/sec on certain links for an Internet video conference. These algorithms, called queuing, or link scheduling, algorithms, include *Weighted Fair Queuing* (WFQ) [64] and *Class Based Queuing* (CBQ) [76]. A protocol called *RSVP* [266] has been developed that allows hosts to dynamically signal to routers which applications should get special queuing treatment. However, RSVP has not yet been deployed, with some people arguing that queuing preference could more simply be indicated by using the precedence bits in the IP header [45].

Often other functions, less directly related to packet forwarding, get incorporated into TCP/IP routers. The reason for modifying the routers is usually that there are fewer routers than hosts, and router software is typically much easier to upgrade. Examples of these nonforwarding functions include

- *Security functions*. Companies often put a router between their company network and the Internet and then configure the router to prevent unauthorized access to the company's resources from the Internet. This configuration may consist of certain patterns (for example, source and destination address and TCP port) whose matching packets should not be forwarded or of more complex rules to deal with protocols that vary their port numbers over time, such as the File Transfer Protocol (FTP) [199]. Such routers are called *firewalls* [41]. Similarly, Internet Service Providers often configure their routers to verify the source address in all packets received from the ISP's customers. This foils certain security attacks and makes other attacks easier to trace back to their source. Similarly, ISPs providing dial-in access to their routers typically use *Remote Authentication Dial-In User Service* (RADIUS) [214] to verify the identity of the person dialing in.

- *Packet tracing.* People often use their routers to collect packet traces, in order to diagnose network problems. With an implementation of the *Remote Monitoring MIB* (RMON) [256], a router can be turned into a network analyzer, although usually one with considerably less function and performance than a dedicated analyzer, such as a Network General Sniffer (see Section 12.8).

- *Statistics collection.* Some people collect traffic statistics on their routers: how many packets and bytes are forwarded per each IP source and destination combination. This may be too fine a granularity, and statistics may be kept instead per source and destination Autonomous System (AS, the administrative groupings of routers within the Internet, as described in Section 2.2) or simply per receiving and transmitting interface on the router. These statistics are used for future capacity planning. However, in the future, such statistics may be used by ISPs to implement usage-based charging schemes for their customers or as a way to implement settlement schemes between the ISPs themselves.

Finding the First-Hop Router

We have described how routers forward IP packets. However, to get the ball rolling, the source host must find a router to send the packet to in the first place. This has always been a weak spot in the IP protocol suite. IP does not have a good way to find the best first-hop router to use for a particular destination and for a long time had no way to dynamically find any router.

Let us first step back a bit. How does a host determine whether a router has to get involved at all? The host checks to see whether the destination belongs to one of its directly attached network segments. For example, suppose that a host has a single interface onto a network segment with address of 128.186.1/24 (see Section 1.2.1). This means that all hosts with addresses 128.186.1.x also are directly attached to the segment. Packets can be sent directly to these hosts without using a router. However, if the host wants to send a packet to 192.9.32.1, it must first send the packet to a router attached to the 128.186.1/24 segment.

Traditionally a host would have a configured set of one or more default gateways (*gateway* being the previous term for what we now call a router) to send the packet to. Out-of-service default gateways would be pruned from the list by periodically sending *ICMP Echoes* to the list and checking for *ICMP Echo Replies* (that is, *pinging* the list). In 1991 ICMP Router Discovery [57] was developed, allowing hosts to dynamically find routers by listening for ICMP Router Discovery messages.

However, the configured default, or discovered, router may not be the best router to use for the given destination. For example, in Figure 1.4, the router 128.186.1.254 is on the best path to the destination 192.9.32.1. If the host's default router is 128.186.1.253, the packet will transit the network segment twice, first to the default router and then to 128.186.1.254 on the way to the destination. IP removes this extra hop via ICMP. The default router, realizing that it is forwarding the packet back onto the segment where it originated, sends an ICMP Redirect message back to the host (128.186.1.1), informing the host that future packets to 192.9.32.1 should be sent directly to the first-hop router 128.186.1.253. The host then stores this information in its routing table. Such redirect information must be timed out and refreshed periodically lest the disappearance of the first-hop router (which possibly could be detected by ICMP router discovery, or `ping`) cause the destination to be permanently unreachable.

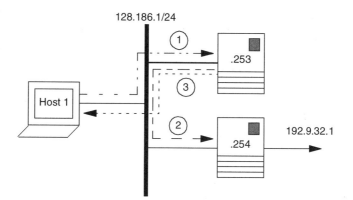

Figure 1.4 ICMP Redirect messages remove extra router hops. (1) Host sends packet to suboptimal first-hop router; (2) that router forwards the packet on to the real next hop, and (3) sends an ICMP Redirect back to the host so that future packets will be sent directly to best next hop (.254).

Unfortunately redirect timeouts are often quite long, causing transport connections to fail before old redirect information is removed. For this reason, router vendors have developed protocols whereby another router can take the place of the failed router (assuming its IP and MAC addresses) without the host's knowledge. One such example is Cisco Systems' "hot standby router protocol" [136]. Another example is the Virtual Router Redundancy Protocol [100] being developed within the Internet Engineering Task Force (IETF). This protocol introduces the concept of a "virtual IP address." This virtual IP address can be used as a next hop for a segment's hosts, and the responsibility for the virtual IP address is dynamically allocated to one of the segment's routers via an election algorithm.

Another common method for finding the best router for a particular destination is to have the host participate in the IP routing protocols (sometimes referred to as *wiretapping*, since the host is really only eavesdropping on the routers' routing protocols), although this solution is discouraged by IP purists. RIP (Section 13.1) is commonly used for this purpose, with most UNIX systems shipped running the `routed` program [222], an implementation of RIP. The OSPF implementation included in the companion to this book (*OSPF Complete Implementation*) allows hosts to wiretap the OSPF protocol.

1.2.1   IP Addresses

An IP packet is routed on the basis of the 32-bit destination IP address found in the packet's IP header. IP addresses are generally represented in *dotted decimal notation:* the decimal value of each byte of the address, separated by periods. For example, the IP address whose hexadecimal value is 0xc0090102 is written as 192.9.1.2.

By looking at the IP address, a router can determine quickly whether it is a unicast, broadcast, or multicast address, as shown in Table 1.1. The address space is broken into three chunks: the majority used for unicast, a range of multicast addresses (see Chapter 9, Internet Multicast Routing), and a small portion at the top of the address space that is reserved for future applications. There are also some special-purpose addresses. A host uses 0.0.0.0 as the IP source in its packets when the host is attempting to learn its IP address through the BOOTP [53] or DHCP [67] protocols, for example. Packets sent onto a network segment with IP destination set to the broadcast address 255.255.255.255 will be received by all other IP hosts and routers on the segment; this feature is used by such routing protocols as RIP to disseminate routing updates (Section 13.1).

Table 1.1 Division of IP Address Space by Function

Address Range	Address Functionality
1.0.0.0–223.255.255.255	IP unicast addresses
224.0.0.0–239.255.255.255	IP multicast addresses
240.0.0.0–255.255.255.254	Reserved for future use
0.0.0.0	Specifies unknown IP address
255.255.255.255	Local segment broadcast

A TCP/IP network segment (for example, an Ethernet segment, FDDI ring, or Frame Relay subnet) is assigned a set of globally unique unicast addresses by assigning a unicast *address prefix* to the segment. Hosts and router interfaces attaching to the segment are then assigned unicast addresses from the set. For example, the network segment in Figure 1.4 has been assigned the range of addresses 128.186.1.0–128.186.1.255, which is also represented as the address prefix 128.186.1.0/24; the 24 indicates that all addresses in the segment agree in their first 24 bits. This is also sometimes written as the address, mask pair [128.186.1.0, 255.255.255.0], with the 1 bits in the mask representing those bits in the address that stay constant over the segment's addresses. The host and two routers in Figure 1.4 have been assigned addresses from the prefix for their interfaces to the segment (128.186.1.1, 128.186.1.253, and 128.186.1.254, respectively).

The highest address in the prefix is assigned as the broadcast address for the segment. For example, 128.186.1.255 is the broadcast address for the network segment in Figure 1.4. A packet sent to this address will be delivered to all hosts and routers attached to the segment.

As mentioned earlier, TCP/IP routers route to segments. When forwarding a packet, a router looks in its routing table (see Section 2.1) to find the segment to which the packet's destination address belongs and then forwards the packet toward the matching segment. However, it is more correct to say that routers route to prefixes. Routers cannot possibly keep track of every segment in the Internet. Instead a segment's addressing information is aggregated into shorter prefixes at points in the Internet. It is routes to these shorter prefixes, which may have been aggregated up to three or four times from the original segment prefixes, that are kept in the router's routing table.

An example of aggregation is shown in Figure 1.5. Router G is aggregating the addresses of the four segments on its right (128.1.1/24, 128.1.3/24, 128.1.4/24, and 128.1.62/24), advertising instead a single prefix of 128.1/16 to the routers to its left. This means that routers A–F are not aware of the four segments to G's right but instead have a single routing table entry for 128.1/16 pointing (eventually) to router G.

Prior to 1993, prefixes were forced into a small number of fixed-sized lengths, based on address *class* (see Section 1.2.2). When this restriction was lifted, allowing arbitrary prefix lengths, much more aggressive aggregation became possible, allowing for greater conservation of IP address space and a slowing of the growth rate of the Internet core routers' routing tables (see Section 2.1). Routing on arbitrary prefix length became known as *Classless Inter-Domain Routing*, or CIDR [81]. The prefix/length notation, such as 128.186.1.0/24, became known as *CIDR notation*.

A hierarchy of Internet Registries is responsible for assigning the globally unique Internet TCP/IP address space [102]. At the top of the hierarchy is the Internet Assigned Number Authority (IANA), which allocates pieces of the Internet address space to regional Internet Registries. To date, three regional Internet Registries have been established: InterNIC for North America, RIPE NCC for Europe, and APNIC for Asia Pacific. ISPs apply to these regional Internet Registries for blocks of IP addresses. The ISPs in turn assign parts of these address blocks to their customers (businesses, individuals, or smaller ISPs). Termed *provider addressing*, this procedure encourages address aggregation; the ISP can aggregate its customer's addresses and advertise only the larger

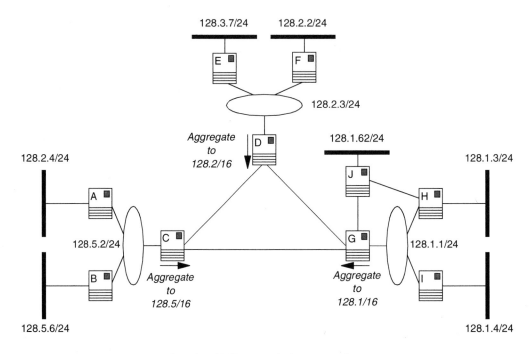

Figure 1.5 Sample TCP/IP network showing prefix aggregation.

address blocks to other ISPs. A side effect of provider addressing occurs when a customer wants to change ISPs. To maintain address aggregation, the customer is encouraged to give back its old addresses and to renumber its network segments into one of its new ISP's address blocks [209]. Hence the assignment of addresses from ISPs to their customers is termed *address lending*. Renumbering TCP/IP network segments can be quite difficult however [19], [74].

Table 1.2 Special-Purpose IP Unicast Addresses

Prefix	Address Range	Reserved Purpose
10/8	10.0.0.0–10.255.255.255	Private Internet addresses
127/8	127.0.0.0–127.255.255.255	Loopback addresses
172.16/12	172.16.0.0–172.31.255.255	Private Internet addresses
192.168/16	192.168.0.0–192.168.255.255	Private Internet addresses

Over time, certain IP unicast addresses have accrued special meaning, as shown in Table 1.2. The development of BSD UNIX and the TCP/IP protocol suite proceeded hand in hand for many years. In particular, many BSD UNIX TCP/IP conventions and protocols have been adopted by the TCP/IP community at large. As one example, the loopback address 127.0.0.1 is used by a BSD system to send IP packets to itself. This led to the entire prefix 127/8 being officially reserved as loopback addresses. Certain other address prefixes have been allocated for use by private TCP/IP internets and are not routable (since they cannot be ensured to be unique) on the public Internet. For private TCP/IP internets that are not attached to the public Internet, the fact that the addresses are not globally routable is of little issue. However, even when using these private, nonunique addresses, private internets may be attached to the public Internet through Network Address Translation (NAT) [79] devices. These devices convert the addresses in packets destined for the public Internet, substituting dynamically assigned globally unique addresses for all private addresses appearing within the packet.

1.2.2   A Short History of Internet Addressing

Internet unicast addresses were not always assigned as arbitrary-length prefixes. In the beginning, the Internet address space was carved up into fixed networks of three sizes: *Class A, B, and C networks.* Class A networks, which we would now call a CIDR prefix of length 8, could contain more than 16 million hosts. Similarly each Class B network was a CIDR prefix of length 16 containing more than 65,000 hosts, and each Class C network was a CIDR prefix of length 24 containing up to 254 hosts. Whether any particular address belonged to a Class A, B, or C network could be determined quickly by looking at the address's first byte, as shown in Table 1.3. Class D addresses were later assigned for IP multicast, with Class E remaining reserved for future use.

Table 1.3 Historical Class Division of IP Address Space

First Byte	Class	Example
0–127	A	16/8
128–191	B	128.186/16
192–223	C	192.9.1/24
224–239	D	224.1.1.1 (multicast)
240–255	E	reserved

It soon became clear that assigning an entire Class A or B network number to a single physical network segment was wasteful. How often would several thousand hosts be attached to a single Ethernet segment? Also, assigning each physical network segment a separate network number would force the Internet's routing table to grow linearly with the number of segments. To avoid these problems, *subnetting* was invented [166], adding another level of hierarchy to the Internet's routing and addressing. With subnetting, each Class A, B, or C network number could be broken up into fixed-sized pieces called *subnets*, with each subnet assigned to a different physical segment.

Take, for example, the Class B network 128.186/16; some number of the lower 16 bits reserved for host addressing could be used to indicate a *subnet number*. If the third byte were used for this purpose, 128.186/16 could be divided into 254 subnets (subnets 0 and 255 being reserved), each containing 254 hosts; this practice was also called using a *subnet mask* of 255.255.255.0. In this way, a single Class B network could be used to address hundreds of segments, a Class A network thousands. Outside of the subnetted network, all of the segments would be covered by a single Class A, B, or C routing table entry.

In the presence of subnets, additional broadcast addresses were defined in RFC 922 [164]. Setting all of a subnet's host bits to 1 resulted in the subnet's *directed-broadcast* address. This address could be used to send a packet to all hosts on the subnet, even when the packet was originated from a distant segment. For the subnetted network, setting both the subnet and the host bits to 1 resulted in the *all-subnets-broadcast* address. Although never widely implemented, a packet sent to this address was supposed to be delivered to all hosts on all subnets of the given Class A, B, or C network. Using the earlier example of the Class B network 128.186/16 subnetted on the third byte, 128.186.10.255 would be the directed-broadcast address for subnet 10 and 128.186.255.255 the all-subnets-broadcast address for the entire Class B network. Forwarding of IP broadcasts is described in Section 9.3.

Unfortunately the BSD UNIX project used the setting of the host bits to 0 to indicate broadcast addresses. So in the previous example, 128.186.10.0 would be the BSD directed-broadcast address for subnet 10 and 128.186.0.0 the all-subnets-broadcast address for 128.186/16. For a long time, routers would have to support both the RFC 922 broadcast addresses and the BSD broadcast addresses.

Eventually the restriction that all subnets be the same size was found too limiting. Subnet size was driven by the segment having the largest number of hosts, wasting addresses on the smaller segments. In our example, if the 128.186/16 subnetted network had one segment with 1,000 hosts, you would be limited to 62 subnets (again avoiding subnets of all 0s and all 1s) of 1,022 hosts each. To solve this problem, people began dividing their Class A, B, and C networks into subnets of varying sizes; this has been called *variable-length subnet masks,* or VLSMs. As just one combination, 128.186/16 could now be divided into three subnets capable of holding 254 hosts (128.186.1–3/24), one subnet with 1,022 hosts (128.186.4/22), and 3,966 subnets of 14 hosts each.

With VLSMs, schemes were developed allowing subnet masks to be adjusted as the host population of segments changed, without renumbering hosts [250]. The *Fuzzball* routers in the original NSFNET were the first routers to allow VLSMs [161]. Newer routing protocols, such as OSPF, were designed with VLSM support.

Subnet numbers usually were assigned to immediately follow the network prefix. If there was a gap between the network prefix and the subnet number, the subnet mask was termed *discontiguous.* An example of a discontiguous subnet mask is using the fourth byte of a Class B network to indicate the subnet number, resulting in a subnet mask of 255.255.0.255. The combination of VLSMs and discontiguous subnet masks was a bad one, for two reasons. First, certain assignments of discontiguous subnet masks could result in multiple subnets matching the same number of bits, making the concept of best match ambiguous! Second, common routing table lookup algorithms, such as Patricia (see Section 2.1), could not handle discontiguous masks efficiently. With discontiguous subnet masks already discouraged by RFC 922, the introduction of VLSMs made them virtually unsupported. Discontiguous subnet masks are now prohibited by the latest router-requirements RFC [12].

In 1993, concern grew over the possibility of the Internet address space becoming exhausted. A good percentage of the Class B addresses had already been assigned, and the Internet number authorities wanted to start assigning multiple Class C networks instead. However, since each Class A, B, and C network appeared as individual entries in the Internet core routers, assigning multiple Class Cs ran the risk of exhausting the table space of the Internet's routers. The idea of using a single routing table entry to represent routes to a collection of class C networks led to CIDR and the current prefix-based, classless Internet routing paradigm. For example, the prefix 192.24.16/20, which formerly was represented by the 16 separate Class C networks 192.24.16.0 through 192.24.31.0, could now be a single routing table entry. Such an entry is sometimes referred to as a *supernet*.

With CIDR, the restriction on all 0s and all 1s subnets was also removed; with CIDR, even the idea of a subnet loses most of its meaning. Internet routing protocols that encoded their routes based on the now defunct Class A, B, and C network divisions were either discarded (for example, EGP) or updated to new versions customized for CIDR, advertising arbitrary address prefixes (for example, BGP-3 to BGP-4, RIP to RIPv2, and IGRP to EIGRP).

1.2.3 Tunneling

Suppose that routers A and B know how to forward datagrams addressed to the IP destination X but that the intervening routers between A and B do not. In order to deliver packets to X, a *tunnel* is configured between routers A and B: When A receives a packet destined for X, it alters that packet to look as though the destination is really router B, in essence tricking the intervening routers to forward the packet. When B receives the packet, it returns the packet to its original state (possibly altering its TTL; see [188]) and forwards it on toward X.

Why would the intervening routers between routers A and B not know how to forward to X? The most common example in the Internet is the Internet's *Multicast Backbone* (MBONE); see Section 9.4. The MBONE consists mostly of a collection of UNIX workstations running the DVMRP routing protocol. DVMRP calculates paths for multicast datagrams. However, most of the Internet's routers do not run DVMRP and so are not aware of these multicast paths. This forces the MBONE routers to be interconnected by tunnels.

As another example, in many regions of the Internet, only those routers participating in BGP (see Section 13.3) obtain routing information for the full set of Internet destinations. In order to forward data traffic to certain destinations, tunnels must be configured between BGP routers.

Two separate mechanisms may be used to implement such a tunnel. The first is the source route option. When forwarding datagrams addressed to X, router A puts router B's address into the IP header as destination address and moves address X into a loose source route option. The second mechanism is to encapsulate the packet by a complete extra IP header. This IP header is again addressed to router B, and the protocol number in this header is set to 4, telling B that it should strip the IP header and forward the encapsulated packet [188]. The second mechanism is usually preferred, due to the significant performance degradation seen in most Internet routers when IP options are employed.

Although tunnels are sometimes necessary, they are usually to be avoided. The process of adding and stripping information (be it source routes or extra IP headers) at the tunnel end points (routers A and B) decreases forwarding performance in those routers. The additional information also makes it more likely that fragmentation will be necessary, although hosts can avoid fragmentation by using the Path MTU discovery algorithm [165], which can take tunneling into account. Worst of all, tunneling can subvert firewalls and in general make traffic monitoring more difficult; the real destination is buried in the options field or in additional IP headers. In particular, many ISPs get annoyed when people configure MBONE tunnels through the ISP's network, in the process masking high-bandwidth video feeds as innocuous unicast data.

1.3   IPv6

Prompted by the fear of exhausting the Internet's address space, designers began work in 1993 on a new version of IP with larger addresses. This culminated in 1996 with the publication of a full set of network-layer protocol specifications (the other layers of the protocol stack remaining unchanged) for IPv6 [49], [61], [99], [181], with the Internet's currently deployed IP being referred to in comparison as IPv4.

We touch only briefly on IPv6 in this book. Why? Mainly because IPv6 is not all that much different from IPv4. IPv6 has made a number of incremental improvements over IPv4 yet can be summarized roughly as "IPv4 with 128-bit addresses." In particular, the IP routing and addressing architecture remains largely unchanged. An IPv6 router makes its forwarding decisions on the basis of a routing table of CIDR-like address prefixes; address assignment is likely to be provider based; and IPv4's existing routing protocols—OSPF [46], RIP [151], and BGP [208]—are being modified to carry IPv6's larger addresses.

IPv6 also has not been widely deployed, probably for several reasons. First, the original fear that IPv4's address space soon may be exhausted now seems an overreaction. The deployment of CIDR has improved the efficiency of address usage, and fear has now shifted to the routing tables' expanding beyond the capacity of the Internet's core routers—a problem that IPv6 does not solve. The possibility of organizations using the private Internet address space (see Section 1.2.1) and connecting to the Internet through Network Address Translation (NAT) [79] boxes has also lessened the demand for Internet addresses. Since IPv6 does not enable any new classes of network applications, conversion of the large base of routers and hosts running IPv4 is likely to be delayed until IPv4 address exhaustion again seems imminent.

IPv6 can be thought of as an attempt to capture current IPv4 usage in protocol specifications. Those IPv4 features that are either unused (for example, TOS-based routing) or discouraged (such as fragmentation by intermediate routers) have been deleted from the IPv6 protocol specifications. IPv6 has made mandatory several IPv4 features that are desirable but have yet to see widespread deployment: IP multicast and security. In addition, address scoping has been made an initial part of the IPv6 addressing architecture [99], building on IPv4 experience with private internet addresses [210] and proposals for IPv4 multicast address scope [158]. Address scoping is a way of dropping the global-uniqueness requirement for certain addresses. IPv6 supports link-local (unique only on a given segment) and site-local (unique only within a certain "site") address scopes, as well as the usual globally unique addresses.

Differences from IPv4

As mentioned earlier, the major difference between IPv6 and IPv4 is the size of addresses: 128 bits for IPv6 versus IPv4's 32-bit address. In IPv6, addresses are no longer written in dotted decimal notation. Instead the IPv6 address is broken into eight 16-bit pieces, and each piece is then expressed in hexadecimal, with the pieces separated by colons. An example of an IPv6 address is 4722:0c62:0:0:2:1298:0CC:A096. As a shortcut, the longest string of 16-bit 0s within an address can be abbreviated as :: (but only one string within an address, to avoid ambiguities); our example address can also be written as 4722:0c62::2:1298:0CC:A096. IPv6's notation for CIDR prefixes is similar to IPv4's, with the prefix defined by the first four bytes of our address written as 4722:0c62/32.

Because of the increase in address size, the IPv6 packet header is somewhat larger than IPv4's header, with the minimum size IPv6 header twice the size of the minimum IPv4 header. The IPv6 network layer header is depicted in Figure 1.6.

All of the fields in the IPv6 header were also present in IPv4, with the exception of the Flow Label, although some fields have been renamed. The Version field is, of course, set to 6. The Priority field carries similar semantics to IPv4's precedence field, carrying an indication of a packet's transmission queuing priority, although IPv6 allows this field to be rewritten at each router hop. The Payload Length is simply the length of the packet in bytes. The Next Header field is the same as IPv4's Protocol field, even going so far as to use the same encodings. For example, a Next Header field of 6 (see Figure 1.3) indicates that TCP data is encapsulated. The Hop Limit field is IPv4's TTL field renamed, an

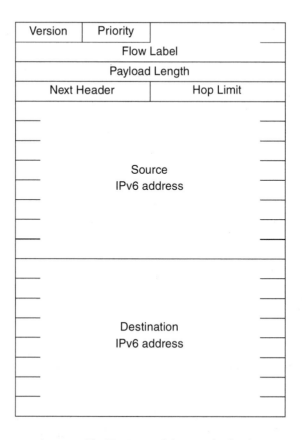

Figure 1.6 The IPv6 network-layer packet header.

admission of the TTL field's real function in IPv4. Use of the Flow Label in IPv6 has not yet been completely determined, although the general idea is to provide a forwarding hint to routers for particular packet streams.

IPv6 uses different data-link encapsulations than IPv4 does. Although the Version field would in theory allow both IPv4 and IPv6 to use the same data-link encapsulations, experience with the ST2 protocol (an experimental flow-oriented network-layer protocol that was assigned IP version number 5; see [63]) indicated that many IPv4 implementations do not bother to check the Version field and would get very confused on receiving an IPv6 packet. Defining new data-link encapsulations is mostly an administrative task; for example, IPv6 has been assigned the Ethernet type of 0x86DD [52], as opposed to IPv4's Ethernet types 0x800. Still, there are plenty of new RFCs describing how IPv6 works over the various data links in use in the Internet.

IPv6 has distilled and simplified IPv4's packet-forwarding process. IPv6 has no TOS field, which had gone pretty much unused in IPv4. The Header Checksum field has also disappeared; those applications that include the IPv6 source and destination addresses as part of their connection identifier must include part of the IPv6 header in an application checksum (much as is done for TCP in IPv4) or risk having corrupted packets associated with the wrong connections. Routers also do not fragment packets, something always thought best avoided in IPv4. Instead they simply send an error back to the source when they are unable to fit the packet onto the next data link.

IPv6 supports header options as IPv4 does, such as source routing. In IPv6, however, options are encoded as a separate header between the IPv6 header and application data. Additional headers may also be inserted before the application data, to implement authentication, security, and source-packet fragmentation. Each header indicates the function of the next-in-line encapsulated header by proper setting of the Next Header field.

IPv6 also has an ICMP [49] that is very similar to its IPv4 counterpart; in IPv6, the Internet Group Membership Protocol (IGMP, see Section 9.2.1) has been absorbed into ICMP as well. IPv6 does not use ARP. Instead the ARP function has been incorporated into the *IPv6 Neighbor Discovery* protocol [181], which is also part of IPv6 ICMP. In addition to implementing the ARP function, IPv6 neighbor discovery encompasses IPv4's ICMP router discovery and redirect functions. In addition, IPv6 neighbor discovery implements two functions not present in IPv4: address autoconfiguration and duplicate-address detection.

Further Reading

Many good books and papers detail the history of the ARPANET network and the Internet. See, for example, the papers by Leiner et al. [135] and Clark [44].

This book assumes that you have a basic knowledge of the TCP/IP protocol suite and data communications in general. The books by Comer [48] and Stevens [240] provide an excellent introduction to TCP/IP. Bertsekas and Gallagher's text *Data Networks* [20] is a thorough introduction to data communications for the theoretically inclined. Anyone looking just for a survey of networking protocols may be more comfortable with Tanenbaum [242].

The router-requirements RFC [12] is necessary reading for anyone designing or implementing an IP router. The RFC provides many years of collected wisdom on what one should and should not do when building a router.

Books on IPv6 are just starting to come out. The collection of essays edited by Bradner and Mankin [26] provides insight into the requirements and design decisions that resulted in the IPv6 protocols. For general information on IPv6 protocols, see Huitema's book [103].

2

Internet Routing Protocols

In this chapter, we explore the Internet's dynamic routing protocols. TCP/IP has many routing protocols, with OSPF, BGP, RIP, IGRP, and Integrated IS-IS all in use in today's Internet. Before getting to the routing protocols themselves, we first discuss the database that all routing protocols produce: the router's routing table. An examination of the Internet's routing architecture introduces the concept of Autonomous Systems and Interior and Exterior Gateway Protocols (IGPs and EGPs). We end the chapter with a description of the two main routing technologies in use today: Distance Vector and link state.

2.1   Routing Tables

All TCP/IP routing protocols have ways of discovering the reachable IP address prefixes and, for each prefix, the next-hop router to use to forward data traffic to the prefix. As the network changes—leased lines fail, new leased lines are provisioned, routers crash, and so on—the routing protocols continually reevaluate prefix reachability and the next hop to use for each prefix. The process of finding the new next hop after the network changes is called *convergence*. We prefer routing protocols that find the new next hop quickly, that is, protocols having a short *convergence time*. However, for any routing protocol, as the size and complexity of the network increase, so does convergence time.

A router's routing table instructs the router how to forward packets. Given a packet, the router performs a routing table lookup, using the packet's IP destination address as key. This lookup returns the best-matching routing table entry, which tells the router which interface to forward the packet out of and the IP address of the packet's next hop.

There is a separate routing table entry for each address prefix that the router knows about. Entries in the routing table are also commonly referred to as *routes*. For example, Figure 1.5's router C would have the routing table listed in Table 2.1. The next hop of "self" for prefix 128.5.2/24 indicates that that segment is directly connected to router C; C will deliver packets destined to that prefix directly to their destination. Note that although there is a network segment with the prefix 128.2.2/24, that prefix is hidden from C by the aggregate 128.2/16 advertised by router D. Similarly router G on the right of Figure 1.5 hides a number of more specific prefixes from C by advertising the single aggregate 128.1/16.

Table 2.1 The Routing Table of Figure 1.5's Router C

Prefix	Next Hop
128.1/16	Router G
128.2/16	Router D
128.2.4/24	Router A
128.3.7/24	Router D
128.5.2/24	Self
128.5.6/24	Router B

If a packet's IP destination falls into the range of addresses described by a particular routing table entry's prefix, we say that the entry is a *match*. In our example, the entry for 128.3.7/24 in Table 2.1 matches all destinations of the form 128.3.7.*x*. In our example, many destinations do not have a matching entry—28.4.56.77, 192.9.1.3, 11.11.11.11 are a few examples. If router C receives a packet addressed to any of these destinations, it simply throws the packet away and attempts to send an ICMP Destination Unreachable message back to the packet's source to inform it about the error.

In Table 2.1, the destination 128.2.4.5 matches two routing table entries: 128.2/16 and 128.2.4/24. This is not at all uncommon. In these cases, the entry with the longest prefix, 128.2.4/24, is selected as the *best match* (sometimes also referred to as *longest match*); we also say that 128.2.4/24 is *more specific* than 128.2/16. One way that multiple matches can occur is when the provider addressing model is being used. An organization takes a range of addresses from its Internet Service Provider and later on changes providers but does not wish to change addresses. The new ISP then ends up advertising a more specific route for a piece of the old provider's address space (this is now officially discouraged by the address lending policy, which would instead force the organization to renumber when changing providers; see [209]).

Many routers have a *default route* in their routing table. This is a routing table entry for the zero-length prefix 0/0. The default route matches every destination, although it is overridden by all more specific prefixes. For example, suppose that an organization's intranet has one router attaching itself to the public Internet. All of the organization's other routers can then use a default route pointing to the Internet connection rather than knowing about all of the public Internet's routes.

Each router has a different routing table, reflecting its unique position within the Internet. From router to router, not only do the next hops of routing table entries change, but even the prefixes that each router knows can be different, as addresses are aggregated into large prefixes. In Figure 1.5, routers D, E, and F are aware of the prefix 128.2.2/24, but all other routers see only the aggregate 128.2/16. Routers at the edge of the Internet may rely heavily on the default routing table entry, with only a few hundred or more specific entries in their routing table. Core routers in the Internet, however, have upwards of 45,000 entries. These routers, which do not use a default route, are said to hold the full Internet routing table. The size trend of the full Internet routing table is shown in Figure 2.1. The contents of a router's routing table can be viewed through SNMP and the IP forwarding-table MIB of RFC 2096 (see Section 12.6).

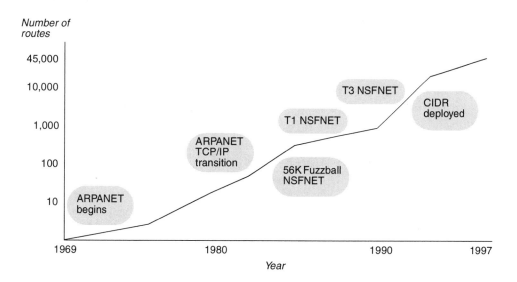

Figure 2.1 Size increases in the Internet's routing tables (logarithmic scale).

In our example, we have been assuming that router C is building its routing table through the use of dynamic routing protocols—the aggregates 128.1/16 and 128.2/16 are being advertised to C (by routers G and D, respectively) through some protocol, as are the paths to other remote segments. Dynamic routing protocols are certainly the norm, although they do not need to be used. Instead routing table entries can be explicitly configured, called *static routing*, by a network operator. For example, to install the route to 128.3.7/24 in router C, a network operator may type the command **add route 128.3.7/24** a*ddress-of-router-D*. Running an entire network via static routing is too difficult to manage, requiring modification of static routes as the network changes or even during network failures. In our example, if the link between routers C and D fails, the operator would have to tell router C to route packets destined to 128.3.7/24 through G instead, something that a dynamic routing protocol would do automatically. However, static routes are still used today in the Internet to augment dynamic routing. For example, two organizations may not trust each other enough to run dynamic routing at the interorganization boundary, relying instead on a set of configured static routes.

Implementation of Routing Tables

Forwarding performance, usually expressed in packets/second, is the most valued commodity in a router. Therefore makers of routers try to arrange their routers' routing tables so that the best match operation can be performed as quickly as possible.

A common routing table arrangement is a *Patricia tree* (see [129] and [230])—a special kind of radix tree that minimizes bit comparisons and, when used as a routing table, requires only a single mask-and-match operation. These trees are binary trees, whereby the tree traversal depends on a sequence of single-bit comparisons in the key, the destination IP address.

A Patricia tree that might be used to implement the lookup for the routing table in Table 2.1 is shown in Figure 2.2. Suppose that the router is trying to route a packet to the destination 128.2.5.6. The router starts at the top of the Patricia tree, testing bit 13 in the destination address (bits are numbered starting at 0 for the most significant bit of the address). Since this bit is 0, the router branches left, testing in sequence bits 14 (which is a 1), 15 (a 0) and 21 (a 1). This ends up at the entry specifying no bit comparison, so the tree traversal stops; traversal would also stop if the new bit to test were less than or equal to the last bit tested. When the traversal stops, the destination is compared to the prefix in the entry to see whether there is a match. In our example, 128.2.5.6 does not match 128.2.4/24. The router must then check for matches against shorter prefixes of 128.2.4/24; following the prefix pointer back to 128.2/16 yields the best-matching routing table entry.

With a routing table containing 45,000 entries, the router will perform on average 16 bit comparisons for each lookup. However, the performance of Patricia is somewhat data dependent. With a particularly unfortunate collection of prefixes in the routing table, the lookup of certain addresses can take as many as 32 bit comparisons, one for each bit of the destination IP address.

Although radix tree variants such as Patricia are most common, other routing table lookup algorithms are also employed in TCP/IP routers. For example, the OSPF implementation in the companion book to this book uses a balanced binary tree (see [129]).

Another way to speed up the routing table lookup is to try to avoid it entirely. The routing table lookup provides the next hop for a given IP destination. Some routers

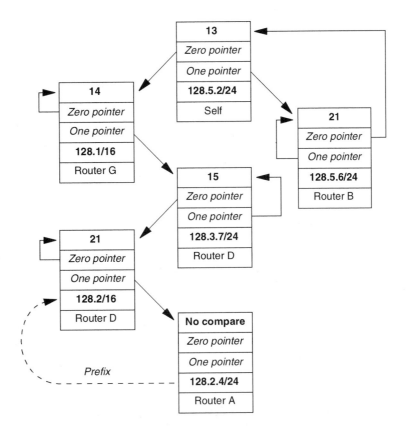

Figure 2.2 Patricia-tree implementation of routing table lookup.

cache this IP destination-to-next-hop association in a separate database that is consulted before the routing table lookup (one might say as the *front end* to the routing table). Finding a particular destination in this database is easier because you are doing an exact match instead of the more expensive best-match operation of the routing table. As a concrete example, this front-end database might be organized as a *hash table* (see [129]). If the *hash function* were the sum of the third and fourth bytes of the IP destination, a couple of buckets within the hash table might look as in Figure 2.3 after the router had forwarded several packets. Now if the router sees any of these destinations again (a *cache hit*), their lookup will be very quick. Packets to new destinations will be slower, however, because the cost of a failed hash lookup will have to be added to the normal routing table lookup.

Front-end caches to the routing table can work well at the edge of the Internet or within organizations. However, cache schemes do not seem to work well in the Internet's core. The large number of packet destinations seen by the core routers can cause caches to overflow or for their lookup to become slower than the routing table lookup itself. For example, cache schemes are not really a win when the hash bucket

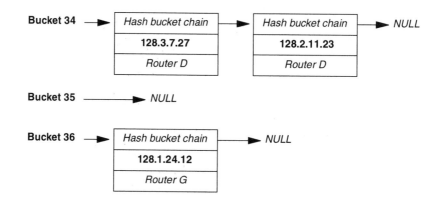

Figure 2.3 Hash-table front end to a routing table.

size—the number of destinations that hash to the same value—starts getting large. Also, the frequent routing changes seen in the core routers can force them to invalidate their caches frequently, leading to a small number of cache hits.

Although IP addressing has been around for more than 20 years, new routing table lookup algorithms are still being developed in attempts to build ever faster routers. The two papers on routing table design presented at SIGCOMM '97, [27] and [257], are recent examples.

2.2   Internet Routing Architecture

The Internet is organized into regions called *Autonomous Systems* (ASs). Each AS consists of a collection of routers under the control of a single administrative entity—for example, all the routers belonging to a particular Internet Service Provider, corporation, or university.

The collection of ASs is organized in a rough hierarchical fashion. The closer to the top of the hierarchy—the core of the Internet—the more routes appear in the AS. At the same time, the individual prefixes within the routers' routing tables get shorter. The ASs at the core of the Internet carry the complete routing table, currently 45,000 routes, and do not use a default route (they are in the so-called *default-free zone*). All other ASs use a default route, pointing up the hierarchy, enabling them to carry only a subset of the Internet's routes. This arrangement of ASs is pictured in Figure 2.4.

ASs that are in the business of providing Internet connectivity are called *Internet Service Providers* (ISPs). The network operators that configure and manage the interconnection of ISPs have a language all their own. When two providers connect, they usually establish a *peering agreement*. If the two providers are at the same level of the hierarchy, this is simply an agreement to exchange routing information. However, when one AS is lower in the hierarchy (*downstream*), this AS is sometimes entering into a

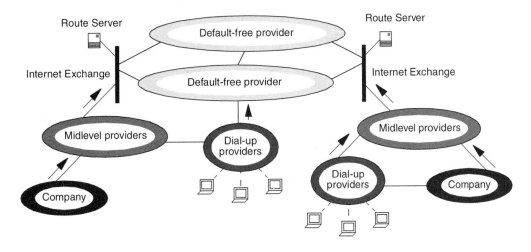

Figure 2.4 Organization of the Internet into Autonomous Systems. Solid lines indicate peering relationships. The arrows indicate the direction of the default route.

customer relationship with the *upstream provider*. This means that the upstream provider will advertise the downstream's addresses to the rest of the Internet and will forward the downstream's packets to other providers and their customers as appropriate—that is, the upstream provider provides *transit* for the downstream provider. Interprovider operational issues are discussed in various forums, such as the North American Network Operators Group (NANOG) [183]; peering issues are a major topic.

Internet prefixes are now assigned to achieve the best aggregation under CIDR. Providers that are large enough can get assigned their own address prefixes, also referred to as *CIDR blocks*. Other smaller providers and their customers must use addresses from the CIDR blocks of their upstream provider(s). However, many companies are still using addresses assigned before the advent of CIDR and its address conservation policies: large corporations and universities, such as DEC, Xerox, and MIT, have their own Class A addresses, and many individual Class C addresses in the range 192/8 still appear in the routing tables (these Class C addresses are sometimes derisively referred to by the network operators as *the swamp*).

The identity of the ASs at the Internet's core has changed over the years. Originally the ARPANET network [146], [147] was at the Internet's core. Then, in 1985, the National Science Foundation funded a new Internet core, called the NSFNET. The NSFNET began as a collection of LSI-11-based routers, affectionately called Fuzzballs, interconnected by 56Kb leased lines [161]. In 1987, the NSFNET was upgraded to IBM RT-based routers interconnected with T1 lines, and in 1992, the line speed was upgraded to T3. The NSFNET was decommissioned in 1995 [93]. Today the Internet's core consists of around half a dozen commercial Internet providers, including UUNET, MCI, and Sprint.

In a variety of facilities around the world, an ISP can place a router and peer with other ISPs. These facilities are commonly given names such as *Network Access Points* (NAPs), *Metropolitan Area Ethernets* (MAEs), or *Commercial Internet Exchanges* (CIXs). Physically these exchanges are usually implemented as bridged FDDI/Ethernet combinations or as ATM subnets. Dozens of providers may connect at a single exchange point. The ISPs connecting to the exchange, and those they are peering with, is often public knowledge. See, for example, [148] for the ISPs connected to MAE East. Some exchanges also supply a specially instrumented router to ease the distribution of routing information between connected providers. These routers are called Route Servers, and were developed by the NSF-funded *Routing Arbiter* project [223]. Instead of each provider establishing a routing protocol session with every other, a provider instead establishes a single session with the Route Server. The Route Server then redistributes the information learned to the other providers at the exchange.

Two providers may also peer directly over a private connection, such as a high-speed leased line or an ATM circuit. This kind of private peering is becoming common between the top-level ISPs making up the Internet core.

As originally designed, routers within an AS exchanged routing information via a common routing protocol (called an *Interior Gateway Protocol*, or IGP), whereas a different routing protocol (called an *Exterior Gateway Protocol*, or EGP) was used to exchange routing information between ASs. The single-IGP rule was soon broken, however, with many ASs running multiple IGPs concurrently—for example, both RIP (see Section 13.1) and OSPF. A collection of routers running a common IGP is often called a *routing domain*; in this case, an AS may consist of multiple routing domains.

The first EGP was also called the Exterior Gateway Protocol [162]. It did a poor job of loop detection and so forced a strict hierarchy of ASs. EGP was eventually replaced by the *Border Gateway Protocol,* or BGP (see Section 13.3), which is the EGP in use in the Internet today. With BGP, ASs no longer need to be organized in a strict hierarchy. BGP is run between providers or between providers and the Route Servers at the various Internet exchanges. A peering agreement almost always includes a commitment to exchange some amount of BGP routing information. To facilitate configuration and management of the BGP protocol exchanges, each AS is assigned a unique 16-bit *AS number*. For example, BBN Planet has been assigned AS 1, UUNET AS 284, and Sprint AS 1239.

You might ask why there is a distinction between IGPs and EGPs. Some people think that the EGP/IGP split is simply a historical accident. However, I believe that the requirements for an IGP differ from those for an EGP, which drives different protocol designs. In an IGP, one wants a protocol that can calculate efficient routes and that recalculates quickly when the network changes. In an EGP, one is more interested in the ability to express particular routing policies and to aggregate routing information. As we shall see in the next section, these differing requirements often lead to using link-state routing technology in the IGP, whereas EGPs are invariably based on Distance Vector routing technology.

2.3   Distance Vector Algorithms

In a *Distance Vector* protocol, the routers cooperate in performing a *distributed computation*. Distance Vector algorithms calculate the best path to each destination prefix separately, usually trying to find paths that minimize a simple metric, such as the number of router hops to the destination. At each intermediate step in the algorithm, each router has its current best path to the destination prefix. The router then notifies all of its neighbors of its current path; concurrently the router's neighbors are also notifying the router of their path choices. The router, seeing the paths being used by all of its neighbors, may find a better (that is, lower-cost) path through one of its neighbors. If so, the router updates its next hop and cost for the destination and notifies its neighbors of its new choice of route, and the procedure iterates. After some number of iterations, the choice of route will stabilize, with each router having found the best path to the destination.

The main advantage of Distance Vector algorithms is their simplicity. These algorithms are also amenable to route aggregation, and relatively simple routing policies (for example, the router should route certain prefixes through a given neighbor but not others) are easy to implement.

The canonical example of a Distance Vector protocol is the Internet's *Routing Information Protocol* (RIP). Using RIP and the network in Figure 2.5 as a concrete example, we'll examine a Distance Vector algorithm's distributed computation in a little more detail.

Distance Vector Convergence

RIP routers augment each destination's routing table entry (see Section 2.1) with a metric field. This metric indicates the minimum number of router hops required to reach the destination; the prefixes for directly attached network segments always have their metric set to 1. Every 30 seconds, each RIP router broadcasts RIP updates to its neighboring RIP routers; these updates list the prefixes in the router's routing table, together with their current metrics. When a RIP router receives a RIP update from its neighbor X, the router examines all the prefixes within the update. If the number of hops to reach a given prefix through X (obtained by adding 1 to the metric advertised by X for the prefix) is better than the metric the router has for the prefix, the router updates its routing table. The updated routing table entry has its next hop set to X and its metric set to one more than the metric advertised by X.

The example shown in Table 2.2 assumes that at time T1 the interface on router I to 192.1.4/24 in Figure 2.5 has just become operational and that at times T1–T4, each of the routers A–I sends routing updates simultaneously to its neighbors. The column under A shows the routing table entry for 192.1.4/24 in router A as time progresses. After time T4, the routing table entries remain stable, and RIP has converged.

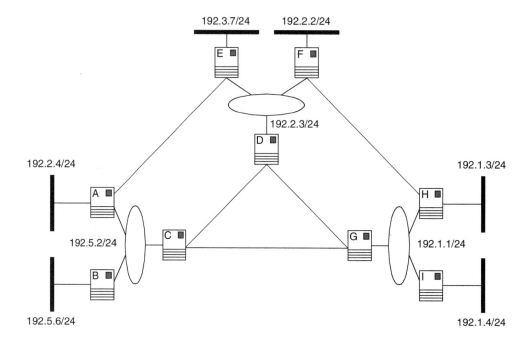

Figure 2.5 Sample network topology to illustrate Distance Vector protocol behavior.

Table 2.2 RIP Convergence When Subnet 192.1.4/24 Is Added to Figure 2.5.
(Routing table changes appear in bold, with each metric printed as a cost, next-hop pair.)

Time	A	B	C	D	E	F	G	H	I
T1	∞	∞	∞	∞	∞	∞	∞	∞	1
T2	∞	∞	∞	∞	∞	∞	**2,I**	**2,I**	1
T3	∞	∞	**3,G**	**3,G**	∞	**3,H**	2,I	2,I	1
T4	**4,C**	**4,C**	3,G	3,G	**4,D**	3,H	2,I	2,I	1

Distance Vector protocols get their name from the form their routing updates take: a list (or *vector*) of metrics (or *distances*), one for each advertised prefix. If you look at the distributed calculation that a Distance Vector algorithm is performing over the network as a whole, as illustrated in Table 2.2, you see that it is a distributed application of the Bellman-Ford algorithm for finding shortest paths [18]. For this reason, Distance Vector algorithms are also sometimes called Bellman-Ford algorithms (although this is somewhat confusing, since link-state algorithms can also use the Bellman-Ford algorithm to perform their routing calculations; see [86]).

Table 2.2 shows what happens when a new, shorter path to a destination prefix is discovered. However, sometimes the current shortest path is no longer available, because of link or router failures, and routing must revert to a longer path. A router discovers this failure in two ways. Sometimes the router's current best hop will merely send an update saying that the best path just got longer. Other times, the lack of updates received from the current next hop tells the router that the next hop is probably no longer operational, and so the router selects a new next-hop router advertising an equal or longer path. A Distance Vector protocol's convergence behavior in these failure conditions is a little more interesting, and we talk about this in the next section.

Counting to Infinity

A Distance Vector protocol's distributed calculation is quite robust, converging after network changes even if the updates from the various routers are not synchronized (in fact, synchronization of updates can cause problems; see [78]) or if the routers use varying update intervals [20], [241]. However, Distance Vector protocols can take a long time to converge in the face of certain network failures. Suppose, for example, that the interface from router I to 192.1.4/24 in Figure 2.5 becomes inoperational. Table 2.3 shows the behavior of RIP, again making the artificial assumption that each of the routers A–I sends updates synchronously at the time intervals T1–T15.

Table 2.3 Distance Vector Convergence When Subnet 192.1.4/24 Is Deleted from Figure 2.5. (Routing table changes are printed in bold, with each metric printed as a cost, next-hop pair.)

Time	A	B	C	D	E	F	G	H	I
T1	4,C	4,C	3,G	3,G	4,D	3,H	2,I	2,I	∞
T2	4,C	4,C	3,G	3,G	4,D	3,H	**3,H**	**3,G**	**3,G**
T3	4,C	4,C	**4,G**	**4,G**	4,D	**4,H**	**4,H**	**4,G**	**4,G**
T4	**5,C**	**5,C**	**5,G**	**5,G**	**5,D**	**5,H**	**5,H**	**5,G**	**5,G**
T5	**6,C**	**6,C**	**6,G**	**6,G**	**6,D**	**6,H**	**6,H**	**6,G**	**6,G**
T6	**7,C**	**7,C**	**7,G**	**7,G**	**7,D**	**7,H**	**7,H**	**7,G**	**7,G**
				...T7–T13...					
T14	**15,C**	**15,C**	**15,G**	**15,G**	**15,D**	**15,H**	**15,H**	**15,G**	**15,G**
T15	∞	∞	∞	∞	∞	∞	∞	∞	∞

As you can see, it takes quite a while before the routers decide that the prefix 192.1.4/24 is unreachable. During this time, forwarding loops may very well form; in our example, there is a forwarding loop between routers G and H from time T2 until time T14. Notice that in any given router, the cost of prefix 192.1.4/24 continually increases until it reaches the RIP infinity of 16. This behavior is called *counting to infinity* and is the reason that the maximum path cost is generally set to a small value in Distance Vector protocols: The larger the maximum path cost, the longer counting to infinity can last, consuming network and router CPU bandwidth in the process. Distance Vector protocols, such as RIP, exhibit similar properties when a network failure simply lengthens the path to a destination. The general convergence behavior in this case can be characterized as follows: On the way to its new metric value, the router's routing table entry assumes the lengths of all possible paths (to the destination) existing in the routing domain *before* the failure [120].

Improving Convergence

In order to improve Distance Vector protocol convergence, many modifications to Distance Vector protocols have been implemented at one time or another.

- In order to reduce convergence time, many routers running Distance Vector protocols send updates immediately when their routing tables change instead of waiting for the next 30-second interval. These updates are called *triggered updates*.

- To help prevent forwarding loops during convergence, Distance Vector protocols usually employ a procedure called *split horizon*. In split horizon, when a router sends a routing update out its interface X, the router omits all routes from the update whose outgoing interface is equal to X. For example, at time T1 in Table 2.3, router G would not be broadcasting an update for 192.1.4/24 to routers H and I. In a modification to split horizon, called *infinite split horizon*, or *split horizon with poison reverse*, updates sent out interface X advertise routes with outgoing interface X as being unreachable (that is, with a cost of 16). Infinite split horizon is more effective than split horizon in reducing forwarding loops, in fact completely doing away with loops consisting of only two routers. However, since infinite split horizon makes updates larger, split horizon is more common.

- In another modification, called *hold down*, a router refuses to accept updates for a route for some period of time after the route has initially been declared unreachable. For example, if router I in Table 2.3 had been performing hold down, it would refuse to accept routing updates from its neighbors for several time periods after time T1. Hold down can inhibit the forming of forwarding loops in certain situations, although it lengthens convergence time in others. For that reason, it is not often employed by protocols such as RIP but is still used in other Distance Vector protocols, such as IGRP (see Section 13.4) and DVMRP (Section 14.2).

These modifications can improve a Distance Vector protocol's convergence properties but cannot completely eliminate the formation of routing loops during convergence or the counting-to-infinity behavior. There are two known ways to solve these problems in a Distance Vector protocol. The first method, employed by the Internet's BGP, is to advertise the complete path (that is, sequence of routers) to each destination prefix rather than just the prefix's metric (see Section 13.3). The second method, described in various papers ([82], [119], [157]) and implemented by EIGRP (Section 13.4), is to strictly control the order of routing updates between nodes. These latter methods can guarantee loop-free routing but generally complicate the protocol significantly and can in fact increase convergence time.

2.4   Link-State Algorithms

Instead of the incremental, distributed calculation used by a Distance Vector algorithm, *link-state routing* algorithms employ a *replicated distributed database* approach. Each router in a link-state algorithm contributes pieces to this database by describing the router's local environment: the set of active links to local IP network segments and neighboring routers, with each link assigned a cost. This is where link-state algorithms get their name: Instead of advertising a list of distances to each known destination, a router running a link-state algorithm advertises the states of its local network links. These link-state advertisements are then distributed to all other routers. The end result is that all routers obtain the same database of collected advertisements, together describing the current map of the network. The cost of a path in the network is assigned as the sum of the costs of the links comprising the path. From the network map, each router then runs a shortest-path calculation, typically the Dijkstra algorithm, although other algorithms, such as Bellman-Ford, are also sometimes used, producing the shortest path to each destination prefix.

Part II of this book is dedicated to the detailed description of a particular link-state routing protocol: OSPF. We defer explanation of many link-state mechanisms until then. Link-state algorithms were originally designed to get around performance problems in Distance Vector protocols [146]; however, arguments about the relative merits of Distance Vector and link-state protocols persist (see Section 3.2). Link-state algorithms are generally considered to have good convergence properties: When the network changes, new routes are found quickly and with a minimum of routing protocol overhead. Since link-state database protocols have more data at their disposal (namely, a complete description of the network) than do Distance Vector protocols, they can easily calculate paths with more sophisticated characteristics than simply paths with least cost. For example, link-state protocols have been designed for the Internet to calculate separate paths for each IP Type of Service (see Section 7.1), calculate paths obeying a wide range of policy constraints (IDPR, in Section 13.6), or calculate paths that can deliver certain quality-of-service guarantees [86].

Link-state routing protocols are definitely more complicated to specify than are Distance Vector protocols, as you can tell by comparing the size of the OSPF and RIP specifications. However, once you modify a Distance Vector algorithm to obtain some of the standard link-state properties (resistance to routing loops, transmit only routing changes instead of frequent refresh of routing data), you end up with a protocol that is just as difficult to implement as a link-state protocol. For example, writing good OSPF and BGP implementations are roughly equivalent tasks.

The EGP/IGP split allows the Internet to get the best features of both routing protocol technologies. For example, using OSPF as the IGP enables fast local convergence, whereas BGP between ASs facilitates route aggregation and policy-based routing. Of course, these two technologies can also be mixed within a single protocol—the two-level hierarchy within OSPF, a link-state protocol, uses Distance Vector mechanisms (see Chapter 6, Hierarchical Routing in OSPF).

Further Reading

Part II of this book covers the OSPF protocol in detail. Chapter 13, Unicast Routing Protocols, compares and contrasts the unicast routing protocols in use in the Internet today: RIP, OSPF, BGP, IGRP, and Integrated IS-IS.

Routing in the Internet by Huitema [104] does a good job of explaining the motivation and theory behind the Internet's routing protocols.

Part II

The OSPF Protocol

In Part II, we discuss the OSPF protocol. We start in Chapter 3, Developing the OSPF Protocol, by discussing why OSPF was developed in the first place and the original requirements and design decisions. We also discuss how OSPF has evolved, first as the result of interoperability testing and Internet deployments and then in reaction to evolution of the Internet itself.

Chapter 4, OSPF Basics, discusses the basic protocol mechanisms of OSPF. Link-state routing was originally designed for networks whose packet-switching computers were interconnected by point-to-point links, and so we restrict ourselves to those topologies. At the core of a link-state protocol is the link-state database, and in Chapter 4, we discuss the contents of individual pieces of the database, how the database is distributed and synchronized between routers, and the routing calculations that produce a routing table from the link-state database.

In Chapter 5, OSPF Network Types, we discuss how OSPF runs differently over segments other than point-to-point links. OSPF contains special support for broadcast segments, such as Ethernets, and for nonbroadcast yet multiaccess network segments, such as Frame Relay and ATM subnets. We discuss how OSPF performs neighbor discovery and database synchronization over these segment types and how these segments are represented within the link-state database. OSPF can run in two distinct modes over nonbroadcast subnets: Point-to-MultiPoint and NBMA. We compare and contrast these two modes of operation.

The implementation of hierarchical routing using OSPF is the subject of Chapter 6, Hierarchical Routing in OSPF. We describe how an OSPF routing domain can be split into areas and discuss the rules covering area organization, including when and where virtual links must be deployed. We then describe how routing information learned from other protocols, called external routes, can be advertised by OSPF. The chapter ends with a discussion of the interaction between external routes and areas. This includes a description of the two area types, stub areas and NSSAs, that can be used to control the spread of external routing information.

OSPF has been extended in various ways over the years. These optional extensions are described in Chapter 7, OSPF Extensions. Stub areas and NSSAs are described in more detail. The Demand Circuit extensions are a way of running OSPF efficiently over dial-up and low-speed links. The Database Overflow extensions enable a router to gracefully degrade when the size of the link-state database exceeds the router's capacities. The proposed external-attributes-LSA would enable OSPF to be used to propagate BGP path information across an OSPF routing domain, as an alternative to IBGP. We also describe an extension that has recently been removed from the OSPF specification: the ability to route packets differently, based on their specified TOS. A discussion of MOSPF, an extension enabling the forwarding of multicast datagrams, is deferred until Chapter 10, MOSPF.

Part II ends with Chapter 8, An OSPF FAQ. This chapter provides a list of frequently asked questions about OSPF and their answers.

3

Developing the OSPF Protocol

The development of the OSPF routing protocol began in 1987. OSPF was one of the first protocols to be developed completely within the Internet Engineering Task Force (IETF). A decade later, the IETF's OSPF Working Group still exists, and the OSPF protocol continues to be extended, although the basic OSPF protocol was established with the first publication of the OSPF Version 2 (OSPFv2) specification in 1991.

Tracing OSPF development allows us to introduce the features of OSPF—not just what they are but also why they were considered important. Like the Internet, OSPF has evolved over time. Some current features of OSPF, such as the Point-to-MultiPoint interface, were never envisioned in the original OSPF design. Other features, such as TOS-based routing, were included in the design but never deployed. A timeline showing the major milestones in the development of OSPF is shown in Figure 3.1.

In this chapter, we describe the features of OSPF and the basic design decisions that formed the OSPF protocol. We begin with the first meeting of the OSPF Working Group, at the November 1987 IETF meeting in Boulder, Colorado.

3.1 Functional Requirements

To understand the initial goals of the OSPF Working Group, you need to consider what the Internet of 1987 looked like. It was largely an academic and research network, funded by the U.S. government. At the core of the Internet, the ARPANET had been replaced by the NSFNET backbone and its regional networks. Much of the Internet used

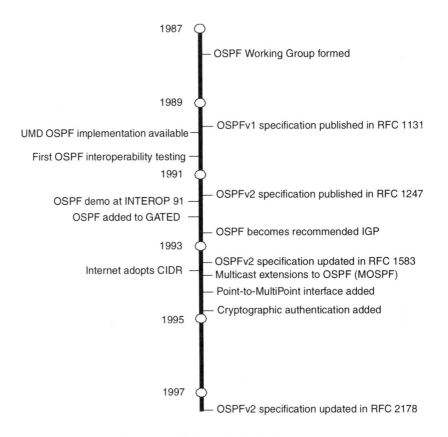

1987 ⊙
— OSPF Working Group formed

1989 ⊙
UMD OSPF implementation available —
— OSPFv1 specification published in RFC 1131
First OSPF interoperability testing —
1991 ⊙
OSPF demo at INTEROP 91 —
— OSPFv2 specification published in RFC 1247
OSPF added to GATED —
— OSPF becomes recommended IGP
1993 ⊙
— OSPFv2 specification updated in RFC 1583
Internet adopts CIDR —
— Multicast extensions to OSPF (MOSPF)
— Point-to-MultiPoint interface added
— Cryptographic authentication added
1995 ⊙

1997 ⊙
— OSPFv2 specification updated in RFC 2178

Figure 3.1 Timeline of OSPF development.

static routing; those Autonomous Systems employing dynamic routing used the Routing Information Protocol (RIP), while the Exterior Gateway Protocol (EGP) was used between Autonomous Systems.

Both of these protocols were having problems. As the size of Autonomous Systems grew and as the size of the Internet routing tables increased, the amount of network bandwidth consumed by RIP updates was increasing, and route-convergence times were becoming unacceptable as the number of routing changes also increased. EGP's update sizes were also increasing, and the topological restrictions imposed by EGP (which technically required a tree topology, coining the term "reachability protocol" instead of a routing protocol) were rapidly becoming unmanageable.

We decided to tackle the problem of producing a RIP replacement. The reasons for trying to solve the RIP problem instead of the EGP problem were twofold. First, the RIP problem seemed easier—being of local-scale scope—than a protocol that has to run over the entire Internet as EGP did. Second, a RIP replacement would have wider applicability, being of use both in the Internet and in commercial TCP/IP networks (what people today call *intranets*). Tackling the EGP problem was left to the designers of BGP [208].

Thus the major requirement was to produce an intra-AS routing protocol (also called an Interior Gateway Protocol, or IGP) that was more efficient than RIP. We wanted a protocol that both consumed fewer network resources than RIP and con- verged faster than RIP when the network changed. Examples of network changes are when communication links, router interfaces, or entire routers fail. After the failure, the best paths to certain destinations change. It takes some time for any routing protocol to find the new best paths, and the paths used in the meantime are sometimes suboptimal or even nonfunctional. The process of finding the new path is called *convergence*.

Other initial functional requirements for the OSPF protocol included the following.

- *A more descriptive routing metric.* RIP uses hop count as its routing metric, and path cost is allowed to range from 1 to 15 only. This created two problems for network administrators. First, it limited the diameters of their networks to 15 router hops. Second, administrators could not take into account such factors as bandwidth and/or delay when configuring their routing systems. For OSPF, we settled on a configurable link metric whose value ranges between 1 and 65,535, with no limitation on total-path cost. This design decision removes network- diameter limitations and allows for configurations such as that in Figure 3.2, where a two-hop terrestrial path (OSPF cost of 200) can be preferred over a direct satellite connection (OSPF cost of 1,000). See Section 4.8 for more details on OSPF's routing metric.

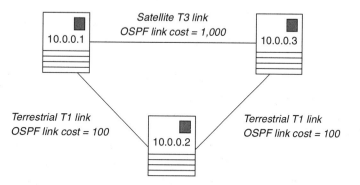

Figure 3.2 Configuring metrics to avoid links with high delay.

- *Equal-cost multipath.* We wanted OSPF to be able to discover multiple best paths to a given destination, when they exist. However, we did not mandate how routers should use these multiple best paths for forwarding data packets. It did not seem necessary to standardize the choice of which of the multiple paths to use for a given packet. There are many strategies: round-robin on a packet-by-packet basis, a hash on the source address, and so on. However, routers with different strategies can be mixed together freely, and a working network will still result.

- *Routing hierarchy.* We wanted to be able to build very large routing domains, on the order of many thousands of routers. The only known way to scale routing to such a size is by introducing hierarchy. The OSPF hierarchy was implemented via a two-level area routing scheme, as described in Section 6.1.

- *Separate internal and external routes.* Autonomous Systems running RIP were having trouble knowing which information to trust. You always want to trust information gained first hand about your own internal routing domain over external routing information that has been injected into your domain. RIP did not distinguish between the two types of information. In OSPF, external routing information is labeled and is explicitly overridden by any internal routing information; see Section 6.2.

- *Support of more flexible subnetting schemes.* When OSPF was first being designed, the Internet was still using Class A, B, and C addresses. IP subnetting did exist, but subnets were always allocated by dividing a given Class A, B, and C address into equal-sized pieces [166]. However, we felt that people were going to want to make more efficient use of the address space, so we made it a requirement that OSPF be able to route to arbitrary [address, mask] combinations. In particular, we wanted to be able to accommodate so-called variable-length subnet masks (VLSMs), whereby a Class A, B, or C address could be carved into unequal-sized subnets.

  This requirement pretty much anticipated classless Internet routing (CIDR). However, it would have to be adjusted slightly to accommodate CIDR completely (see Section 3.7).

- *Security.* We wanted to be able to administratively control which routers joined an OSPF domain. A common problem with RIP is that anyone can bring up a bogus RIP router advertising the default route (or any other route, for that matter), disrupting routing. By authenticating received OSPF packets, a router would have to be given the correct key before it could join the OSPF routing domain.

  This requirement led us to reserve space in OSPF packets for authentication data. But the development of nontrivial authentication algorithms for OSPF would have to wait for several years (see Section 3.7).

- *Type of Service routing.* We wanted to be able to calculate separate routes for IP Type of Service (TOS). TCP/IP supports five classes of TOS: *normal service, minimize monetary cost, maximize reliability, maximize throughput*, and *minimize delay*. The idea behind TOS is that IP packets can be labeled with a particular TOS, which would then influence the handling of the packets, including possibly the route that the packet would take through the Internet (called TOS-based routing).

OSPF supported TOS-based routing from the beginning, allowing the assignment of separate link metrics and building separate routing tables for each TOS. For example, in Figure 3.2, a second metric can be assigned for the maximize-bandwidth TOS, allowing the satellite link to be preferred for file-transfer traffic at the same time that the link is avoided by all other traffic types. TOS support was made optional, giving rise to many arguments about what should happen to a packet designated with, for example, minimize monetary cost when a path minimizing monetary cost does not exist but a normal service path does: Should the packet be discarded, or should it be forwarded along the normal service path instead?

All these design efforts and arguments were really for naught. Although several implementations of OSPF TOS-based routing were developed, TOS-based routing has never been deployed in the Internet. This is probably for lack of a real need for TOS and also because of a chicken-and-egg problem: The hosts do not label packets with TOS because the routers do not act on TOS, and the routers do not act on TOS because the packets are not labeled.

3.2   Design Decisions

After establishing the requirements for the new protocol, the design could begin. This section describes some of the major design decisions made during initial development of OSPF. Some of the decisions were controversial; others were not.

One noncontroversial design decision was the formatting of the OSPF packet. As is done for most TCP/IP protocols, we wanted OSPF packets to be aligned so that they could be processed easily within common computer architectures: 4-byte fields starting at offsets of a multiple of 4 bytes, 2-byte fields starting at even offsets, and so on. Nicely aligned packets also allow protocol implementors in languages such as C to use data structures as "packet templates," simplifying the implementation of packet reception and transmission.

The most major design decision, and also the most controversial one, was choosing the underlying routing protocol technology. At the time, there were two major technologies, which are the same two choices one would have if designing a routing protocol today: link-state and Distance Vector.

Link-State versus Distance Vector

Distance Vector protocols were in common use in the Internet, with RIP being the major example. Distance Vector protocols employ a *distributed-processing model*. Each router participating in a Distance Vector algorithm performs a routing calculation based on the current information received from the router's neighbors. The router then sends the intermediate results of this calculation (which is typically the router's current routing table) to all of its neighbors, causing them to redo their calculations based on this updated information. The neighbors in turn send their updated routing tables to their neighbors, and so on. This process then iterates until all routers converge on the best paths to the destination networks. (For a more detailed description of the Distance Vector algorithm, see Section 2.3.)

Link-state protocols (also called shortest-path first, or SPF, protocols because they commonly use Dijkstra's Shortest Path First algorithm in their routing calculations) employ a *distributed database model*. Each router running a link-state algorithm describes its local environment in link-state advertisements, or LSAs. Local environment includes the router's operational interfaces, the cost to send user data traffic out the interface, and to what the interface connects. These LSAs are distributed to all other routers by a procedure called *flooding*. All routers end up with the same set of LSAs, called the link-state database. From this database, the routers calculate their routing tables, using shortest-paths algorithms, such as Dijkstra's algorithm. (For a more detailed description of link-state algorithms, see Chapter 4, OSPF Basics.)

As mentioned earlier, RIP was having trouble in some of the Internet's larger Autonomous Systems. RIP was taking a long time to converge and was consuming considerable network bandwidth in the process. In addition, RIP is slow to flush unreachable destinations from the network, going through a procedure called counting to infinity (see Section 2.3). Indeed, as shown in [20] and [120], when a network change causes the best path to a destination to lengthen, the routing table entry for the destination in a Distance Vector algorithm will, under some circumstances, take all intermediate values between the old and new costs before finally converging to the new value.

BBN saw similar behavior in the original ARPANET routing algorithm, which was based on Distance Vector. That algorithm's deficiencies included slow response to topological changes, large update packets that interfered with data traffic, and a tendency to form loops that would persist for seconds at a time [147]. In response to these problems, BBN had developed the first link-state routing algorithm, which had performed well in replacement of the original ARPANET routing algorithm ([146], [147], and [220]).

After observing BBN's success in the first link-state algorithm, we decided to develop a link-state routing algorithm for TCP/IP. There was considerable dissent on this issue, however. Link-state routing protocols are more complicated to specify and implement than are Distance Vector protocols. And although link-state routing looked promising to many people, a multivendor link-state routing protocol had never been developed—and some people believed that it could not be done.

In fact, there was enough dissent that we were forced to change the name of the working group from its original Open Interior Gateway Protocol (OIGP) Working Group to the Open Shortest Path First Interior Gateway Protocol (OSPFIGP, later mercifully shortened to OSPF) Working Group, and a short-lived Open Distance Vector Working Group was formed in direct competition.

In retrospect, the industry trend has been toward link-state routing algorithms. Besides OSPF for TCP/IP, link-state routing protocols have been developed for all other major protocol suites: IS-IS for OSI, NetWare Link Services Protocol (NLSP) for Novell Netware, Advanced Peer-to-Peer Networking (APPN) for IBM's SNA, and Private Network-to-Network Interface (PNNI) for ATM. However, the debate about link state versus Distance Vector does continue in a more muted form. Research continues in removing the deficiencies of Distance Vector algorithms [82], with some of these improvements being fielded in an enhancement to Cisco's proprietary Distance Vector algorithm IGRP [96]. RIP, the quintessential Distance Vector algorithm, has been extended to carry CIDR routes [149] and remains widely used in the Internet. The Internet's BGP [208] is also Distance Vector based.

Link-State Basis

Having chosen to create a link-state TCP/IP routing protocol, we found quite a bit of existing technology to draw on. BBN had pioneered link-state routing, having deployed the first link-state routing protocol in May 1979 in the ARPANET network. The ARPANET was both a simple and challenging environment for a routing protocol. The ARPANET was a packet-switching network that provided services at level two of the OSI reference model, similar to an X.25 Public Data Network (PDN). The ARPANET environment was simple because of its uniformity: All switches were manufactured by the same vendor, were running the same software, and were interconnected by serial lines with line rates between 9.6Kb and 56Kb. However, routing within the ARPANET was tasked with a job that no TCP/IP routing protocol has ever taken on: Not only did ARPANET routing route around network failures, but it also detected and routed around network congestion (see Chapter 8, An OSPF FAQ).

The ARPANET link-state protocol had established all of the basic mechanisms of a link-state routing protocol: the link-state database, distribution of the database via a flooding algorithm, and shortest-path routing calculations. An area routing scheme had also been developed for the ARPANET, although it had never been deployed [231]. However, the ARPANET protocol still had room for improvement. For example, the background level of routing traffic was fairly high, since in the ARPANET algorithm, the refresh rate of the link-state database was inversely proportional to the time it took to bring up a new serial line between switches. And in a famous network outage, a vulnerability in the ARPANET flooding algorithm caused a failure of the entire network that could be reversed only by power cycling all the switches concurrently (see Section 4.2.2). Corrective measures for these problems were proposed in a 1983 paper by Perlman [189].

BBN also had converted the ARPANET link-state protocol to a TCP/IP routing protocol [152]. However, this protocol was too inefficient over link technologies common in the Internet, such as Ethernet, because this protocol simulated the ARPANET environment by treating a collection of routers connected to an Ethernet as if they were pairwise-connected by serial lines.

At the same time that we were developing OSPF for TCP/IP, the ISO standards organizations were developing a link-state routing protocol called IS-IS for the OSI protocol stack [112]. The emerging IS-IS protocol had already developed an efficient mechanism for running link-state protocols over broadcast links, such as Ethernet LANs, electing a Designated Router to control flooding and to perform information reduction for each LAN.

These were the link-state routing experiences that we could use as a basis for our protocol design. At the time, some people posed the question, "Why not simply adopt the IS-IS OSI routing protocol as your new routing protocol?" IS-IS was being developed at the same time that we were undertaking development of OSPF. Looking at the emerging IS-IS protocol, we saw a number of barriers to its becoming a TCP/IP routing protocol. We mention a few of these problems by way of example. First, IS-IS ran directly over the link layer, which we thought was the wrong choice for a TCP/IP routing protocol, as explained next. At the time, IS-IS had no way to fragment LSAs, with a router having to originate all of its routing data within a single LSA. In some TCP/IP environments in which routers import many external routes, such a design would be unworkable. IS-IS had an area routing scheme, but one that did not allow any shortcuts between areas that we thought were necessary for an Internet routing protocol. Also, IS-IS made no attempt to align fields in their packet formats, making life more difficult for protocol implementors.

Given these and other technical issues, we considered it simpler to design a new protocol rather than to attempt to modify a protocol such as IS-IS. There were also non-technical considerations. Many people felt that it was better that the IETF have complete control over the OSPF protocol design rather than depend on an ISO committee whose goals, namely, to produce a routing protocol for the OSI protocol stack, were somewhat different. Equally as controversial as the decision about link state versus Distance Vector, the decision to design a brand-new routing protocol would remain a bone of contention for years, until 1992, when OSPF was selected as the Internet's recommended IGP (see Section 3.6).

Encapsulation

When designing a TCP/IP routing protocol, you have three choices for encapsulation of your new protocol's packets: They can run directly over the link layer, directly over the IP network layer, or over IP's transport protocols UDP or TCP.

Running directly over the link layer is problematic, for the following reasons. Most link layers do not provide fragmentation and reassembly services, so your routing protocol would have to implement its own fragmentation. You would also have to get code points assigned for all of the various link layers that your protocol runs over, for example an *Ethernet type* for running over Ethernet.

Running over IP allows your protocol to use all of IP's network-layer services. You can use IP fragmentation and reassembly instead of creating your own. IP runs over virtually any link type; so if your protocol runs over IP, you do not have to worry about allocation of code points for the various link layers. If you want to send your routing protocol packets more than one hop and if you are careful, you can even use the forwarding services of the IP layer (OSPF does this for its virtual links; see Section 6.1.1). You have to be careful, though, that you do not enter into a chicken-and-egg situation, whereby your routing protocol depends on the forwarding, which in turn depends on the data supplied by your routing protocol.

Using UDP gives you a couple of additional benefits. It provides you with an optional checksum to verify integrity of your protocol packets. Each UDP protocol is assigned a UDP port for multiplexing over the UDP layer, and these UDP ports are much more abundant than IP protocol numbers, coming from a 16-bit rather than an 8-bit space. Also, UDP protocols are easier to deploy on many operating systems: Often, sending or receiving packets directly over IP requires special privileges (for example, being "superuser" on a UNIX system), whereas the UDP interface is usually available to all users and their applications. If running over TCP, an additional benefit is running over a reliable byte stream (for example, BGP [208]).

We did not need the reliability of TCP; link-state routing protocols have their own reliability built into their flooding algorithms, and TCP would just get in the way. Also, the ease of applications in UNIX and other operating systems to send and receive UDP packets was seen by some as a disadvantage; the necessity of gaining OS privileges was seen as providing some small amount of security. The additional small benefits of UDP encapsulation were outweighed by the extra 8 bytes of UDP header overhead that would appear in every protocol packet. So we decided to run OSPF directly over the IP network layer, and we received an assignment of IP protocol number 89 from the IANA [212].

One other issue involving encapsulation appeared when running over broadcast subnets, such as Ethernet LANs. Existing TCP/IP routing protocols, such as RIP, transmitted routing protocol packets as IP broadcasts on these networks. However, this meant that all hosts on the LAN would receive the RIP packets, even if they were not running RIP (or even if they were not running the TCP/IP stack). An emerging technology—IP multicast—solved this problem by allowing a single IP packet to be sent and then received only by those hosts interested in the packet. The problem with IP multicast was that it was not supported in most operating systems. For example, if you wanted to use IP multicast on a UNIX workstation, you would have to build your own UNIX kernel with the multicast additions. But multicast was clearly a better solution than broadcast, and so we bit the bullet and requested a pair of IP multicast addresses for use by OSPF over Ethernet and other broadcast subnets (see Section 5.2).

LSA Fragmentation

Switches running a link-state routing protocol advertise their routing information in link-state advertisements, or LSAs. If a switch advertises all of its information in a single LSA, that LSA could get very large indeed. For example, an IP router may want to advertise many thousands of routes about destinations elsewhere in the Internet. Instead of advertising a single large LSA, most link-state protocols allow the switches to originate multiple smaller LSAs. We call this behavior *LSA fragmentation.*

In OSPF, we could have made the LSAs quite large; since OSPF has access to the IP network layer's fragmentation and reassembly services, OSPF LSAs could have been up to 65,000 bytes long. However, IP fragmentation should usually be avoided [125]. So we definitely wanted to make OSPF LSAs smaller than common link MTUs found in the Internet. The smallest common MTU is Ethernet's 1,500 bytes [165].

Making LSAs as large as possible minimizes the static size of the link-state database, because the bookkeeping portion of the LSA header is amortized over more data. However, we opted to keep OSPF LSAs as small as possible, advertising each separable piece of routing data in a distinct LSA. Making the link-state database somewhat larger in fact minimizes the total amount of routing traffic; when something in the OSPF routing domain changes, only the changed routing information gets reflooded.

Keeping the data within LSAs small and of fixed format also made LSAs easy to build and parse. This was important to those of us who had spent a lot of time writing code to build packets in those routing protocols, such as EGP [162], with complicated packet formats.

Note that we did not make the LSA format flexible and open-ended, as is done in other link-state protocols. Although flexible formats allow some implementations to experiment with efficient packing algorithms, they make the development of packet reception code and interoperability testing more difficult by increasing the number of test cases. Worse, flexible formats leave the network vulnerable to bad packing algorithms in other implementations.

Common Mechanisms over Disparate Link Layers

Many kinds of link-level technologies, with different properties, are in use in the Internet. Some connect only two routers, such as synchronous serial lines. Others may connect many routers, such as a large Frame Relay public-data network. Some may allow packets to be broadcast or multicast, such as Ethernet. Others may not, such as an ATM subnet. Link technologies also have different MTUs, transmission speeds, and error rates. Link-state routing as originally developed for the ARPANET was designed for switches interconnected via leased serial lines (called point-to-point links in OSPF). However, we wanted OSPF to work over all of the Internet's link technologies and to work the same way over each link technology, or at least to minimize any link-specific functionality. A few examples follow.

The first example was the flooding of LSAs over broadcast LANs. We could have modeled a collection of *n* routers attached to a broadcast LAN as $n * (n - 1) / 2$ point-to-point connections (one for each pair of routers) and then run the point-to-point flooding algorithm over each connection. Although simple, this approach costs too much in terms of the amount of flooding traffic that would be sent over the LAN. Instead we added a level of indirection: We modeled the LAN connectivity, from the flooding algorithm's point of view, as a star network of *n* point-to-point connections. A special router, called the Designated Router, on the LAN is elected, and all other routers on the LAN need to flood LSAs to/from the Designated Router only. Running a slight variant of the point-to-point flooding algorithm over these *n* connections then does a nice job of minimizing flooding traffic on the LAN (see Section 5.2.2).

Another example is the operation of OSPF over X.25 PDNs. Except for the missing broadcast/multicast capability, as far as the operation of a link-state protocol was concerned, an X.25 subnet had the same properties as an Ethernet: many routers connected to a common medium, each pair of which can communicate directly. We coined the term *NBMA* (nonbroadcast multiaccess) for these subnets. Operation of OSPF over NBMAs is almost identical to operation of OSPF over broadcast LANs: Flooding uses the Designated Router, and both subnets are represented identically within the OSPF link-state database by network-LSAs (see Section 5.2.3). The only real difference between broadcast subnets and NBMA subnets is in the discovery of neighboring routers. On broadcast networks, a router can discover its neighbors dynamically by sending multicast probes (called Hello packets in OSPF); on NBMA networks, a router's neighbors may have to be configured (see Section 5.3.1).

Unfortunately not all link technologies could be mapped directly to leased serial lines or Ethernets. For example, to support OSPF over dial-up telephone lines, a collection of significantly different mechanisms had to be developed (see Section 7.3).

Backup Designated Router

When running over broadcast and NBMA segments, OSPF relies on the Designated Router. All LSAs flooded over a broadcast or NBMA subnet go through the subnet's Designated Router, which is responsible for reporting the subnet's local topology within a network-LSA. This behavior, however, leads to a robustness problem. When the Designated Router fails, neither LSAs nor user data can be forwarded over the subnet until after a new Designated Router is established.

Even inadvertently replacing the current Designated Router with another causes some disruption, as all routers must synchronize with the new Designated Router and a new network-LSA is flooded to all OSPF routers, causing all routers to rerun their routing calculations. To make sure that a switch of Designated Router happens only on failures, we designed the Designated Router election so that routers newly added to the subnet always defer to the existing Designated Router.

Then, to ensure that the switchover occurs as quickly as possible on failures, we introduced the concept of a *Backup Designated Router*. The Backup Designated Router also is elected and then prequalified to take over as Designated Router, all while the current Designated Router is operating normally. If the Designated Router fails, the Backup Designated Router keeps the flooding over the subnet going, even before the Designated Router's failure is detected (see Section 5.2.2). As soon as the failure is discovered, the Backup Designated Router is promoted to Designated Router; since all other routers on the subnet have already synchronized with the Backup Designated Router, the switchover is relatively painless.

External Route Tag

We had designed a way to import external routes into an OSPF routing domain. External routes are those routes learned from other sources: routes learned from routing protocols, such as RIP or BGP, or static information configured by network managers. Each external route is imported in its own LSA. At the urging of one of the OSPF Working Group's members, Milo Medin, we also imported each route with a 32-bit tag called the external route tag. This tag is not used by the OSPF protocol itself but instead was to be used to convey information, transparently to OSPF, across an OSPF routing domain. Although when OSPF was initially designed, we did not know exactly what the tag would be used for, it has proved to be very useful over the years.

The first use for the tag was to convey policy information between routers on the boundary of the OSPF domain. In the Internet, a single router may import thousands of external routes into an OSPF routing domain. Other routers on the boundary of the OSPF domain must decide, after learning of the routes, whether to readvertise them to other routing domains. A router usually makes this decision by scanning manually configured lists of routing filters. The tag simplifies the configuration of routing filters by allowing routes to be grouped together by policy when imported into the OSPF domain. Then a routing policy can simply say, "Readvertise routes with tag X," rather than "Readvertise routes X_1, X_2, ..., X_n." The same sort of functionality is provided in BGP when using BGP communities [39].

Rules were written on how to exchange routing information between the OSPF and BGP routing protocols (see Section 11.6.1). Use of the external route tag allows OSPF routers to import routes (namely, RIP routes, statically configured routes, or BGP-learned routes with short AS paths) with enough additional information to construct correct BGP attributes at the other side of the OSPF routing domain. This ability removes the necessity to also advertise such routes across the OSPF routing domain in IBGP. Although not yet implemented, use of the tag also allows complete replacement of IBGP by an alternative OSPF mechanism (see Section 7.6).

Hierarchical Abstraction

In order to be able to build large OSPF networks, we allowed an OSPF routing domain to be split into regions, or *areas*. Details of any particular area were to be hidden from all other areas, and addressing information would be aggregated when advertised across area boundaries. Both of these functions would reduce the size of a router's routing table and link-state database, thereby enabling the size of the overall routing domain to grow larger. Splitting an OSPF routing domain into areas could also be considered to be a two-level hierarchical routing scheme (see Chapter 6, Hierarchical Routing in OSPF).

Several design decisions needed to be made about the area organization. First, what would be on the area boundary—routers, network segments, or both? As discussed in Chapter 2, Internet Routing Protocols, the Internet is split into Autonomous Systems, the boundaries of which are composed of network segments. For OSPF areas, however, we took the opposite tack, choosing routers as the area boundaries. This decision meant that each network segment would belong to one and only one area, a property that we thought would make the aggregation of addresses across area boundaries easier.

Second, how would we describe an area to other areas? In order to achieve the scaling properties we desired, we had to reduce the information associated with an area before advertising it to other areas. This information reduction is called *abstraction*. Abstraction in a link-state routing algorithm is a difficult problem. We considered an analog of the OSPF network-LSA, which abstracts the OSPF connectivity across a given broadcast subnet (see Section 5.2.3); however, that kind of abstraction has a tendency to distort metric information. Instead we decided to simply summarize a list of addresses reachable within the area. These addresses are then passed from area to area, just as routes are advertised from router to router within a Distance Vector protocol (see Section 2.3). For other link-state routing abstraction schemes, see [9] and [38].

Although we were using Distance Vector mechanisms between areas, we wanted to avoid the common pitfalls of Distance Vector algorithms. So we required that all areas be directly connected to a special area, called the *backbone area*. By forcing all of an area's routing information to go through the backbone area on the way to other areas, we thus mandated a simple hub-and-spoke area organization that standard Distance Vector mechanisms could handle without problems.

Yet forcing all areas to be physically connected to a single backbone area seemed to be too onerous. To get around this restriction, we enabled the logical extension of the backbone area through the configuration of what we called *virtual links*. Virtual links allowed us to tunnel routing information through areas, creating a logical hub-and-spoke topology on any arbitrary physical area topology (see Section 6.1.2).

3.3   OSPFv1: A False Start

The OSPF protocol specification was first published in October 1989, as RFC 1131 [174]. Like most Internet protocols, OSPF has a version number. RFC 1131 documented version 1 of the OSPF protocol.

The IETF's motto is *rough consensus and running code*. Completing the OSPF design was the first part of the OSPF Working Group's job; now we had to prove that the protocol worked by implementing it.

Two implementations of OSPFv1 were written, one to run on Proteon's routers, and another, written by Rob Coltun at the University of Maryland, to run on UNIX workstations. The latter implementation was made available in source code form for a very nominal fee. This implementation later became quite widespread and is now available as part of the GATED distribution [83].

The implementation of a new protocol invariably uncovers problems, and OSPFv1 was no exception. The first problem we noticed was that OSPFv1 had trouble deleting information from the routing system. Information is deleted in OSPF through the use of so-called MaxAge LSAs (see Section 4.7.2). However, in OSPFv1, MaxAge LSAs often circulated through the routing system long after they had served their function. Besides being somewhat disconcerting, this behavior could prevent new information from being introduced. Although we fixed this problem in the next version of OSPF, problems with deleting MaxAge LSAs persisted in many implementations for years.

Another problem was more hypothetical. The original ARPANET link-state routing protocol had a flaw that could cause an entire network to "melt down" as routing updates would continue to circulate at great speeds throughout the network until the network itself was shut down as a corrective action [221]. At the root of this problem was the way in which the ARPANET protocol detected whether an LSA was being updated. In all link-state algorithms, LSAs have sequence numbers: When a router receives two copies of the same LSA, the copy with the "higher" sequence number is an update of the other copy. Just what "higher" means depends on how the sequence space is organized. In the original ARPANET algorithm, the sequence number space was circular, and data corruption could confuse the determination of which LSA was the update. In OSPFv1, we had made the corrections suggested in [189] to avoid this problem, but these corrections were not quite foolproof. To patch the last vulnerability, we needed to change the LSA sequence space to a simple linear space, as described in Section 4.2.2.

Implementation of OSPFv1 uncovered several places where OSPF could be optimized. For example, OSPFv1 specified that after a router interface became operational, the router had to wait a fixed time interval before establishing OSPF neighbor relationships over the interface. However, it turned out that information contained in OSPF packets received over the interface could make this interval much smaller. As another example, OSPF requires that you exchange information about the full link-state database with a newly discovered OSPF neighbor. OSPFv1 specified that you had to send a description of your full database before requesting to receive pieces of your neighbor's database. However, it turned out to be much more efficient for OSPF routers to mix database descriptions and requests.

It also became clear that a number of points in the OSPFv1 specification were not completely specified. For example, OSPFv1 gave a detailed description of how to build an OSPF router's routing table but did not explain how a router performs a routing table lookup: choosing the "best-matching" routing table entry for a given IP destination. In fact, up until this point, no IP routing protocol had a completely specified routing table lookup.

All of these issues led us to revise the OSPFv1 specification. A fix to the LSA sequence space could not be backward compatible; any change to the LSA sequence space would lead to LSA sequence-number confusion between routers running the old and new versions of the specification, which is what we were trying to avoid in the first place. Hence we incremented the OSPF version number, producing a specification for OSPFv2, which was eventually published as RFC 1247 in July 1991 [176].

The failure of OSPFv1 and OSPFv2 to interoperate was not an issue, since OSPFv1 was never deployed. Since we did not have to worry about backward compatibility, we took this opportunity to simplify the OSPF packet formats. It also had become clear that there were some OSPF features, such as the ability of OSPF routing to take into account an IP packet's Type of Service label, which were not going to be implemented by everyone. In order to make such features optional, we introduced a way for routers to negotiate capabilities, by adding an Options field to OSPF packets and LSAs (see Chapter 7, OSPF Extensions).

Going from OSPFv1 to OSPFv2 was the last time that we could make sweeping changes to OSPF. OSPFv2 would soon be deployed in the Internet, and all future changes would have to be made with an eye toward keeping the installed base of OSPF routers running. Although the OSPF specification has been reissued several times since the publication of RFC 1247, the current specification still has the OSPF version number set to 2 and still interoperates with implementations of the original RFC 1247.

3.4   Interoperability Testing

Making sure that multiple independent implementations of a protocol can interoperate is essential to the creation of a good protocol. Until interoperability is demonstrated, one can never be sure that the protocol specification is clear and unambiguous. Often interoperability testing will uncover holes in the protocol specification; unwritten assumptions made by protocol designers are not always apparent to implementors when they read the specification for the first time. Interoperability testing is especially important for routing protocols, which are distributed algorithms that require the concerted interaction of many routers (instead of just the interoperability of two hosts, as, for example, with transport algorithms such as TCP). For this reason, interoperability of independent implementations is one of the requirements for advancement of routing protocols in the IETF's standard process [98].

Six organized interoperability sessions were held during the initial development of the OSPF protocol, in the years 1990 through 1994. These sessions were really more like the *bake-offs* held periodically for various Internet protocols. One company would volunteer to host an interoperability session, and then OSPF developers from other companies would arrive with their routers for several days of testing. The first session was held at Proteon, Inc., and involved three router vendors. Then came sessions hosted by SURANet (an NSF regional network, since purchased by BBN Planet), 3Com, FTP Software, and Xyplex. A final session, held by the Corporation for Open Systems' lab in Reston, Va., attracted 12 router vendors.

These tests were loosely organized, with a collegial atmosphere. Much of the first day was typically spent stringing Ethernet and serial cables. We would then agree on several network topologies and failure scenarios to try. Along the way, we would find bugs, usually in the implementations, although sometimes in the OSPF protocol itself. Sometimes several developers would examine a packet trace to try to isolate a problem. After having found a bug, developers would typically change their code (some had brought their complete development environments on portable PCs, whereas others telnetted back to their companies' development systems), reload their routers, and try the tests again. It was a common occurrence at these sessions to see developers from several companies all leaning over a competitor's shoulder, trying to fix a bug!

Test topologies were typically small, since each router vendor could bring only a couple of routers. For example, one of the network topologies used during the testing session at 3Com is pictured in Figure 3.3. In this testing session and others, a live Internet connection (this time to BARRNet, the Bay Area NSF Regional Network, which has since been purchased by BBN Planet) was used in order to import some Internet routes into the testing environment.

OSPF bake-offs are no longer scheduled today. Nonetheless, there are still places that vendors can take their OSPF implementations for testing, such as University of New Hampshire's InterOperability Lab [251].

Tools

To determine how well OSPF was working and to track down problems when they arose, we needed some tools. To discover whether OSPF was building the correct routes, we used standard Internet tools, such as `traceroute` and `ping` (see Chapter 12, Debugging Routing Problems). But in order to monitor OSPF protocol performance, new tools had to be created.

First, we needed a way to see the OSPF packets that were being sent and received during the testing. Network analyzers, such as the Network General Sniffer, were attached to our test network in order to perform packet collection (see Section 12.8). However, these analyzers did not know how to decode OSPF packets, and manually

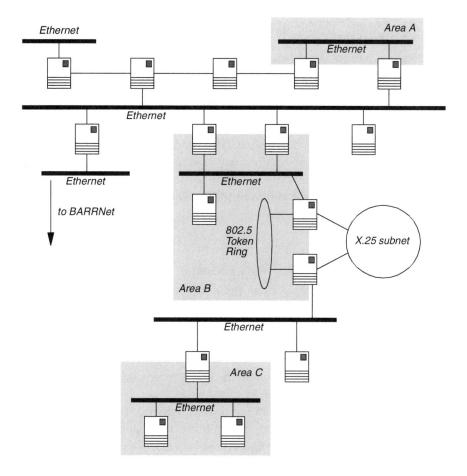

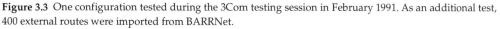

Figure 3.3 One configuration tested during the 3Com testing session in February 1991. As an additional test, 400 external routes were imported from BARRNet.

decoding hexadecimal packet dumps was cumbersome. So we modified the analyzers' software to decode OSPF packets and to be able to filter out non-OSPF packets, in order to make analysis of the remaining OSPF packets easier.

Most of the job of a link-state protocol such as OSPF is to keep the database of LSAs synchronized between routers. But determining whether the database was synchronized proved difficult. Having each router list its complete set of LSAs and then comparing the list was very time consuming and error prone—even in our small test setups, the OSPF database often had hundreds of LSAs. Having each router print how many LSAs were in its database was useful, but just because each router had the same number of LSAs did not mean that the databases were synchronized. For example, one router might have more up-to-date copies of particular LSAs than another router. To detect these situations, we had each router report a 32-bit checksum of its database, which proved a reliable indication of database synchronization.

The database checksum and other statistics that we found useful during testing were eventually added to the OSPF Management Information Base (see Section 11.2), so that the information could be extracted via SNMP.

Most of the interoperability testing was limited to small networks. However, at the 1994 COS testing, Rob Coltun modified his OSPF implementation so that a UNIX workstation could both participate in the testing as an OSPF router and simulate an additional number of OSPF routers. This modified implementation allowed us to test how other OSPF implementations behaved in relatively large networks, by increasing the OSPF area size to 240 routers and importing a number of external routes equal to the full Internet routing table at that time (10,000 entries).

Problems Found

Most problems found during interoperability testing were implementation problems. Developers participating in interoperability tests quickly learn to bulletproof their implementations. Interoperability tests produce all kinds of behavior, some of which is counter to the protocol specifications. Malformed protocol packets are the most common violation. A robust protocol implementation detects these violations and responds gracefully.

However, quite a few errors in the OSPF specification were also found during the testing. Some representative examples follow.

The most common problem was incomplete specification, usually in the OSPF packet and LSA formats. For example, in the first round of testing, there was a disagreement on how to represent the default route in OSPF. Routes are represented in OSPF as [network, mask] pairs. However, the OSPF specification defined the default route as a route with network equal to 0.0.0.0, without specifying the associated mask value. During testing, one implementation originated a route with network equal to 0.0.0.0 and a nonzero mask. Some implementations interpreted this as a default route, but others did not, because they were expecting a mask of 0.0.0.0.

Testing often produced a rapidly changing environment, with routers being continually rebooted, interfaces going up and down, addresses changing, and so on. These rapid changes stressed the OSPF protocol mechanisms. For example, after discovering each other, neighboring OSPF routers synchronize their OSPF databases by a procedure called Database Exchange (see Section 4.7.1). This procedure assumed that the sequence number in LSAs always progressed. But in a rapidly changing network, we saw that this was not necessarily the case. It was possible that during Database Exchange, an LSA could be deleted and then reoriginated with the initial (smallest) sequence number, giving the appearance that the LSA's sequence number was going backward! The specification of Database Exchange had to be modified accordingly; for more details on this issue, see the FAQ entitled "Why install MaxAge LSAs in the link-state database when there are no previous instances?" in Chapter 8.

Selection of the network configurations to test was fairly random, with several people drawing on the whiteboard at once. This sometimes yielded situations not anticipated when OSPF was designed. For example, in the fifth round of testing, a virtual-link configuration was constructed that caused the OSPF routing calculation to fail. As a result, the calculation of OSPF routes when virtual links are in use was significantly changed when the OSPF specification was republished in March 1994 [177].

INTEROP Demo

In October 1991, we performed interoperability testing of a different type: We held an interoperability demonstration at the INTEROP 91 Fall trade show. Unlike previous OSPF tests, the OSPF routers this time were being used in a production environment, comprising INTEROP's ShowNet. The ShowNet provided TCP/IP connectivity between the trade show booths and the Internet, providing Ethernet and/or Token Ring drops to each booth. FDDI rings connected the Ethernet and Token Ring segments, and a router running EGP was connected via a T1 connection to the Internet. A diagram of the INTEROP 91 ShowNet is shown in Figure 3.4. All routers pictured ran OSPF, and there were additional OSPF routers in the booths of the 11 vendors supplying OSPF routers.

It is difficult to create a flashy demonstration of a routing protocol. When the routing protocol is working, one does not really notice that it is there at all. We did have an HP Openview Network Management Station, modified to display the OSPF routers' database checksums. Looking at the display, one could tell when new OSPF information was being flooded. We also had an Excelan LANalyzer network analyzer modified to show the level of OSPF protocol traffic, separated by OSPF packet type (see Section 4.5).

The INTEROP 91 OSPF demonstration was a one-time event. Succeeding INTEROP ShowNets ran OSPF not as a demo but as an integral part of their operational environments.

3.5   Field Trials

Interoperability testing is very valuable when developing a routing protocol, but there is no substitute for seeing how well the protocol works in a production environment. For that reason, concurrent with the interoperability test sessions, we started looking for places in the Internet to deploy OSPF.

But first we had to start using it ourselves. The best way to get a superior product is to have the people who are developing the product use it on a day-to-day basis. In 1990, when I was working at Proteon, Inc., we had an in-house router network that was used

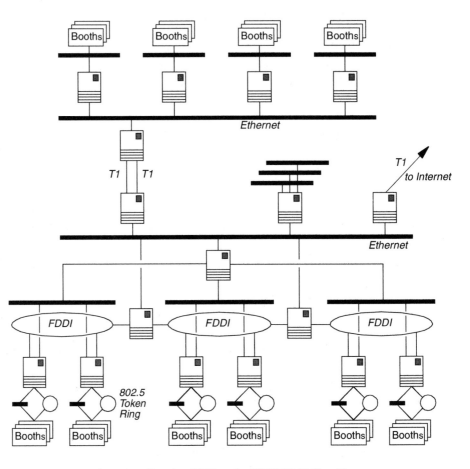

Figure 3.4 Running OSPF on the INTEROP 91 ShowNet.

to carry on the business of the company. If the network failed, you knew it instantly, as the workstation or PC on your desk would pretty much cease to function. This network consisted of about 20 routers running RIP, interconnecting Ethernet and 802.5 Token Ring LANs with a high-speed proprietary LAN technology called Pronet-80. One evening in 1990, after the Proteon OSPF implementation was well tested in a lab environment, I started converting the Proteon network from RIP to OSPF. After about the sixth router was converted, the routers began crashing. So I turned OSPF off and tried again the next night after making appropriate changes to the software. This scenario continued for several nights in a row, until the network ran smoothly. At that point, I left the network running OSPF. Over time, Proteon's operational network grew to more than 60 routers, and it was always an important proving ground for new releases of OSPF software. In time, the Proteon network also ran OSPF extensions, such as MOSPF and the OSPF database-overflow mechanisms.

At this point, we knew that OSPF could be run in an operational network, but we were not sure that OSPF could be managed by people other than the OSPF software developers. We began looking for other networks to run OSPF. The NSF regional networks seemed likely candidates. These networks were the largest and most demanding of all the TCP/IP networks that existed at the time, and it was these networks that drove the design of the OSPF protocol in the first place (see Section 3.1).

The first network that we attempted to convert to OSPF was the NSF regional network SURANet, in 1990. At that time, SURANet had about 60 routers, all running RIP. We decided to convert the network incrementally, converting one router at a time from RIP to OSPF. In order to do an incremental conversion, one has to have routers running both protocols simultaneously, converting RIP routes to OSPF routes and vice versa; this can be dangerous if not handled correctly (see Section 11.6). In addition, two other requirements were imposed on the transition. First, the routing tables in the routers were to look the same regardless of whether the router was running OSPF, RIP, or both protocols simultaneously (see Section 11.6.2). Second, during the transition, we had to manage all routers through the in-band mechanisms of TELNET consoles and SNMP. With these restrictions, conversion of SURANet was abandoned after several attempts. Such a conversion today would be easy, but then it was too difficult to monitor the conversion using in-band management, and the mechanisms for running OSPF and RIP simultaneously had not been adequately designed, producing instead an overabundance of routing traffic.

The first deployment of OSPF in the Internet was in April 1990. Milo Medin and Jeff Burgan converted the NASA Science Internet network from RIP to OSPF, and a day later Vince Fuller started running OSPF on the NSF regional network BARRNet [170]. In both cases, all routers were converted at one time. In the NASA Science Internet network, this was made easier because all routers could be managed out-of-band via modem connections to the routers' consoles.

Feature Requests

Deployment of a protocol often reveals places where it can be improved. The Internet standards process recognizes the importance of deployment, emphasizing protocol implementation and operational experience as a protocol advances up the Internet standards ladder [98]. Deployment of OSPF led to a number of protocol modifications to increase the protocol's usefulness in the Internet.

People who manage Internet networks are very concerned about optimizing the paths that data takes across their networks. They do not like packets taking extra hops. As soon as OSPF was deployed in the Internet, it was found that OSPF could produce extra hops at the boundary between the OSPF routing domain and another Autonomous System. At the time, these boundaries were called DMZs, borrowing military terminology, and were typically implemented as shared Ethernets where routers from two or more ASs would connect and exchange routing information via the EGP protocol. (Today the boundaries are called *Network Access Points* or NAPs, and are typically implemented as FDDI rings, ATM subnets, and so on, and BGP is used instead of EGP, but otherwise the same ideas apply.) An example of the extra hop is shown in Figure 3.5.

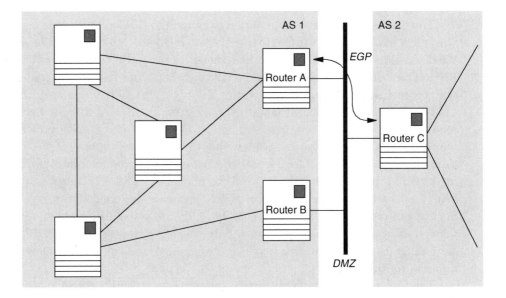

Figure 3.5 Use of OSPF's forwarding address.

The OSPF routing domain in AS 1 has placed two routers on the DMZ Ethernet, but only one of these routers, router A, is exchanging routing information with the router from AS 2, router C. Router A would then import the routes into the OSPF routing domain. However, in importing these routes, router A was saying, "Send me traffic for destinations in AS 2." This meant that router B would send such traffic first to router A instead of directly to router C. To get rid of this extra hop, we introduced the concept of a *forwarding address* into OSPF. This concept allows router A to say, "Send traffic destined for AS 2 directly to router C." The EGP routing protocol also had a forwarding-address concept, called third-party EGP, and forwarding addresses were later added to the BGP and RIP-II routing protocols.

People who deployed OSPF also wanted to run OSPF on as many of their routers as possible so as to minimize the number of routing protocols they had to deal with. However, some of their routers had only minimal resources, especially when it came to available memory. So OSPF *stub areas* were invented—regions at the edge of the Autonomous System whose routers would rely mainly on a default route (see Section 7.2). Routers within stub areas would as a result have only small routing tables but would still be able to participate in OSPF routing.

Production environments often require more flexibility than anticipated by protocol designers. For example, OSPF includes an area routing scheme. At the edge of an area, IP addresses can be aggregated before being advertised further, allowing a reduction in routing table size. Originally it was required that all such aggregations be nonoverlapping. However, the following scenario was common in practice: A range of addresses was assigned to one area, but then later on, some of these addresses were reassigned to other areas. (This is similar to what happens in today's provider-based addressing model when someone changes Internet providers; see Section 2.2.) You then want one area to advertise the original aggregate and other areas to advertise more specific parts of the aggregate. The OSPF specification was amended to allow such a configuration.

Problems Found

Production environments can also often be more demanding than interoperability tests. The most obvious example is network size; it is impractical to put together very large testbeds, and even if you could do so, you would never replicate completely the traffic patterns that you would see in a real network. Thus production networks often reveal protocol problems that have not been seen before. A couple of examples taken from experience with OSPF in real networks follow.

People tried using OSPF on very slow links. Requests to delete OSPF routing information, called MaxAge LSAs, could get queued on these slow links for many seconds during periods of congestion. This in turn could inhibit the origination of new OSPF information, spreading congestion even further. To fix this problem, OSPF's flooding mechanism was altered. Not surprisingly, this flooding alteration was also required to operate OSPF over dial-up links (OSPF's so-called *Demand Circuit extensions*, as described in Section 7.3).

When OSPF was originally designed, only a few different common link technologies were running IP: Ethernet and point-to-point serial lines running proprietary data-link encapsulations. PPP and FDDI were just being developed. Later on, data-link technologies that had a rather ill-defined IP MTU (maximum transmission unit) came into use—802.5 Token Ring and Frame Relay are two examples. Over these data links, it is possible that two neighboring routers will disagree on the largest packet that can be sent over the link, which causes problems in forwarding. As one router sends a packet that is too big for the other to receive, it becomes impossible to deliver large packets over certain paths. (One might think that IP fragmentation would deal with this situation, but although fragmentation nicely handles links with differing MTUs, it assumes that all routers attached to a given link agree on that link's MTU.) As a result, OSPF was modified to detect and avoid links having MTU mismatches.

3.6   On Becoming a Standard

Starting in 1992, the IETF began the process of selecting a common IGP for the Internet. The de facto common IGP, RIP, was no longer viewed as adequate. Two candidates for the common IGP emerged: OSPF and Integrated IS-IS [30].

Both OSPF and the OSI routing protocol IS-IS are link-state protocols. There are, of course, technical differences between them. Integrated IS-IS was an enhancement to IS-IS, allowing both IP and OSI routes to be calculated by a single routing protocol. The OSPF developers thought that their original reasons for not choosing IS-IS as a base (see Section 3.2) were still valid, making OSPF a better choice. The IS-IS developers had their own technical reasons for preferring IS-IS. These technical issues were debated on mailing lists and other technical forums ([156] and [191]).

However, instead of the technical details, two other issues dominated the debate. First, the decision between OSPF and Integrated IS-IS was a continuation of the tension between the TCP/IP and OSI protocol suites, similar to the SNMP versus CMIP debates in previous years and the debate over the various IPv6 choices in later years. Many of the OSPF supporters believed that it was important to have an Internet routing protocol over which the IETF had change control. On the other hand, some Integrated IS-IS supporters viewed the choice of common IGP as an opportunity for significant deployment of the OSI protocol suite within the Internet.

Another issue was over integrated routing itself. If you wanted to simultaneously support two separate protocol suites, such as TCP/IP and OSI, should you do this with a single integrated instance of a routing protocol, or should each protocol suite have its own routing protocol? Supporters of integrated routing argued that it was more efficient and easier for software developers. Opponents of integrated routing, labeled adherents of a Ships-in-the-Night, or SIN approach, argued that only separate routing protocols provided the needed flexibility for deployment of multiple protocols. The integrated-routing debate, just as with the Bellman-Ford versus link-state routing debate, continues today as people consider deploying IPv6 into the existing Internet.

The IETF—whose motto is *rough consensus and running code*—is not set up to make quick decisions when confronted with multiple competing protocols. In the end, the IETF chose OSPF as the common IGP [85], [109]. At that point, however, the choice was anticlimactic, since the market had already made the decision, with all the major routing manufacturers opting to implement OSPF.

At the same time as the choice for the Internet's common IGP was being made, criteria for the standardization of routing protocols were also being determined. Routing protocols typically involve the interoperation of many routers instead of simply a pair of hosts for a transport protocol such as TCP. For this reason, more stringent criteria involving testing, deployment, and multiple independently developed implementations were required [98]. Each Internet routing protocol must document how it meets these criteria; for OSPF, these documents can be found in [170], [173], and [175].

3.7   The Internet Evolves

The basic OSPF design was completed in 1989 and 1990. However, the Internet changes continually, and Internet protocols must adapt to these changes or become obsolete. In this section, we examine how changes in the Internet have led to changes in OSPF.

CIDR

In 1993, it became apparent that the growth in the Internet was going to soon cause the routers at the core of the Internet to run out of routing table space. To keep the Internet running, the previous procedure of chopping the Internet address into fixed-length pieces (called Class A, B, and C addresses and their fixed-length subnets; see Section 1.2.2) was abandoned. Instead Internet routing would be based on address prefixes. Each routing protocol would have to advertise the size of prefixes by advertising the number of significant bits or, alternatively, a mask, with each prefix. This new addressing method was called Classless Inter-Domain Routing (CIDR) [81].

Older Internet routing protocols whose packet formats were based on Class A, B, and C addressing were either discarded or updated. EGP and earlier versions of BGP were rapidly replaced by BGP-4 [208]. RIP and IGRP were updated to become RIP-II and EIGRP, respectively.

OSPF had always advertised each prefix together with its mask and did not depend on Class A, B, and C addressing. As CIDR was deployed, however, one problem became apparent. OSPF imported external routes (for example, routes learned from BGP) into the OSPF routing domain in AS-external-LSAs. When imported by a single router, multiple AS-external-LSAs were distinguished by their Link State ID; the Link State ID was supposed to be set to the address prefix of the imported route. However, sometimes a router might want to import the same prefix with two different lengths—for example, 192.9.0.0/16 and 192.9.0.0/24—and this was impossible, since both would use the Link State ID of 192.9.0.0. As it looked as though such situations might become commonplace—with, for example, an organization shifting Internet providers yet keeping its IP addresses—the rules for setting Link State IDs in AS-external-LSAs had to be modified.

Frame Relay Subnets

OSPF was designed to run over various types of links, including point-to-point links; broadcast subnets, such as Ethernet; and nonbroadcast subnets supporting many routers (see Chapter 5, OSPF Network Types). These nonbroadcast subnets were called nonbroadcast multiaccess networks (NBMAs). When running over NBMAs, OSPF assumes that each router attached to the NBMA can communicate directly. This assumption was valid for X.25 PDNS using SVCs, the original model for an OSPF NBMA.

Later Frame Relay subnets implemented out of PVCs became common in the Internet. Application of NBMAs to Frame Relay subnets met with only partial success. Often PVCs were not configured in a full mesh, or even if they were, individual PVCs were subject to failure; either condition violated the NBMA assumption of direct communication. Configuration guidelines were established to ameliorate these problems by configuring a single Frame Relay subnet as multiple NBMAs [65]. Unfortunately such a configuration is often confusing and error prone.

To solve these problems running OSPF over Frame Relay, the Point-to-MultiPoint subnet was eventually developed as an alternative to OSPF's NBMA support (see Section 5.4). Although not as efficient as OSPF's NBMA support, Point-to-MultiPoint subnets can autoconfigure and are robust against PVC failures.

Multicast

Work began in the 1980s on extending multicast—the ability to send a single packet and have it delivered to multiple recipients—from a single LAN to Internetwide. The seminal work on this subject was done by Steve Deering when he was at Stanford [59], as he developed the receiver-oriented Internet multicast model and the Internet Group Membership Protocol (IGMP), which communicated multicast group membership between hosts and routers [56].

Multicast routing protocols compute the path of a multicast datagram from its sender to its multiple recipients. The first Internet multicast routing protocol was the Distance Vector Multicast Routing Protocol (DVMRP) [202]. DVMRP is implemented for UNIX workstations in the **mrouted** program.

In 1992, the Multicast Backbone, or MBONE, was formed. The MBONE provides multicast routing services to the Internet and is overlaid on the Internet—mainly UNIX workstations running DVMRP interconnected via tunnels. The MBONE broadcasts audio and video from IETF meetings to interested participants around the world and is a breeding ground for multicast applications, such as interactive whiteboards [140]; teleconferencing tools [139], [228]; video conferencing [80], [246]; and large-scale image distribution [55].

As a Distance Vector multicast routing protocol, DVMRP suffers from the same convergence problems as RIP (see Section 3.1). In the hope of getting a more stable and efficient multicast routing protocol and in deploying multicast routing directly in the Internet's routers, the Multicast Extensions to OSPF (MOSPF) were developed in 1992 (see Chapter 10, MOSPF).

Enhanced Security

The first Internet security incident to achieve widespread attention was the Internet worm in 1988. In November of that year, Robert Morris, a graduate student at Cornell University, wrote a computer virus that replicated itself over the Internet, infecting thousands of UNIX workstations by exploiting security flaws in the UNIX operating system [87], [211].

Security firewalls soon became big business as a way of protecting Internet sites from unlawful entry. People also came to believe that the Internet's infrastructure, including its routing protocols, needed to be protected. All new Internet protocol specifications are now required to have a section discussing security concerns, when the protocol is published as an RFC [193]. Proposals were made to secure the Internet's existing protocols [111].

The OSPF protocol had been designed with security in mind. Fields were included in OSPF protocol packets so that the packets could be authenticated. The idea is to validate a set of routers by giving them a key and then to use data contained within a received OSPF packet to verify that it was generated by a router holding the key and that the packet had not been altered. However, no real security mechanism had been implemented for OSPF, only a *clear password* mechanism akin to TELNET passwords before the advent of Kerberos [238] and one-time passwords [90], which can be broken trivially by anyone watching the packet exchanges on the network. To provide nontrivial authentication in OSPF, cryptographic hash algorithms were eventually developed, as described in Section 11.7.

IPv6

Besides the danger imposed by routing table growth to the Internet's routers, the Internet will sometime run out of addresses (when, precisely, this will happen is a matter of some conjecture; see [1]). To prepare for this eventuality, development of the next generation of the Internet Protocol, IPv6, was started in 1995. IPv6 is an evolution of the IPv4 architecture; the routing architecture stays the same, but the size of the address increases from 32 to 128 bits ([49], [61], [99], [181]).

To be able to provide routing services for IPv6, the OSPF protocol was also updated. Since backward compatibility was not an issue, the packet and LSA formats were redone in OSPF for IPv6 [46]. All addressing semantics were removed from packet and LSA headers, allowing OSPF for IPv6 to be used by any protocol stack. All basic OSPF mechanisms, such as flooding, area organization, and routing calculations, were kept the same so that most of the software for OSPFv2 could be reused.

Further Reading

A succession of OSPF protocol specifications have been published as RFCs over the years, each one obsoleting the previous ([174], [176], [177], and [178]). Each specification has an appendix listing changes from the previous, allowing one to track the changes in the OSPF protocol. OSPF features, properties, and performance characteristics are described in [173]. Results of OSPF interoperability testing and OSPF deployments are described in [168] and [175].

4

OSPF Basics

OSPF belongs to the general category of routing protocols called link-state protocols. In the last 10 to 15 years, link-state protocols have become popular alternatives to more traditional Distance Vector algorithms. In addition to the development of OSPF for TCP/IP, link-state routing protocols have been implemented for many other protocol stacks, including the IS-IS protocol for OSI [112], NLSP for Novell's NetWare [184], IBM's APPN network-node routing [84], and the ATM Forum's PNNI routing protocol [9].

The first link-state algorithm was developed by Bolt, Beranek and Newman in 1979 for the ARPANET [147], a packet-switching network that provided data-link services to attached hosts. These hosts used either the X.25 or 1822 protocols to interface with the ARPANET packet switches. Between hosts, the Network Control Protocol (NCP) provided transport services. In 1983, all the hosts were converted to the TCP/IP protocol stack, and routers were attached to the ARPANET, giving birth to today's Internet. The ARPANET remained at the core of the Internet for many years, until it was finally retired in 1989.

The ARPANET's link-state routing algorithm replaced a Distance Vector algorithm that was starting to show signs of wear and tear. The goal of ARPANET routing was to find the least-delay paths through the network. The previous Distance Vector algorithm was taking a long time to converge on correct paths when the network topology changed, and it was generating a lot of control traffic in the process. The new link-state routing protocol was extensively instrumented and monitored, and it was found to meet quite stringent performance goals, consuming less than 1 percent of link bandwidth for control traffic and less than 2 percent of switch CPU for routing calculations, while responding to network changes in less than 100 milliseconds.

At the core of every link-state routing protocol is a distributed, replicated database. This database describes the routing topology—the collection of routers in the routing domain and how they are interconnected. Each router in the routing domain is responsible for describing its local piece of the routing topology in *link-state advertisements,* or *LSAs*. These LSAs are then reliably distributed to all the other routers in the routing domain in a process called *reliable flooding.* Taken together, the collection of LSAs generated by all of the routers is called the *link-state database.* The link-state routing protocol's flooding algorithm ensures that each router has an identical link-state database, except during brief periods of convergence. Using the link-state database as input, each router calculates its IP routing table, enabling the correct forwarding of IP data traffic.

In this chapter, we will examine the basic features of a link-state protocol. These include LSAs, the link-state database, reliable flooding, and routing calculations. We will look at the OSPF protocol in detail.

4.1   An OSPF Example

The ARPANET switches were interconnected via point-to-point leased lines. To this day, all link-state protocols run in a very similar fashion, given such an environment. For this reason, we illustrate the basic concepts of OSPF, using a collection of routers interconnected by point-to-point links. A specific example network topology, shown in Figure 4.1, is used throughout this chapter.

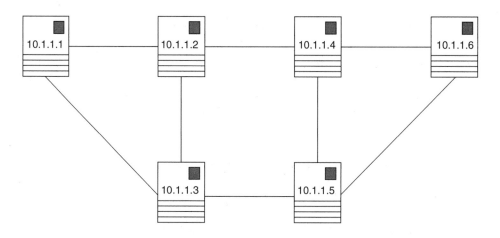

Figure 4.1 Point-to-point network topology.

Suppose that this network has been up and running for some time. All of the six routers pictured will then have identical link-state databases that describe a complete map of the network. Looking at this database, any of the six routers can tell how many other routers are in the network (5), how many interfaces router 10.1.1.4 has (3), whether a link connects 10.1.1.2 and 10.1.1.4 (yes), and so on. The database also gives a cost for each link. Although this cost is not shown in Figure 4.1, let us assume that the cost of each link is 1.

From the database, each router has calculated the shortest paths to all others. For example, router 10.1.1.1 calculates that it has two equal-cost shortest paths to 10.1.1.6, one through 10.1.1.2 and 10.1.1.4 and the other through 10.1.1.3 and 10.1.1.5. (It is interesting to note that since they all have the same database, any router can calculate the routing table of any other; this useful property is taken advantage of by the Multicast Extensions to OSPF, as explained in Chapter 10, MOSPF.)

When the network is in a steady state—that is, no routers or links are going in or out of service—the only OSPF routing traffic is periodic Hello packets between neighboring OSPF routers and the occasional refresh of pieces of the link-state database. Hello packets are usually sent every 10 seconds, and failure to receive Hellos from a neighbor tells the router of a problem in its connected link or neighboring router. Every 30 minutes, a router refloods the pieces of the link-state database that it is responsible for, just in case those pieces have been lost from or corrupted in one of the other routers' databases.

Now suppose that the link between routers 10.1.1.2 and 10.1.1.4 fails. The physical or data-link protocols in router 10.1.1.2 will probably detect this failure in a small number of seconds; as a last resort, the failure to receive OSPF Hellos over the link will indicate the failure in 40 seconds. As soon as it detects the failure, router 10.1.1.2 will update the link-state database by reoriginating its router-LSA. This new router-LSA will say that router 10.1.1.2 has links to routers 10.1.1.1 and 10.1.1.3 but that it no longer has a link to 10.1.1.4. Router 10.1.1.2 will start the flooding of its new router-LSA by sending the LSA to routers 10.1.1.1 and 10.1.1.3. Router 10.1.1.3 will then continue the flooding process by sending the LSA to router 10.1.1.5, and so on.

As soon as each router receives router 10.1.1.2's new router-LSA, the router recalculates its shortest paths. For example, router 10.1.1.1 will now calculate that it has only a single shortest path to 10.1.1.6, the one going through 10.1.1.3 and 10.1.1.5.

In this example, we have identified each router by an IP address, and this is also how OSPF routers commonly identify one another. Each OSPF router has an OSPF *Router ID*. The Router ID is a 32-bit number that uniquely identifies the router within the OSPF routing domain. Although not required by the OSPF specification, the OSPF Router ID in practice is assigned to be one of the router's IP addresses.

4.2   Link State Advertisements (LSAs)

Each OSPF router originates one or more LSAs to describe its local part of the routing domain. Taken together, the LSAs form the link-state database, which is used as input to the routing calculations. In order to provide organization to the database and to enable the orderly updating and removal of LSAs, each LSA must provide some bookkeeping information, as well as topological information. All OSPF LSAs start with a 20-byte common header, shown in Figure 4.2, which carries this bookkeeping information. These bookkeeping functions are described in the following sections.

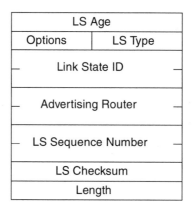

Figure 4.2 The LSA header.

4.2.1 Identifying LSAs

An OSPF link-state database might consist of many thousands of LSAs. Individual LSAs must be distinguished during flooding and the various routing calculations. OSPF LSAs are identified by three fields found in the common LSA header: LS Type, Link State ID, and Advertising Router.

LS Type Field

The LS Type (link-state type) field broadly classifies LSAs according to their functions. Five LS Types are defined by the base OSPF specification. LSAs with LS Type equal to 1 are called *router-LSAs*. Each router originates a single router-LSA to describe its set of active interfaces and neighbors. In a routing domain consisting solely of routers interconnected by point-to-point links, the link-state database consists only of router-LSAs. For this reason, we concentrate on router-LSAs in this chapter.

LSAs with LS Type equal to 2 are called *network-LSAs*. Each network-LSA describes a network segment, such as a broadcast or NBMA network, along with the identity of the network's currently attached routers. The use of network-LSAs is described further in Chapter 5, OSPF Network Types.

LSAs with LS Type equal to 3 (*network-summary-LSAs*), 4 (*ASBR-summary-LSAs*), and 5 (*AS-external-LSAs*) are used to implement hierarchical routing within OSPF. These are discussed further in Chapter 6, Hierarchical Routing in OSPF.

One way of extending the OSPF protocol is to add new LS Types. Two LS Types have been added to those defined by the base specification. LSAs with LS Type equal to 6 are called *group-membership-LSAs* and are used to indicate the location of multicast group members in MOSPF (see Chapter 10, MOSPF). LSAs with LS Type equal to 7 are used in OSPF NSSA areas to import a limited set of external information (see Section 7.4). In addition, an LS Type of 8 has been proposed, the *external-attributes-LSAs*, to carry BGP path information across an OSPF routing domain in lieu of Internal BGP (see Section 7.6).

OSPF routers are not required to store or forward LSAs with unknown LS Type. When OSPF is extended by adding new LS Types, this rule is maintained through use of the Options field. Options bits are added, saying, "I understand this new LS Type," and are exchanged between routers in Database Description packets (see Section 4.7.1). Looking at the Options field advertised by its neighbor, a router then knows which LSAs to forward and which LSAs to keep to itself.

Link State ID Field

The Link State ID field uniquely distinguishes an LSA that a router originates from all other self-originated LSAs of the same LS Type. For compactness and convenience, the Link State ID also often carries addressing information. For example, the Link State ID of an AS-external-LSA is equal to the IP address of the externally reachable IP network being imported into the OSPF routing domain (see Section 6.2).

Advertising Router Field

The Advertising Router field is set to the originating router's OSPF Router ID. A router can easily identify its self-originated LSAs as those LSAs whose Advertising Router is set to the router's own Router ID. Routers are allowed to update or to delete only self-originated LSAs.

Knowing which router has originated a particular LSA tells the calculating router whether the LSA should be used in the routing calculation and, if so, how it should be used. For example, network-summary-LSAs are used in the routing calculation only when their Advertising Router is reachable. When they are used, the cost to the

destination network is the sum of the cost to the Advertising Router and the cost advertised in the LSA.

4.2.2 Identifying LSA Instances

When a router wishes to update one of the LSAs it is originating (called *self-originated
LSAs*), it must have some way to indicate to the other routers that this new LSA instance
is more up to date and therefore should replace any existing instances of the LSA. In
OSPF LSAs, the LS Sequence Number in the common LSA header is incremented when
a new LSA instance is originated. The LSA instance having the larger LS Sequence
Number is considered to be more recent. If the LS Sequence Numbers are the same, the
LS Age and LS Checksum fields of the LSA are compared by the router before it declares
that the two instances are identical.

LS Sequence Number Field

When a router has two instances of a particular LSA, it detects which instance is more
recent by comparing the instances' LS Sequence Numbers. The instance with the *larger*
LS Sequence Number is the more recent. Of course, the meaning of larger depends on
the organization of the sequence number space (see Figure 4.3).

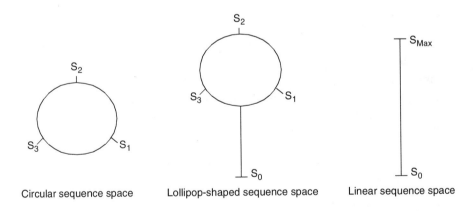

Circular sequence space   Lollipop-shaped sequence space   Linear sequence space

Figure 4.3 Various LS Sequence Number space organizations.

The original ARPANET link-state algorithm used a circular sequence number space.
By carefully controlling the rate at which new LSA instances were generated, all possible sequence numbers for a given LSA were constrained at any one time to lie in a half-
circle (that is, a semicircle). The largest sequence number was then the sequence number
appearing on the counterclockwise edge of the semicircle. However, this scheme was

not robust in the face of errors. In a now famous network failure, bit errors in switch memory caused the accidental introduction of three instances of an LSA having sequence numbers (S_1, S_2, and S_3 in Figure 4.3) that were not constrained to a semicircle. The switches could no longer determine which LSA instance was most recent, since $S_1 < S_2 < S_3 < S_1$. As a result, the three LSA instances were continually flooded throughout the network, each instance replacing the others in turn. This continued until the entire network was power cycled (see [221]). Some people have likened such problems to a virus. Once introduced by a switch, such bad data spreads to all other switches and becomes extremely difficult to eradicate.

To help avoid this network failure (called herein the ARPANET sequence bug), a *lollipop-shaped* sequence number space was proposed [189]. Each LSA is initially originated with the smallest sequence number S_0, which is part of the lollipop's handle. The sequence space then increments until it enters the circular part of the space. Version 1 of the OSPF protocol used the lollipop-shaped sequence space. Although the lollipop-shaped organization provides better protection against the ARPANET sequence bug, since sequence numbers falling into the lollipop handle never create ambiguities, the three sequence numbers S_1, S_2, and S_3 still cause a problem.

OSPFv2 uses a linear sequence space, which completely prevents the ARPANET sequence bug. OSPF LS Sequence Numbers are signed 32-bit values. The first time an OSPF router originates a given LSA, it sets the LSA's LS Sequence Number to the smallest negative value (S_0, called InitialSequenceNumber and having the value 0x80000001). Subsequently each time the router updates the LSA, it increments the LSA's LS Sequence Number by 1. An LSA's LS Sequence Number monotonically increases until the maximum positive value is reached (S_{Max}, called MaxSequenceNumber and with the value 0x7fffffff). At this point, when the router wishes to update the LSA, it must start again with the initial sequence value of S_0, rolling over the sequence space. However, to get the other routers to accept this new LSA instance as the most recent, the router must first delete the LSA instance with sequence number S_{Max} from the routing domain (see Section 4.7.2) before flooding the new instance with sequence number S_0.

One should note that, since OSPF routers are not allowed to update their self-originated LSAs more than once every 5 seconds, in the absence of errors (in either hardware or software implementations), a 32-bit sequence space, such as OSPF's, will take more than 600 years to roll over! However, as we saw in the ARPANET bug, errors can and do happen. Besides using a linear sequence space in its LSAs, OSPF has other features that guard against problems similar to the ARPANET sequence bug. First, all OSPF LSAs contain a checksum, so that data corruption within an LSA is detected. Second, OSPF requires the LS Age field of all LSAs to be incremented at each hop during flooding, which eventually breaks any flooding loop by causing a looping LSA's LS Age field to reach the value MaxAge.

4.2.3 Verifying LSA Contents

An LSA may become corrupted during flooding or while being held in a router's memory. Corrupted LSAs can create havoc, possibly leading to incorrect routing calculations, black holes, or looping data packets. To detect data corruption, redundant information is added to the LSA as a checksum or parity check. In OSPF, this function is provided by the LS Checksum field in the LSA header.

LS Checksum Field

Each OSPF LSA is checksummed to detect data corruption within the LSA header and contents. The checksum is calculated originally by the router that originates the LSA and then is carried with the LSA as it is flooded throughout the routing domain and stored within the link-state database. A router verifies the checksum of an LSA received from a neighboring router during flooding; corrupted LSAs will be discarded by the router, in hopes that the retransmitted LSA from the neighbor will be uncorrupted. A router also periodically verifies the checksums of all the LSAs in its link-state database, guarding against its own hardware and software errors. Detection of such internal errors will generally cause the router's OSPF processing to reinitialize.

After an LSA instance is originated, its checksum is never altered. For this reason, the checksum excludes the LSA's LS Age field, which is modified in flooding. This means that OSPF does not detect corruption of the LS Age field; corruption of the LS Age field will in general cause no more harm than speeding up the rate of LSA originations. A proposal to safeguard the LS Age field (along with other security-related concerns) is given in [179].

The checksum is implemented by using the Fletcher checksum algorithm, which is used in the OSI network and transport layers (see [145]). The reason for using the Fletcher checksum in LSAs is that it is easy to calculate yet catches patterns of data corruption different from the standard Internet ones-complement checksum used by OSPF's protocol packets. During flooding, LSAs are carried in OSPF Link State Update packets. If for some reason data corruption fails to be detected by the Update packet's ones-complement checksum, Fletcher may still detect the corruption within individual LSAs.

The OSPF protocol also uses the LSA checksum as an efficient way to determine whether two instances of the same LSA, both having the same LS Checksum fields and relatively the same age, also have the same contents (and so should be considered the same instance). This is a probabilistic comparison—there is no absolute assurance that when the checksums are equal, so are the contents, although it seems to be highly likely in this context (same LSA, same LS sequence number, and relatively the same LS age). Note that even if the assumption were wrong, OSPF would recover automatically whenever the LSA was refreshed (that is to say, within 30 minutes).

4.2.4 Removing LSAs from the Distributed Database

Under normal circumstances, every LSA in the link-state database is updated at least once every 30 minutes. If an LSA has not been updated after an hour, the LSA is assumed to be no longer valid and is removed from the database. The LS Age field in the LSA header indicates the length of time since the LSA was last updated.

LS Age Field

The LS Age field indicates the number of seconds since the LSA was originated. Under normal circumstances, the LS Age field ranges from 0 to 30 minutes; if the age of an LSA reaches 30 minutes, the originating router will refresh the LSA by flooding a new instance of the LSA, incrementing the LS sequence number and setting the LS age to 0 again.

   If the originating router has failed, the age of the LSA continues to increase until the value of MaxAge (1 hour) is reached. At that time, the LSA is deleted from the database—1 hour is the maximum value that the LS Age field can ever attain. To ensure that all routers remove the LSA more or less at the same time, without depending on a synchronized clock, the LSA is reflooded at that time. All other routers will then remove their database copies on seeing the MaxAge LSA being flooded.

   After an LSA's originating router has failed, it can therefore take as long as an hour for the LSA to be removed from other routers' link-state databases. Such an LSA is certainly advertising out-of-date information; however, OSPF guarantees that the LSA will not interfere with the routing table calculation. How? By requiring that a link be advertised by the routers at both ends of the link before using the link in the routing calculation (see Section 4.8).

   OSPF also has a procedure, called *premature aging,* for deleting an LSA from the routing domain without waiting for its LS Age to reach MaxAge. Sometimes a router wishes to delete an LSA instead of updating its contents. Using premature aging, the router deletes the LSA from the distributed database by setting the LSA's LS Age field to MaxAge and reflooding the LSA. In order to avoid possible thrashing situations whereby one router continually originates an LSA while another continually deletes it, a router is allowed to prematurely age only those LSAs that the router itself originated. If a router crashes or is removed from service without prematurely aging its self-originated LSAs, said LSAs will remain in other routers' link-state database for up to an hour while they age out naturally.

   The age of an LSA is also examined in order to implement other OSPF functions, such as rate limiting the amount of OSPF flooding (see Section 4.7.3). The uses of the LS Age field are shown in Table 4.1.

Table 4.1 Actions Taken by OSPF Router, Based on LS Age Fields

Constant	Value	Action of OSPF Router
MinLSArrival	1 second	Maximum rate at which a router will accept updates of any given LSA via flooding.
MinLSInterval	5 seconds	Maximum rate at which a router can update an LSA.
CheckAge	5 minutes	Rate at which a router verifies the checksum of an LSA contained in its database.
MaxAgeDiff	15 minutes	When two LSA instances differ by more than 15 minutes, they are considered to be separate instances, and the one with the smaller LS Age field is accepted as more recent.
LSRefreshTime	30 minutes	A router must refresh any self-originated LSA whose age reaches the value of 30 minutes.
MaxAge	1 hour	When the age of an LSA reaches 1 hour, the LSA is removed from the database.

4.2.5 Other LSA Header Fields

Options

The Options field in the OSPF LSA header can indicate that an LSA deserves special handling during flooding or routing calculations. In addition to the LSA header, the Options field can appear in OSPF Hello and Database Description packets. The Options field is 1 byte in length. In the base OSPF protocol specification, only two Options bits were defined. With the addition of OSPF protocol extensions, such as MOSPF, NSSA areas, and the Demand Circuit extensions, five of the eight Option bits now have defined meanings.

Length

The Length field contains the length, in bytes, of the LSA, counting both LSA header and contents. Because the Length field is 16 bits long, an LSA can range in size from 20 bytes (the size of the LSA header) to over 65,000 bytes; note that one cannot go all the way to 65,535 bytes, since the LSA must eventually be transported within an IP packet that is itself restricted to 65,535 bytes in length. However, note that all OSPF LSAs are small, with the only LSA type that is likely to exceed a few hundred bytes being the router-LSA. Router-LSAs can be large when a router has many different interfaces, but are still unlikely to exceed a few thousand bytes in length.

4.3   A Sample LSA: The Router-LSA

In the network environment of routers interconnected via serial lines, OSPF uses only
a single LSA type: the router-LSA. Each OSPF router originates a single router-LSA,
which reports the router's active interfaces, IP addresses, and neighbors.

Let's examine the router-LSA originated by router 10.1.1.1 in Figure 4.4. First, a little
more explanation of Figure 4.4 is in order. All serial lines in the figure are unnumbered:
The routers' serial line interfaces have not been assigned IP addresses; nor have IP subnets been assigned to the serial lines. Each router has been assigned an IP address that is
not attached to any particular interface; the routers are labeled with these addresses.
Following the usual convention, OSPF Router IDs have been assigned equal to the routers' IP addresses, although this is not strictly required by the OSPF specification. Finally,
each interface is labeled with a pair of numbers. The first number is the interface's
MIB-II IfIndex value, and the second is the OSPF output cost that has been assigned to
the interface. Figure 4.5 displays the router-LSA that router 10.1.1.1 would originate
after full OSPF relationships to its neighbors have been established.

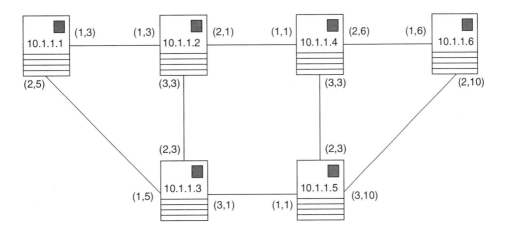

Figure 4.4 Point-to-point network topology, with interface IFIndexes and costs labeled.

Let us first consider the setting of the fields in the standard LSA header. All LSAs
are originated with LS Age set to 0. The Options field describes various optional capabilities supported by the router; see Chapter 7, OSPF Extensions. The Link State ID of
a router-LSA is set to the router's OSPF Router ID. The LS sequence number of the LSA
is 0x80000006, indicating that five instances of the router-LSA have previously been
originated.

Next in the router-LSA comes a byte (labeled *Router Type* in Figure 4.5) describing
the router's role in hierarchical routing, as well as any special roles that router might
have in multicast routing. (See Sections 6.1, 6.2, and 10.4.)

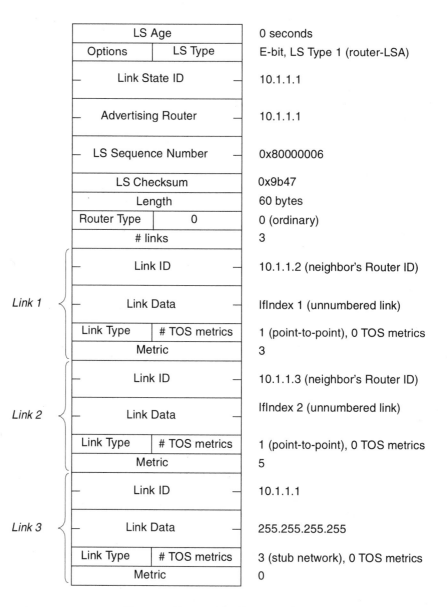

LS Age		0 seconds
Options	LS Type	E-bit, LS Type 1 (router-LSA)
Link State ID		10.1.1.1
Advertising Router		10.1.1.1
LS Sequence Number		0x80000006
LS Checksum		0x9b47
Length		60 bytes
Router Type	0	0 (ordinary)
# links		3

Link 1

Link ID		10.1.1.2 (neighbor's Router ID)
Link Data		IfIndex 1 (unnumbered link)
Link Type	# TOS metrics	1 (point-to-point), 0 TOS metrics
Metric		3

Link 2

Link ID		10.1.1.3 (neighbor's Router ID)
Link Data		IfIndex 2 (unnumbered link)
Link Type	# TOS metrics	1 (point-to-point), 0 TOS metrics
Metric		5

Link 3

Link ID		10.1.1.1
Link Data		255.255.255.255
Link Type	# TOS metrics	3 (stub network), 0 TOS metrics
Metric		0

Figure 4.5 Router 10.1.1.1's router-LSA.

The router-LSA then indicates that three connections (or links) are being reported. The first two links are point-to-point connections to neighboring routers, as indicated by the Link Type field. The Link ID of a point-to-point connection is the neighboring router's OSPF Router ID. Since these connections are unnumbered, the Link Data field indicates the corresponding router interface's MIB-II IfIndex.

Each link also contains a Metric field. This field, ranging from 1 to 65,535, indicates the relative cost of sending data packets over the link. The larger the cost, the less likely that data will be routed over the link. Metrics are configured by the person setting up the network. The metric can mean anything—delay, dollar cost of sending traffic over the link, and so on. The only thing to note is that adding the metrics should be meaningful, since OSPF calculates the cost of the path to be the sum of the cost of the path's component links. This means that delay would be a fine metric. So would transmission time for the link (which is the default value for the metric in the OSPF MIB; see Section 11.2). However, link bandwidth would probably not be a good metric, since adding bandwidth along a path is not very meaningful. Figure 4.4 uses the metric I call *weighted hop count*. One starts by assigning each link a metric of 1 and then increases the cost of the less preferred links until the least-cost paths flow over the more desirable links.

Note that metrics can be asymmetric; one does not have to assign equal metrics to both sides of a link. However, assigning equal metrics to both sides of a link is the norm, as has been done in Figure 4.4. In the original OSPF specification, separate metrics could be assigned for each TOS, although this feature was removed due to lack of deployment of TOS-based routing. For backward compatibility, the router-LSA still has space for TOS metrics, even though in practice the # TOS metrics for each link is always set to 0.

The last link in router 10.1.1.1's router-LSA advertises the router's own IP address. The address is advertised as a stub network connection. Stub networks are allowed to source or sink IP packets, but do not carry transit traffic. The Link ID field of a stub network connection is advertised as the network's IP address, the Link Data field as its IP mask. Connections to stub networks are allowed to advertise a Metric of 0.

As mentioned earlier, the router-LSA is the one type of LSA that can get quite large. All of a router's interfaces must be advertised in a single router-LSA. The fixed part of a router-LSA is 24 bytes in length, with each advertised connection adding an additional 12 bytes. The router-LSA in Figure 4.5 is only $24 + 3 * 12 = 60$ bytes long, but a router-LSA for a router with 100 interfaces would be 1,224 bytes in length.

4.4   The Link-State Database

The collection of all OSPF LSAs is called the *link-state database*. Each OSPF router has an identical link-state database. Link-state databases are exchanged between neighboring routers soon after the routers have discovered each other; after that, the link-state database is synchronized through a procedure called *reliable flooding* (see Section 4.7.2).

The link-state database gives a complete description of the network: the routers and network segments and how they are interconnected. Starting with a link-state database, one can draw a complete map of the network. This property can serve as a powerful debugging tool. By examining a single router's database, one immediately observes the state of all other routers in the network.

Of course, OSPF is not a network-monitoring protocol; it is a routing protocol. In performance of the routing function, a router uses the link-state database as the input to the router's routing calculation (see Section 4.8).

Table 4.2 shows the link-state database for the network in Figure 4.4. Each column in the table represents a single LSA. As mentioned earlier, each LSA is identified by the contents of the table's first three columns; the second three columns identify the LSA's instance.

Table 4.2 Link-State Database for Sample Network

LS Type	Link State ID	Adv. Router	LS Checksum	LS Sequence No.	LS Age
Router-LSA	10.1.1.1	10.1.1.1	0x9b47	0x80000006	0
Router-LSA	10.1.1.2	10.1.1.2	0x219e	0x80000007	1,618
Router-LSA	10.1.1.3	10.1.1.3	0x6b53	0x80000003	1,712
Router-LSA	10.1.1.4	10.1.1.4	0xe39a	0x8000003a	20
Router-LSA	10.1.1.5	10.1.1.5	0xd2a6	0x80000038	18
Router-LSA	10.1.1.6	10.1.1.6	0x05c3	0x80000005	1,680

One can quickly determine in OSPF whether two routers do indeed have synchronized databases. First, determine that the two routers have the same number of LSAs in their link-state databases; second, that the sums of their LSAs' LS Checksum fields are equal. These values are represented in the OSPF MIB by the variables `ospfExternLsaCount`, `ospfExternLsaCksumSum`, `ospfAreaLsaCount`, and `ospfAreaLsaCksumSum`. As with using the LS Checksum field to compare LSA contents, comparing the sum of the LS Checksums to determine link-state database synchronization is probabilistic in nature but useful in practice. For example, according to the database in Table 4.2, all routers should have six LSAs in their link-state database, and the sum of the LSAs' LS Checksums should be 0x2e43b.

Looking at the OSPF database, one can also immediately tell which parts of the network are changing the most—namely, the parts that are described by LSAs whose LS Sequence Numbers are changing the most and whose LS Age field never gets very large. In Table 4.2, for example, you can see that the router-LSAs originated by routers 10.1.1.4 and 10.1.1.5 are changing much more rapidly than LSAs originated by other routers. Looking at the network diagram in Figure 4.4, one would guess that is because the point-to-point connection between 10.1.1.4 and 10.1.1.5 goes up and down frequently. Note that this information can be determined by looking at any router's link-state database, since all routers have exactly the same information.

In our sample network of routers connected via serial lines, the link-state database is very simple and uniform, consisting only of router-LSAs. However, in the presence of network segments other than point-to-point links or when hierarchical routing is employed or when OSPF extensions, such as MOSPF, are deployed, other LSA types are introduced. These LSAs are explained further in Chapters 5, 6, and 10.

4.5   Communicating between OSPF Routers: OSPF Packets

Like most IP protocols, OSPF routers communicate in terms of protocol packets. OSPF runs directly over the IP network layer, doing without the services of UDP or TCP (which are used by RIP and BGP, respectively). When a router receives an IP packet with IP protocol number equal to 89, the router knows that the packet contains OSPF data. Stripping off the IP header, the router finds an OSPF packet. One particular type of OSPF packet, together with its IP encapsulation, is shown in Figure 4.6.

OSPF uses services of the IP header as follows.

- Since most OSPF packets travel only a single hop, namely, between neighboring routers or peers, the TTL in the IP packet is almost always set to 1. This keeps broken or misconfigured routers from mistakenly forwarding OSPF packets. The one exception to setting the TTL to 1 comes in certain configurations of OSPF hierarchical routing (see Section 6.1.1).

- The Destination IP address in the IP header is always set to the neighbor's IP address or to one of the OSPF multicast addresses AllSPFRouters (224.0.0.5) or AllDRouters (224.0.0.6). Use of these two multicast addresses is described in Section 5.2.

- An OSPF router uses IP fragmentation/reassembly when it has to send a packet that is larger than a network segment's MTU. However, most of the time, a router can avoid sending such a large packet, sending an equivalent set of smaller OSPF packets instead (this is sometimes called *semantic fragmentation*). For example, IP fragmentation cannot be avoided when a router is flooding an LSA that is itself larger (or close to larger) than the network segment's MTU. That is to say, there is no semantic fragmentation for OSPF LSAs (although this has been introduced in OSPF for IPv6; see Section 3.7). IP fragmentation is also unavoidable when the router has so many neighbors on a broadcast segment that the size of the Hello packet exceeds the segment's MTU (Section 5.2.1).

- A router sends all OSPF packets with IP precedence of Internetwork Control, in hope that this setting will cause OSPF packets to be preferred over data packets (although in practice, it seldom does).

All OSPF packets begin with a standard 24-byte header, which provides the following functions.

- *An OSPF packet type field.* There are five separate types of OSPF protocol packets: Hello packets (type = 1), used to discover and maintain neighbor relationships and Database Description packets (type = 2), Link State Request packets (type = 3), Link State Update packets (type = 4), and Link State Acknowledgment packets (type = 5), all used in link-state database synchronization (see Section 4.7).

- *The OSPF Router ID of the sender.* Thus the receiving router can tell which OSPF router the packet came from.

- *A packet checksum.* This allows the receiving router to determine whether the packet has been damaged in transit; if so, the packet is discarded.

- *Authentication fields.* For security, these fields allow the receiving router to verify that the packet was indeed sent by the OSPF router whose Router ID appears in the header and that the packet's contents have not been modified by a third party. See Section 11.7 for details.

- *An OSPF Area ID.* This enables the receiving router to associate the packet to the proper level of OSPF hierarchy and to ensure that the OSPF hierarchy has been configured consistently (see Section 6.1).

4.6   Neighbor Discovery and Maintenance

All routing protocols provide a way for a router to discover and maintain neighbor relationships (also sometimes called *peer* relationships). A router's neighbors, or peers, are those routers with which the router will directly exchange routing information.

In OSPF, a router discovers neighbors by periodically sending OSPF Hello packets out all of its interfaces. By default, a router sends Hellos out an interface every 10 seconds, although this interval is configurable as the OSPF parameter HelloInterval. A router learns the existence of a neighboring router when it receives the neighbor's OSPF Hello in turn.

The part of the OSPF protocol responsible for sending and receiving Hello packets is called OSPF's Hello protocol (not to be confused with the old NSFNET routing protocol of the same name). The transmission and reception of Hello packets also enables a router to detect the failure of one of its neighbors; if enough time elapses (specified as the OSPF configurable parameter RouterDeadInterval, whose default value is 40 seconds) without the router's receiving a Hello from a neighbor, the router stops advertising the connection to the router and starts routing data packets around the failure. In most cases, however, the failure of the neighbor connection should be noticed much earlier by the data-link protocol. Detecting neighbor failures in a timely fashion is crucial to OSPF protocol performance. The time to detect neighbor failures dominates convergence time, since the rest of the OSPF protocol machinery (flooding updated LSAs and redoing the routing table calculations) required to route packets around the failure takes at most a few seconds.

Besides enabling discovery and maintenance of OSPF neighbors, OSPF's Hello protocol also establishes that the neighboring routers are consistent in the following ways.

- The Hello protocol ensures that each neighbor can send packets to and receive packets from the other. In other words, the Hello protocol ensures that the link between neighbors is bidirectional. Unless the link is bidirectional, OSPF routers will not forward data packets over the link. This procedure prevents a routing failure that can be caused by unidirectional links in other protocols, which is most easily demonstrated using RIP (see Section 13.1). Suppose that RIP routers A and B are connected and that packets can go from B to A but not vice versa. B may then send routing updates for network N to A, causing A to install B as the next hop for N. However, whenever A forwards a packet destined for network N, the packet will go into a "black hole."

- The Hello protocol ensures that the neighboring routers agree on the HelloInterval and RouterDeadInterval parameters. This ensures that each router sends Hellos quickly enough so that losing an occasional Hello packet will not mistakenly bring the link down.

The OSPF Hello protocol performs additional duties on other types of network segments (see Chapter 5, OSPF Network Types). Also, the OSPF Hello protocol is used to detect and negotiate certain OSPF extensions (see Chapter 7, OSPF Extensions).

Figure 4.6 shows the Hello packet that router 10.1.1.1 would be sending to router 10.1.1.2 in Figure 4.1 after the connection has been up some time. By including router 10.1.1.2 in the list of neighbors recently heard from, router 10.1.1.1 indicates that it is receiving router 10.1.1.2's Hellos. On receiving this Hello packet, router 10.1.1.2 will then know that the link is bidirectional. The fields Network Mask, Router Priority, Designated Router, and Backup Designated Router are used only when the neighbors are connected by a broadcast or NBMA network segment (see Section 5.2). The Options field is used to negotiate optional behavior between the neighbors and is discussed further in Section 7.1.

4.7   Database Synchronization

Database synchronization in a link-state protocol is crucial. As long as the database remains synchronized, a link-state protocol's routing calculations ensure correct and loop-free routing. It is no surprise, then, that most of the protocol machinery in a link-state protocol exists simply to ensure and to maintain synchronization of the link-state database. Of the 76 pages in the OSPF specification detailing protocol functionality, 32 deal exclusively with database synchronization. Of the 5 OSPF protocol packet types, 4 are used for database synchronization.

Database synchronization takes two forms in a link-state protocol. First, when two neighbors start communicating, they must synchronize their databases before forwarding data traffic over their shared link, or routing loops may ensue (Section 4.7.1). Second, there is the continual database resynchronization that must occur as new LSAs are introduced and distributed among routers. The mechanism that achieves this resynchronization is called reliable flooding (Section 4.7.2).

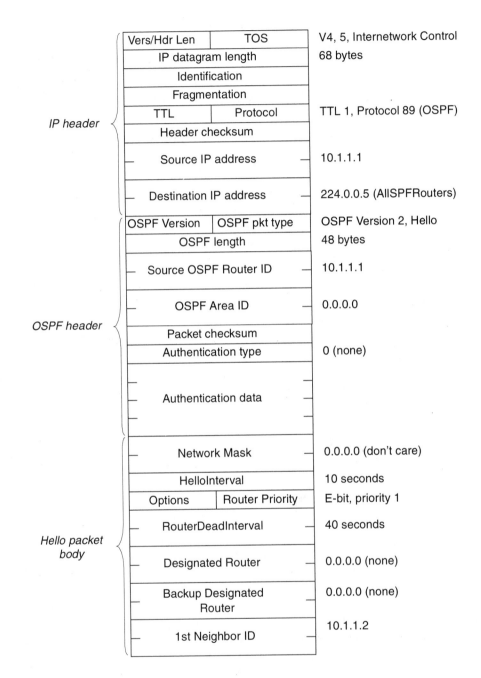

Figure 4.6 An OSPF Hello packet.

4.7.1   Initial Database Synchronization

When the connection between two neighboring routers first comes up, the routers must wait for their link-state databases to be synchronized before forwarding data traffic over the connection. Otherwise discrepancies in the neighbors' databases may lead to their calculating incompatible routing tables, resulting in routing loops or black holes.

In the original ARPANET link-state protocol, achieving this initial synchronization was done without introducing any additional mechanisms. When the connection first came up, reliable flooding began over the connection, but the connection was not used for data traffic until enough time had elapsed to guarantee that the entire database had been either updated or refreshed. In the ARPANET protocol, this time interval was 60 seconds.

The ARPANET strategy, although simple, did have a major drawback. It tied the time to bring up a connection to the database refresh interval. In order to reduce the amount of routing traffic, one would like to increase the database refresh interval; for example, in OSPF, each LSA is refreshed only once every 30 minutes. In the ARPANET strategy, however, this would incur an unacceptable delay in bringing up neighbor connections. To solve this problem, [189] suggested another strategy: an explicit database download when neighbor connections first come up. The OSPF protocol uses this second strategy.

Instead of sending the entire database to the neighbor when the connection comes up, an OSPF router sends only its LSA headers, and then the neighbor requests those LSAs that are more recent. This procedure is more efficient than simply sending the entire database; it is called *Database Exchange* in the OSPF specification.

Database Exchange is what the majority of the OSPF neighbor finite-state machine is tasked to do. As soon as the Hello protocol has determined that the connection between neighbors is bidirectional, the OSPF protocol decides whether databases need to be synchronized—over serial lines, databases are always synchronized, although over other network segments, databases are synchronized only between certain neighbor pairs (see Chapter 5, OSPF Network Types). If a decision to synchronize is made, each neighbor does two things: sends the link-state headers of all the LSAs currently in its database to the other in a sequence of OSPF Database Description packets and starts flooding any future LSA updates over the connection. Commencing the flooding procedure is necessary to ensure that Database Exchange finishes in a deterministic time period.

Transmission and reception of the sequence of Database Description packets by a router resembles the operation of the TFTP protocol. Only one Database Description packet can be outstanding at any one time; the router will send the next Database Description packet only when the previous one is acknowledged through reception of a properly sequenced Database Description packet from the neighbor.

When an entire sequence of Database Description packets has been received, a router knows the link-state headers of all the LSAs in its neighbor's link-state database.

In particular, the router knows which of the neighbor's LSAs it does not have and which of the neighbor's LSAs are more recent. The router then sends Link State Request packets to the neighbor requesting the desired LSAs, and the neighbor responds by flooding the LSAs in Link State Update packets.

After having sent a full sequence of Database Description packets to the neighbor, having received a full sequence of Database Description Packets from the neighbor, and having had all of its Link State Request packets satisfied by Link State Updates received from the neighbor, the router declares the connection synchronized and advertises it as ready to be used for data traffic. At this point, the neighbor is said to be *fully adjacent* to the router (at the beginning of the Database Exchange procedure, the two routers were said to be merely *adjacent*).

Figure 4.7 shows an example of the Database Exchange procedure. Assume that all the routers in Figure 4.1 have synchronized on the database displayed in Table 4.2. Then suppose that router 10.1.1.6 restarts. This temporarily tears down the connections between 10.1.1.6 and its neighbors 10.1.1.4 and 10.1.1.5. These two routers will have updated their LSAs, omitting their connections to 10.1.1.6. The initial exchange of Hellos and the Database Exchange between routers 10.1.1.4 and 10.1.1.6 is then displayed in Figure 4.7.

Note several features of Database Exchange as illustrated in Figure 4.7. The first Database Description packet sent by router 10.1.1.6 indicates that 10.1.1.6 has seen 10.1.1.4's Hellos, so that 10.1.1.4 does not need to wait for 10.1.1.6's next Hello to establish bidirectionality. This same Database Description packet also establishes the sequence number to be used during Database Exchange; the sequence number is incremented for each pair of Database Description packets and serves as an acknowledgment for the previous pair. The last Database Description packet sent by 10.1.1.4 is empty, serving only as an acknowledgment. Examining the Link State Request packet sent by 10.1.1.6, you see that Link State Request packets do not request particular LSA instances but only the current database copy of each LSA listed. Finally, note that although 10.1.1.6 really has the most recent router-LSA for itself, both routers act as if the old router-LSA for 10.1.1.6 in 10.1.1.4 is most recent. After requesting and receiving this old LSA from 10.1.1.4, router 10.1.1.6 immediately issues an updated router-LSA with a larger sequence number.

An interesting property of the combination of the Hello protocol and Database Exchange is the following: It uses both small packets and large packets, multicast (on those segments that support multicast) and unicast. As a result, OSPF tends to detect link-level difficulties, such as MTU mismatches between neighbors, or unicast working but multicast not working, by failing to form a full adjacency. This behavior makes the link-level problems easier to find than does the alternative of tracking down strange failures in TCP/IP applications.

One last thing to note is that a router may have MaxAge LSAs in its link-state database as Database Exchange is begun with a neighbor. Since MaxAge LSAs are in the process of being deleted from the database, the router does not send them in Database

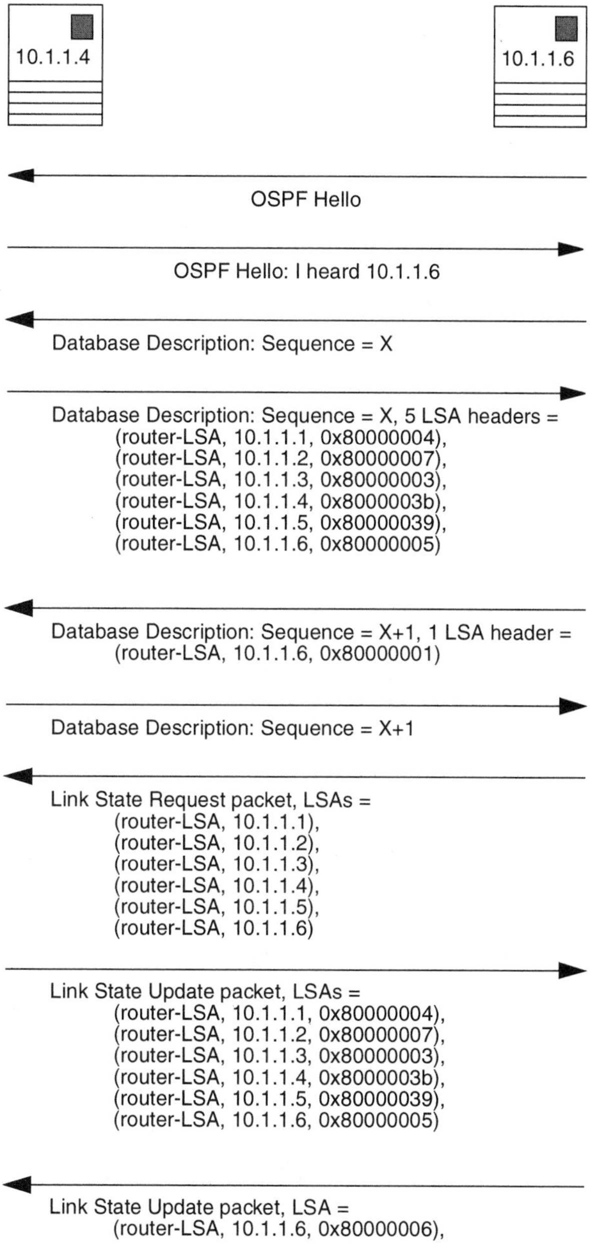

Figure 4.7 Sample Database Exchange.

Description packets to the neighbor; the LSAs may be gone by the time the neighbor gets around to requesting them. Instead the MaxAge LSAs are flooded to the neighbor to make sure that the neighbor also deletes them.

4.7.2 Reliable Flooding

As LSAs are updated with new information, they are sent throughout the routing domain by a procedure called *reliable flooding*. The flooding procedure starts when a router wishes to update one of its self-originated LSAs. This may be because the router's local state has changed—for example, one of the router's interfaces may have become inoperational, causing the router to reoriginate its router-LSA. Or the router may wish to delete one of its self-originated LSAs, in which case it sets the LSA's LS Age field to MaxAge. In any case, the router then floods the LSA, packaging the LSA within a Link State Update packet, which may or may not contain other LSAs, and then sending the Link State Update packet out all of its interfaces.

When one of the router's neighbors receives the Link State Update packet, the neighbor examines each of the LSAs contained within the update. For each LSA that is uncorrupted, of known LS type, and more recent than the neighbor's own database copy (if any), the neighbor installs that LSA in its link-state database, sends an acknowledgment back to the router, repackages the LSA within a new Link State Update packet, and sends it out all interfaces except the one that received the LSA in the first place. This procedure then iterates until all routers have the updated LSA.

In order to achieve reliability, a router will periodically retransmit an LSA sent to a neighbor until the neighbor acknowledges receipt of the LSA by sending a Link State Acknowledgment packet listing the updated LSA's link-state header.

Figure 4.8 shows an example of OSPF's flooding. The example starts with router 10.1.1.3 updating its router-LSA and flooding the LSA to its neighbors at time T1. The example then makes the simplifying assumptions that each router spends an equal time processing the update, that transmission time of the update is equal on all links, and that all of the updates are received intact. Note, then, that after a number of iterations less than or equal to the diameter of the network (in this example, 3), all routers have the updated LSA. Some further explanation of the example is in order. At time T2, router 10.1.1.4 seems to receive the update from both 10.1.1.2 and 10.1.1.5 simultaneously. We assume that the update from 10.1.1.5 is processed first, and so at time T3, 10.1.1.4 sends an update to 10.1.1.2 only. After time T3, acknowledgments are sent. In OSPF, routers generally delay acknowledgment of received LSAs, in hope that they can fit more LSA acknowledgments into a single Link State Acknowledgment packet, which reduces routing protocol processing and bandwidth consumption. Note also that not all updates require explicit acknowledgment. When updates *cross*, with each neighbor sending the other the same update (as in the case of routers 10.1.1.1 and 10.1.1.2 at time T2), the received update is taken as an *implicit acknowledgment,* and no corresponding Link State Acknowledgment packet is required to be sent. In fact, as a result of this property, in any link direction, one update or acknowledgment is sent but never both.

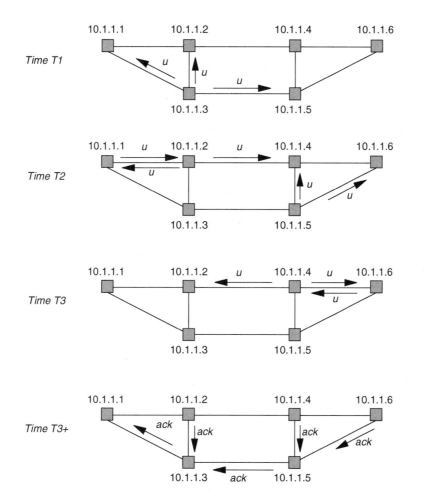

Figure 4.8 Reliable flooding, starting at 10.1.1.3, where *u* is a Link State Update packet and *ack* is a Link State Acknowledgment packet.

The preceding example has described flooding in a network of routers connected via serial lines. When different network segment types, such as broadcast networks, are present or when some routers run optional extensions to the OSPF protocol, flooding can get more complicated, as illustrated in Chapters 5 and 7.

4.7.3 Flooding Robustness

OSPF's reliable-flooding scheme is robust in the face of errors. Just what do we mean by robust in this case? Even when transmission errors, link and/or router failures occur, the network continues to function correctly; link-state databases continue to be synchronized, and the amount of routing traffic remains at an acceptable level. OSPF's flooding achieves this robustness because of the following features.

- Flooding could be restricted to a minimal collection of links interconnecting all routers (called a *spanning tree*). As long as the links in the spanning tree remain operational, router databases would remain synchronized. However, OSPF does not use a spanning tree; it floods over all links. As a result, the failure of any link does not significantly disrupt database synchronization, as LSA updates simultaneously flow on alternate paths around the link failure.

- Because of software errors, a router might accidentally delete one or more LSAs from its database. To ensure that the router eventually regains database synchronization with the rest of the OSPF routing domain, OSPF mandates that all originators of LSAs refresh their LSAs every 30 minutes, incrementing the LSAs' sequence numbers and reflooding them throughout the routing domain.

- To detect corruption of LSAs as they are flooded, each LSA contains a checksum field. An LSA's checksum is originally calculated by the LSA's originator and then becomes a permanent part of the LSA. When a router receives an LSA during flooding, it verifies the LSA's checksum. A checksum failure indicates that the LSA has been corrupted. Corrupted LSAs are discarded and not acknowledged, in hope that the retransmitted LSA will be valid.

- Errors in implementation might lead to situations in which the routers disagree on which LSA instance is more recent, possibly causing flooding loops. An example of this is the problem caused by the ARPANET routing protocol's circular sequence space (see Section 4.2.2). To guard against this kind of problem, an OSPF router increments an LSA's LS Age field when placing the LSA into a Link State Update packet. This behavior eventually breaks flooding loops, as a looping LSA's LS Age field will eventually hit the value MaxAge, at which time the LSA will be discarded. This behavior is similar to the breaking of IP forwarding loops through the use of the IP header's TTL field.

- To guard against a rapidly changing network element (for example, a link between routers that is continually going up and down) causing an excessive amount of control traffic, OSPF imposes rate limits on LSA origination; any particular LSA can be updated at most once in every 5 seconds (MinLSInterval).

- To guard against routers that are updating their LSAs at too high a rate, an OSPF router will refuse to accept a flooded LSA if the current database copy was received less than 1 second ago. For example, suppose that router 10.1.1.1 in Figure 4.1 disregards the MinLSInterval limit and begins updating its router-LSA 100 times a second. Rather than flood the entire network with these excessive updates, router 10.1.1.1's neighbors (10.1.1.2 and 10.1.1.3) will discard most of the updates from 10.1.1.1, allowing only 1 update in 100 to escape into the network at large. This behavior localizes the disruption to 10.1.1.1's immediate neighbors.

Given that (a) when an LSA is flooded, either the LSA or an acknowledgment for the LSA is sent over every link, but not both, (b) each LSA is guaranteed to be flooded at least every 30 minutes (the refresh time), and (c) the most an LSA can be flooded is once every 5 seconds, one can calculate the minimum and maximum amount of link bandwidth consumed by flooding traffic. For example, in Figure 4.1, the sum of LSA sizes is 336 bytes (24 bytes for the fixed portion of each router-LSA and 12 bytes for each link direction). This yields a maximum-link bandwidth consumption by flooding of 537 bits/second and a minimum consumption of 1.5 bits/second. For further performance analysis of OSPF, see [173].

Use of the Demand Circuit extensions to OSPF can further reduce the amount of link bandwidth consumed by flooding, at the expense of reduced robustness. See Section 7.3 for details.

4.8   Routing Calculations

We have spent all of this chapter talking about the link-state database—how it is organized, what the individual pieces (namely, LSAs) look like, and how the database is synchronized between OSPF routers. However, an IP router does not use the link-state database when forwarding IP datagrams. Instead the router uses its IP routing table. Just how does an OSPF router produce an IP routing table from its OSPF link-state database?

The link-state database describes the routers and the links that interconnect them. However, only the links that are appropriate for forwarding have been included in the database. Inoperational links, unidirectional links (detected by the Hello protocol), and links between routers whose databases are not yet synchronized have been omitted from the database.

The link-state database also indicates the cost of transmitting packets on the various links. What are the units of this link cost? OSPF leaves that question unanswered. Link cost is configurable by the network administrator. There are only three restrictions on link cost. First, the cost of each link must be in the range of 1 to 65,535. Second, the more preferred links should have smaller cost. And third, it must make sense to add link costs, since the cost of a path is set equal to the sum of the cost of its constituent links. For example, link delay makes a perfectly good metric. So does hop count: If you set the cost of each link to 1, the cost of a path is the number of links in the path.

The link-state database for the network of Figure 4.1 is shown in Figure 4.9. The metrics used in this example are what some people call *weighted hop count*. Small integers are assigned to each link, with more preferred links getting smaller values than others. Link costs have been assigned symmetrically in this example, although they do not have to be. Each router can advertise a different cost for the router's own link direction. If costs are assigned asymmetrically, paths will in general be asymmetric, with packets in one direction taking a given path and responses traveling a different path. IP works fine in the face of such asymmetric paths, although many network administrators dislike asymmetry, because it makes routing problems more difficult to debug.

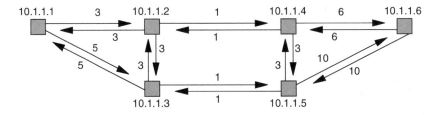

Figure 4.9 Link-state database as directed graph.

Note that each link is advertised by two routers, namely, those at either end of the link. For example, the link between 10.1.1.2 and 10.1.1.4 is advertised by both routers in their router-LSAs, each with a cost of 1. In order to avoid using stale information in the routing calculation, OSPF requires that both routers advertise the link before it can be used by the routing calculation. For example, suppose that router 10.1.1.4 in Figure 4.9 fails. Router 10.1.1.4's router-LSA, advertising the now inoperational links to routers 10.1.1.2, 10.1.1.5, and 10.1.1.6, will persist in the link-state database for up to an hour. But since these routers will no longer be advertising their halves of the links to 10.1.1.4, data traffic will be successfully rerouted around the failure.

The link-state database in Figure 4.9 reconstitutes the network map, in the form of a directed graph. The cost of a path in this graph is the sum of the path's component link costs. For example, there is a path of cost 4 from router 10.1.1.3 to 10.1.1.4, going through router 10.1.1.5. On the graph, a router can run any algorithm that calculates shortest paths. An OSPF router typically uses Dijkstra's Shortest Path First (SPF) algorithm [230] for this purpose.

Dijkstra's algorithm is a simple algorithm that efficiently calculates all at once the shortest paths to all destinations. The algorithm incrementally calculates a *tree* of shortest paths. It begins with the calculating router adding itself to the tree. All of the router's neighbors are then added to a *candidate list*, with costs equal to the cost of the links from the router to the neighbors. The router on the candidate list with the smallest cost is then added to the shortest-path tree, and that router's neighbors are then examined for inclusion in (or modification of) the candidate list. The algorithm then iterates until the candidate list is empty.

As an example, Table 4.3 shows Dijkstra's algorithm as run by router 10.1.1.3 in Figure 4.9. At each iteration, another router is added to the tree of shortest paths. While on the candidate list, each destination is listed with its current cost and next hops. These values are then copied to the routing table when the destination is moved from the candidate list to the shortest-path tree. The boldface type in Table 4.3 indicates those places where a destination is first added to the candidate list or when its values on the candidate list are modified. For example, in iteration 4, destination 10.1.1.6's entry on the candidate list is modified when a shorter path is discovered by going through router 10.1.1.4.

Table 4.3 Dijkstra Calculation Performed by Router 10.1.1.3

Iteration	Destination Added to Shortest-Path Tree	Candidate List Destination (cost, next hops)
1	10.1.1.3	**10.1.1.5 (1, 10.1.1.5)** **10.1.1.2 (3, 10.1.1.2)** **10.1.1.1 (5, 10.1.1.1)**
2	10.1.1.5	10.1.1.2 (3, 10.1.1.2) **10.1.1.4 (4, 10.1.1.5)** 10.1.1.1 (5, 10.1.1.1) **10.1.1.6 (11, 10.1.1.5)**
3	10.1.1.2	**10.1.1.4 (4, 10.1.1.5, 10.1.1.2)** 10.1.1.1 (5, 10.1.1.1) 10.1.1.6 (11, 10.1.1.5)
4	10.1.1.4	10.1.1.1 (5, 10.1.1.1) **10.1.1.6 (10, 10.1.1.5, 10.1.1.2)**
5	10.1.1.1	10.1.1.6 (10, 10.1.1.5, 10.1.1.2)
6	10.1.1.6	Empty

As you can see by going through the example, Dijkstra's algorithm ends up examining each link in the network once. When examining the link, the algorithm may place a destination onto the candidate list or modify a destination's entry on the candidate list. This operation also requires a sort of the candidate list, because we always want to know which destination on the candidate list has the smallest cost. Since the sort is an $O(\log(n))$ operation and the size of the candidate list never exceeds the number of destinations, the performance of Dijkstra's algorithm is $O(l * \log(n))$, where l is the number of links in the network and n is the number of destinations (in our example, equal to the number of routers). In some books on data structures, Dijkstra's algorithm is stated somewhat differently for fully mesh-connected networks (every router directly connected to every other router); for these networks, the algorithm's performance can be seen to be $O(n^2)$.

The resulting shortest paths calculated by router 10.1.1.3 in our sample network are displayed in Figure 4.10. Multiple shortest paths have been found to 10.1.1.4, allowing load balancing of traffic to that destination (called *equal-cost multipath*). An OSPF router knows the entire path to each destination. However, in IP's hop-by-hop routing paradigm, only the first hop is needed for each destination. Extracting this information from the collection of shortest paths yields the IP routing table, as displayed in Table 4.4.

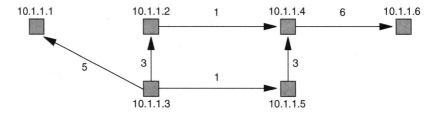

Figure 4.10 Shortest paths, as calculated by router 10.1.1.3.

Table 4.4 Router 10.1.1.3's IP Routing Table

Destination	Next Hop(s)	Cost
10.1.1.1	10.1.1.1	5
10.1.1.2	10.1.1.2	3
10.1.1.4	10.1.1.2 10.1.1.5	4
10.1.1.5	10.1.1.5	1
10.1.1.6	10.1.1.2 10.1.1.5	10

The routing calculation is the simplest part of OSPF. However, in the presence of network segments other than point-to-point links or when OSPF hierarchical routing or some of the OSPF extensions are used, the routing calculations get a little more complicated, as we will see later.

Further Reading

The ARPANET's link-state routing algorithm is described in [147]. The problem caused by the ARPANET's circular sequence space is described in [221]. Suggestions for fixes to prevent future occurrences of the ARPANET's sequence are given in [189].

The OSPF specification can be found in [177]. The first three chapters give an overview of the OSPF protocol, although the rest of the specification is really geared to protocol implementers.

For descriptions of other link-state protocols, see [237].

Exercise

4.1   Calculate the size in bytes of each of the LSAs in Table 4.2.

5

OSPF Network Types

Until now, we have addressed how the OSPF protocol runs in network topologies consisting of routers interconnected with serial lines. Such topologies are where link-state protocols were originally developed (namely, the ARPANET network), and they demonstrate all the basic elements of a link-state protocol. The bulk of the routing literature also concentrates on point-to-point network topologies.

However, the Internet contains many other subnet (that is, data-link) technologies, all capable of joining more than two routers to a single medium: Ethernets, 802.5 Token Rings, FDDI rings, Frame Relay subnets, ATM, SMDS, packet radio, and so on. OSPF runs over these subnet technologies, although somewhat differently from the way it runs over point-to-point links. In the OSI reference model, these differences would be called *subnetwork-dependent convergence functions*.

The differences in the way that OSPF runs over the various subnet technologies can be grouped as follows.

- *Neighbor discovery and maintenance.* OSPF always accomplishes this task through its Hello protocol, but the Hello protocol runs differently on different subnet types.

- *Database synchronization.* How does one synchronize the link-state database over the subnet? Which routers become adjacent, and how does reliable flooding take advantage of any special properties that the subnet might provide?

- *Abstraction.* In the OSPF link-state database, how does one represent the subnet and router connectivity over the subnet?

OSPF divides the various subnet technologies into the following classes: point-to-point subnets, broadcast subnets, nonbroadcast multiaccess (NBMA) subnets, and Point-to-MultiPoint subnets. The point-to-point subnet case has already been discussed. Before exploring these other subnet technologies in Sections 5.2, 5.3, and 5.4, we must first understand how OSPF uses the IP subnet model.

5.1   The IP Subnet Model

In TCP/IP, every link (or physical subnet) is assigned one or more address prefixes. Each address prefix is called an *IP subnet*. For example, suppose that an Ethernet segment was assigned the set of addresses beginning with the first 24 bits of 10.3.2.0. This is usually written as the prefix 10.3.2.0/24. Sometimes it is also said that the Ethernet segment's subnet number is 10.3.2.0 and that its subnet mask is 255.255.255.0. The subnet mask may also be written as the hexadecimal 0xffffff00. In any case, it means that all routers and hosts connected to the Ethernet segment have IP addresses in the range 10.3.2.0 to 10.3.2.255.

IP routes to subnets, not to individual hosts. IP routing protocols advertise routes to address prefixes, and each entry in an IP routing table is an address prefix.

The IP subnet model generally contains the following rules.

- Two hosts on different IP subnets cannot send IP packets directly to each other (or, as we say, cannot talk directly) but instead must go through one or more IP routers.

- In the converse of the preceding rule, it is assumed that two hosts/routers on a common subnet can send packets directly to each other.

- Two routers cannot exchange routing information directly unless they have one or more IP subnets in common. (This is true only for routers exchanging information via Interior Gateway Protocols. When running Exterior Gateway Protocols, such as BGP, two routers generally need either a common IP subnet or to belong to the same Autonomous System.)

Multiple subnets (in other words, IP prefixes) can be assigned to a physical link. In this case, the IP subnetting rules say that two hosts on separate subnets cannot talk directly, even if they are on the same physical link. Figure 5.1 gives an example of an Ethernet segment that has been assigned two IP subnets: 10.3.2.0/24 and 10.3.3.0/24. Each subnet has two hosts, and a router has addresses on both. The physical connectivity shows all hosts and the router on a common link, and the IP connectivity shows two separate segments connected by an IP router (see Figure 5.2).

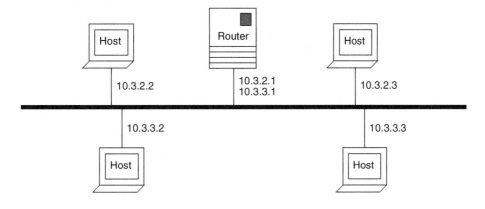

Figure 5.1 Ethernet segment with two IP subnets.

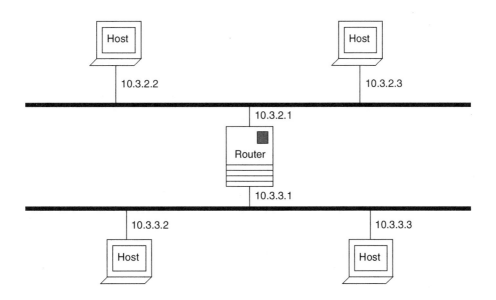

Figure 5.2 Resulting IP connectivity.

Of course, rules in IP are made to be broken, or at least bent, and the IP subnet model is no exception. For example, [24] proposes removing the restriction that two IP entities must share a common IP prefix in order to talk directly. The Next Hop Resolution Protocol (NHRP) [123] actively tries to find shortcuts between routers on different subnets. In IPv6, two nodes can talk directly whenever they are connected to the same physical media, regardless of their addresses. Even OSPF's Point-to-MultiPoint network model breaks the rule that two routers on the same subnet must be able to talk directly.

IP multicast does not use the IP subnet model either. When a multicast datagram is sent onto a physical link, usually as a data-link multicast, all IP multicast routers on the link get it, regardless of IP subnet boundaries. IGMP ignores IP subnets also.

However, OSPF in general enforces the IP subnet model. Two OSPF routers will never form a neighbor relationship and hence will never forward packets directly between each other unless they share a common prefix. This behavior is accomplished via OSPF's Hello protocol. An OSPF router creates a separate OSPF interface for each IP subnet that the router connects to (that is to say, has addresses in). When an OSPF router sends a Hello packet out an interface, the router sets the IP source address in the Hello to the router's IP address on the subnet and includes the subnet mask in the body of the Hello. Routers receiving the Hello will accept it only if (a) both routers agree on the subnet mask and (b) both router interfaces (sender and receiver) attach to the same subnet.

For example, suppose that all the hosts and routers in Figure 5.1 were OSPF routers. Then the router with two addresses would have two OSPF interfaces and would be sending Hellos out both interfaces, even though the Hellos in either case would appear on the same Ethernet segment. The Hello sent out the router's 10.3.2.1 interface would be accepted by both routers 10.3.2.2 and 10.3.2.3 but would be rejected by routers 10.3.3.2 and 10.3.3.3 for being associated with the wrong IP subnet. The Hello sent out the router's 10.3.3.1 interface would be handled similarly, with the result being the OSPF neighbor relationships as shown in Figure 5.2.

A number of problems have been caused by the fact that MOSPF is built on top of a protocol that respects that IP subnet model (namely OSPF), whereas IP multicast does not. These problems will be considered in Chapter 10, MOSPF.

5.2   Broadcast Subnets

A *broadcast subnet* is a data link whereby an attached node can send a single packet that will be received by all other nodes attached to the subnet. The canonical example is an Ethernet. When a station on an Ethernet sends an Ethernet packet, all other stations hear the packet, but their Ethernet adapters discard the packet unless it is addressed to either the adapter's own unique 48-bit Ethernet MAC address or to the Ethernet broadcast address 0xffffffffffff. The latter type of packet is termed a *broadcast packet*. Broadcast is very useful for (a) autoconfiguration and (b) replicating information, as we will see. Other examples of broadcast subnets are 802.5 Token Rings, FDDI rings, and SMDS subnets.

An additional useful capability of some broadcast networks is multicast. *Multicast* is the ability of a node to send onto the subnet a single packet that will be accepted by some subset of nodes on the subnet. Again using Ethernet as an example, Ethernet multicast addresses are those 48-bit Ethernet addresses having the least significant bit of the most significant byte set to 1 (namely, 0x01xxxxxxxxxx). A node typically can program its Ethernet adapter to accept one or more specific multicast addresses. Then, when packets are sent to a given multicast address, only those nodes interested in the multi-cast address will accept the packet. This behavior allows a subset of nodes on the Ethernet to converse, without adversely affecting the other nodes on the Ethernet. Some subnet technologies, such as Ethernet and FDDI (Fiber Distributed Data Interface), offer very good multicast capabilities. Other broadcast subnets offer no multicast capabilities, or their multicast is of such limited scope (such as Token Ring and SMDS) as to be of no use to TCP/IP applications such as OSPF.

5.2.1 Neighbor Discovery and Maintenance

Consider the five OSPF routers connected to an Ethernet segment in Figure 5.3, all attached to the IP subnet 10.4.7.0/24. Each OSPF router joins the IP multicast group AllSPFRouters (224.0.0.5). On Ethernets, IP multicast addresses map algorithmically to Ethernet multicast addresses: The last 23 bits of the IP multicast address are appended to the multicast block 0x01005exxxxxx. So the OSPF routers end up programming their Ethernet adapters to accept Ethernet multicasts to 0x01005e000005.

Each OSPF router then periodically multicasts its Hello packets (once every HelloInterval seconds, just as on point-to-point links) to the IP address 224.0.0.5. When router 10.4.7.1 multicasts its Hello packet, routers 10.4.7.2–10.4.7.5 all receive the Hello. Router 10.4.7.1 also indicates that it can hear the other routers' Hellos, by listing all of their OSPF Router IDs in the body of the single Hello (see Section 4.6). In this way, router 10.4.7.1 maintains its relationships with all other OSPF routers by sending a single packet instead of sending a separate packet to each neighbor on the Ethernet.

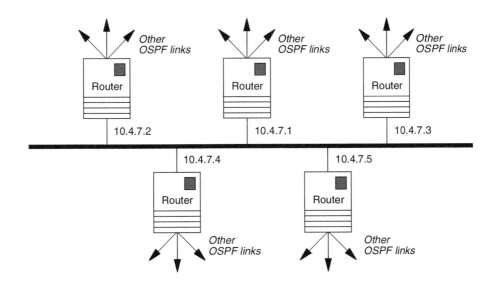

Figure 5.3 Ethernet segment with five OSPF routers attached.

The advantages of OSPF's Hello protocol over broadcast subnets are as follows.

- *Automatic discovery of neighbors.* By multicasting to a well-known address, neighboring routers discover each other without needing any configuration.

- *Efficiency.* When n OSPF routers are on a broadcast segment, there are $n * (n - 1) / 2$ neighbor relationships. However, these neighbor relationships are maintained by sending only n Hellos, one by each router, every HelloInterval seconds.

- *Isolation.* If the broadcast subnet has sufficient multicast capability, such as Ethernet, the Hello protocol operates without disturbing non-OSPF nodes on the broadcast segment. If multicast is not supported, OSPF's AllSPFRouters address gets mapped into the data-link broadcast address. The disadvantage of using the data-link broadcast address is that all nodes on the Ethernet, whether they are OSPF routers or not, will receive the OSPF Hello packets. Nodes other than OSPF routers would discard the packets, of course, but the act of discarding them still consumes valuable processing time.

5.2.2 Database Synchronization

On a broadcast subnet with n OSPF routers, there are $n * (n - 1) / 2$ neighbor pairs. If you try to synchronize databases between every pair of routers, you end up with a large number of Link State Updates and Acknowledgments being sent over the subnet.

OSPF solves this problem by electing a Designated Router for the broadcast subnet. All other routers keep their databases synchronized with the Designated Router, using the normal procedures of Database Exchange and reliable flooding (see Section 4.7). Instead of $n * (n - 1) / 2$ adjacencies over the broadcast subnet, there are now only n.

Using a Designated Router is more efficient than synchronizing between every pair of routers attached to the broadcast subnet, but it is less robust. If the Designated Router fails, so does database synchronization over the broadcast subnet. OSPF deals with this problem by electing a Backup Designated Router for the broadcast subnet. All routers now synchronize with both the Designated Router and the Backup Designated Router, and the Backup Designated Router acts as a hot standby in case the Designated Router fails. In fact, even before the failure of the Designated Router is noticed, the Backup Designated Router keeps reliable flooding running smoothly over the broadcast subnet. With the advent of the Backup Designated Router, there are now $2n - 1$ adjacencies over the broadcast subnet.

For example, suppose that in Figure 5.3, router 10.4.7.3 has been elected Designated Router and 10.4.7.2 Backup Designated Router. The set of adjacencies formed over the Ethernet segment are then indicated in Figure 5.4.

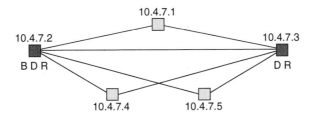

Figure 5.4 Flooding adjacencies when 10.4.7.3 and 10.4.7.2 are Designated Router and Backup Designated Router, respectively.

To see how reliable flooding works over a broadcast subnet, suppose that, in Figure 5.4, Router 10.4.7.5 receives a new LSA from one of its other links. The router then installs the LSA in its link-state database and then wants to flood it to both 10.4.7.3 and 10.4.7.2 (the Designated Router and Backup Designated Router, respectively). To do so, router 10.4.7.5 sends a Link State Update to the IP multicast address AllDRouters (224.0.0.6), which only the Designated Router and the Backup Designated Router listen to. Both the Designated Router and the Backup Designated Router then receive the LSA; the Designated Router sends the LSA back onto the Ethernet segment in a Link State Update addressed to AllSPFRouters, updating the rest of the routers on the Ethernet. The Backup Designated Router has deferred its flooding responsibilities on the Ethernet to the Designated Router; however, if the Backup Designated Router does not see the Link State Update from the Designated Router within the LSA retransmission interval (typically 5 seconds), it will step in and flood the LSA back onto the Ethernet in order to keep the database synchronization going.

Designated Router Election

The Designated Router election process works as follows, using data transmitted in Hello packets. The first OSPF router on an IP subnet always becomes Designated Router. When a second router is added, it becomes Backup Designated Router. Additional routers added to the segment defer to the existing Designated Router and Backup Designated Router; the only time the identity of the Designated Router or Backup Designated Router changes is when the existing Designated Router or Backup Designated Router fails.

In the event of the failure of a Designated Router or Backup Designated Router, there is an orderly changeover. Each OSPF router has a configured Router Priority value, a value between 0 and 127 inclusive. When, for example, the Designated Router fails, the Backup Designated Router is promoted to Designated Router, and the remaining router having the highest Router Priority becomes the Backup Designated Router, using the routers' OSPF Router ID to break ties. Then the new Backup Designated

Router has to start the time-consuming procedure of initial database synchronization or Database Exchange with all other routers on the subnet.

Since being Designated Router or Backup Designated on a subnet consumes additional resources, you may want to prevent certain routers from assuming these roles. This is done by assigning those routers a Router Priority of 0.

One other time that Router Priority comes into play is in partitioned subnets. When a subnet is partitioned into two pieces, two Designated Routers are elected, one for each partition. When the partition heals, the Designated Router with the higher Router Priority assumes the role of Designated Router for the healed subnet.

5.2.3 Abstraction

The common theme in running OSPF over broadcast subnets is reducing an $O(n^2)$ problem to $O(n)$. Representation of broadcast subnets in the link-state database is no exception. We want to capture the fact that each of the routers connected to the broadcast subnet can talk to each other directly. The obvious way to do this is for each router to include links to all other routers in its router-LSA. But this would introduce $n * (n - 1)$ links into the OSPF database. So instead, OSPF creates a new LSA type, called the *network-LSA*, to represent the broadcast subnet. Each router-LSA then has a link to the broadcast subnet's network-LSA, and the network-LSA has links to each of the router-LSAs, reducing the number of links from $n * (n - 1)$ to $n * 2$. These two alternatives are shown in Figures 5.5 and 5.6.

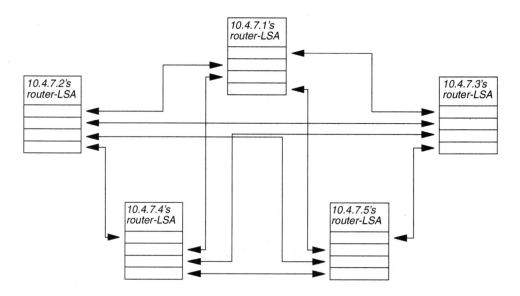

Figure 5.5 One possible representation of router connectivity of a broadcast subnet.

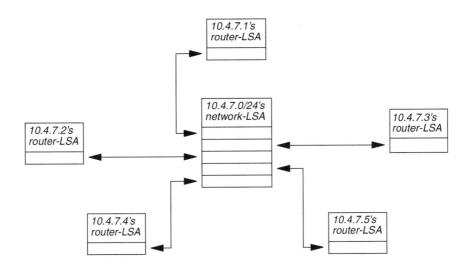

Figure 5.6 OSPF's representation of a broadcast subnet, using a network-LSA.

Of course, most broadcast subnets do not have a computer processor, and so the subnet cannot originate the network-LSA itself. Instead the Designated Router originates the network-LSA on the subnet's behalf. OSPF also uses the network-LSA to indicate the state of database synchronization. The Link State ID of the network-LSA is the IP address of the Designated Router; when a router-LSA includes a link to the network-LSA, the originating router is saying, "I have an interface on this subnet and my database is synchronized with the Designated Router." Likewise the network-LSA lists those routers whose databases have been synchronized with the Designated Router. As in the point-to-point network case, this synchronization property ensures that routers will calculate shortest-path trees containing only those routers that are able to make consistent routing calculations, which in turn ensures loop-free forwarding (see Section 4.8).

This synchronization guarantee provides another example of why OSPF uses a Backup Designated Router. When a Designated Router fails, a new network-LSA must be originated by the new Designated Router. Timely promotion of the Backup Designated Router, which is already synchronized with the other routers, ensures that this new network-LSA will immediately list all the subnet's routers and hence that forwarding of data traffic over the subnet will continue uninterrupted.

The network-LSA for the subnet in Figure 5.3, assuming that 10.4.7.3 has been elected Designated Router, is shown in Figure 5.7. This figure assumes that 10.1.1.3 is the Designated Router's OSPF Router ID, which is probably an address assigned to another of the router's OSPF interfaces.

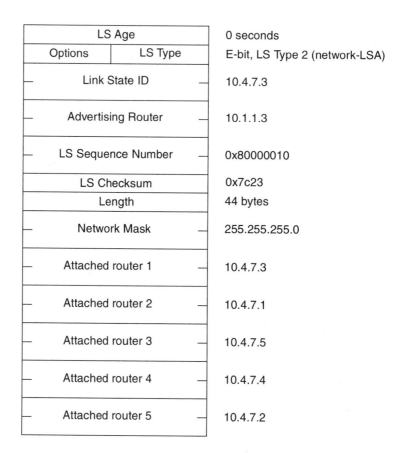

Figure 5.7 Network-LSA for subnet 10.4.7.0/24, assuming that router 10.4.7.3 has been elected Designated Router.

5.2.4 Problems

When OSPF runs over broadcast networks, it assumes transitive connectivity: If router A can talk to the Designated Router and if the Designated Router can talk to router C, then routers A and C can also talk directly. This assumption underlies the network-LSA abstraction in the previous section; using the network-LSA generated by the Designated Router, A will calculate routes with router C as next hop, possibly without ever having exchanged any packets (including Hellos) with router C directly.

Fortunately the transitivity assumption is valid for most common broadcast subnet technologies, such as Ethernet. However, it is not always valid for subnet technologies that are themselves composed of data-link switches, such as SMDS (we also call these *cloud subnets*). These subnets may sometimes be better candidates for the Point-to-MultiPoint subnets (see Section 5.4).

Packet-radio subnets also fail the transitivity assumption, due to line-of-sight problems. Packet radio subnets are good candidates for treatment as Point-to-MultiPoint subnets, with the OSPF Demand Circuit extensions enabled to reduce routing traffic to a minimum because of packet radio's bandwidth limitations (see Section 7.3).

5.3   NBMA Subnets

Nonbroadcast multiaccess (NBMA) segments support more than two routers and allow any two routers to communicate directly over them but do not support a data-link broadcast capability. Examples include X.25, Frame Relay, or asynchronous transfer mode (ATM) subnets that support either (a) switched virtual circuits (SVCs) or (b) a full mesh of PVCs connecting each pair of routers.

Any NBMA subnet can also be modeled as a Point-to-MultiPoint segment (see Section 5.4). NBMA segments are efficient in terms of neighbor maintenance, database synchronization, and database representation, reducing $O(n^2)$ relationships to $O(n)$ by using similar mechanisms to those used for broadcast subnets. However, NBMA segments have weird failure modes when two attached routers cannot communicate directly (see Section 5.3.4), sometimes making the Point-to-MultiPoint model the more robust, although less efficient, choice.

An example of an NBMA segment is shown in Figure 5.8. A collection of six routers is attached to a Frame Relay subnet, with each router connected to every other router via a Frame Relay PVC. A single IP subnet will be assigned to the NBMA segment, with all routers having IP interface addresses on the segment.

5.3.1   Neighbor Discovery and Maintenance

Since there is no broadcast capability on an NBMA subnet, OSPF neighbors must be discovered initially through configuration. Configuration is restricted to routers eligible to become Designated Router (that is, those whose Router Priority on the NBMA subnet is nonzero). To make administration easier and to reduce the amount of Hello traffic, most routers attached to the NBMA subnet should be assigned a Router Priority of 0. In routers eligible to become Designated Router, the identity of all other routers attached to the NBMA subnet must be configured, as well as whether those routers themselves are eligible to become Designated Router.

In order to implement Designated Router election, routers that are eligible to become Designated Router send one another Hellos every HelloInterval (typically 10) seconds. Additionally the routers that have been elected Designated Router and Backup Designated Router send Hellos to all other routers on the NBMA subnet. These Hellos are initially sent also every HelloInterval seconds, but since typical NBMA networks have a habit of charging per packet, the rate of sending Hellos when the other router

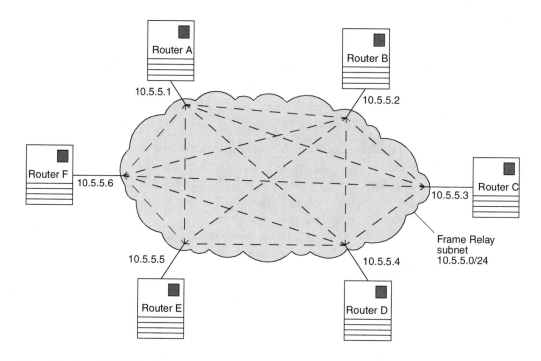

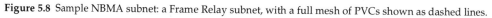

Figure 5.8 Sample NBMA subnet: a Frame Relay subnet, with a full mesh of PVCs shown as dashed lines.

does not respond slows eventually to PollInterval seconds (typically 120). In contrast, routers with Router Priority of 0 simply send Hellos to the current Designated Router and Backup Designated Router every HelloInterval seconds.

For example, in Figure 5.8, assume that routers A and B have been elected Designated Router and Backup Designated Router, respectively; that router F has a Router Priority of 1; and that all other routers have a Router Priority of 0. Assume further that router C has been inoperational for some time. Then routers A and B will be sending separate Hellos to each of D, E, and F every 10 seconds and will be polling router C every 2 minutes to see whether it has come up. Also, D, E, and F will be responding to A and B with Hellos of their own every 10 seconds.

5.3.2 Database Synchronization

Database synchronization on NBMA networks works the same as on broadcast networks. A Designated Router and Backup Designated Router are elected; all other routers initially perform Database Exchange with the Designated Router and Backup Designated Router, and flooding over the NBMA always goes through the Designated Router on the way to the other routers attached to the NBMA subnet. The only difference is that, where on broadcast subnets one would be sending Link State Updates to the multicast addresses AllSPFRouters and AllDRouters, on NBMA subnets, Link State Updates must be replicated and sent to each adjacent router separately.

5.3.3 Abstraction

Representation of an NBMA subnet within the OSPF link-state database is indistinguishable from the representation of a broadcast subnet. A network-LSA is originated for the NBMA subnet by the Designated Router, and all router-LSAs originated by the subnet's routers contain links to the network-LSA.

5.3.4 Problems

Many nonbroadcast subnets cannot support a large number of routers, with each router pair being able to communicate directly. In a subnet providing only a PVC service, the cost of this many PVCs may be prohibitive. For example, to connect 100 routers in a full mesh over a Frame Relay subnet would require 4,950 PVCs. Even when SVCs are used, capacity limitations may prohibit pairwise connectivity. Unless each router on the subnet can communicate directly with every other router, the NBMA model cannot be used.

However, a partial mesh can be turned into multiple NBMA networks, although the configuration can get quite complicated (see [65]). Consider, for example, the Frame Relay subnet in Figure 5.9. Although PVCs do not interconnect every pair of routers, three overlapping router subsets can be found, each of which is full-mesh connected: {F,A,B}, {B,C,D}, and {D,E,F}. Each of these subsets is assigned its own IP subnet. Those routers attached to more than one subnet then end up with multiple IP addresses and OSPF interfaces, each attaching to a different IP subnet.

NBMA networks are only as robust and reliable as the underlying data-link service. If, for example, a PVC fails or is misconfigured or if an SVC cannot be established, due to capacity or policy reasons, routing over the NBMA subnet will fail. And, unfortunately, often the reason for the failure will not be immediately obvious to the network operator.

Take, for example, the network in Figure 5.8. Suppose that router A has been elected Designated Router. If then the PVC between routers E and B fails, all routing tables would look correct in the routers, but any packets that B was supposed to forward to E, or vice versa, would fall into a black hole. If instead the PVC between A and F fails, routing between routers A through E would continue to work, but F would be isolated from all other routers on the NBMA subnet, even from those with which it continues to maintain PVCs.

The Point-to-MultiPoint model can always be applied to rectify these problems, although at some loss of efficiency. This model is described next.

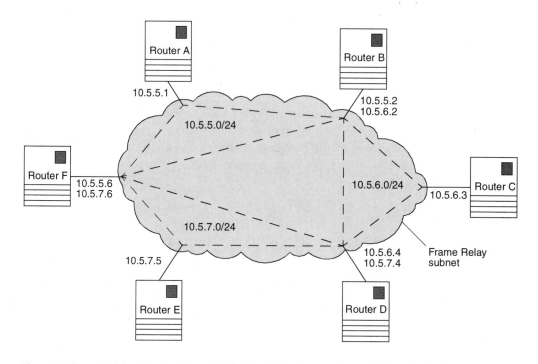

Figure 5.9 Frame Relay network with partial PVC mesh, implemented as multiple NBMA subnets.

5.4 Point-to-MultiPoint Subnets

The Point-to-MultiPoint model can be used on any data-link technology that the NBMA model can be used on. Usually these subnets are connection-oriented subnets, such as Frame Relay and ATM. In addition, the Point-to-MultiPoint model drops the requirement that all routers on the subnet be able to communicate directly, making it possible to model partial PVC meshes as single Point-to-MultiPoint networks. Dropping the full-mesh requirement also allows the modeling of more exotic data-link technologies, such as packet radio, as Point-to-MultiPoint networks.

For example, the partial PVC mesh in Figure 5.9 can be turned into the single OSPF Point-to-MultiPoint subnet with prefix 10.6.6.0/24 as pictured in Figure 5.10. Each OSPF router would have a single IP address on the subnet: Router A would be assigned the IP address 10.6.6.1, and so on. Each router would have a single OSPF interface to the subnet, although multiple OSPF neighbor relationships would form over that interface: Router A would form neighbor relationships with F and B; B with A, C, D, and F; and so on.

When the Point-to-MultiPoint model is used on a subnet built out of PVCs, the operation of OSPF is very similar to treating each PVC as if it were a serial line, as we shall see in the following sections. The advantage of using the Point-to-MultiPoint

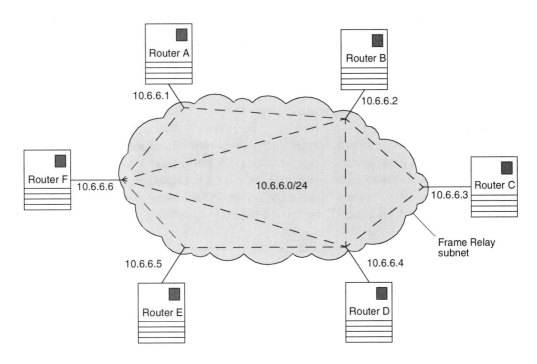

Figure 5.10 Turning the partial mesh of Figure 5.9 into a Point-to-MultiPoint subnet.

model is in the possibility of autoconfiguration and the model's robustness. Since the Point-to-MultiPoint model deals well with partial connectivity between attached routers, the failure of an occasional PVC or SVC causes no problems. In addition, the Point-to-MultiPoint model plays well with the Demand Circuit extensions to OSPF (see Section 7.3).

5.4.1 Neighbor Discovery and Maintenance

There are no Designated Routers or Backup Designated Routers on Point-to-MultiPoint subnets. On these subnets, the job of the Hello protocol is simply to detect active OSPF neighbors and to detect when communication between neighbors is bidirectional.

Because Point-to-MultiPoint networks do not have a broadcast capability, it is sometimes necessary to configure the identity of OSPF neighbors in an OSPF router. However, sometimes a router can detect its neighbors dynamically. For example, on a Frame Relay subnet using PVCs, a router could use the Link Management Interface (LMI) protocol to learn the identity of the PVCs provisioned on the Point-to-MultiPoint interface and could then use Inverse ARP (see [25]) to discover the IP addresses of the neighbors on the other end of the PVC.

A router on a Point-to-MultiPoint subnet periodically sends OSPF Hellos to all other routers on the subnet with which the router can converse directly. For example, in Figure 5.10, router A would send separate Hellos to routers F and B every 10 seconds; router B would send separate Hellos to routers A, C, D, and F; and so on.

5.4.2 Database Synchronization

On a Point-to-MultiPoint subnet, each router becomes adjacent to all other routers with which it can communicate directly, performing initial database synchronization through Database Exchange, then participating in reliable flooding with its neighbors. For example, in Figure 5.10, each PVC is an OSPF adjacency. In order to flood an LSA from router A to router D, the LSA first goes to router B (or one of several alternative paths).

5.4.3 Abstraction

A router on a Point-to-MultiPoint subnet includes the following links in its router-LSA: a point-to-point connection for each of its neighbors on the Point-to-MultiPoint subnet and a single stub network connection to its own IP interface address (see Section 4.3). For example, router D in Figure 5.10 would include four point-to-point connections in its router-LSA (one each to routers B, C, E, and F) and a single stub network connection for its address of 10.6.6.4. Note, then, that to route from 10.6.6.4 to 10.6.6.1, the OSPF routing calculation will calculate a next hop of 10.6.6.2. Even to go between two routers on the same IP subnet, an intermediate router must be traversed.

5.4.4 Problems

What the Point-to-MultiPoint model gains in autoconfiguration and robustness, it loses in efficiency. The closer the underlying physical subnet comes to providing full-mesh connectivity, the less efficient Point-to-MultiPoint becomes. In fact, a full-mesh Frame Relay or ATM subnet can be configured as a Point-to-MultiPoint network, and you may even have to configure it so, if the underlying data-link service is unreliable. However, when operating a full-mesh Frame Relay or ATM network in Point-to-MultiPoint mode, the work involved in neighbor maintenance, flooding, and database representation increases as $O(n^2)$, where n is the number of OSPF routers attached to the subnet, instead of the $O(n)$ behavior that can be achieved with the NBMA model.

Further Reading

See [24] for a description of the enhancements that have been proposed to the IP subnet model, mainly to support the connection of a large number of routers to connection-oriented subnets, such as Frame Relay and ATM. One of the technology pieces used in these extensions is NHRP, the protocol described in [123]. Splitting up a partial-mesh Frame Relay or ATM subnet into multiple OSPF NBMA subnets is explained in [65].

Exercises

5.1   In Figure 5.8, when the circuit between router A, the Designated Router, and router F fails, why is router F isolated from all other routers on the NBMA subnet?

5.2   In Figure 5.10, what are all the possible paths that an LSA might take as it is flooded from router A to router D? Assuming that transmission times on all PVCs are equivalent and that router-handling times in all routers are equivalent, how many copies of the LSA is router D likely to receive?

5.3   Give the router-LSA that will be produced by router A in Figure 5.10.

6

Hierarchical Routing in OSPF

Hierarchical routing is a technique commonly used when building large networks. As a network grows, so do the resource requirements for the network's management and control functions. In a TCP/IP network, resource consumption includes

- Router memory consumed by routing tables and other routing protocol data. In an OSPF network, this other data would include the OSPF link-state database.

- Router computing resources, used in calculating routing tables and other routing protocol functions. In an OSPF network, these resources include the CPU required to calculate shortest-path trees.

- Link bandwidth, used in distributing routing data. In an OSPF network, this includes the bandwidth consumed by OSPF's database synchronization procedures.

It is inevitable that resource requirements grow as the network grows. But the question is, How quickly do resource requirements need to grow? Let's take routing table size as an example. Employing the OSPF protocol as described in Chapter 4, one sees that routing table size increases linearly (specifically, one for one) as the number of TCP/IP segments grows. We call this *flat routing*; each router in the network is aware of the existence and specific addresses belonging to each and every network segment.

However, by employing hierarchical routing, we can slow the rate of routing table growth to the order of the logarithm of the number of segments, written as $O(\log(n))$, where n is the number of network segments. Figure 6.1 illustrates the difference between linear and logarithmic routing table growth.

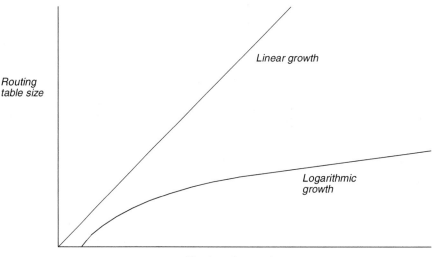

Figure 6.1 Linear versus logarithmic growth.

In hierarchical routing, an internet is partitioned into pieces, which in turn are grouped recursively into levels. At the lowest level, inside one of the lowest-level partitions, routing is flat, with all routers knowing about all network segments within the partition. But the routers have only sketchy information about other partitions. When forwarding a packet addressed to a remote destination, the routers rely on the higher levels of hierarchical routing to navigate the internet, eventually locating the partition containing the destination address.

Figure 6.2 shows an internet organized into a three-level hierarchy. All addresses come from the address range 10.0.0.0/8. There are three second-level partitions, with the lower left containing the 10.1.0.0/16 addresses, the lower right 10.2.0.0/16, and the upper partition 10.3.0.0/16. The nine first-level partitions contain even more specific addresses, with the lower-left first-level partition containing the addresses 10.1.1.0/24, and so on.

Suppose that an IP packet is sent by host 10.1.1.6 to the destination 10.3.3.5. The packet first appears in the first-level partition 10.1.1.0/24. Since the destination is not in the range 10.1.1.0/24, it is handed to second-level routing in the 10.1.0.0/16 partition and then similarly handed to third-level routing. At this point, the packet is forwarded to the correct second-level partition (10.3.0.0/16) and then by second-level routing to the correct first-level partition (10.3.3.0/24), whereupon first-level routing delivers the packet to the destination. This pattern of forwarding the packet up the hierarchy—first level to second to third and then back down again—is what gives hierarchical routing its name.

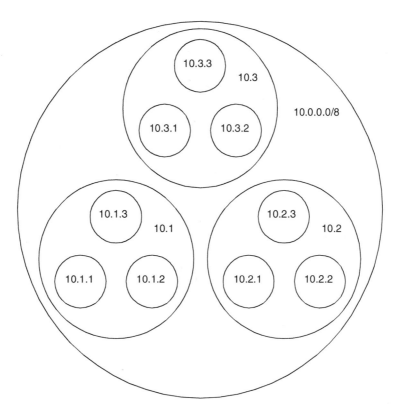

Figure 6.2 An internet employing hierarchical routing.

Hierarchical routing reduces routing table size. Suppose that 16 network segments are in every first-level partition in Figure 6.2. Let us look at routing from the perspective of a router in the first-level partition labeled 10.1.1. If flat routing were deployed throughout the figure, the router would have a routing table consisting of 9 ∗ 16 = 144 entries, one for every network segment. However, because of the three-level hierarchy, the router has 16 entries for the local segments within 10.1.1.0/24 and additional entries for 10.1.2.0/24, 10.1.3.0/24, 10.2.0.0/16, and 10.1.0.0/16, for a total of 20 routing table entries, a marked reduction from 144.

There is often a trade-off involved in the routing table size reduction (and reduction in other resources) that can be accomplished with hierarchical routing. Namely, the information reduction can lead to suboptimal forwarding. Although packets are still forwarded to their destinations, the packets may take a longer path than can be found in a flat routing system. This is illustrated further in Section 6.1.1.

To keep the routing table sizes, and therefore the memory and CPU demands, on its routers to a manageable level, the worldwide Internet employs hierarchical routing. IP subnetting and CIDR addressing (see Chapter 2) are tools used to implement the Internet's routing hierarchy. IP's 32-bit address generally limits the number of hierarchical levels to around four, although with IPv6's 128-bit addresses (see Section 1.3), more levels of hierarchy may be possible in the future.

OSPF implements a two-level hierarchical routing scheme through the deployment of OSPF areas, as described in Section 6.1. Furthermore, OSPF allows an internet to be split into additional levels by incorporating two levels of external routing information into the OSPF routing domain, as explained in Section 6.2.

Hierarchical routing protocols are difficult to design. Most of the protocol bugs found in OSPF over the years have been in the area routing support, some of which have been discovered only recently. See Section 3.5 for a description of the various hierarchical routing bugs that have been encountered and repaired in OSPF since its original design.

6.1   OSPF Areas

OSPF supports a two-level hierarchical routing scheme through the use of OSPF areas. Each OSPF area is identified by a 32-bit Area ID and consists of a collection of network segments interconnected by routers.

Inside any given OSPF area, OSPF runs as described in Chapters 4 and 5. Each area has its own link-state database, consisting of router-LSAs and network-LSAs describing how the area's routers and network segments are interconnected. Routing within the area is flat, with each router knowing exactly which network segments are contained within the area. However, detailed knowledge of the area's topology is hidden from all other areas; the area's router-LSAs and network-LSAs are not flooded beyond the area's borders.

Routers attached to two or more areas are called *area border routers*, or ABRs. Area border routers leak IP addressing information from one area to another in OSPF summary-LSAs. This enables routers in the interior of an area to dynamically discover destinations in other areas (the so-called *inter-area* destinations) and to pick the best area border router when forwarding data packets to these destinations.

Figure 6.3 shows a sample OSPF area configuration having four OSPF areas. Area 0.0.0.0's link-state database consists of four router-LSAs. Area 0.0.0.1's link-state database has four router-LSAs. Area 0.0.0.2's link-state database has three router-LSAs and a network-LSA. Area 0.0.0.3's link-state database has three router-LSAs. Since all of area 0.0.0.1's addresses fall into the range 10.2.0.0/16, routers B and C can be configured to aggregate area 0.0.0.1's addresses by originating a single summary-LSA with destination of 10.2.0.0/16. Likewise router A can be configured to aggregate area 0.0.0.2's addresses by advertising a single summary-LSA with destination equal to 10.1.0.0/16.

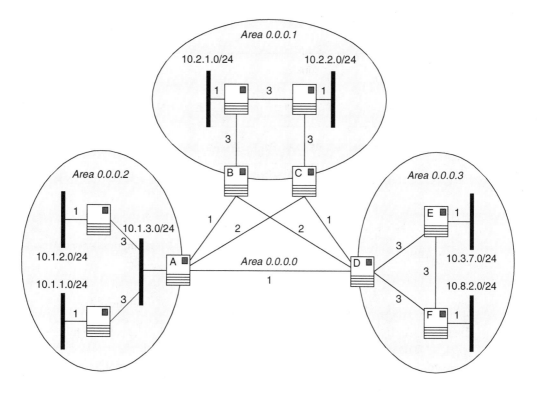

Figure 6.3 A sample area configuration.

However, area 0.0.0.3's addresses do not aggregate, so router D will end up originating two summary-LSAs, one for 10.3.7.0/24 and one for 10.8.2.0/24.

Figure 6.4 displays in detail the summary-LSA that router B uses to leak area 0.0.0.1's addressing information into area 0.0.0.0. Router B has been configured to aggregate all of area 0.0.0.1's addresses into a single advertisement for the prefix 10.2.0.0/16. The Link State ID for the summary-LSA is the prefix address 10.2.0.0. The prefix mask, 255.255.0.0, is included in the body of the summary-LSA. Also included in the summary-LSA is the cost from the advertising router (router B) to the prefix. Since 10.2.0.0/16 is an aggregation, the cost in this case is set to the cost from router B to the most distant component of 10.2.0.0 (in this case, 10.2.2.0/24, at a cost of 7).

Area 0.0.0.1's addresses are distributed throughout area 0.0.0.0 as the summary-LSA is flooded throughout area 0.0.0.0. From area 0.0.0.0, the addresses are advertised into the other areas, as described in Section 6.1.1.

Splitting an OSPF routing domain into areas reduces OSPF's demands for router and network resources. Since the area's link-state database contains only router-LSAs and network-LSAs for the area's own routers and networks, the size of the link-state database is reduced, along with the amount of flooding traffic necessary to synchronize

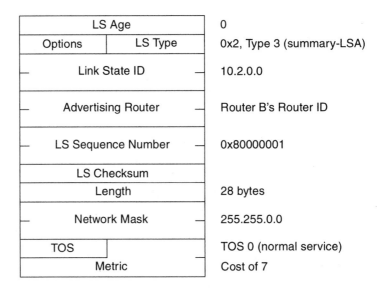

LS Age		0
Options	LS Type	0x2, Type 3 (summary-LSA)
Link State ID		10.2.0.0
Advertising Router		Router B's Router ID
LS Sequence Number		0x80000001
LS Checksum		
Length		28 bytes
Network Mask		255.255.0.0
TOS		TOS 0 (normal service)
Metric		Cost of 7

Figure 6.4 Summary-LSA advertised by router B into area 0.0.0.0.

the database. If aggregation is employed at area boundaries, routing table size is also reduced. The cost of the shortest-path calculation is $O(i * \log(n))$, where i is the number of router interfaces, and n is the number of routers (see Section 4.8); so as the routing domain is split into areas, the cost of the shortest-path calculation also decreases.

Of course, splitting the routing domain adds some amount of summary-LSAs to the database and routing calculations. However, summary-LSAs are smaller than router-LSAs, and the routing calculations involving summary-LSAs are cheaper than the shortest-path calculation. In fact, the routing calculation for all summary-LSAs in an area is like the processing of a single RIP packet (see Section 6.1.1).

In 1991, [173] recommended that the size of an OSPF area be limited to 200 routers, based solely on the cost of the shortest-path calculation. However, this estimate is probably dated, as router CPU speeds have increased considerably since then. In reality, maximum area size is implementation specific. Some vendors of OSPF routers are building areas of 500 routers, whereas others recommend that the number of routers in an area be limited to 50.

In addition to allowing one to build much larger OSPF networks, OSPF areas provide the following functionality.

- *Increased robustness.* The effects of router and/or link failures within a single area are dampened external to the area. At most, a small number of summary-LSAs are modified in the other areas, and, when aggregation is employed, possibly nothing will change in the other areas at all.

- *Routing protection*. OSPF always prefers paths within an area (intra-area paths), over paths that cross area boundaries. This means that routing within an area is protected from routing instabilities or misconfiguration in other areas. For example, suppose that a corporation runs OSPF and assigns the engineering department as one area and the marketing department as another. Then, even if the marketing department mistakenly uses some of the engineering address prefixes, communication within engineering will continue to function correctly.

- *Hidden prefixes*. One can configure prefixes so that they will not be advertised to other areas. This capability allows one to hide one or more subnets from the rest of the routing domain, which may be wanted for policy reasons: The subnets may contain servers that should be accessed only by clients within the same area.

6.1.1 Area Organization

When an OSPF routing domain is split into areas, all areas are required to attach directly to a special area called the OSPF *backbone* area. The backbone area always has Area ID 0.0.0.0. In the sample area configuration of Figure 6.3, areas 0.0.0.1, 0.0.0.2, and 0.0.0.3 attach directly to area 0.0.0.0 via the area border routers A, B, C, and D.

The exchange of routing information between areas is essentially a Distance Vector algorithm (see Section 2.3 for a discussion of Distance Vector algorithms). Let us use router D in Figure 6.3 as an example. The exchange of routing information includes the following steps.

1. The area border routers A through D advertise the addresses of their directly connected areas by originating summary-LSAs into the backbone.

2. Router D receives all the summary-LSAs through flooding.

3. For any given destination, router D examines all summary-LSAs advertising that destination, using the best summary-LSA to create a routing table entry for the destination, and then readvertises the destination into its attached area 0.0.0.3 in summary-LSAs of its own.

In particular, for the destination 10.2.0.0/16, router D sees two summary-LSAs, one from router C and one from router D, each advertising a cost of 7. Router D then selects the summary-LSA from C as best because C is closer (a distance of 1 instead of 2). Router D then installs a routing table entry for 10.2.0.0/16 with a cost of 8: the cost advertised in router C's summary-LSA plus the cost from D to C. Finally, router D originates a summary-LSA for 10.2.0.0/16, with a cost of 8, into area 0.0.0.3 so that area 0.0.0.3's routers will know how to reach 10.2.0.0/16.

The similarities between the distribution of area routing information in OSPF and the operation of the canonical Distance Vector algorithm, RIP, is given in Table 6.1.

Table 6.1 Distribution of Area Routing Information, Using Distance Vector Mechanisms

Area Routing Function	Analogous RIP Function
Originate summary-LSAs for directly attached areas into backbone.	Send directly attached nets in RIP packets.
Receive summary-LSAs via flooding.	Receive RIP packets from neighbors.
Add cost in summary-LSA to distance to summary-LSA's originator.	Add 1 to cost of each received route.
Choose best summary-LSA.	Choose best route advertised by neighbor.
Originate own summary-LSAs into directly attached areas.	Advertise updated routing table in RIP packets sent to neighbors.

The use of Distance Vector mechanisms for exchanging routing information between areas is the reason for requiring all areas to attach directly to the OSPF backbone. The larger the number of redundant paths in a network, the worse a Distance Vector algorithm's convergence properties (see Section 2.3). Requiring all areas to attach directly to the backbone limits the topology for inter-area routing exchange to a simple hub-and-spoke topology (see Figure 6.5), which eliminates redundant paths and is not subject to Distance Vector convergence problems, such as counting to infinity. However, requiring direct connection of all areas to the OSPF backbone does not mean requiring physical connectivity to the backbone, as we shall see in the discussion of virtual links later on in this section.

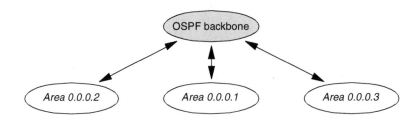

Figure 6.5 Inter-area routing exchange in the sample OSPF network of Figure 6.3.

The example at the beginning of this section also illustrates that the loss of information that enables OSPF area routing to scale also can lead to the selection of less efficient paths. If router D forwards a packet to the IP destination 10.2.1.20, it will forward the packet to router C instead of along the shorter path through router B. This behavior is due to the fact that router D does not even realize the existence, much less the location, of the network segment 10.2.1.0/24 and so forwards using the aggregated routing table entry of 10.2.0.0/16 instead.

6.1.2 Virtual Links

OSPF requires that all areas attach directly to the backbone area but not that the attachment be physical. Indeed, one can take any physical arrangement of areas and attach them logically to the backbone through the use of OSPF *virtual links.*

For example, suppose that the organization whose network is pictured in Figure 6.3 purchases two smaller companies and adds their networks as separate OSPF areas, as pictured in Figure 6.6. The two new areas do not attach physically to the backbone, so two virtual links are configured through area 0.0.0.3, the first having as end points routers D and E, the second having as end points routers D and F. Virtual links allow summary-LSAs to be tunneled across nonbackbone areas, maintaining the desired hub-and-spoke topology for inter-area routing exchange. In Figure 6.6, router A receives the summary-LSA from router E, after the summary-LSA has been tunneled across area 0.0.0.3. In order to evaluate the relative cost of the summary-LSA, router A sums the cost of the backbone path to router D, the cost of the virtual link to router E, and the cost advertised in router E's summary-LSA. In this fashion, the virtual link acts like a point-to-point link that has been added to the backbone.

However, although the exchange of routing topology continues to follow a simple hub-and-spoke topology, the forwarding of data packets does not. The OSPF routing calculations for virtual links have a built-in shortcut calculation, allowing data packets to avoid the backbone area when the backbone is not on the shortest path. Using Figure 6.6 again as an example, routing information from area 0.0.0.4 goes to the backbone before being redistributed to area 0.0.0.5, but data traffic from area 0.0.0.4 to 0.0.0.5 simply traverses area 0.0.0.3, avoiding the backbone altogether.

Unfortunately many people find it difficult to decide when and where to configure virtual links. It is possible to design algorithms so that the routers themselves can dynamically establish virtual links; an example of such an algorithm can be found in [267]. In the future, these algorithms may relieve network operators of the burden of configuring virtual links.

6.2   Incorporating External Routing Information

Of course, the entire Internet is not run as a single OSPF domain. Many routing protocols are in use in the Internet simultaneously: OSPF, RIP, BGP, IGRP, and IS-IS, to name a few of the most common (see Chapter 2). On the edge of an OSPF routing domain, generally you will find routers that run one or more of these routing protocols, in addition to OSPF. It is the job of these routers, called *AS boundary routers* (ASBRs), to import the

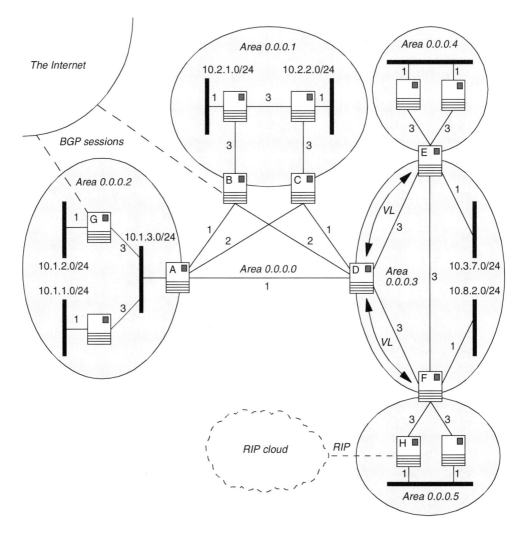

Figure 6.6 Virtual links incorporate new networks. External routing information is imported by the routing domain's AS boundary routers.

routing information learned from these other routing protocols into the OSPF routing domain. This behavior allows routers internal to the routing domain to pick the best-exit router when routing to destinations outside the OSPF routing domain, just as summary-LSAs allow routers within an OSPF area to pick the right area exit when forwarding to inter-area destinations.

Information learned from other routing protocols and for destinations outside of the OSPF routing domain is called *external routing information*, or *external routes*. External routes are imported into the OSPF routing domain in AS-external-LSAs originated by the AS boundary routers. Each AS-external-LSA advertises a single prefix.

Consider, for example, the network in Figure 6.6. Routers B and G are running BGP sessions to learn of destinations in the Internet at large. Tens of thousands of routes may be learned in this way; to date, the default-free core of the Internet carries more than 40,000 routes. However, probably not all of these routes would be imported into the OSPF domain. Routers B and G would import only those routes where the choice of B or G was important; when either exit would do, default routes imported by B and G would suffice. Still it would not be unusual for B and G to originate several thousand AS-external-LSAs into the routing domain. In addition, router H is exchanging RIP information with an isolated collection of RIP routers. Router H then imports each prefix that it learns from the RIP routers in an AS-external-LSA.

Paths internal to the OSPF routing domain are always preferred over external routes. External routes also can be imported into the OSPF domain at two separate levels, depending on metric type. This gives a four-level routing hierarchy, as shown in Table 6.2. Paths that stay within one level are always preferred over paths that must traverse the next level.

Table 6.2 OSPF's Four-Level Routing Hierarchy

Level	Description
1	Intra-area routing
2	Inter-area routing
3	External Type 1 metrics
4	External Type 2 metrics

For example, in the network of Figure 6.6, router H may import its RIP routes into OSPF as external Type 1 metrics, and routers B and G import their routing information as external Type 2 metrics. Then the routing preferences introduced by OSPF hierarchy in Figure 6.6 are as follows, from most preferred to least preferred: (1) routing within any given OSPF area, (2) routing within the OSPF routing domain itself, (3) routing within the OSPF domain and RIP cloud, taken together, and (4) routing within the Internet as a whole.

Besides establishing two different routing levels, external Type 1 and Type 2 metrics have different semantics. The use of external Type 1 metrics assumes that in the path from OSPF router to destination, the internal component (path to the ASBR advertising the AS-external-LSA) and external component (cost described by external Type 1 metric) are of the same order. For example, if the OSPF routing domain used hop count as its metric (namely, setting each interface cost to 1) and RIP routes were imported as external Type 1 metrics, the combined OSPF and RIP system would operate more or less seamlessly, selecting paths based on minimum hop count even when they cross the OSPF-to-RIP boundary.

In contrast, external Type 2 metrics assume that the external part of the path (cost given by the external Type 2 metric) is always more significant than the internal cost to the AS boundary router. This would be the case when BGP routes were imported as external Type 2 metrics, with metric set equal to the BGP route's AS path length—no matter what the cost to the advertising AS boundary router, the whole OSPF routing domain is still only a single AS.

Figure 6.7 displays an AS-external-LSA. This AS-external-LSA assumes that router B has learned the prefix 8.0.0.0/8 through BGP, with an AS path length of 12, and that AS path length is being used as the OSPF external Type 2 metric. Note that the format of the AS-external-LSA is very similar to the summary-LSA: The Link State ID for both is the address prefix of the route being advertised, and both LSAs contain the network mask and route cost in the body of the LSA.

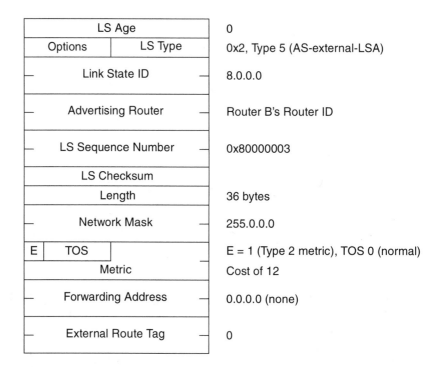

Figure 6.7 An AS-external-LSA.

There are two fields in the AS-external-LSA of Figure 6.7 that have not been mentioned so far. The Forwarding Address field in this particular AS-external-LSA has been set to 0.0.0.0 to indicate that traffic destined for 8.0.0.0/8 should be forwarded to router B, the originator of the AS-external-LSA. However, by specifying another router's IP address in the Forwarding Address field, router B can have traffic forwarded to another router instead. This feature is used to prevent extra hops at the edge of the routing domain and would be done automatically by router B when necessary. See Section 3.5 for further information.

The External Route Tag field is not used by OSPF itself but instead is used to convey information between the routing protocols being run at the edge of the OSPF routing domain (BGP and RIP in Figure 6.6). For example, in the BGP-OSPF interaction specified in [252], the External Route Tag is set when importing external routes on one edge of the routing domain, to give routers on the other side of the routing domain information as to whether, and if so how, they should export this routing information to other Autonomous Systems (see Section 11.6.1). The External Route Tag is also used by the external-attributes-LSA, proposed in [73] as an alternative to IBGP (see Sections 7.6 and 13.3).

6.2.1 Interaction with Areas

How is external routing information conveyed across area borders in OSPF? One way this could have been done in OSPF was to reoriginate the AS-external-LSAs at area borders, just as OSPF does with summary-LSAs for inter-area routes. However, this would have been expensive in terms of database size. When there are multiple area border routers for a given area, multiple AS-external-LSAs would be originated for each original AS-external-LSA: one origination per area border router. And within the area border routers, the situation would have been even worse, with each area border router holding a slightly different version of each AS-external-LSA for each attached area.

So OSPF takes a different tack, simply flooding AS-external-LSAs across area borders. For example, the AS-external-LSA in Figure 6.7 is flooded throughout all areas in Figure 6.6; all routers in the network then hold this exact AS-external-LSA in their link-state databases.

In particular, router H in area 0.0.0.5 has the AS-external-LSA in its link-state database. However, in order to make use of this information, router H must know the location of the originator of the AS-external-LSA—in this case, the ASBR router B. For this reason, OSPF advertises the location of ASBRs from area to area, using Type 4 summary-LSAs (also called ASBR-summary-LSAs). The ASBR-summary-LSA that the area border router F originates into the area 0.0.0.5 in order to advertise the location of ASBR B is shown in Figure 6.8. The Link State ID of the ASBR-summary-LSA is the OSPF Router ID of the ASBR whose location is being advertised. Other than that, the format, origination, and processing of ASBR-summary-LSAs is identical to that of summary-LSAs.

The AS-external-LSA is the only type of OSPF LSA, other than the proposed external-attributes-LSA of Section 7.6, that is flooded throughout the entire OSPF routing domain. We say that OSPF AS-external-LSAs have *AS flooding scope*, whereas

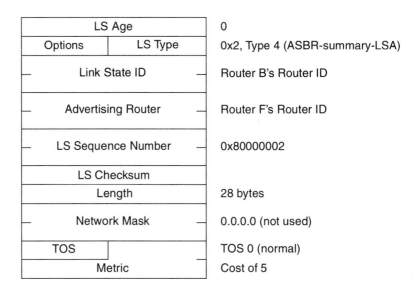

LS Age	0
Options / LS Type	0x2, Type 4 (ASBR-summary-LSA)
Link State ID	Router B's Router ID
Advertising Router	Router F's Router ID
LS Sequence Number	0x80000002
LS Checksum	
Length	28 bytes
Network Mask	0.0.0.0 (not used)
TOS	TOS 0 (normal)
Metric	Cost of 5

Figure 6.8 ASBR-summary originated by router F into area 0.0.0.5.

router-LSAs, network-LSAs, and summary-LSAs, which are not flooded across area borders, have *area flooding scope*.

There can be thousands of external routes imported into an OSPF routing domain in AS-external-LSAs, forming a large part of an OSPF area's link-state database. For this reason, additional OSPF area types have been defined that restrict the amount of external routing information within an area, thereby limiting the resources that OSPF consumes in the area's routers and links, at the expense of reduced functionality. These area types are the subject of Section 6.3.

6.3   OSPF Area Types

Normal OSPF areas have some desirable properties. Normal areas can be placed anywhere within the OSPF routing domain, although possibly requiring configuration of virtual links. Normal areas calculate efficient, although not always optimal, inter-area and external routes through the use of summary-LSAs, ASBR-summary-LSAs, and AS-external-LSAs. And normal areas support ASBRs, directly importing external routing information from other routing protocols and then distributing this information to other areas.

However, this support requires processing and bandwidth resources that may not be available everywhere. To have areas with smaller routers and to have low-bandwidth links, OSPF forgoes some of these desirable properties and introduces two restricted area types: *stub areas* and *NSSAs*.

6.3.1 Stub Areas

Of all OSPF area types, stub areas consume the least resources. Stub areas, part of the original OSPF design, were designed to contain routers that had limited resources, especially when it came to router memory.

To conserve router memory, the link-state database in stub areas is kept as small as possible. AS-external-LSAs are not flooded into stub areas; instead routing to external destinations within stub areas is based simply on default routes originated by a stub area's area border routers. As a result, ASBRs cannot be supported within stub areas. To further reduce the size of the link-state database, origination of summary-LSAs into stub areas is optional. Inter-area routing within stub areas can also follow the default route. Without AS-external-LSAs and summary-LSAs, stub areas cannot support virtual links either and so must lie on the edge of an OSPF routing domain.

As a result of these restrictions, not all areas can become stub areas. For example, in Figure 6.6, only areas 0.0.0.1 and 0.0.0.4 could be configured as stub areas. The backbone area can never be configured as a stub; areas 0.0.0.2 and 0.0.0.5 support ASBRs; and area 0.0.0.3 needs to support virtual links.

Even if you can configure an OSPF area as a stub area, you may not want to. The lack of AS-external-LSAs (and possibly summary-LSAs) means that routing to external (and possibly inter-area) destinations can take less efficient paths than in regular areas. This fits in with the observation made at the end of Section 6.1.1: The trade-off for the improved scaling properties of hierarchical routing is the possibility of suboptimal routes. With the even better scaling properties of stub areas comes the possibility of even more suboptimal routes.

6.3.2 NSSAs

NSSAs, or not-so-stubby areas, were defined in [47] as an extension to stub areas. Although most of the stub area restrictions, such as preventing the flooding of AS-external-LSAs into the area and not allowing configuration of virtual links through the area, were deemed acceptable by the NSSA designers, they wanted the ability to import a small amount of external routing information into the NSSA for later distribution into the rest of the OSPF routing domain.

A typical example of an NSSA is area 0.0.0.5 in Figure 6.6. You want to import routes learned from the RIP cloud into area 0.0.0.5 and then to distribute these routes throughout the rest of the OSPF routing domain. However, area 0.0.0.5 does not need the collection of AS-external-LSAs imported by routers B and G as a result of their BGP sessions. Instead routing in area 0.0.0.5 to these BGP-learned destinations can be handled by a single default route pointing at router F.

External routing information is imported into an NSSA by using Type-7-LSAs (LS Type = 7). These LSAs have area flooding scope and are translated at the NSSA boundary into AS-external-LSAs that allow the external routing information to be flooded to other areas. The NSSA border serves as a one-way filter for external information, with external information flowing from NSSA to other areas, but not vice versa. For further information on NSSAs, see Section 7.4.

Further Reading

The seminal paper on hierarchical routing is [128]. Scaling properties of hierarchical routing are analyzed in [88]. An interesting proposal to add area routing to the original ARPANET link-state routing algorithm, although never implemented, is presented in [231].

The interaction between BGP and OSPF, defining what information should be leaked between the two routing protocols and how it should be leaked, is defined in [252]. The specification for NSSAs is provided in [47].

Exercises

6.1   Calculate routing table for routers A through D in Figure 6.3.

6.2   Calculate the routing table for router A in Figure 6.6.

6.3   In Figure 6.6, how many summary-LSAs does router E originate into area 0.0.0.4? How many ASBR-summary-LSAs? What are their associated costs?

6.4   By combining two areas in Figure 6.6, how could one avoid the need for any virtual links?

7

OSPF Extensions

The base OSPF protocol has changed only slightly since the OSPF Version 2 specification was first published in [176] in 1991. The OSPF version number is still 2, and today's OSPF implementations still interoperate with those written in 1991. However, this is not to say that nothing has changed in OSPF since 1991. There have been a number of bug fixes and optimizations made to the specification as a result of field experience and an increasing number of independent OSPF implementations, as documented in Chapter 3. Also, there have been a steady stream of optional extensions to OSPF, ranging from multicast routing to protocol extensions enabling efficient use of dial-up circuits, such as ISDN. These optional extensions—their content and the OSPF mechanisms that enable their addition in a backward-compatible way—are the subject of this chapter.

It was fortunate that there were two optional capabilities built into the OSPF Version 2 specification at the very beginning, namely, TOS-based routing and stub area support. These capabilities caused extension mechanisms to be built into OSPF from the start. One usually goes about extending OSPF by employing one or more of the following methods.

- Enrich the network description as implemented by the OSPF link-state database by adding either data to existing LSA types or new LSA types. For example, the multicast routing extensions to OSPF, referred to as MOSPF, add group-membership-LSAs (LS Type 6) to indicate the location of multicast group members.

- Add new routing calculations to accommodate more sophisticated forwarding rules. For example, OSPF's optional TOS-based routing performs separate routing calculations for each of the five IP Type of Service values [3]. This behavior allows routers to forward IP packets based on the packet's TOS designation, as well as on the packet's IP destination address.

- Alter OSPF database synchronization to achieve different performance points. For example, the *Demand Circuit extensions* to OSPF remove the periodic refresh of OSPF LSAs in order to make more efficient use of dial-up link technology.

Of course, OSPF extensions must be defined in such a way that they are backwardly compatible with existing OSPF routers. Since one cannot expect to deploy an OSPF extension in all routers at once, one needs to ensure that a mix of new and old OSPF routers (a) continues to forward IP data traffic successfully and (b) does not exhibit any anomalous behavior, such as continual retransmissions of LSAs. To enable backward compatibility, OSPF includes an 8-bit Options field in OSPF Hello packets, Database Description packets, and OSPF LSAs. The Options field allows automatic discovery of which routers support a given extension and what routing information the extension can use.

The Options field is displayed in Figure 7.1. In general, one bit of the Options field has been allocated to each OSPF extension. As a result, the OSPF Options field is almost used up, which has led to an increase in size to 24 bits in OSPF for IPv6 (see Section 3.7). Explanation of the current use of the Options bits can be found in Table 7.1 and elsewhere in this chapter.

		DC-bit	EA-bit	N/P-bit	MC-bit	E-bit	T-bit

Figure 7.1 The OSPF Options field.

Mismatches in router capabilities in an OSPF routing domain, with some routers supporting an option and others not, can trigger the following OSPF mechanisms in order to retain backward compatibility.

- Routers may refuse to become adjacent. For example, two routers that disagree on whether an OSPF area has been configured as a stub will refuse to become adjacent, because otherwise routing loops might occur (see Section 7.2).

- An OSPF router will not flood an extension's new LSA type to a neighbor unless the neighbor implements the extension. In other words, routers are required to store and flood only those LSAs that they understand. For example, group-membership-LSAs are sent only to those routers supporting MOSPF.

- Certain router-LSAs and other LSA types may be ignored during routing calculations. For example, in OSPF TOS-based routing, paths are calculated around those routers that do not support TOS.

Table 7.1 summarizes the current OSPF extensions and how they are implemented. The remainder of this chapter discusses each extension in more detail. Detailed discussion of MOSPF, the largest extension, is postponed until Chapter 10, MOSPF.

Table 7.1 Summary of OSPF Extensions

Extension	Option Bits Used	Additional LSA Types	Updates Routing Calculations?
TOS-based routing	T-bit	Additional data in router-LSAs	Yes
Stub areas	E-bit	None	No
Demand Circuit extensions	DC-bit	None	No
NSSA areas	N/P-bit	Type-7-LSAs (LS Type 7)	Yes
Database overflow	None	None	No
External-attributes-LSAs	EA-bit	External-attributes-LSA (LS Type 8)	No
Multicast routing extensions to OSPF (MOSPF)	MC-bit	Group-membership-LSA (LS Type 6)	Yes

7.1   TOS-Based Routing

IP supports five different Types of Service (TOS) for datagram delivery: normal service, minimize monetary cost, maximize reliability, maximize throughput, and minimize delay. An application indicates which TOS it wishes to be applied to the application's datagrams by setting the TOS field in its datagrams' IP headers. The routers may then route both on the datagrams' IP destination and on their TOS, forwarding datagrams requesting normal service one way, datagrams requesting to minimize monetary cost another way, and so on.

Consider the network in Figure 7.2. Link costs have been configured symmetrically, with the cost of a link for normal service pictured. As a result, router 10.9.0.6 will deliver datagrams destined for 10.9.0.4 over the path of cost 8 through 10.9.0.1. However, if the link between 10.9.0.3 and 10.9.0.4 is a satellite link, router 10.9.0.6 may send datagrams requesting to minimize delay over the alternative path through 10.9.0.5.

TOS-based routing has recently been omitted from the OSPF specification [178], due to lack of deployment experience. TOS-based routing has seen limited deployment within TCP/IP networks and for this reason, has also been omitted from the IPv6 specifications (see Section 1.3). Lack of TOS-based routing has been a chicken-and-egg problem: Host vendors have not changed their applications to request TOS, because the

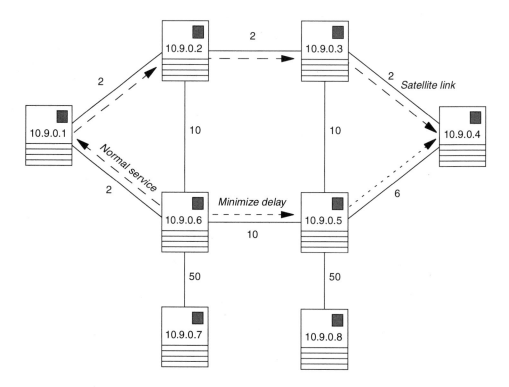

Figure 7.2 Sample network implementing TOS-based routing.

routers do not forward based on TOS; the routers do not forward based on TOS, because few applications request TOS. There are, however, a few TCP/IP hosts (such as Cray supercomputers) that can be configured to request maximize throughput TOS for FTP sessions, and so on. Although there are no commercially available router implementations of TOS-based routing, there have been two separate implementations of OSPF TOS-based routing in the past, one done for the Research Internet Gateway project [105] and the other by 3Com. In the rest of this section, we describe how TOS routing was implemented within the original OSPFv2 specification [176].

Each link within a router-LSA (see Section 4.3) could advertise separate costs for each TOS value; if the router-LSA failed to list a cost for a TOS value, the cost defaulted to that specified for normal service, which was always present. An OSPF router implementing TOS-based routing then ran separate routing calculations for each TOS, each time using the costs specified for the given TOS. In Figure 7.2, the costs pictured are for the TOS value of normal service. In order to get router 10.9.0.6 to forward traffic requesting minimize-delay service toward 10.9.0.5, router 10.9.0.3 simply advertised the cost of its attached satellite link as greater than 10 for the TOS value of minimize delay.

Backward-Compatibility Provisions

The preceding discussion assumed that all routers within the routing domain were capable of routing based on TOS. However, it is more likely that certain routers would support TOS and that others would not.

OSPF allowed a mix of TOS capability within a routing domain through the use of the T-bit in the Options field of router-LSAs, summary-LSAs, and AS-external-LSAs. By setting the T-bit in its router-LSA, a router indicated that it was performing TOS-based routing. Summary-LSAs and AS-external-LSAs with the T-bit set indicated that they were describing TOS-capable paths all the way to their advertised destinations. An OSPF router performing TOS-based routing then performed its routing calculations, for all TOS other than normal service, on the subset of the link-state database having the T-bit set.

As a result of these procedures, an OSPF router supporting TOS may have had a normal service path to a destination but not paths for other TOS values. In this case, when a router forwarded datagrams that requested other than normal service to the destination, the normal-service path was used anyway. In this way, the datagram was forwarded on the best-effort path until a path for the specific TOS value was encountered, and then the datagram used the path for the specific TOS the rest of the way to the destination, resulting in loop-free routing.

For example, suppose in Figure 7.2 that routers 10.9.0.1, 10.9.0.3, 10.9.0.4, and 10.9.0.5 supported TOS routing, yet the others did not. In that case, a datagram with destination 10.9.0.4 and requesting to minimize delay would be forwarded by router 10.9.0.1 along the normal-service path through 10.9.0.2 to 10.9.0.3, whereupon it would take the shortest minimize-delay path through 10.9.0.5 on its way to 10.9.0.4.

7.2   Stub Areas

Stub areas arose from the desire to deploy routers having limited memory and processing resources, even within a large OSPF routing domain. To support such limited routers, an OSPF routing domain is split into areas, and the resource-limited routers are assigned to special areas, called stub areas, at the edge of the OSPF routing domain. AS-external-LSAs are not flooded into stub areas, relying instead on default routing in the stub areas to forward traffic addressed to external destinations. The default route also can be used for inter-area destinations, removing the need for summary-LSAs within stub areas.

Removing AS-external-LSAs and summary-LSAs can significantly reduce the link-state database size, and hence the memory and processor consumption, of routers within a stub area. To give a numerical example, suppose that, on average, router-LSAs consume 192 bytes of router memory and that AS-external-LSAs consume another 64 bytes. In an OSPF router domain consisting of 200 routers and 10,000 AS-external-LSAs, the link-state database would consume approximately 678K of router memory. However, if in this same routing domain, a particular router was isolated within a stub area of 10 routers, the router's link-state database would be a meager 2K in size.

Stub areas are a part of the base OSPF specification [177]. For further information on stub areas, see Section 6.3.1.

Backward-Compatibility Provisions

It is important for all routers within a stub area to agree that the area is a stub area. If certain routers treated the area as a stub area and others did not, two problems might ensue. First, there might be continual retransmissions of LSAs, with those routers believing that the area was not a stub trying unsuccessfully to flood AS-external-LSAs to those routers believing that the area was a stub. Worse yet, disagreements on a stub- area status might cause routing loops, with some routers in the area using AS-external-LSAs in their routing calculations and others simply using default routes.

To prevent these problems, OSPF mechanisms ensure that all routers agree on whether the area is a stub. When an OSPF router's interface connects to a stub area, the router sends Hellos out onto the associated network segment, with the E-bit clear in the Hello packets' Options field. Other OSPF routers receiving the Hello will accept it for further processing only if they too agree that the associated segment belongs to a stub area. This means that two routers disagreeing on stub-area status will never achieve bidirectional communication, and so will never start database synchronization (thereby avoiding potential flooding problems), and will not become fully adjacent (thereby avoiding using each other for forwarding).

7.3   Demand Circuit Extensions

The OSPF Demand Circuit extensions are specified in [169]. *Demand circuits* are point-to-point or Point-to-MultiPoint links (see Chapter 5) that incur usage-based costs. An example is an ISDN basic-rate service, whereby you might pay for your connect time and also pay a per packet or per bit rate for the data you transmit or receive. Other examples include standard dial-up links and router-to-router links implemented through X.25, Frame Relay, or ATM switched virtual circuits (SVCs). In all these circumstances, to save money, you want to send the bare minimum of routing protocol traffic over the demand circuit, ideally establishing the underlying data-link connection only when there is user-data traffic to transmit. These are the goals of OSPF's Demand Circuit extensions.

OSPF routing protocol traffic is of two types. First, there are the periodic Hello packets that are sent over each link for neighbor discovery and maintenance (see Section 4.6). Second, there is the OSPF protocol traffic to achieve and maintain link-state database synchronization between routers. The Demand Circuit extensions remove the periodic nature of both traffic types. These extensions reduce the amount of OSPF routing traffic, removing all OSPF protocol traffic from a demand circuit when the routing domain is in a steady state (in other words, in the absence of link and router failures).

Over a demand circuit, OSPF Hellos are sent only until initial link-state database synchronization is achieved. Then Hellos are suppressed, depending completely on the data-link protocol to indicate link failures. For example, when the demand circuit is implemented as an X.25 SVC, the router will receive an X.25 Clear message with an appropriate diagnostic code when the link is no longer usable.

To remove the periodic nature of OSPF database synchronization, simple refreshes of LSAs are not flooded over demand circuits. When a router receives a new LSA instance, the router compares the contents of the new LSA instance to the current LSA copy in the router's database. If the contents have not changed, the new LSA is not flooded over the router's attached demand circuits. Therefore the last copy of the LSA to be flooded over the demand circuit reflected some change in the OSPF routing domain. To prevent the routers on the other side of the demand circuit from aging out this LSA, the router indicates that the LSA should not be aged, by setting the LSA's DoNotAge bit when flooding the LSA over the demand circuit.

As an example of the Demand Circuit extensions, suppose that in Figure 7.2, the link between routers 10.9.0.6 and 10.9.0.7 is a demand circuit, implemented as a dial-up link. When router 10.9.0.7 is first booted, the dial-up connection to 10.9.0.6 is established, Hellos are exchanged, and then link-state database synchronization is performed between 10.9.0.6 and 10.9.0.7. During database synchronization, each LSA flooded by 10.9.0.6 to 10.9.0.7 (and vice versa) has the DoNotAge bit set, so they will not have to be refreshed. Then, after some period of time without network changes and/or user-data traffic, the dial-up connection between 10.9.0.6 and 10.9.0.7 is torn down, to be reestablished when necessary: A refresh of 10.9.0.2's router-LSA would not cause a new dial-up connection, but if the link between 10.9.0.2 and 10.9.0.3 fails, the dial-up connection would be reestablished in order to flood updated router-LSAs from 10.9.0.2 and 10.9.0.3.

The OSPF Demand Circuit extensions can be used to good effect even when demand circuits are not in use. On low-bandwidth broadcast links and permanent point-to-point links, such as packet radio, the Demand Circuit extensions can reduce routing protocol traffic, making more of the link bandwidth available for user-data traffic. The Demand Circuit extensions typically avoid LSA refreshes over links labeled as demand circuits, but in OSPF networks with large databases, LSAs can even be originated with the DoNotAge bit set in order to avoid LSA refreshes on all links.

The DoNotAge Bit

The DoNotAge bit is defined as the most significant bit of the LS Age field. LSAs having the DoNotAge bit set are not aged as they are held in an OSPF router's link-state database. This means that these LSAs do not have to be refreshed every 30 minutes. However, stale LSAs with the DoNotAge bit set are still eventually removed from the link-state database. The rule is that these LSAs can be removed from the database when both (a) they have been in the database for at least an hour and (b) the LSAs' originator has also been unreachable for at least that period of time. The time constant of 1 hour was chosen to prevent temporary unreachability conditions from causing LSA thrashing—the flushing of LSAs only to see them immediately originated again.

In all other link-state database operations—comparing two instances of the same LSA, deciding whether an LSA is to be updated or deleted, and so on—an LSA with an age of DoNotAge + x is treated identically to an LSA with an age of x. In particular, to protect against flooding loops, the LS Age of a DoNotAge LSA is incremented at each flooding hop. Should the LSA's LS Age reach DoNotAge + MaxAge, the LSA is removed from the routing domain.

Caveats

Since the Demand Circuit extensions remove all OSPF protocol traffic when the routing domain is in a steady state, the data-link connection underlying the demand circuit can be closed when not being used for user-data traffic. This behavior saves money but can delay notification of link failures: If the underlying data-link connection is closed due to lack of traffic, the inability to establish a new data-link connection (in other words, a link failure) will not be noticed until there is new user-data traffic to send. As a result, longer rerouting times may occur.

Also, the Demand Circuit extensions remove some of OSPF's robustness. The removal of periodic Hellos means that the method of last resort to detect neighbor failures is no longer available. Further, the removal of LSA refreshes over demand circuits means that the automatic correction for link-state database corruption does not take place across demand circuits.

When there is a real change in an OSPF routing domain, for example, when a link becomes inoperational or a new piece of external routing information is imported, updated LSAs are flooded over demand circuits. In a large routing domain, these changes may be frequent enough to keep a demand circuit's underlying data-link connection continuously open. One way to isolate a demand circuit from these changes is to assign the demand circuit to an OSPF stub area or NSSA (see Section 6.3).

Backward-Compatibility Provisions

In order to suppress Hellos on demand circuits, an OSPF router must establish that the OSPF router on the other end of the link also is going to treat the link as a demand circuit. Otherwise, suppressing Hellos will just cause the neighbor to declare the link inoperational. Therefore a link's demand-circuit status is negotiated. A router wanting to treat a link as a demand circuit sends its first Hello on the link with the DC-bit set in the Hello's Options field (see Figure 7.1). If the router on the other end of the link is able and willing to treat the link as a demand circuit, it responds with a Hello also having the DC-bit set.

Use of the DoNotAge bit also must be negotiated, although this negotiation is networkwide instead of just between the end points of a demand circuit. All routers in an OSPF routing domain must be capable of understanding the DoNotAge bit before any one router starts setting the DoNotAge bit in LSAs. The reason is that the reaction of an unmodified OSPF router to the DoNotAge bit is unpredictable; at best, an unmodified router will treat an LSA with DoNotAge set as a MaxAge LSA, causing the unmodified router to ignore the LSA.

A router indicates that it is capable of understanding the DoNotAge bit by setting the DC-bit in the Options field of the LSAs that the router itself originates. Routers can then set the DoNotAge field in LSAs if, and only if, all LSAs in the link-state database have the DC-bit set.

The presence of routers that do not understand DoNotAge must be indicated across area boundaries, to prevent the flooding of AS-external-LSAs with DoNotAge set. This is accomplished by area border routers. Noticing routers incapable of DoNotAge processing in one area, an area border router floods a dummy ASBR-summary-LSA (see Section 6.2.1, and Section 2.5.1 of [169]) with DC-bit clear into its other attached areas.

7.4   NSSA Areas

Defined in [47], not-so-stubby areas (NSSAs) are an extension of OSPF stub areas. Like stub areas, NSSAs enable routers with limited resources to participate in OSPF routing. Like stub areas, NSSAs limit resource consumption by preventing the flooding of AS-external-LSAs into NSSAs, relying instead on default routing to external destinations. As a result, both stub areas and NSSAs must be placed at the edge of an OSPF routing domain.

However, NSSAs are more flexible than stub areas. An NSSA can import a selected number of external routes into the OSPF routing domain, enabling the NSSA to provide transit service to small stub routing domains that themselves are not part of the OSPF routing domain. For example, in Figure 6.6, area 0.0.0.5 can be configured as an NSSA, protecting its internal routers from all the AS-external-LSAs imported by the OSPF routing domain's BGP routers (routers B and G), but allowing attachment of the isolated RIP cloud.

External routing information is imported into an NSSA in Type-7-LSAs. Type-7-LSAs are identical in format to AS-external-LSAs. However, unlike AS-external-LSAs, Type-7-LSAs have only area flooding scope. In order to further distribute the NSSA's external routing information, Type-7-LSAs are selectively translated into AS-external-LSAs at the NSSA border.

Translation is performed by the area border router with the highest OSPF router ID. Aggregation is also possible at translation time through the configuration of address ranges within the area border router. The N/P-bit in a Type-7-LSA's Options field indicates whether the Type-7-LSA should be translated: Only those LSAs with the N/P-bit (where the *P* in this case stands for *propagate*) are translated. There are several reasons why you might not want a Type-7-LSA translated.

- *For policy reasons.* The Type-7-LSA may describe a private external route that should be used only by the routers within the NSSA area.

- *For protocol reasons.* Default routing within an NSSA, which is necessary because the NSSA does not receive the OSPF domain's AS-external-LSAs, is implemented by the NSSA's area border routers originating Type-7-LSAs advertising the default route. These Type-7-LSAs must not be translated into a default for the entire OSPF routing domain.

- *When an area border router is also an AS boundary router.* In this case, proper AS-external-LSAs exist without having to translate Type-7-LSAs.

Going back to the example in Figure 6.6, suppose that router H learns a route to 192.9.1.0/24 via RIP with a cost of 3. Router H may then import into area 0.0.0.5 the Type-7-LSA pictured in Figure 7.3, which would then be translated into an AS-external-LSA by router F for distribution to other OSPF areas.

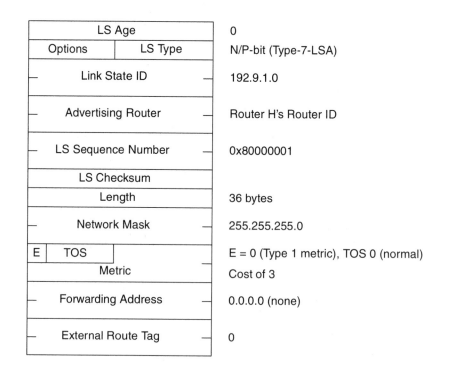

Figure 7.3 An example Type-7-LSA.

Backward-Compatibility Provisions

Just as for stub areas, all routers in an NSSA area must agree that the area is an NSSA, to prevent continual retransmissions of LSAs or, even worse, routing loops. This agreement is ensured in a similar fashion to that for stub areas. A router will set the N/P-bit in the Options field of Hello packets that it transmits out its interfaces connecting to NSSA areas. On these interfaces, the router will not accept Hello packets unless their N/P-bit is also set. In this way, two OSPF routers that disagree on whether an area is an NSSA will never attempt database synchronization; nor will they use each other in routing calculations.

7.5   Database Overflow Support

The OSPF *Database Overflow extensions* are designed to deal with resource shortages in OSPF routers. When such shortages are known ahead of time, the routers with limited resources may be consigned to OSPF stub areas or NSSAs. It is the job of OSPF's database-overflow support to deal with unexpected shortages.

The Database Overflow extensions work by limiting the size of the link-state database. Only the number of nondefault AS-external-LSAs is restricted. The decision to limit only these LSA types was based on the following considerations.

- Nondefault AS-external-LSAs often comprise the lion's share of the link-state database, as discussed in [173].

- The number of these LSAs that will be present day to day is most unpredictable. The Internet is always growing, causing more external routes to be imported in each OSPF domain. Also, a configuration error in an AS boundary router importing BGP-learned routes easily can lead to thousands of extra external routes being imported by mistake.

- These LSAs are, in some sense, optional. If removed from the link-state database, routing within the OSPF routing domain will continue to function. In particular, the OSPF routers still should be manageable; thus if the reason for the database overflow was a configuration error, the error can be corrected. In addition, without these LSAs, any default routing in the AS will continue to work, ideally meaning that the majority of external destinations will still be reachable.

To enforce this limit, the maximum allowed number of nondefault AS-external-LSAs, **ospfExtLsdbLimit**, is configured in each router. The **ospfExtLsdbLimit** must be set identically in each router; its value can be calculated as a function of the smallest router's memory size. At no time will any OSPF router accept more than **ospfExtLsdbLimit** nondefault AS-external-LSAs; excess LSAs are silently discarded without being acknowledged. In addition, when a router reaches its limit of **ospfExtLsdbLimit** LSAs, it goes into *database-overflow* state. In database-overflow state, a router deletes its self-originated nondefault AS-external-LSAs from the routing domain and refuses to originate any more.

When the number of nondefault AS-external-LSAs exceeds `ospfExtLsdbLimit`, some number of Link State Update retransmissions will occur. However, since all routers agree on the value of `ospfExtLsdbLimit`, it is guaranteed that within a short period of time, enough routers will enter database-overflow state and flush their self-originated LSAs that the database will converge to a state having less than `ospfExtLsdbLimit` nondefault AS-external-LSAs. Convergence on a common link-state database is crucial, as this is the only guarantee that loop-free routing will continue.

Although `ospfExtLsdbLimit` should be set the same in each router, there is no protocol mechanism guaranteeing an equal setting. Instead `ospfExtLsdbLimit` is set in each router via SNMP (see Section 11.1).

The database-overflow condition may be transitory. To return the routing domain to complete operation without human intervention, a timer may be configured in each router so that it automatically transitions out of database-overflow state after some period of time, reoriginating its nondefault AS-external-LSAs in the process. This timer need not be the same length in all routers. Indeed, you may want to configure a shorter timer in the routers that originate the more critical AS-external-LSAs.

The database-overflow support limits only AS-external-LSAs. Similar techniques can be applied to control the number of other LSA types, such as summary-LSAs and group-membership-LSAs.

Backward-Compatibility Provisions

The OSPF database-overflow support has no explicit support for backward compatibility with unmodified OSPF routers. In the same routing domain, you can mix routers supporting the Database Overflow extensions with unmodified routers, just as you can mix routers having `ospfExtLsdbLimit` set to differing values. In these cases, however, the only routers guaranteed to detect the database-overflow condition are those having the smallest `ospfExtLsdbLimit` value. Unless this subset of routers can bring the link-state database size under their `ospfExtLsdbLimit` by themselves, the routers in the OSPF domain may fail to synchronize on a common link-state database. This failure, in turn, can lead to continual retransmissions of Link State Updates and to routing loops when sending to external destinations.

7.6   The External-Attributes-LSA

The Internet is split up into Autonomous Systems (ASs). Routers within an AS run an Interior Gateway Protocol (IGP) in order to forward traffic within the AS. Examples of IGPs include OSPF and RIP. Routers at the edge of an AS exchange routing information with other ASs using an Exterior Gateway Protocol (EGP). The Border Gateway Protocol (BGP; see Section 13.3) is the EGP used in the Internet.

When an AS is providing transit service for other ASs, routers on one side of the AS must transmit the BGP information across the AS where other routers will in turn readvertise the information to their BGP peers. The original mechanism to propagate BGP information across an AS was called Internal BGP, or IBGP. In IBGP, each BGP router on the edge of a given AS must form an IGBP peering session with every other BGP router in the AS. The problem with this scheme is that the number of IBGP sessions rapidly becomes intractable, growing as n^2, where n is the number of BGP routers in the AS.

Methods for distributing BGP information across an AS have been proposed that provide better scaling than IBGP: BGP confederations [248], BGP route reflectors [17], and BGP route servers [94]. The first two methods have seen significant deployment in the Internet.

When an AS runs OSPF as its routing protocol, the external-attributes-LSA (LS Type 8) provides another alternative to IBGP. The BGP information that needs to be communicated consists of a set of BGP attributes for each BGP destination, the foremost attribute being the path of ASs (the so-called AS path), which must be traversed to reach the destination. The AS path is necessary to provide loop detection within the BGP protocol and also is used to implement BGP routing policies (see Section 13.3).

In order to use the external-attributes-LSA to replace IBGP, each BGP router at the edge of the OSPF Autonomous System imports its BGP-learned destinations in AS-external-LSAs. Each AS-external-LSA has a 4-byte tag field that can be used to carry extra information about the external route (see Figure 6.7). If the BGP attributes for the destination can be squeezed into these 4 bytes, an external-attributes-LSA is unnecessary; for example, this is the case when the destination belongs to a neighboring AS (see Section 11.6.1 and [252]). However, if the destination's AS path is longer, a separate external-attributes-LSA is originated with contents equal to the destination's BGP attributes. Then, in order to associate the destination's AS-external-LSA with the correct BGP attributes, the Tag field in the AS-external-LSA is set equal to the Link State ID of the appropriate external-attributes-LSA.

Advertising the BGP attributes separately from the destinations saves space in the link-state database when multiple destinations have the same BGP attributes. This is commonly the case. To date, an example default-free router had 40,000 BGP routes but only 13,000 associated BGP attributes.

As an example, suppose that in Figure 6.6, the OSPF Autonomous System is assigned AS 33 and provides transit service for several other ASs. Suppose further that router B has a BGP session with a router in AS 171 and that router G has a BGP session with a router in AS 265. When router B installs in its routing table a BGP route to 132.166.0.0/16 with an AS path of [AS 171, AS 68, AS 373], router B passes this information along to G by originating an external-attributes-LSA and an AS-external-LSA. The external-attributes-LSA, having a Link State ID of 0xf000000a, is pictured in Figure 7.4.

The AS-external-LSA would advertise 132.166.0.0/16, inserting 0xf000000a in the AS-external-LSA's Tag field. If on receipt of these two LSAs, router G installs the route into its routing table, G would in turn advertise 132.166.0.0/16 to its BGP peer in AS 265, with a new AS path of [AS 33, AS 171, AS 68, AS 373]. The Format ID field in the body of the external-attributes-LSA enables the external-attributes-LSA to transmit data for protocols other than BGP.

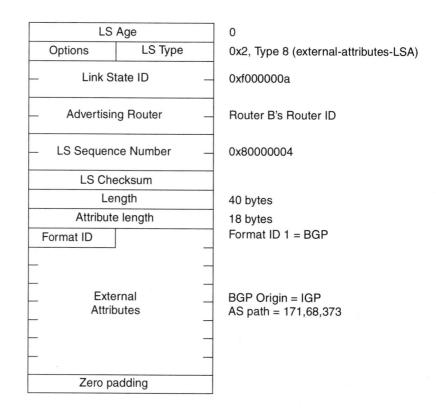

Figure 7.4 The external-attributes-LSA.

Use of the external-attributes-LSA has a clear advantage over IBGP, analogous to the advantage of multicast over multiple unicasts. When a router uses the external-attributes-LSA to advertise its BGP information to other routers in its AS, the router is guaranteed that each advertised BGP route will traverse each network segment at most once; this is a generic property of OSPF flooding (see Section 4.7.2). In contrast, when using IBGP, the same BGP information may be sent over a network segment many times, as multiple IBGP peering sessions each may traverse the network segment. The external-attributes-LSA also has an advantage over other IBGP scaling methods, such as route reflectors and BGP communities, in that the external-attributes-LSA requires no additional configuration. The one potential downside of the external-attributes-LSA is that it requires routers on the interior of the AS (although not all routers) to store BGP information in the form of external-attribute-LSAs, when before they did not have to.

Although the external-attributes-LSA is an attractive alternative to IBGP, it has never been implemented or deployed. This is probably due to the reluctance of network operators to import all of their BGP-learned routes (to date, more than 40,000 in the default-free networks) into their IGP.

Backward-Compatibility Provisions

As with all optional LSA types, the external-attributes-LSA is flooded only between those routers that understand the LSA. A router conveys its understanding to its neighbors by setting the EA-bit in the Database Description packets that the router sends during initial database synchronization (see Section 4.7.1).

Restricting external-attributes-LSAs to modified routers is both a feature and a bug. On the positive side, it relieves unmodified routers from the burden of storing the external-attributes-LSAs. On the negative side, however, it can prevent the external-attributes-LSA from replacing IBGP functionality. If two BGP routers are not interconnected by routers supporting the external-attributes-LSA, the two routers will still be aware of the BGP routes each is trying to exchange with the other through examination of AS-external-LSAs. But they will not be able to associate BGP path attributes with the routes, since they will not receive each other's external-attributes-LSAs. Worse yet, if two BGP routers were, but are no longer, interconnected by routers capable of flooding external-attributes-LSAs, the two BGP routers may end up associating incorrect BGP path attributes with the BGP routes. This latter problem is due to the fact that the external-attributes-LSAs that each router holds may in that case be out of date.

Considering these problems, it may have been better if all routers were capable of flooding external-attributes-LSAs. For this reason, the OSPF for IPv6 specification introduced a category of LSA types that are stored and flooded even by routers that do not understand the LSA type (see [46]).

Further Reading

OSPF hierarchical routing, including a discussion of OSPF stub areas and NSSAs, is covered in Chapter 6. The NSSA protocol specification is given in [47].

For a more detailed explanation of Type of Service routing, see the discussions on IP forwarding rules in the IP router-requirements document [12].

The OSPF Demand Circuit extensions are defined in [169]. These extensions have also been defined for RIP. Defined in [159] and [160], the RIP extensions provide similar functionality to the OSPF Demand Circuit extensions. However, the mechanisms to provide such functionality in a Distance Vector algorithm, such as RIP, are quite different.

For further information on BGP, see Section 13.3 and the BGP specification [208]. BGP extensions addressing ways to more efficiently propagate BGP routing information across an AS are described in [17], [94], and [248].

Exercises

7.1   Consider the area configuration in Figure 6.6. Assume that router B imports 1,000 external routes into OSPF as AS-external-LSAs and that router G imports another 1,000. Assume that area 0.0.0.4 is an OSPF stub area and that area 0.0.0.5 is an NSSA, with router H originating 100 Type-7-LSAs. What is the size of the link-state database in area 0.0.0.1? In area 0.0.0.4? In area 0.0.0.5?

7.2   Consider the network in Figure 7.2. Suppose that the link between routers 10.9.0.1 and 10.9.0.2 incurs a high per packet charge. For that reason, for traffic between 10.9.0.6 and 10.9.0.4, you want packets that request to minimize monetary cost (IP TOS 16) to avoid that link. What is the smallest TOS 16 cost that can be configured for the link in order to achieve this goal?

7.3   Section 7.3 gave an example of X.25 networks indicating link failures through certain diagnostic codes in Call Clear indications. Give other examples of data-link protocols that can indicate link failures. Which common data links do not provide link-failure notifications?

7.4   Assume the following configuration in Figure 7.2. Only routers 10.9.0.6 and 10.9.0.2 implement the OSPF Database Overflow extensions, with both setting their **ospfExtLsdbLimit** to 5,000. Suppose that each of the eight routers in the AS originates 1,000 AS-external-LSAs. Does the link-state database reach a synchronized state in this case? How about if **ospfExtLsdbLimit** is set to 6,500 in both 10.9.0.6 and 10.9.0.2?

7.5   Assume that the external-attributes-LSA is used to replace IBGP in an AS in which 40,000 BGP routes must be exchanged between BGP routers, with 14,000 distinct AS paths, of average length 6 ASs. What would the size of link-state database be in bytes, assuming no overlap of destinations and/or AS paths advertised by the BGP routers? Is the latter a reasonable assumption?

8

An OSPF FAQ

In this chapter, we answer some frequently asked questions (FAQs) about the OSPF protocol. Many of these questions have been raised on the OSPF Working Group's mailing list. The questions that follow are roughly organized from general to specific.

Q: *Where can I get OSPF software?*

A: The original freely available OSPF implementation was written by Rob Coltun when he was at the University of Maryland (UMD). That implementation was written in C for UNIX systems and for a long time was available via anonymous FTP over the Internet.

Although no longer available in its original form, the UMD OSPF implementation has since been incorporated into the GATED program. GATED was originally developed at Cornell University and is now maintained and enhanced by Merit Network Inc., a nonprofit corporation located in Ann Arbor, Michigan. GATED, a routing daemon for UNIX platforms, can be used as a replacement for the standard UNIX `routed` routing daemon. In addition to `routed`'s RIP support, GATED also supports OSPF and BGP. GATED is also commonly used as a development platform for routing protocol software, so you can often find modified GATEDs supporting other protocols: DVMRP, PIM Sparse, IS-IS, and so on.

Although freely available for individual use, you must execute a GATED redistribution license when incorporating GATED software into commercial products. Software support for GATED is available through joining the Merit GATED Consortium. For more information on GATED, consult **http://www.gated.org**.

In addition to being incorporated into GATED, the UMD implementation has also been ported into many commercial routers. As such, it is by far the most common OSPF implementation in use today.

Besides the UMD OSPF implementation, the only other freely available OSPF implementation is the one contained in the companion book to this book (*OSPF Complete Implementation*), which is covered by the GNU General Public License.

Q: *How can I participate in discussions about OSPF?*

A: Discussions about the OSPF protocol, including possible bugs and enhancements, are carried on the OSPF Working Group's mailing list: **ospf@gated.cornell.edu**. To join the mailing list, send a subscription request to **ospf-request@gated.cornell.edu**. There are also sometimes interesting OSPF discussions on the various GATED mailing lists (**see http://www.gated.org**).

The OSPF Working Group is one of the Internet Engineering Task Force's (IETF) many Working Groups. The IETF is the protocol engineering and development arm of the Internet. Anyone is free to participate in the IETF through any of the many IETF mailing lists. The IETF also holds three face-to-face meetings a year. Most IETF Working Groups produce documents called Internet Drafts, some of which will eventually be published as RFCs. For information on IETF Working Groups, how to join IETF mailing lists, how to receive or submit Internet Drafts, and so on, consult **http://www.ietf.org**. For a general description on how the IETF works, see [108].

Q: *What units is the OSPF link-state metric measured in?*

A: OSPF does not specify how costs are assigned to links. Assignment of link costs is left up to individual network administrators. Within one OSPF routing domain, link cost may be set to the link's fixed delays (propagation), whereas another routing domain may use the monetary cost of transmission over the link, and so on. As far as OSPF is concerned, links costs are just numbers subject to the following restrictions.

- The cost of any link must lie in the range 1 to 65,535 inclusive. In other words, link cost is a positive 16-bit integer.

- The cost of a path is the sum of the cost of the path's constituent links. Paths with smaller cost are shorter and preferred over paths with larger cost. As a result, links with smaller cost are more likely to carry data traffic.

- When virtual links are used, the cost of paths within a transit area should be kept less than or equal to 65,535. If path cost in a transit area exceeds this value, virtual links may not become operational.

As an example, when all links are assigned a cost of 1, OSPF routing will always choose minimum-hop paths. The default value for link cost in the OSPF MIB [12] indicates link-transmission speed. For more information on metric-setting strategies, see Chapter 11, OSPF Management.

Q: *Does OSPF routing respond to network load?*

A: No, OSPF metrics are static. OSPF dynamically routes around link failures, but it does not route around network congestion. Changing paths in response to network load is difficult to do well in a distributed routing protocol: Routing has a tendency to thrash, with all routers choosing the shortest path initially, then moving en masse to a lightly loaded secondary path, and then back again.

The only link-state routing protocol to react to network load was the BBN ARPANET routing algorithm [147], which used a link-state metric that varied with the length of the link's output queue. The ARPANET experienced route thrashing, but BBN fixed the problem by limiting the dynamic metric range to reduce the response to congestion. The effect of limiting the metric is shown in [127], which contains a great figure that shows graphically that within a limited range, metric changes encourage an equilibrium but that large metric changes cause wild oscillations in routes.

Having routing respond to network load is easier in virtual-circuit networks than in datagram networks like the Internet. The reason is that virtual-circuit networks naturally limit the response to congestion: Changes in metric due to congestion levels typically affect only new circuits, leaving existing circuits on their old paths (see [20]). For this reason, you do see link-state algorithms in virtual-circuit networks that route circuits based in part on network load conditions.

Q: *Why is the representation of point-to-point links in OSPF so strange?*

A: The representation of point-to-point links in OSPF is a little strange. But before explaining why it is so strange, we should describe how point-to-point links are represented. Figure 8.1 shows three routers connected by point-to-point links. Each router has assigned an IP address to each of its point-to-point interfaces. These addresses are totally unrelated; the addresses assigned to either end of a point-to-point link need not fall into a common subnet. Each router has also independently assigned a cost to each point-to-point interface. In the resulting router-LSAs, which also are pictured in Figure 8.1, each router advertises a point-to-point connection to the other and a stub link to the *other* router's IP address.

Advertising the neighboring router's IP address instead of the router's own address is what people find so strange. To make this even more confusing, after the router runs its OSPF routing calculation, it finds that the resulting routing table says to forward packets for its own address out the point-to-point interface to the neighboring router! Although it was always assumed that a router would not forward a datagram

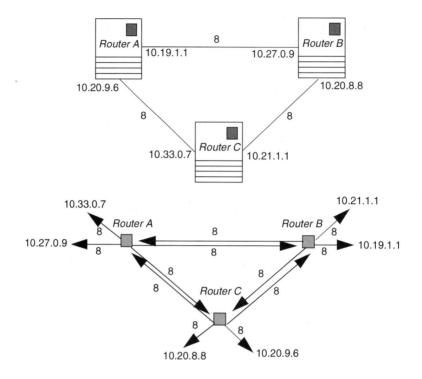

Figure 8.1 Point-to-point representation in OSPF.

addressed to one of its own addresses, this property does make routing table dumps look a little weird.

So what are the reasons behind this strange representation? First, the noncontroversial part: Advertising the interface addresses separately instead of advertising a single route for the point-to-point link, as is done in the RIP, frees the network administrator from assigning separate subnets to each point-to-point link. This allows better conservation of the ever scarcer IP address space.

But why advertise the neighbor's IP address instead of your own? The following obscure reasons explain why.

- The neighbor's address is advertised even before an OSPF neighbor relationship is formed. This allows network booting over the point-to-point link. Assume in Figure 8.1 that router B is trying to boot a software image that is located on a server somewhere else in the network. The network boot loader running in router B is probably a small program without an OSPF application. However, having router A advertise B's address allows router B's address to be routable anyway.

- Advertising the neighbor's address has a tendency to bias routing in a way that is useful for diagnostic purposes. You'd like to use **ping** to determine whether an interface is operational. So when pinging an interface address, it would be useful if the ping were routed into the addressed interface. This is more likely, although not guaranteed, when advertising the neighbor's IP address. For example, in Figure 8.1, when router B sends a ping to router A's address 10.20.9.6, it is in fact routed through router C and then into the correct interface. (Of course, to some people, this just looks like suboptimal routing!)

The representation of point-to-point links in OSPF is confusing enough that an option was added to represent the links in a fashion identical to that used by RIP: Assign a subnet to the point-to-point link and have the router at each end of the link advertise a stub link to the subnet. In OSPF for IPv6 (see Section 3.7), in which backward compatibility with the installed base of OSPF routers is not an issue, each end point of the link advertises its own address instead of its neighbor's address.

Q: *Must both sides of a point-to-point link agree whether the link is numbered or unnumbered?*

A: Yes. To see the problems that such a disagreement causes, let us look at an example. Suppose that in Figure 8.1 router B thinks that its link to router A is unnumbered but that all other interface addresses are as pictured. In this case, router B, thinking that no addresses had been assigned to the link, would fail to advertise A's interface address, 10.19.1.1. As a result, that address would become unreachable.

Q: *Why is OSPF so difficult to configure?*

A: It isn't, or at least it shouldn't be. A router's OSPF implementation should not be any more difficult to configure than its RIP implementation. OSPF does have a large number of tunable parameters that can make configuration seem complicated. However, most of these parameters should be set to default values in an OSPF implementation.

The complete set of OSPF configurable parameters can be found in the OSPF MIB [12]. The MIB is organized into 12 groups (a thirteenth group, **ospfAreaRangeTable**, is obsolete and is included only for backward compatibility), containing 99 variables in all. However, more than half (61) of these variables are read-only, used for statistics collection, reporting the contents of the link-state database, and so on. The remaining variables are used to configure not only the base OSPF protocol but also OSPF extensions, such as MOSPF, NSSA areas, and the Demand Circuit extensions (see Chapter 7).

To get OSPF running on a router, all you really need to do is configure the IP addresses of the router's OSPF interfaces (variable **ospfIfIpAddress**). The other variable that is frequently set is the cost of an OSPF interface (**ospfIfMetricValue**).

OSPF has a number of configurable per interface timers, whose values should almost always remain at their default settings. The default settings are listed in the OSPF MIB. If running OSPF over satellite links or very low-speed links (for example, 1200-baud modems), you may need to change the values of the timers **ospfIfTransitDelay, ospfIfRetransInterval, ospfIfHelloInterval**, and `ospfIfRtrDeadInterval`. Running OSPF over nonbroadcast networks, such as Frame Relay and ATM, may also require some configuration, especially when using NBMA mode (see Chapter 5).

Splitting an OSPF routing domain into areas always requires additional configuration. First, you must establish area boundaries by configuring the area that each router interface attaches to (`ospfIfAreaId`). Then, to achieve address aggregation at area borders, one or more entries in the area border routers' `ospfAreaAggregateTable` must be configured. In addition, if not all nonbackbone areas attach to a single backbone area, one or more virtual links must be configured between area border routers (`ospfVirtIfTable`). For detailed information on configuring OSPF, see Chapter 11, OSPF Management.

Q: *What OSPF interface type should I use when running OSPF over a Frame Relay subnet?*

A: Your two options are the OSPF NBMA and Point-to-MultiPoint interface types. The NBMA interface type treats the Frame Relay network sort of like a simulated Ethernet segment, whereas Point-to-MultiPoint models Frame Relay PVCs as if they were individual point-to-point links. NBMA is more efficient than Point-to-MultiPoint but is generally more difficult to configure and less robust against PVC failures and other failures within the Frame Relay subnet. See Sections 5.3 and 5.4 for more details.

Q: *How should my routers advertise information between the OSPF and RIP protocols?*

A: Unfortunately there are no standards in this area. Every router vendor has worked out its own mechanisms controlling the interactions of OSPF and RIP. So the place to start in answering this question is probably the configuration guide provided by your router vendor(s). Two simple models for the interaction of OSPF and RIP are given in Section 11.6.2.

Q: *I see a lot of "2-Way" states in my OSPF router's neighbor statistics. Don't I want the operational states of all my OSPF router's neighbors to be "Full"?*

A: No. State "2-Way" is often correct for neighbors over broadcast and NBMA segments. On these segment types, only a small percentage of the neighbors become fully adjacent (that is, achieve state "Full"). All routers become fully adjacent to the segment's Designated Router and Backup Designated Router but go no further than "2-Way" with other neighbors on the segment. See Section 5.2 for more details.

Q: *When the Designated Router is operational, is the Backup Designated Router duplicating the work done by the Designated Router?*

A: No. The Backup Designated Router is mainly just waiting to take over Designated Router duties should the present Designated Router fail. The only function that the Backup Designated Router will perform until that failure occurs is to help a little in flooding. The Designated Router is responsible for maintaining the reliability of flooding over its segment. However, should retransmissions of LSAs become necessary, the Backup Designated Router will step in to perform the necessary retransmissions even if the Designated Router is still active. In all other duties, such as origination of the network-LSA for the segment and initial flooding of LSAs over the segments, the Backup Designated Router always defers to the active Designated Router. See Section 5.2 for more details.

Q: *How big can I build my OSPF areas?*

A: Maximum area size really depends on your router vendor (or vendors). In 1991, the guideline was at most 200 routers in a single area [173]. The larger an OSPF area gets, the more resources the OSPF protocol consumes in the area's OSPF routers. These resources include router memory, CPU cycles, and network bandwidth.

To date, some vendors have deployed OSPF areas of up to 350 routers. In contrast, other router vendors recommend that areas should be limited to 50 or fewer routers. Most vendors will include in their documentation the maximum area size they will support.

In general, you should not make your areas too small. Areas require additional configuration (see the previous question) and can create suboptimal routing.

Q: *Where should I put area boundaries?*

A: This is a complicated question, one without a single answer. Placement of area borders can depend on the following factors.

- *Addressing structure.* In a routing domain in which segments have already been assigned address prefixes, you want to configure area boundaries so that OSPF can aggregate prefixes at area borders. For example, in Figure 6.3, area 0.0.0.1 has been assigned so that a single aggregate of 10.2.0.0/16 can be advertised to other areas for the prefixes 10.2.1.0/24 and 10.2.2.0/24. Aggregation reduces routing table size, lessening the resource requirements.

- *Area size.* As mentioned, vendors usually have a limit to the size of areas they can support. Area size comes into play in another way also. Suppose that you have not yet assigned address prefixes to your routing domain's segments. You can then minimize routing domain size by simultaneously (a) assigning prefixes along area boundaries, (b) assigning equal-sized areas, and (c) making the number of areas equal to the common area size (see [128]). For example, if you have 25 network segments in your routing domain, assign 5 areas of 5 segments each, taking the addresses for all segments within a single area from a single aggregated prefix.

- *Topology considerations.* Area boundaries can induce suboptimal routing. To reduce the amount of suboptimal routing, minimize the physical connections between areas. Minimizing physical connection between areas also minimizes the number of area border routers, which reduces the number of summary-LSAs and hence limits link-state database size.

- *Policy considerations.* OSPF protects routing inside area from outside interference. If you are running a single routing domain that consists of multiple organizations, each organization may wish to be configured as its own area. Such a configuration protects against misconfiguration of one organization (for example, mistakenly assigning a subnet belonging to another organization) from disturbing the other organization's internal infrastructure. Also, by using stub areas or NSSAs, one organization can be assured that the other organizations will not use its links for transit (that is, all traffic on the organization's links will either be originated by, or destined for, the organization itself). In addition, when configured as separate areas, organizations can hide selected addresses from each other by configuring "no-advertise" aggregates at area boundaries.

Q: *Should I use virtual links?*

A: Sure, if your area configuration requires them. Virtual links free you from having to worry about maintaining physical connectivity of the backbone area. Simply configure area boundaries based on addressing, topology, and/or policy considerations and then connect the backbone area (including all area border routers) with virtual links as needed. These days, almost all router vendors support virtual links.

Virtual links do have some disadvantages, however. They require manual configuration. Also, when using virtual links, you cannot aggregate addresses assigned to network segments belonging to the backbone area; if you do, the routers will simply ignore the aggregation directives.

Q: *Is an area border router simply a router that attaches to multiple areas, or does it also have to be attached to the backbone area?*

A: Any router that attaches to multiple areas is called an area border router. Area border routers label themselves as such in their router-LSAs, originate summary-LSAs into their attached areas, and are capable of forwarding datagrams between their attached areas.

However, unless an area border router is also attached to the backbone area, either physically or via a configured virtual link, the area border router will not be fully functional. Without an attachment to the backbone area, the area border router is prohibited from using summary-LSAs in its routing calculations and so cannot calculate routes to destinations in remote areas.

Consider, for example, the area configuration in Figure 6.6. Even without the virtual link to router D, router F would still be considered an area border router. Without the virtual link, router F would still be able to forward traffic from area 0.0.0.3 to destinations in area 0.0.0.5, and vice versa. But until the virtual link to router D is

established, router F would be unable to forward traffic to destinations in remote areas
(areas 0.0.0.0, 0.0.0.1, 0.0.2, and 0.0.0.4).

Q: *When I create virtual links, does OSPF force the data traffic to flow along the same paths as
the virtual links?*

A: No. OSPF control traffic follows the path of the virtual links, with information con-
cerning one nonbackbone area being sent to the backbone, where it is then distributed to
the other areas. But data traffic can take shortcuts between nonbackbone areas, flowing
along paths not described by any virtual link. You can think of virtual links as enabling,
but not restricting, transit traffic.

Consider the area configuration in Figure 6.6. The two virtual links in area 0.0.0.3
allow that area to carry transit traffic between the rest of the routing domain and areas
0.0.0.4 and 0.0.0.5. However, data traffic between areas 0.0.0.4 and 0.0.0.5 will flow
across the direct link between routers E and F rather than follow the virtual links
through router D. In contrast, the OSPF control traffic does follow the virtual links.
For example, routing information about the destinations in area 0.0.0.5 is flooded by
router F along the virtual link to router D, from where it is further distributed along the
virtual link to router E and also to routers A, B, and C in area 0.0.0.0.

Q: *Why are LSA instances with larger checksums necessarily more recent?*

A: Obviously just because one instance has a larger checksum does not mean that the
LSA has been more recently generated. However, assuming that both instances have the
same LS Sequence Number and relatively the same age (see Section 4.2.2), OSPF treats
the LSA instance having the larger checksum as being more recent. This behavior solves
the following problem.

Suppose that router X has originated a router-LSA with an LS Sequence Number of
0x80000006. Router X is then taken down to install a new interface card, and is restored
5 minutes later. Router X has no idea which LS Sequence Numbers it has used in the
past; suppose that the new router-LSA that router X originates also has an LS Sequence
Number of 0x80000006 but different contents to reflect the newly added interface. Now
there are two router-LSAs for router X present in the network simultaneously. How are
all the routers to agree on which LSA has the more recent data?

OSPF's rule selecting the LSA having the largest checksum is arbitrary but produces
the desired result. In the situation of the previous paragraph, there are three cases. In the
first case, the new router-LSA has a larger checksum than the old LSA. In this case, as
it is flooded throughout the routing domain, the new LSA replaces the old, and everything is well.

In the second case, the new LSA has a smaller checksum and is therefore ignored.
However, in the process of performing initial database synchronization with its neighbors (see Section 4.7.1), router X will learn about the old LSA instance and, since the old

would be preferred over router X's current LSA, will increase its router-LSA's sequence number to 0x80000007 and reflood to overcome the problem.

In the most unlikely case, both old and new LSAs will have identical checksums, even though they have different contents. In this case, router X's updated LSA will be ignored. It may then take as long as the LSA refresh interval (30 minutes, at which time router X will refresh its LSA with an incremented LS Sequence Number) before the other routers accept the new information from router X.

Q: *Does OSPF aging require synchronized clocks?*

A: No. OSPF does not even require that routers have time-of-day clocks. OSPF does require that a router keep track of how long ago each LSA was originated. This requirement forces all OSPF routers to have some kind of internal clock so that they can age the LSAs within their link-state databases. The age of an LSA is between 0 and 60 minutes. As long as the age of a given LSA does not vary from router to router by more than 15 minutes (the OSPF architectural constant MaxAgeDiff), OSPF continues to work correctly. Allowing a variation of 15 minutes out of a maximum of 60 means that one router's internal clock can be up to 25 percent faster than another's without any adverse effects.

There is one case in which all routers have to agree more closely on the age of an LSA. When an LSA reaches the age of MaxAge (60 minutes), it is removed from consideration by the OSPF routing calculation. To ensure that this happens roughly at the same time in all routers, when an LSA reaches MaxAge in one router's link-state database, that router refloods the LSA to tell the other routers to also remove the LSA.

Q: *I've read that OSPF refreshes its link-state database every 30 minutes. Does the whole database get reflooded all at one time?*

A: No. LSAs, the individual pieces of the link-state database, get refreshed independently. If an LSA's LS Age reaches 30 minutes, the OSPF router that originated the LSA will update the LSA, increasing the LSA's LS Sequence Number, resetting the LS Age field to 0, and reflooding the LSA. Since the LS Age fields of the LSAs within the link-state database usually become fairly randomly distributed, you tend to get a constant dribble of LSA refreshes rather than having all the LSAs refresh at once.

Take, for example, the link-state database pictured in Figure 12.10. The two summary-LSAs originated by router 165.29.1.6 (lines beginning `3 165.29.1.0 165.29.1.6` and `3 165.29.1.64 165.29.1.6`) are due to be refreshed in 6 seconds. After that, the next LSA refresh will be for router 170.211.176.12's router-LSA (line beginning `1 170.211.176.12 170.211.176.12`), which will occur 201 seconds later.

Q: *If I import the whole Internet routing table into OSPF, will my OSPF routers be able to keep up with the LSA refresh traffic?*

A: Most routers will be able to handle this amount of OSPF control traffic, although it should be mentioned that to date, no Internet Service Provider imports the whole routing table (around 45,000 entries) into its IGP. Every OSPF LSA gets refreshed every 30 minutes, so with 45,000 LSAs, you would see on average 25 LSA refreshes a second. Multiple LSAs are likely to be packaged within a single OSPF Link State Update packet, but you'd still probably see several Link State Update packets a second, on every link in the network (see Section 4.7.2). This amount of processing is within reach of modern OSPF implementations but of course will continually increase as the size of the Internet's routing table increases.

There is one way that router vendors can dramatically decrease the amount of OSPF control traffic: They can program their OSPF routers to originate LSAs with the DoNotAge bit (see Section 7.3) set. This removes the requirement to refresh LSAs, resulting in OSPF routers sending only changes, similar to protocols such as BGP. However, this behavior would reduce the protocol's robustness—if you remove OSPF's LSA refreshes, damage to an LSA while in a router's database will not be corrected automatically.

Just because a router originates its LSAs with the DoNotAge bit set, it doesn't mean that the router is prevented from refreshing its LSAs. By setting the DoNotAge bit, the router can choose to refresh its LSAs at whatever rate the router chooses—never, once every 3 hours, once a day, or even at a rate that is inversely proportional to the link-state database size.

There is another possible modification. Just as in the Database Overflow extensions to OSPF (Section 7.5), you can rank the LSAs according to their importance. In the Database Overflow extensions, when a router's capacity is exceeded, it discards the least crucial part of its OSPF database, namely, AS-external-LSAs for destinations other than the default route. These too could be the only LSAs with the DoNotAge bit set, leaving the more important parts of the database to refresh every 30 minutes. Refreshes of these more crucial parts of the database would guarantee that the OSPF routing domain would eventually return to a manageable state automatically, even in the presence of hardware and software errors within the routers that were causing LSAs to be lost or damaged.

Q: *If a router detects that another OSPF router has become unreachable, should it delete the LSAs that that router had originated from the link-state database?*

A: Absolutely not! The only LSAs that the router is allowed to flush are the LSAs that the router itself has originated. The problem with flushing another router's LSAs when that router has become unreachable is that the unreachability condition may be short lived. If so, when that router again becomes reachable, it would have to reoriginate its

LSAs, and all the routers in the network would have gone through the work of flushing and then immediately reinstating the LSAs just to get back to the status quo.

As an example of a temporary unreachability condition, see the network map in Figure 5.3. If there is a Designated Router change on the Ethernet, there may be a short disruption in reachability as a new network-LSA and matching router-LSAs are flooded. During this time, you wouldn't want to flush LSAs originated by routers beyond the segment, even if they are momentarily unreachable, because the contents of these LSAs are going to be the same before and after the Designated Router change.

Another reason for a router not flushing LSAs originated by others is the desire to avoid circular dependencies. The routing table calculation depends on the contents of LSAs, so you don't in turn want the existence of the same LSAs to depend on the routing calculation.

There are two obscure exceptions to the rule about not flushing other routers' LSAs. The first comes about when a router has changed its OSPF Router ID. In this case, old network-LSAs originated with the router's previous Router ID may still be in the link-state database, and these the router is allowed to (in fact, is required to) flush (see Section 13.4 of [178]). The second is when there are LSAs in the database with the DoNotAge bit set (Section 7.3). Since these LSAs never age out, a router removes them from its database when the LSAs' originating router has been unreachable for at least an hour. A time constant as large as a hour was chosen to break the circular dependency described in the previous paragraph.

Q: *Why install MaxAge LSAs in the link-state database when there are no previous instances?*

A: MaxAge LSAs in OSPF are just instructions to delete a particular LSA from the link-state database. So why store a deletion request itself in the database? Most of the time, you do not, but occasionally you do to deal with possible race conditions in OSPF's Database Exchange process (Section 4.7.1).

A router performs Database Exchange with a neighbor as soon as bidirectional communication has been established with the neighbor. The idea is for the router to describe a snapshot of its database to the neighbor and then to let the neighbor pick and choose which pieces of the database (that is, LSAs) the neighbor needs to become up to date. The connection between the two routers is available to forward data packets as soon as Database Exchange completes. However, while the database snapshot is being sent to the neighbor, the database is potentially changing as a result of new LSAs received by the router from other neighbors. These database changes create a window where the snapshot sent to the neighbor can itself be out of date. Depending on how an implementation chooses a snapshot, this window can be small or rather large.

In most cases, having the snapshot go out of date is handled naturally by the Database Exchange process: As long as LS Sequence Numbers don't go backward, the process works correctly. The only time LS Sequence Numbers can go backward in OSPF is when LSAs are deleted. In these cases, having the OSPF routers involved in the Database Exchange store the MaxAge LSAs prevents LS Sequence Numbers from going backward during the extent of the Database Exchange.

Q: *Why does OSPF go through a separate Database Exchange process on link start-up, instead of simply reflooding the entire database over the link?*

A: There are three reasons. First, OSPF wants to know when synchronization has completed, so that it can then start advertising the link in LSAs. In this way, OSPF prevents data traffic from being forwarded over the link until the two ends of the link have synchronized databases. The end of the Database Exchange is a clear indication that synchronization has completed.

Second, Database Exchange proceeds at a controlled rate, with one packet outstanding at any one time, similar to TFTP. On the other hand, simply reflooding the database at link-up would cause a large blast of update traffic.

Third, under most circumstances, Database Exchange ends up transmitting somewhat less data, with only the 20-byte LSA header going over the link instead of the entire LSA.

Q: *How many router vendors support MOSPF?*

A: To date, you can find MOSPF support in products from five routers vendors: 3Com, Bay Networks, IBM, Proteon, and Xyplex.

MOSPF, like the other dense-mode multicast routing protocols DVMRP and PIM Dense, is effective in commercial internets. These protocols calculate efficient paths, are robust, and are simple to configure. In addition, both MOSPF and DVMRP allow multicast routing to be deployed incrementally by supporting multicast topologies that are different from the unicast routing topology.

DVMRP is the protocol in use in the majority of the MBONE (see [131]). However, pieces of the MBONE run MOSPF, as described in Section 10.6.

MOSPF is the only currently deployed multicast routing protocol that can be configured for hierarchical multicast routing (Section 10.4). MOSPF is also the only multicast routing protocol with explicit support for IP multicast's expanding ring search (Section 10.1.1).

Q: *Why does MOSPF use reverse costs when calculating inter-area and inter-AS multicast paths?*

A: Readers interested in the answer to this question will probably have to read Chapter 10, MOSPF, first. Everyone probably agrees that multicast datagram paths are best calculated using forward costs—that is, the cost of links in the direction from the datagram's source to the group members, or the direction in which the datagram will be forwarded. MOSPF does this when the source and group members are within the same area. However, when the datagram must cross area or AS boundaries, MOSPF needs to use summary-LSAs or AS-external-LSAs to approximate the neighborhood of the source. Unfortunately these two LSAs, used mainly for unicast routing calculations, advertise reverse costs from MOSPF's perspective: toward instead of away from the source.

One could still imagine combining the reverse costs advertised by summary-LSAs with forward-link costs in router-LSAs. However, to do so can prevent delivery of datagrams to some group members. Using forward-link costs in these situations could cause an area border router's summary-LSA to look much more attractive for multicast than it really is. These problems begin showing up only in area configurations with virtual links, such as the one displayed in Figure 8.2.

This network diagram has a single multicast source, labeled S1, and located on segment 10.15.6.0/24. Three multicast sources, labeled G1, are located in areas 0.0.0.1, 0.0.0.2, and 0.0.0.3. Asymmetric link costs have been configured on several links. For example, the cost to forward traffic from router D to router C is 1, whereas the cost to forward traffic in the reverse direction is 10. (Links with symmetric costs are displayed with a single cost in the middle of the link, as we have done throughout most of the network diagrams in this book.) As a result of these asymmetric costs, router E forwards unicast traffic to S1 along the circuitous path of cost 7 through routers F, D, C, and A (remember that in OSPF, the cost of the link between a network and a router is always 0).

To calculate the path of a multicast datagram originating from S1, the routers use the summary-LSAs generated for 10.15.6.0/24. These summary-LSAs are listed in Table 8.1. Note that some possible summary-LSAs have not been advertised, due to OSPF's split-horizon rules. For example, router D does not advertise a summary-LSA for 10.15.6.0/24 into area 0.0.0.1, since router D's next hop for that destination is in area 0.0.0.1.

When calculating the multicast path for a datagram with source S1 and destination group G1, router D will be selected as the entry into area 0.0.0.2 and router F as the entry into Area 0.0.0.3. However, if forward costs were used in area 0.0.0.1's multicast routing calculation, router E would be selected erroneously as the entry into area 0.0.0.1, and as a result, none of the group members in areas 0.0.0.1, 0.0.0.2, or 0.0.0.3 would receive the multicast datagram. But since MOSPF uses reverse costs everywhere in the inter-area and inter-AS cases, router C is chosen as the entry point into area 0.0.0.1, and the multicast datagram is delivered successfully.

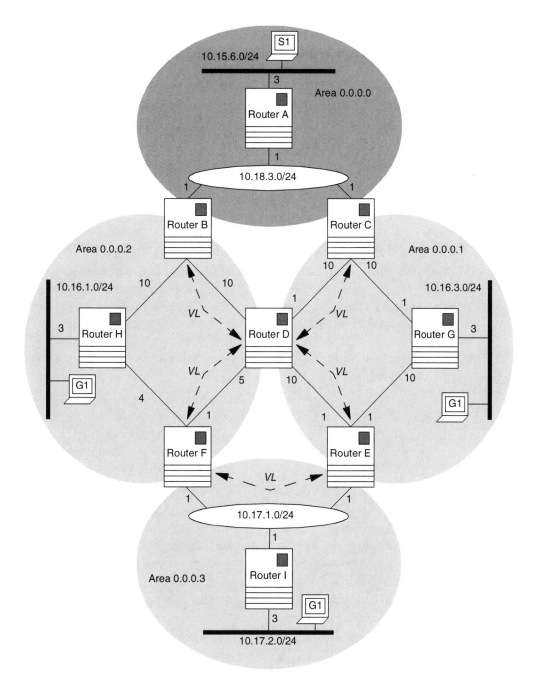

Figure 8.2 An MOSPF example requiring reverse-link costs.

Table 8.1 Summary-LSAs Generated for Segment 10.15.6.0/24

Originating Router	Area	Cost
Router C	0.0.0.1	4
Router E	0.0.0.1	7
Router B	0.0.0.2	4
Router D	0.0.0.2	5
Router F	0.0.0.3	6

Q: *If you could design OSPF again from scratch, what would you do differently?*

A: The Internet is continually evolving, and its protocols must evolve with it. Once you deploy a protocol, you can change it only so much, because you want to remain backwardly compatible with your installed base; once people start using a protocol, you no longer have the luxury of starting with a blank slate when sitting down to solve a problem.

However, if we could start again from scratch, these are some of the things that I would do differently.

- *Representation of point-to-point links.* Having the routers at either end of a point-to-point link advertise one anothers' addresses has been the single most confusing part of OSPF over the years (see earlier question in this FAQ). Although now ameliorated somewhat by allowing a RIP-style advertisement of point-to-point links, it probably would have been better to have each router advertise its own interface address; we have done this in OSPF for IPv6 [46].

- *Having LS Age field count down instead of up.* This would allow a router to lower its LSA refresh rates by increasing the initial LS Age values for LSAs. However, with the advent of the demand-circuit support for OSPF (see Section 7.3), lowering the LSA refresh rate can also be accomplished through setting the LSA's DoNotAge bit.

- *Matching two halves of a link within the link-state database.* When there are multiple links between a pair of routers, it is not possible in OSPF to match the link half advertised by one router with the link half advertised by its neighbor. Although not an issue for IP unicast traffic, which is inherently unidirectional, the inability to match link halves did cause some problems when MOSPF needed to choose the incoming interface for multicast datagrams (see Section 10.3.1).

- *Looking up network-LSAs during the Dijkstra.* In the OSPF routing calculation, you must find a network-LSA knowing only its Link State ID but not its Advertising Router. This has caused some confusion when, for example, the OSPF Router ID of the Designated Router changes and there are for a while two network-LSAs with the same Link State ID present in the database. This problem has been fixed in OSPF for IPv6 [46].

- *Configuring MOSPF on a per-physical link basis.* Instead of configuring MOSPF on a per IP subnet basis, it makes more sense to configure MOSPF on each physical link. IP multicast forwarding, since it uses data-link multicast services, wants to make sure that only one copy of each datagram is sent onto a link, no matter how many IP subnets are configured on the link. In the current MOSPF specification, all but a single subnet on each link must be disabled for multicast forwarding (see Section 6.3 of [171]).

Part III

Internet Multicast Routing

In Part III, we describe the basics of Internet multicast routing. Chapter 9, Internet Multicast Routing, provides an introduction to IP multicast forwarding. The interaction between multicast hosts and routers is covered, including IGMP. The role of a multicast router is described in detail. The difference between source-based tree and shared-tree protocols is also explained. The chapter ends with a discussion of the Internet's multicast service, called the MBONE.

Chapter 10, MOSPF, gives a detailed description of one of the Internet's multicast routing protocols, the Multicast Extensions to OSPF (MOSPF). The interaction of MOSPF and IGMP, the MOSPF routing calculations, the operation of MOSPF's two-level hierarchy, and the interoperation of MOSPF and DVMRP on the MBONE are all covered.

9

Internet Multicast Routing

This chapter lays the foundation for a discussion of multicast routing protocols. The duties of a multicast router, including the interaction between multicast hosts and routers, are explained. Beginning with a historical examination of broadcast forwarding, the two multicast forwarding paradigms, source-based trees and shared trees, are presented. We end with a description of the MBONE, the Internet's multicast routing overlay.

9.1   Internet Multicast Model

A network multicast capability allows an application to send a single datagram that will be delivered to multiple recipients. Applications exhibiting one-to-many and many-to-many communication patterns find multicast extremely useful—the alternative, namely, sending multiple copies of each datagram, consumes more network bandwidth and incurs additional delay to recipients. These applications include multiperson teleconferences and videoconferences, distance learning, and bulk transfer of the same set of data to a large number of recipients, such as the distribution of stock quotations to stockbrokers.

Multicast services are available at the data-link layer of many LAN technologies. For example, in Ethernet, all MAC addresses having the least significant bit in their first byte set to 1 are multicast addresses. A host's Ethernet adapter can usually be programmed with a set of multicast destinations to accept. For example, ten hosts attached to an Ethernet segment may all program their Ethernet adapters to accept the Ethernet multicast address 01-00-5E-00-00-01. If any host on the Ethernet then sends an Ethernet packet with destination 01-00-5E-00-00-01, all ten hosts will receive and process the packet accordingly.

IP multicast is a generalization of these LAN multicast services. The IP multicast model is defined in [56]. A multicast destination is referred to as a *multicast group*. Each group is represented as a single Class D address (224.0.0.0–239.255.255.255). Group members can be scattered across an IP internet. A sender of a datagram addressed to the group does not know where the group members are; in fact, the sender does not know how many group members there are or whether there are any group members at all (this kind of information may be available from the multicast transport protocol in use, but here we are just talking about the network-layer multicast service). The sender, in fact, does not have to be a member of the multicast group itself. To send a datagram to the group, the sending host just sets the IP datagram's destination IP address to the group's Class D address and then transmits the datagram as a data-link multicast onto the local network segment. From there, it is the job of the *multicast routers* to forward the datagram to all group members, replicating the datagram when necessary (Section 9.3.1).

Group membership is dynamic. A host can join and leave multicast groups at will, using the *Internet Group Membership Protocol* to keep the multicast routers informed of the host's current membership status. There are no limits to the size of a multicast group, and a host can belong to multiple groups at the same time.

Multicast routers use *multicast routing protocols* to determine the path of the multicast datagram from sending host to group members. A number of multicast routing protocols have been developed for the Internet; these protocols are discussed in Chapter 14, Multicast Routing Protocols.

Throughout this chapter, we will use the network in Figure 9.1 to demonstrate various IP multicast principles. That figure shows three members of multicast group G1, located on network segments 192.5.1/24, 195.5.2/24, and 192.7.1/24. These group members would use IGMP to convey their group membership to their local routers (routers R5, R6, and R10 and R11, respectively). We assume that all routers R1–R11 are participating in multicast routing. The senders to group G1, marked by circles with an inscribed S, are located on segments 192.6.1/24, 192.5.2/24, and 128.4.1/24. As mentioned earlier, the sender on segment 128.4.1/24 is not aware of the number or location of group G1 members; in fact, the sender need not even be aware of the existence of its local multicast router R8. Two workstations, W1 and W2, have also been included to illustrate MBONE functions in Section 9.4.

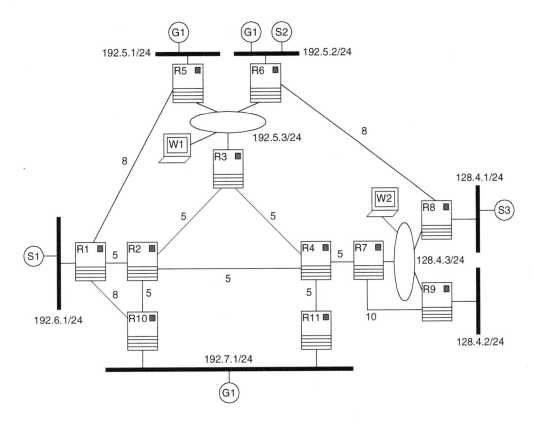

Figure 9.1 Network diagram illustrating IP multicasting principles.

9.2   The Multicast Protocol Stack

The IP protocol stack differs somewhat for multicast and unicast (Section 1.1). From the physical through the network layers, the two stacks coincide, albeit with some modifications made for multicast.

At the data-link layer, multicast makes use of the data-link multicast services, when they exist. When a multicast datagram is transmitted over a data link supporting multicast, by either the sending host or an intermediate multicast router, the data-link destination is set to a multicast address. The mapping of IP Class D address to data-link multicast address is always algorithmic; address resolution protocols, such as ARP, are not required. For example, when transmitting an IP multicast datagram over an Ethernet segment, the low-order 23 bits of the IP destination Class D address are placed into the Ethernet multicast address 01-00-5E-00-00-00 to produce the destination Ethernet address [56]; thus an IP datagram addressed to 224.1.1.1 will always be transmitted on Ethernet segments using the Ethernet destination 01-00-5E-01-01-01. (Why not 24 bits, you ask? The Internet's Assigned Number Authority, IANA, always likes to reserve part of each address space for further use, as you can also see in the encoding of Classes A–E addresses in [212].) If a data link supports broadcast but not multicast, the multicast datagram is transmitted as a data-link broadcast. Although IP hosts wishing to receive multicast datagrams cannot attach to network segments supporting neither multicast nor broadcast, multicast routers (and indeed hosts wishing to send only multicasts) can; over these nonbroadcast network segments, multicast datagrams are transmitted identically to unicasts (see Section 10.3.1).

At the network layer, multicast datagrams have their IP destinations set to Class D addresses. Class D addresses are restricted to appear only as destination addresses; they cannot be used as IP source addresses; nor can they appear in IP source routes (Section 1.2).

Also at the network layer, multicast hosts and routers use IGMP, instead of ICMP, to exchange control information necessary for multicast datagram delivery. The only ICMP packets used for multicast are the ICMP Echo and Echo Reply—you can ping a multicast address (see Section 12.4). However, ICMP errors are never sent in response to IP multicast datagrams; as a result, there is no multicast equivalent of Path MTU discovery, and multicast traceroute employs a completely different mechanism than its unicast inspiration (Sections 12.5 and 12.11). Also, since senders of IP multicast datagrams do not need to know about the local multicast router(s), multicast does not need ICMP router discovery or ICMP redirects.

At the transport layer, the multicast and unicast stacks diverge. The standard unicast transport protocol, TCP, does not work with multicast. In fact, there is no standard IP multicast transport protocol (many IP multicast protocols employ UDP for its multiplexing service but use additional transport mechanisms as well). Many of the initial IP multicast applications, developed on the MBONE (Section 9.4), invented their own transport mechanisms. Applications such as teleconferencing do not need completely reliable delivery of packets but instead want to flag out-of-order packets and to provide a mechanism to detect variations in delay so that the application can adjust its playback buffer. Experience with such MBONE applications as **vat** [139], **nevot** [228], and **nv** [80] has led to the development of a standard multicast transport, called *Real-Time Transport Protocol* (RTP) [229], for these kinds of applications. Numerous other proposals have been made for multicast transport protocols, including [5] and [167].

A large number of applications have been developed for the MBONE, including teleconferencing (**vat**, **nevot**), videoconferencing (**nv**, **ivs** [246]), interactive whiteboards (**wb** [140]), large-scale distribution of imaging data such as weather maps (**imm** [55]), experiments with the multicast delivery of Net news, and so on. The conferencing applications typically need some kind of session control to specify how people can join and leave conferences, as well as monitoring conference quality. Session control can be provided by RTP or by other applications, such as the session directory (**sd** [138]) and multimedia conference control (**mmcc** [227]) tools. The **sd** tool is used to dynamically allocate multicast addresses to new conferences as they start up on the MBONE; the protocol that **sd** implements is described in [91].

IP Multicast Addresses

Parts of IP multicast address space have been allocated for specific purposes, as shown in Table 9.1. The all-systems address of 224.0.0.1 contains all the IP multicast hosts and routers on a given network segment. This address is used by multicast routers to query the segment for group membership. The all-routers address contains all the multicast routers on a given network segment and again is used by IGMP.

Table 9.1 IP Multicast Address Assignments

Address Range	Usage
224.0.0.1	All systems
224.0.0.2	All routers
224.0.0.1–224.0.0.255	Local segment usage only
239.0.0.0–239.255.255.255	Administratively scoped multicast
239.192.0.0–239.195.255.255	Organization local scope
239.255.0.0–239.255.255.255	Local scope

Multicast addresses of the form 224.0.0.*x* are always local to a given network segment and are never forwarded by multicast routers. These addresses are typically used by routing protocols that wish to exchange routing updates over the segment—for example, OSPF uses 224.0.0.5 and 224.0.0.6, RIPv2 uses 224.0.0.9, and so on.

The document [158] proposes that a range of IP multicast addresses be reserved for administrative scoping, along the lines of IPv6's administrative scoping [99]. The idea behind administrative scoping is that these addresses can be locally assigned and that people do not have to worry about their being unique across the entire Internet or even across organizations. For example, the network in Figure 9.1 could be a single organization attached to the Internet. The network's Internet connection would then be its "organization local scope boundary"; inside the organization, a group, such as 239.192.0.1, could be used by an application without fear of interfering with (or interference from) another multicast application running in the Internet at large. The "local scope" range allows the organization itself to be divided into smaller pieces, each with its own private multicast address space. Administratively scoped addressing is intended to replace the TTL-based scoping that is currently deployed in the MBONE.

Other IP addresses have been reserved for certain applications, as documented in [212]. For example, IP multicast addresses in the range 224.252.0.0–224.255.255.255 have been reserved for the Distributed Interactive Simulation (DIS) [106] applications.

9.2.1 IGMP

The *Internet Group Management Protocol* (IGMP) [56] is the multicast equivalent of ICMP, implementing the necessary communication between hosts and multicast routers for the successful delivery of multicast datagrams. As we have seen, no communication is necessary between the sender of multicast datagrams and its first-hop router. However, a host wishing to receive multicast datagrams sent to a particular multicast group must inform its local routers of its group membership by sending IGMP *Host Membership Reports*.

A host sends a Host Membership Report when (a) it first joins a particular multicast group and (b) in response to an IGMP *Host Membership Query* received from a router. A separate Host Membership Report is sent for each group that the host belongs to.

On each network segment, one of the multicast routers becomes the *Querier*, responsible for periodically sending Host Membership Queries onto the segment in order to dynamically keep track of the segment's group membership. In the original IGMP, which we now call IGMPv1, the Querier was elected by the multicast routing protocol in use. In the second version of IGMP, the Querier is elected by IGMP itself (see the discussion of IGMPv2 that follows). Host Membership Queries are sent to the all-systems multicast address 224.0.0.1. If after some time Host Membership Reports for a given group cease to be heard in response to Host Membership Queries, it is assumed that there are no members of that group on the segment.

Routers are interested in knowing whether they need to forward multicast datagrams addressed to a particular group G1 onto the network segment. To make that decision, they need to know whether there are any members of G1 on the segment, but they do not need to know which hosts belong to G1 or even how many hosts. This fact allows IGMP to employ an interesting algorithm to minimize the number of Host Membership Reports sent: When a host receives a Host Membership Query, it randomly delays before sending Reports on its groups. If it hears a report for one of its groups before sending its own report, it then simply cancels the pending report transmission. As a further optimization, reports are addressed to the group address being reported (with a TTL of 1 so that they are not forwarded off the local network segment), so that only group members and multicast routers, which receive all multicasts, will hear the report. Figure 9.2 shows a report sent for the group 224.1.1.1.

IGMP operates only on segments having data-link multicast or broadcast capabilities. Nonbroadcast segments must simulate a data-link multicast capability in order to run IGMP. Examples of simulated data-link multicast include LAN emulation [8] and MARS [4], both developed for ATM subnets.

When a host attaches to multiple network segments, it must join groups separately on each segment. The host may belong to a group on one segment but not another, or it may join the group on both segments. In the latter case, the host will likely get two copies of each datagram.

```
SUMMARY  Delta T     Destination   Source        Summary
  32     2.0615  [224.1.1.1]    [193.1.200.12]   IGMP

      IGMP:  ----- IGMP header -----
      IGMP:
      IGMP:  Version     = 1
      IGMP:  Type        = 6 (IGMPv2 Membership Report)
      IGMP:  Checksum    = 08FD (correct)
      IGMP:  Group Address = [224.1.1.1]
```

Figure 9.2 IGMP Host Membership Report.

IGMP runs over IP, as IP protocol number 2. All versions of the IGMP protocol use the same packet format, with a Type field indicating the packet function. This Type field is a combination of the Version and Type fields present in the original IGMP specification. To make things a little more confusing, some of the multicast routing protocols, such as DVMRP, and some diagnostics, such as multicast traceroute, also use IGMP packet types. The resulting list of IGMP packets by type is shown in Table 9.2.

Table 9.2 IGMP Packet Types

Type Code (hexadecimal)	Packet Function
0x11	Host Membership Query
0x12	Host Membership Report
0x13	DVMRP packets (Section 14.2)
0x16	IGMPv2 Membership Report
0x17	IGMPv2 Leave Group message
0x1e	Multicast traceroute response (Section 12.11)
0x1f	Multicast traceroute query/request (Section 12.11)
0x22	IGMPv3 Membership Report

IGMPv2

The second version of IGMP, IGMPv2, is being deployed to replace IGMPv1. The two versions have two main differences.

First, IGMPv2 improves the so-called *leave latency*, the time it takes a router to notice that no more members of a given group are on the network segment. This improvement is important for applications that send a lot of data or for when many groups come and go. In either case, taking a long time to notice that a group has gone away means that unnecessary bandwidth has been consumed forwarding multicast datagrams to a place where nobody is listening.

To decrease the leave latency, a new IGMP packet is added: the IGMP *Leave Group* message. When a host leaves a group, it immediately multicasts a Leave Group message to the all-routers address of 224.0.0.2. On receiving the Leave Group, the Querier for the network is not sure whether any group members are left on the segment. To find out, the Querier then multicasts a Membership Query for the specific group in question; this query is addressed to the group and has a TTL of 1. If no hosts respond with Membership Reports, it is assumed that group members are no longer present.

Second, IGMPv2 elects the Querier on each segment rather than leaving election up to the multicast routing protocol. When a multicast router first attaches to a network segment, it assumes that it will be the Querier. However, if the router receives a Membership Query on the segment from a router with a lower IP address, the router relinquishes its Querier duty. If, at some point in the future, the router ceases to hear these Membership Queries, the router will again become Querier.

IGMPv3

A third revision of the IGMP is under development [28]. In this version of IGMP, group members will be able to request source filtering, using a new Membership Report (Table 9.2). When joining a group, a host can request that it wants to receive multicast datagrams only from a particular set of sources (called *source-specific joins*) or, alternatively, that it wants to exclude a set of sources (called *source-specific leaves*). One application of such a mechanism would be if you were participating in a teleconference and one of the other participants were playing a radio so loudly that you could not hear anyone else talking. Using IGMPv3's source-specific leave mechanism, you could simply block that participant's packets.

9.3   Broadcast Forwarding

With the advent of IP multicast, Internet broadcast addresses (Section 1.2.2) have become less and less used, especially directed and all-subnets-broadcast addresses. In addition, with the removal of the Class A, B, and C addresses in favor of CIDR, all-subnets broadcast addresses are no longer well defined. However, we discuss broadcast forwarding in this section, using the network in Figure 9.1, which provides a good introduction to IP multicasting mechanisms.

Suppose first that router R7 wants to send a RIPv1 update message to both routers R8 and R9. Router R7 can set the IP destination address of the update to the local segment or local-wire broadcast address of 255.255.255.255 and then send the packet as a data-link broadcast onto the segment 128.4.3/24. Both R8 and R9 will then receive the update and process it accordingly. Packets addressed to 255.255.255.255 are never forwarded.

Suppose instead that S1 wishes to send a packet that will be received by all hosts on a particular remote segment, say, 128.4.2/24. For example, the packet might be a ping, allowing the sending host to detect which hosts are currently attached to 128.4.2/24. The ping would then be addressed to the directed-broadcast address of 128.4.2.255. The ping would then be forwarded exactly as if it were to a unicast address on 128.4.2/24, going through routers R1, R2, R4, and R7 until it reached router R9. At this point, router R9 would send the packet onto 128.4.2/24 as a data-link broadcast, so that it would be received and processed by all attached hosts. Directed broadcasts such as these are also sometimes humorously referred to as *letter bombs*.

Finally, suppose that S1 wants to send a ping to every host attached to a subnet of 128.4/16 (whether this is a good idea is left as an exercise for the reader). The ping is then addressed to the all-subnets-broadcast address of 128.4.255.255 and is forwarded as a data-link unicast until it reaches router R7. At this point, in order to be received by all hosts on all 128.4/16 subnets, the packet will be forwarded instead as a data-link broadcast. However, to avoid disastrous forwarding loops, a procedure called *reverse-path broadcasting* [54] must be employed (similar precautions are used by IP multicast routing). The reverse-path broadcasting inhibits forwarding in certain circumstances: When a router receives the data-link broadcast, it checks to see whether the interface it received the packet on would be used to forward unicast traffic back to the packet source. If so, the packet is accepted and forwarded out all other interfaces belonging to the subnetted network. If not, the packet is dropped.

In our example, the entry router to the subnetted network 128.4/16, router R7, will broadcast the ping onto subnet 3, where it will be received by routers R8 and R9 and broadcast onto subnets 1 and 2, respectively. R7 will also send a copy of the ping over its point-to-point connection to router R9. R9, however, will discard the ping received over the point-to-point link, since its route back to the ping's source, S1, goes over the LAN segment 128.4.3/24 instead of the point-to-point link to R7. By discarding the ping received over the point-to-point link, router R9 avoids forwarding duplicate pings onto subnet 2.

9.3.1 Multicast Forwarding

The path that a multicast datagram takes, from source host to group members, depends on the type of multicast routing protocol in use. In all cases, the datagram's path forms a tree.

In the case of *source-based multicast routing protocol*s (DVMRP, MOSPF, PIM Dense), a separate tree is calculated for each combination of multicast source and destination group. Assuming that the LAN segments in Figure 9.1 have cost 1 and that the costs of the point-to-point links are as labeled, the three source-based trees that would be calculated for group G1 are as shown in Figure 9.3. "Tree" means that there is exactly one path from the source to each group member, illustrated by the path from source S2 to the group G1 member on 192.7.1/24. There are two possible equal-cost paths to the group member, one through R11 and the other through R10. If both paths were used, two copies of each datagram would be received by the group member; therefore the path through R10 is pruned, leaving only the path through R11. All source-based multicast routing protocols have ways to prune these equal-cost paths.

In the shared-tree protocols (PIM Sparse, CBT) a single tree is built for each group, regardless of source. A router is selected as the root for the group's tree, with the group members added as leaves. In PIM, this router is called the *Rendezvous Point* (RP); in CBT, this router is called the *core*. In our example, if router R4 is selected as the RP, the shared tree that would result for group G1 is as shown in Figure 9.4.

The shared tree consists of routers R3, R4, R5, R6, and R11. Multicast datagrams from sources that are not on the shared tree (S1 and S3 in our example) are encapsulated by the first-hop routers (R1 and R8, respectively) and then forwarded to the Rendezvous Point, R4, as unicasts (shown in Figure 9.4 as directed dashed lines). At that point, R4 decapsulates the datagram and multicasts the datagram down the shared tree toward the group members. In both PIM Dense and CBT, an optimization is made if the first-hop router is already on the shared tree (as would be the case when the sender was also a group member). In this case, the multicast is multicast along the shared tree by the first-hop router, both downstream (away from the RP) and upstream toward the RP— exactly as you would forward multicast datagrams at the link-layer in a spanning-tree bridged network [107]. This optimization is performed by default in CBT. In PIM Sparse, it requires explicit action by the RP, which tells the routers between the source and RP to revert to source-based routing (as in PIM Dense) for the particular source (S2 in Figure 9.4).

Shared-tree multicast routing algorithms were designed in an attempt to scale multicast to larger network sizes than were possible with the older, source-based algorithms DVMRP and MOSPF. The idea behind shared-tree protocols is to reduce information that routers need to maintain. You can see this in comparing Figures 9.3 and 9.4; routers running a source-based multicast algorithm may have to keep track of three trees, whereas routers running the shared-tree algorithm need keep track of only the single tree. Yet shared-tree protocols create problems of their own, which have so far prevented their adoption.

- *Less efficient paths.* As you can see by comparing the path between source S1 and the group member on 192.5.1/24 in Figures 9.3 and 9.4, the shared-tree protocols chose a longer path than the path found by the source-based protocols.

- *Traffic concentration.* As you can see by looking at the two figures, the source-based protocols use more links than the shared-tree protocols do. By concentrating the same amount of traffic on fewer links, shared-tree protocols may create bandwidth shortages.

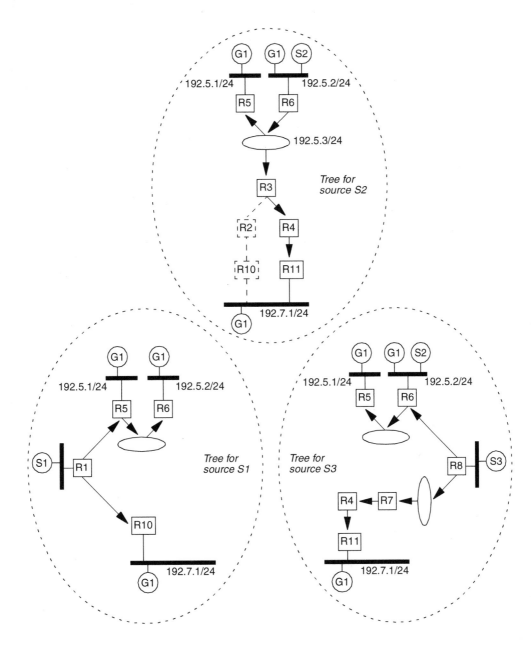

Figure 9.3 Source-based trees for group G1.

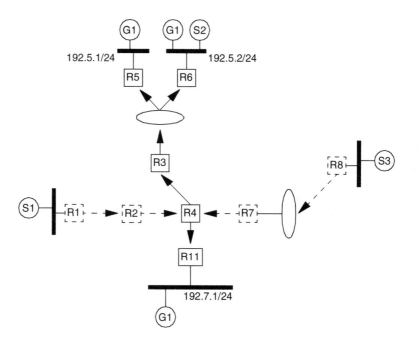

Figure 9.4 Shared multicast tree for group G1.

- *Robustness.* Source-based protocols are distributed and are not affected much by the failure of a single router. However, in shared-tree protocols, the failure of the RP is a big problem.

- *RP selection.* In shared-tree protocols, an extra step must be performed in order to get multicast forwarding working: An RP must be selected. This selection can be done manually. Bootstrap algorithms allowing automatic selection of RPs have also been proposed [70].

Multicast Router Processing

Here we examine how a multicast router forwards IP multicast datagrams, along the lines of the unicast-forwarding discussion in Section 1.2. The forwarding process starts when the source host transmits the datagram onto the local segment as a data-link multicast. The local multicast router (in fact, all multicast routers attached to the local segment) receives it, because it has "opened up" its data-link multicast filters so that it receives all multicasts, regardless of destination. The router then verifies the IP header as it would for a unicast packet, including checking that the TTL in the datagram's IP header is greater than 1. If there are any problems with the IP header, the packet is discarded silently—no ICMP errors are ever sent in response to a received IP multicast datagram.

The router then decrements the TTL in the IP header by 1 (modifying the header checksum accordingly) and finds the matching multicast routing table entry for the multicast datagram. These entries are also called *multicast cache entries*, since some multicast routing protocols create entries dynamically as matching datagrams are received (see Section 10.3). The matching multicast routing table entry tells the router whether it is on the multicast forwarding path (which, as we have seen, forms a tree) for the datagram and, if so, how the router should forward the datagram farther down the path.

If a source-based routing protocol is being used, the routing table entries are indexed on source and destination group, whereas shared-tree protocols index their entries on destination group only. Figure 9.5 shows sample multicast routing table entries for router R6 that match a datagram having source S3 and destination G1. In either case, the routing table entry specifies an incoming interface and a list of outgoing interfaces. If the incoming interface is empty or if there are no outgoing interfaces, the router is not on the datagram's path, and the datagram is silently discarded. If the datagram was received on an interface other than the incoming interface found in the routing table entry, the datagram is again discarded. This circumstance typically indicates the existence of multiple paths.

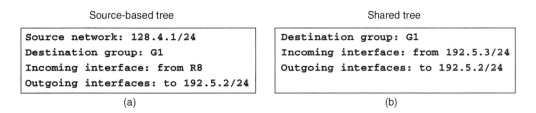

Figure 9.5 Router RT6's multicast routing table entry matching a datagram with source S3 and destination G1. (a) The matching entry for a source-based multicast routing protocol; (b) the entry for a shared-tree protocol.

If the incoming interface in the entry matches the interface on which the datagram was received, the datagram is transmitted as a data-link multicast out the outgoing interfaces specified in the entry. It is possible that the datagram will have to be fragmented before being transmitted on some interfaces, especially since there is no equivalent to Path MTU discovery for multicast.

Each outgoing interface may have additional parameters. For example, the entry may specify a TTL threshold for an outgoing interface: Datagrams whose TTL is less than the threshold will not be forwarded out the interface. TTL threshold may be performed as a way to control the scope of multicast datagrams (see Section 9.4) or as an optimization noting the number of router hops to the nearest group member (Section 10.1.1). The outgoing interface also may be configured as an administrative boundary, preventing the forwarding of administratively scoped multicast groups (Section 9.2).

Multicast forwarding entries are described further in Section 10.3.1. A multicast traceroute facility (Section 12.11) has been developed and deployed, enabling debugging of multicast forwarding in the MBONE. There is also an IP multicast routing MIB [142], allowing a network administrator to examine multicast routing table entries.

The forwarding process then repeats at the next-hop multicast router, until all the group members have been reached. Note that multicast datagrams are replicated during the forwarding process as the paths to the group members diverge. Sometimes this replication is done by the router (router R1 at the lower left of Figure 9.3) and sometimes as a by-product of transmitting the datagram as a data-link multicast (segment 192.5.3/24 at the top of Figure 9.3).

9.4   MBONE

The Internet's multicast service is provided by the Multicast Backbone (MBONE). The MBONE was first created in March 1992, organized to audiocast proceedings at an IETF meeting to those people who could not attend [69]. Today the MBONE is still used to broadcast IETF meetings (now both audio and video), for teleconferences and interactive meetings between researchers, and to broadcast interesting events, such as launches of the space shuttle. The MBONE is also a breeding ground for the development of multicast tools, routing protocols, and applications (Section 9.2). However, the MBONE is still not yet a production service—ISPs are still reluctant to run IP multicast code in their routers, and the MBONE is not available to the public at large (that is, the average 19.2K/sec dial-up user).

Since most of the Internet's routers do not have multicasting forwarding capabilities (or at least do not have it turned on), the MBONE's routers are typically UNIX workstations running the **mrouted** program [62], which is an implementation of the DVMRP routing protocol. To get multicast packets through the Internet's multicast-ignorant routers, these **mrouted** workstations are connected via tunnels (Section 1.2.3). This creates a virtual multicast topology, overlaid on the Internet's unicast topology.

For example, suppose that none of the routers in Figure 9.1 had multicast capability. To establish multicast connectivity between sources and group members, each source and destination would run the **mrouted** program, including the workstations W1 and W2. The **mrouted** routers would then be connected via tunnels, resulting in the virtual topology of Figure 9.6.

The tunnel topology in Figure 9.6 is fairly rational; the real tunnel topology in the MBONE is definitely less planned. In fact, that is one of the things that network operators dislike about MBONE tunnels—it is difficult to tell when someone has configured an MBONE tunnel through one's network. MBONE tunnels can carry a lot of data traffic, such as packet video, so network operators like to know of their existence in advance. Figure 9.6 demonstrates another problem with the tunnel topology: You can get multiple copies of a multicast datagram going over a single segment. Suppose that

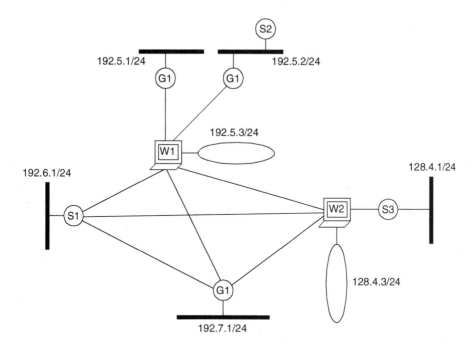

Figure 9.6 Constructing an MBONE topology from Figure 9.1.

S1 were also a member of group G1. Then if S3 sent a multicast datagram to group G1, separate copies would get forwarded by W2 over the tunnels to W1, S1, and the group member on 192.7.1/24. Unfortunately the latter two tunnels both go over the link between routers R7 and R4.

Besides the multicast traceroute facility, the MBONE has other diagnostic tools as well. The `mrinfo` program can be used to query the configuration of a DVMRP router. The `map_mbone` program can use the same query mechanism to produce a map of the MBONE tunnel topology.

The core of the MBONE uses DVMRP exclusively. But other routing protocols, such as MOSPF and PIM, are sometimes used at the edges.

TTL Thresholds

The MBONE also uses IP TTL in a novel way. A network administrator can configure TTL thresholds on the tunnels into the administrator's site. When a threshold is configured, packets having TTL less than the threshold are discarded instead of being forwarded across the tunnels. Conventions were then established for the initial TTLs used by common MBONE applications. If the administrator then wanted to prevent certain applications from entering the administrator's site, the TTL threshold would be configured higher than that application's initial value.

Table 9.3 shows the initial TTLs for common MBONE applications, taken from the MBONE FAQ [36]. For example, if you want to allow only the four IETF audio channels into your site, you would configure a threshold of 128.

Table 9.3 Default TTL Values for MBONE Applications

MBONE Application	Initial TTL	Threshold
IETF channel 1 low-rate GSM audio	255	224
IETF channel 2 low-rate GSM audio	223	192
IETF channel 1 PCM audio	191	160
IETF channel 2 PCM audio	159	128
IETF channel 1 video	127	96
IETF channel 2 video	95	64
Local event audio	63	32
Local event video	31	1

It turns out that discarding packets due to TTL threshold has an adverse effect on DVMRP's pruning mechanism (Section 14.2). If a router discards a packet due to insufficient TTL, it cannot tell whether any group members are downstream and so cannot determine whether it should send prunes upstream. For that reason, TTL thresholds are being phased out in favor of administratively scoped group addresses (Section 9.2).

Further Reading

In Chapter 10, MOSPF, we examine the MOSPF multicast routing protocol in detail. The multicast routing protocols that have been developed for the Internet (DVMRP, MOSPF, PIM Dense and PIM Sparse, and CBT) are compared and contrasted in Chapter 14, Multicast Routing Protocols.

IP multicast routing began with Deering's papers [58] and [59], written while he was working on his Ph.D. at Stanford. These papers are required reading for anyone interested in multicast routing. Similarly, Wall's thesis [258] and [259] is the basis of the shared-tree multicast routing protocols CBT and PIM Sparse. Dalal and Metcalfe [54] is the original paper on reverse-path forwarding.

The IETF's IDMR Working Group has produced a good introduction to multicast routing in [154].

Those people interested in joining the MBONE should consult the excellent MBONE FAQ [36]. An entire book has also been published detailing the MBONE and its operational aspects [131].

10

MOSPF

Continuing our discussion of multicast routing, this chapter examines a particular multicast routing protocol, the Multicast Extensions to OSPF (MOSPF). MOSPF is an extension of OSPF, allowing IP multicast routing to be introduced into an existing OSPF unicast routing domain.

MOSPF has seen considerable deployment in private internets. When a network is already running OSPF, MOSPF is probably a better choice than the more common DVMRP when introducing a multicast routing capability. Both MOSPF and DVMRP calculate source-based trees. However, unlike MOSPF's link-state basis, DVMRP uses Distance Vector routing technology and is susceptible to all the normal convergence problems of Distance Vector algorithms (Section 2.3). MOSPF also always limits the extent of multicast traffic to group members, something that a broadcast-and-prune algorithm (Section 14.1), such as DVMRP, cannot always do. Restricting the extent of multicast datagrams is desirable for high-bandwidth multicast applications or limited-bandwidth network links (or both). A more detailed comparison of existing TCP/IP multicast routing algorithms is given in Chapter 14, Multicast Routing Protocols.

The introduction of MOSPF to an OSPF routing domain can be gradual; MOSPF will automatically route IP multicast datagrams around those routers incapable of multicast routing (see Section 10.5), whereas unicast routing continues to function normally. MOSPF introduces multicast routing by adding a new type of LSA, the group-membership-LSA, to the OSPF link-state database and by adding calculations for the paths of multicast datagrams.

From a multicast datagram's source to any given group member, the path that MOSPF calculates for the datagram is always the shortest in terms of the OSPF link metric. MOSPF also provides explicit support for IP multicast's expanding ring search, inhibiting all but the necessary multicast datagram traffic as a host looks for the nearest server (see Section 10.1.1). When the OSPF routing domain is split into areas, MOSPF employs a hierarchical multicast routing scheme, as described in Section 10.4.

MOSPF can be, and is in isolated places, deployed in the MBONE. A MOSPF domain can be attached to the edge of the MBONE, or can be used as a transit routing domain within the MBONE's DVMRP routing system. To use MOSPF within the MBONE, one must exchange multicast source and group membership information between MOSPF and DVMRP, analogous to the exchange of routing information between unicast routing protocols. This exchange is described further in Section 10.6.

10.1   An Extended Example

Figure 10.1 shows a MOSPF routing domain. All routers pictured are running MOSPF. Five MOSPF routers are attached to a central FDDI ring. These routers in turn attach five Ethernet segments. To get to segment 128.186.4.0/24, a point-to-point link (between either routers C and E or routers D and G) must be traversed. Additional point-to-point connections between routers A and B and between routers D and F have been provided for backup purposes. Each router interface is labeled with its OSPF cost. Two multicast groups are shown. Group G1 has members on segments 128.186.4.0/24, 128.186.5.0/24, and 128.186.6.0/24, whereas group G2 has a single member on segment 128.186.4.0/24.

First, we examine the forwarding of multicast datagrams when the network is in steady state: All links are operational, and all group members have joined their respective groups. Then we examine MOSPF's response to network changes. These changes include hosts joining and leaving multicast groups and network links and routers becoming inoperational and then returning to operation.

10.1.1 Steady-State Forwarding Behavior

Let us consider how an Internet radio transmission might work. In Figure 10.1, workstation S1 is the originator of a radio station, sending digital audio packets on its "radio channel," the multicast group address G1. G1 itself is a Class D IP address; we'll use the address 226.1.7.6 in this example. Radio listeners have tuned their workstations into S1's radio station by joining the group G1. There are listeners on the LAN segments 128.186.4.0/24, 128.186.5.0/24, and 128.186.6.0/24.

S1 sends its audio packets out onto its local Ethernet segment, 128.186.1.0/24, encapsulated in IP headers whose destination address is set to 226.1.7.6. These packets are multicast onto the Ethernet segment at the data-link level; the IP multicast

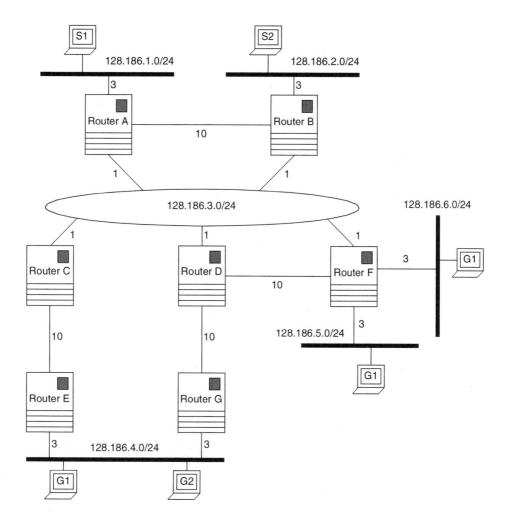

Figure 10.1 An MOSPF routing domain.

destination of 226.1.7.6 is algorithmically mapped to an Ethernet data-link multicast address of 0x01005e010706 (see [56], [212]).

Since the audio packets are multicast onto S1's Ethernet segment, hosts and routers connected to 128.186.1.0/24 can receive the audio packets by properly programming their Ethernet adapters. A radio listener connected to the segment (of which there are none) would program its Ethernet adapter to receive packets sent to 0x01005e010706. A multicast router, such as router A, programs its Ethernet adapter to receive *all* multicast packets; this is sometimes said to be putting the adapter into *promiscuous mode*.

Thus router A receives the audio packets. Recognizing that it is on the shortest path between S1 and one or more members of G1 (in this case, it is on the path to all G1 members), router A then multicasts the audio packets onto the FDDI segment 128.186.3.0/24.

As for Ethernet, there is an analogous mapping between the IP multicast address and an FDDI multicast address, resulting in the audio packets' being multicast onto the FDDI segment at the data-link level.

Routers B, C, D, and F receive the audio packets multicast onto the FDDI segment. Router B simply discards the audio packets, since it is not on the shortest path between S1 and any G1 group member. Routers C and D are both on shortest paths between S1 and the group member on segment 128.186.4.0/24. Only one router will forward the packets, otherwise unwanted replication of the audio stream will result. MOSPF invokes tie-breaking procedures to choose one shortest path over another (see Section 10.3). In this case, assuming that router G has a higher OSPF Router ID than router E does, the shortest path through router D will be chosen. This means that router C will discard the audio packets received from the FDDI segment. Router D will forward the packets to router G, which in turn will multicast them onto the Ethernet segment 128.186.4.0/24, which contains one of the listeners. Finally, when router F receives an audio packet from the FDDI segment, it will forward copies onto the Ethernet segments 128.186.5.0/24 and 128.186.6.0/24, where the other two radio listeners are located.

Expanding Ring Search

Expanding ring search is a procedure for finding the nearest server. Suppose that in Figure 10.1, S2 wishes to find the nearest time server. Suppose further that all time servers belong to a multicast group G2. To find the nearest time server, S2 performs an expanding ring search: first multicasting a query to multicast group G2 with IP TTL 1, then with TTL 2, and so on, until S2 receives a response. The response will be from the nearest time server, in terms of router hops.

MOSPF makes expanding ring search more efficient. Let's look at the expanding ring search performed by S2 in more detail. First, S2 sends a multicast datagram to G2 with a TTL of 1. Router B receives this datagram but is not allowed to forward the datagram, since the TTL is too small. Router B then silently discards the datagram; ICMP error messages, such as TTL Exceeded, are not sent in response to multicast datagrams. (Note that this means that the unicast **traceroute** utility does not work for multicast; see Section 12.11.)

S2 next sends a query to G2 with a TTL of 2. Router B receives this datagram and is allowed to forward it. However, router B knows that the datagram will never reach the nearest member of group G2, because of insufficient TTL, and so discards this datagram too instead of wasting network bandwidth and computing resources. Similarly, it discards the next query sent by S2. Only when S2 sends a query with TTL of 4 will router B forward the query onto the FDDI segment 128.186.3.0/24; this query will be forwarded all the way to the group member on 128.186.4.0/24, where it will produce the appropriate reply.

10.1.2 Response to Change

We now illustrate the reactions of the MOSPF algorithm to changes within the MOSPF domain: hosts joining and leaving multicast groups, links going in and out of service, and so on. We again consider the Internet radio example of Figure 10.1, but this time, we assume that the radio station has not yet started its broadcast and that no hosts have yet tuned in to the radio channel.

Now we assume that the following sequence of events transpires.

1. *Host S1 starts its radio broadcast.* S1 simply starts sending audio packets to the IP multicast destination group G1. On receiving the first of these packets, router A calculates the shortest paths between the multicast packet's source (segment 128.186.1.0/24) and the members of G1. Note that router A waits until receiving the packet before calculating a route for the packet. This on-demand calculation (see Section 10.3) is in contrast to unicast routing, whereby routes are always calculated in advance.

    Since there are no members of G1, router A simply discards the audio packets without forwarding them.

2. *The listener on segment 128.186.4.0/24 tunes in.* The listener joins multicast group G1 by sending an IGMP Host Membership Report for G1 onto segment 128.186.4.0/24. The OSPF Designated Router for the segment, which we assume is router E, then originates a group-membership-LSA and floods the LSA throughout the MOSPF domain. The group-membership-LSA informs all routers within the MOSPF domain that 128.186.4.0/24 has a G1 member (see Section 10.2).

    Router A will receive the group-membership-LSA. The next audio packet router A receives will cause it to recalculate the path of the audio packets. This time, the calculation will tell A to forward the multicast onto the FDDI ring 128.186.3.0/24. Routers B, C, D, and F will then calculate the path of the datagram, with only D forwarding. When G receives the datagram from D, it too will run the MOSPF routing calculation before multicasting the packet onto 128.186.4.0/24.

3. *The listener on segment 128.186.5.0/24 tunes in.* This time, router F will originate a group-membership-LSA announcing a G1 member. However, this group-membership-LSA will not label 128.186.5.0/24 with group G1 membership but will instead label router F itself as requesting packets for group G1. This happens because 128.186.5.0/24 is a stub network, and labeling the router instead of the stub network segment accomplishes some aggregation of group membership information.

    All routers will receive the group-membership-LSA originated by router F. Then, on receiving the next audio packet, they will all rerun their routing calculation for the audio packet's path. However, only router F's forwarding behavior changes; router F will now forward the packet by multicast onto 128.186.5.0/24.

4. *The listener on segment 128.186.6.0/24 tunes in.* Because 128.186.6.0/24 is another stub network connected to router F, router F does not need to originate another group-membership-LSA. Router F simply starts forwarding the audio packets onto 128.186.6.0/24, without any other routers in the MOSPF domain even noticing.

5. *The point-to-point connection between routers D and G fails.* Routers D and G originate new OSPF router-LSAs announcing the link failure and flood the LSAs throughout the MOSPF domain. After the flood, the next audio packet received will trigger a path recalculation in routers A, B, C, D, and F. This time, router C will start forwarding the audio packets to router E, which will then multicast the packets onto 128.186.4.0/24.

6. *The listener on segment 128.186.4.0/24 tunes out.* Router E (the Designated Router on the segment) will eventually notice that the listener has tuned out: The listener either sends an IGMP Leave Group message (IGMPv2 only; see [71]) when tuning out or simply stops responding to IGMP Host Membership Queries (see Section 10.2). Router E then flushes the group-membership-LSA that it had previously originated, thereby telling the MOSPF domain that there is no longer a G1 member on 128.186.4.0/24. The next audio packet causes a path recalculation in routers A, B, C, D, and F. Only router C's forwarding behavior will change; router C will no longer forward audio packets on to router E.

10.2 Group-Membership-LSAs

The Internet Group Membership Protocol (IGMP; see [56]) is used to communicate group membership information from hosts to multicast routers, regardless of the multicast routing protocol in use. LAN-attached hosts multicast an IGMP Host Membership Report onto the LAN when they join a multicast group, informing all local multicast routers. As long as it remains a member of the group, the host will respond to IGMP Host Membership Queries sent by the LAN's IGMP Querier, by again sending a Host Membership Report for the group. Multicast routers need keep track only of whether there are one or more group members on the LAN; the routers are not concerned with which hosts belong to the group. For this reason, a host delays for a random amount of time before answering the Host Membership Query; seeing another Host Membership Report in the meantime obviates the host's need to respond with its own report.

When it leaves a multicast group, a host stops answering Host Membership Queries. Some time after the last host on the LAN has left the group, the LAN's multicast routers will realize that there are no longer any group members. This time period is called the *leave latency*. If the hosts and routers are using IGMPv2 [71], leave latency is reduced by having the hosts send IGMP Leave Group messages when they leave the multicast group.

In IGMP as specified in [56], it is up to the multicast routing protocol to select the IGMP Querier. MOSPF assigns IGMP Querier responsibilities to the LAN's OSPF Designated Router. IGMPv2 provides facilities to elect the IGMP Querier, removing the need for the multicast routing protocol to select the Querier.

Regardless of which router is providing the query function on the LAN, it is the job of the LAN's OSPF Designated Router to listen to the Host Membership Reports sent in response, thereby keeping track of the LAN's group membership. The Designated Router then reports the LAN's group membership to the rest of the routers in the MOSPF routing domain by originating group-membership-LSAs.

Group-membership-LSAs have an LS Type of 6. A group-membership-LSA reports group membership in a single group; the Link State ID of the group-membership-LSA is the multicast group's Class D IP address. The body of the group-membership-LSA lists the location of group members by referencing router-LSAs and network-LSAs. If the router detects group members on one or more of its directly connected stub networks (or if the router itself is running multicast applications), it tells the other MOSPF routers to forward multicasts to the router itself by referencing its own router-LSA. For those transit networks having group members and for which the router is acting as Designated Router, the router tells the other MOSPF routers to forward multicasts to the network by referencing the network's network-LSA. These LSAs are referenced by including their LS Type and Link State ID fields in the body of the group-membership-LSA.

Let us go back to the example in Section 10.1.2. Router E (OSPF Router ID 128.186.4.1) has been elected Designated Router on LAN 128.186.4.0/24. As a result, it is also serving as the IGMP Querier, periodically sending IGMP Host Membership Queries. In the beginning, no group members are on the LAN, and the queries go unanswered. Then a host joins group G1 (226.1.7.6), sending a Host Membership Report in the process. This report causes router E to originate and to flood the group-membership-LSA in Figure 10.2. The body of the group-membership-LSA reports a G1 member on 128.186.4.0/24 by referencing that LAN's network-LSA. This network-LSA, also originated by router E, has Link State ID equal to 128.186.4.1.

When the other group G1 members join G1, there will be an additional group-membership-LSA, this one originated by router F. Since 128.186.5.0/24 and 128.186.6.0/24 are both stub networks connected to router F, F simply lists itself in the body of the group-membership-LSA by referencing its own router-LSA (Referenced LS Type = 1, Referenced Link State ID = router F's Router ID).

Group-membership-LSAs have area flooding scope. They are used to distribute group membership information throughout a single area only. Distribution of group membership information across area and Autonomous System boundaries is one of the functions of hierarchical multicast routing, the subject of Section 10.4.

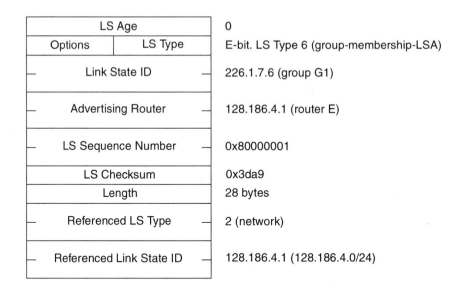

LS Age		0
Options	LS Type	E-bit. LS Type 6 (group-membership-LSA)
Link State ID		226.1.7.6 (group G1)
Advertising Router		128.186.4.1 (router E)
LS Sequence Number		0x80000001
LS Checksum		0x3da9
Length		28 bytes
Referenced LS Type		2 (network)
Referenced Link State ID		128.186.4.1 (128.186.4.0/24)

Figure 10.2 Sample group-membership-LSA.

10.3 MOSPF Routing Calculations

Section 10.1 introduced the multicast paths that MOSPF routers calculate between a multicast source and the destination group's members. This section goes into more detail about those paths, answering the following questions.

1. How many different multicast paths are there?

2. How often are paths calculated? When do paths need to be recalculated?

3. What data derived from the multicast path calculation does a MOSPF router store and use in forwarding?

4. If the multicast path calculation is a shortest-path calculation, how is this calculation different from the OSPF unicast routing calculation, if at all?

The answer to the first question is easy. MOSPF has different paths for each combination of source network and destination multicast group. This can be many separate paths. However, the calculation burden that a MOSPF router bears is reduced by the fact that the multicast routing calculation is performed on demand: A MOSPF router calculates a multicast path for a given source network and multicast group only when the router receives a matching datagram.

This behavior accomplishes two things. First, it spreads the number of routing calculations out over time, as opposed to the unicast routing behavior of calculating all the routes at once. Second, a MOSPF router will never have to calculate paths for a given source network and destination group combination unless the router is along the path between source and one or more destination group members. Often, however, MOSPF routers along the multicast path will not forward the datagram, as the example in Section 10.1 demonstrates. The aggregation of sources and destination groups achieved when organizing MOSPF routing hierarchically (Section 10.4) further lessens, sometimes drastically, the number of paths that a MOSPF router calculates.

Multicast paths must be recalculated when network conditions change—routers or links go in and out of service or when hosts join or leave multicast groups. We will go into the causes of path recalculation in more detail after we discuss the precise data that a MOSPF router must store from a multicast routing calculation—the multicast forwarding cache entry.

10.3.1 The Multicast Forwarding Cache

MOSPF routers calculate the path of the multicast datagram from the datagram's source to its destination group members. However, it is not necessary for the MOSPF router to store the entire path. Only the router's position with respect to the path is important. This position is stored within a multicast forwarding cache entry.

As mentioned earlier, there are separate paths, and therefore separate forwarding cache entries, for each source network and destination group combination. Each of the router's forwarding cache entries contains information about

- *The router or network from which the router must receive matching datagrams.* This information is needed because multicast datagrams are replicated when forwarded. In order to ensure that only one copy of each datagram is received on any particular segment, those replications taking more circuitous paths must be discarded.

  It would be more natural to specify the receiving router interface for each datagram. MOSPF instead specifies the network or router from which the datagram must be received because in one case, MOSPF cannot determine the receiving interface exactly: when multiple point-to-point links connect the router to the neighbor. For example, suppose that in Figure 10.1, there are two point-to-point links between routers D and G. When building the path of a multicast datagram sent from S1 to group G1, MOSPF can determine which link router D will send the datagram on, but router G cannot determine which of the two links it will receive the datagram on—router D advertises the sending half of the links and router G the receiving half, but there is insufficient information within the OSPF link-state database to match the sending and receiving halves.

- *The interfaces out which the router should forward matching datagrams.* For nonbroadcast networks, either NBMA or Point-to-MultiPoint, a router keeps track of which neighbors the datagrams must be sent to, since datagrams must be forwarded separately to each neighbor. Regardless of whether an interface or neighbor appears in the forwarding cache entry, the number of hops to the nearest group members reached via the interface or neighbor is also recorded. This information indicates the minimum TTL that multicast datagrams sent via the interface/neighbor must have in order to reach any group member and enables optimization of MOSPF's expanding ring search (see Section 10.1.1).

As an example of a forwarding cache entry, consider again the MOSPF routing domain in Figure 10.1. In router D, the forwarding cache entry for source network 128.186.1.0/24 and destination group G1 would indicate that matching datagrams must be received from network 128.186.3.0/24, in which case they are forwarded out the interface to router G, where the nearest group member is one hop away.

There is a multicast routing table MIB, described in [142], that allows you to examine multicast forwarding cache entries via SNMP. This MIB describes cache entries and multicast routing statistics in a way that pertains not only to MOSPF but also to other multicast routing protocols, such as DVMRP and PIM.

A router can clear one or more of its multicast cache entries at any time. The multicast cache entries will simply be rebuilt the next time a matching multicast datagram is received. However, certain multicast cache entries must be deleted in order to force rebuilding when network conditions change, as explained next.

10.3.2 Maintaining the Multicast Forwarding Cache

When changes occur within the MOSPF routing domain, certain multicast paths also change, requiring that forwarding cache entries be rebuilt. However, MOSPF routers do not rebuild the forwarding cache entries directly. Instead they simply delete the cache entries. These entries will then be rebuilt as matching datagrams are received, in exactly the same manner as the entries were constructed in the first place. Building the forwarding cache entries as matching datagrams are received spaces the routing calculations out over time rather than trying to recalculate all cache entries at once.

Which entries need to be deleted, forcing a later recalculation? The answer depends on the nature of the change within the MOSPF domain. A MOSPF router knows that something has changed when it receives an updated LSA whose contents have been altered. The LSA's type indicates the nature and extent of the change.

Reception of a modified router-LSA or network-LSA indicates a router or link failure (or restoral), or maybe a change in link cost. In these cases, it is impossible to tell precisely which multicast paths will be affected, so a MOSPF router deletes all cache entries. In contrast, reception of a modified group-membership-LSA indicates that the membership of a particular group has changed. In this case, a MOSPF router needs to delete only those cache entries that pertain to the particular group.

Going back to our example in Figure 10.1, if the link between routers D and G fails, new router-LSAs for D and G will be flooded throughout the MOSPF domain, which will in turn cause all forwarding cache entries (in all routers) to be cleared. If, however,

the group G2 member on segment 128.186.4.0/24 leaves G2, router E will flood a
new group-membership-LSA for G2, and only cache entries pertaining to G2 will be
deleted.

When examining hierarchical multicast in MOSPF (Section 10.4), we will see that in
general, the farther away the change is from a given router, the fewer cache entries the
router has to delete. This is an important property for the scaling of multicast routing in
a MOSPF domain.

10.3.3 Calculating a Multicast Datagram's Path: Details

As mentioned previously in this chapter, the MOSPF multicast routing calculation is
very similar to OSPF's unicast routing calculation. Both calculate shortest-path trees,
using Dijkstra's algorithm. However, as we examine the details of MOSPF's routing calculation, we will notice some differences.

In OSPF's unicast routing calculation, the shortest-path tree is rooted at the calculating router itself. A router can get away with this because it does not care about which
interface a unicast datagram is received from—the datagram is going to be forwarded
based purely on its IP destination address. Rooting the shortest-path tree at the calculating router also allows the router to calculate routing table entries for all destinations at
once. However, in order to control replication of multicast datagrams, the MOSPF
forwarding decision must be based on both the datagram's source and destination
addresses. This forces the shortest-path trees calculated by MOSPF to be rooted at the
datagram source. One additional consequence of root placement is that, whereas unicast
calculations are always specific to the router doing the calculation, every MOSPF router
performs the exact same calculation for a given multicast datagram.

Figure 10.3 shows the shortest-path tree calculated for a multicast datagram sent by
source S1 to destination group G1 in Figure 10.1. Routers A–G all calculate the same
tree, in which the backup links between routers A and B and between routers D and F
have been pruned.

Another difference between unicast and multicast calculations occurs in the treatment of stub networks. In the MOSPF routing calculation, excepting the source network,
stub network segments do not appear. In MOSPF, group membership of a stub network
is aggregated and advertised by the stub network's router. In Figure 10.3, router F is
advertising membership in group G1 for its two attached stub networks.

We have been using the term *tree* a little loosely in this discussion. The unicast OSPF
calculation keeps redundant shortest paths for its equal-cost multipath load-balancing
feature. However, in multicast forwarding, redundant paths would cause unwanted
datagram replication. In order to remove the redundant paths, the MOSPF calculation
introduces tiebreakers that cause one shortest path to be preferred over another: When
multiple shortest paths exist to a network or router, the path whose previous hop router
or network has the highest address is chosen. In Figure 10.3, two shortest paths exist to

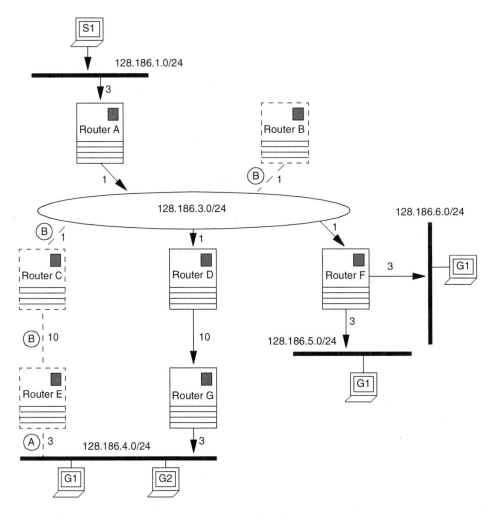

Figure 10.3 MOSPF shortest-path tree. Dashed links labeled with A are pruned when removing redundant shortest paths. Dashed lines labeled with B are pruned when removing links that do not lead to group G1 members.

network 128.186.4.0/24. Assuming that router G has a higher Router ID than router E does, the path through router G is chosen, causing the connection from router E to 128.186.4.0/24 to be pruned from the tree.

One case in which MOSPF cannot automatically detect the presence of redundant paths is when multiple IP subnets have been assigned to the same physical segment (see Section 5.1). MOSPF sees such subnets as completely separate entries, yet for the purpose of multicast forwarding, they are the same segment, because IP multicast forwards datagrams as data-link multicast, thereby transcending IP subnet boundaries.

These types of redundant paths must be removed through configuration (see Section 6.3 of [171]).

Dijkstra's algorithm calculates routes to all destinations at once. However, the MOSPF calculation is concerned only with calculating the paths from a source to a specific group. Therefore the final part of the MOSPF routing calculation prunes those paths that do not lead to members of the group. In our example in Figure 10.3, routers B, C, and E and their links are pruned from the tree because they do not lead to members of group G1.

10.4 Hierarchical Multicast in MOSPF

The goal of hierarchical multicast routing is the same as for hierarchical unicast routing: reduce the resources consumed by the routing algorithms, thereby enabling the network to scale to large sizes. OSPF implements a two-level hierarchical routing scheme for unicast routing by splitting an OSPF routing domain into areas (see Chapter 6). MOSPF uses this OSPF area organization to implement a hierarchical multicast routing scheme.

Hierarchical routing in MOSPF allows both datagram source information and multicast group membership to be aggregated at area boundaries. This aggregation can drastically reduce the number of forwarding cache entries in a router, thereby reducing the number of routing calculations a MOSPF router must perform. However, just as for unicast routing, hierarchy can have disadvantages. The disadvantage of hierarchy for unicast traffic was that you sometimes get suboptimal paths (see Section 6.1). In MOSPF, the disadvantage of hierarchy is that multicast datagrams are sometimes forwarded unnecessarily, only to be discarded later (see Section 10.4.1).

We explore the effects of hierarchy on MOSPF in two parts. In Section 10.4.1, we show how the location of datagram sources and multicast group membership is conveyed across area boundaries. In Section 10.4.2, we describe how the MOSPF routing calculation changes in the face of hierarchy and the effect on the paths of multicast datagrams. In both sections, we give examples, using the hierarchical MOSPF domain pictured in Figure 10.4. The example consists of four separate areas, in which virtual links have been configured between router D and each of the routers B, C, E, and F in order to connect all areas to the backbone area. Area 0.0.0.3 has no configured virtual links and so does not provide transit service. Area 0.0.0.3 is configured to aggregate its two subnets, advertising the aggregate 10.17.0.0/16 to the other areas in OSPF summary-LSAs.

A MOSPF domain (also called Autonomous System) can be embedded in a larger multicast routing domain. In that case, further levels of multicast hierarchical routing can be achieved, essentially replicating the MOSPF area mechanisms at the AS boundary, where datagram source information and group membership can be further aggregated. This case is explored further in Section 10.6, using the example of embedding a MOSPF domain inside a DVMRP routing system.

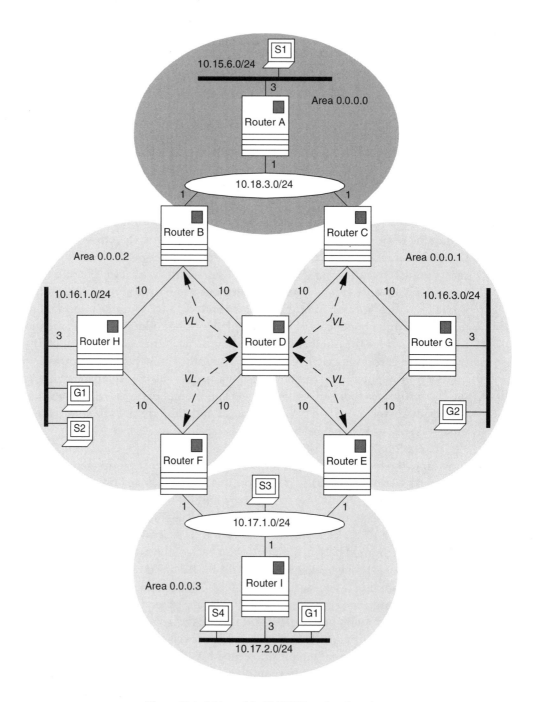

Figure 10.4 A hierarchical MOSPF routing domain.

10.4.1 Advertising MOSPF Information in the Presence of Hierarchy

Area border routers advertise unicast routing information across area boundaries in the form of summary-LSAs (see Section 6.1.1). These same summary-LSAs also serve to communicate the presence and location of multicast sources, as long as the MC-bit is set in the summary-LSAs' Options field. An area border router can aggregate multicast source information by advertising an address prefix that incorporates multiple IP subnets. Aggregation of multicast sources reduces the number of multicast forwarding cache entries required, reducing resource requirements on the MOSPF routers.

For example, in Figure 10.4, router F advertises a single summary-LSA for the prefix 10.17.0.0/16 into area 0.0.0.2. By setting the MC-bit in this summary-LSA, router F lets the routers within area 0.0.0.2 know that the prefix contains multicast sources. By aggregating IP subnets 10.17.1.0/24 and 10.17.2.0/24 into a single summary-LSA, router F allows routers internal to area 0.0.0.2 (for example, router H) to cover both sources S3 and S4 with a single forwarding cache entry.

Multicast group membership in nonbackbone areas is always advertised into the backbone area (area ID 0.0.0.0). An area border router aggregates the group membership of its attached nonbackbone areas by originating group-membership-LSAs into the backbone area. Analogous to the way MOSPF hides which specific stub networks contain group members, the area border router simply lists itself as wanting to receive multicasts for certain groups. Again using Figure 10.4 as an example, we see that router B requests datagrams addressed to G1 by advertising a group-membership-LSA for group G1 into the backbone area. Routers within the backbone area will then forward group G1 traffic to router B, even though they do not know which nonbackbone areas attached to router B have group G1 members. Similarly routers D, E, and F also advertise G1 membership into the backbone, whereas routers C, D, and E advertise G2 membership.

In this way, the MOSPF routers within the backbone area know the identity, but not necessarily the precise location, of all groups within the MOSPF routing domain. However, routers internal to nonbackbone areas do not even know which groups have members within other areas. To deliver multicast datagrams to other areas, the multicast equivalent of default routing is employed: The nonbackbone area's area border routers advertise themselves as wildcard multicast receivers. *Wildcard multicast receivers* are those MOSPF routers that wish to receive all multicast datagrams, regardless of destination group. By labeling all area border routers as wildcard multicast receivers, all multicast datagrams originating in nonbackbone areas are forwarded to the backbone area, where they can be forwarded in turn to area border routers requesting the particular multicast group.

In our example, routers B, D, and F advertise themselves as wildcard multicast receivers in area 0.0.0.2. If S2 then sends a multicast datagram to group G2, router H will forward the datagram on to routers B and F, even though router H has no idea whether any group members of G2 exist. From there, the multicast datagrams are forwarded to those backbone routers requesting G2 datagrams (C and D); finally, router C (chosen over router D by the MOSPF hierarchical routing calculation; see Section 10.4.2) will forward the datagram to router G, which will multicast the datagram onto the 10.16.3.0/24 segment.

The path just described shows the trade-off made in MOSPF hierarchical routing: network bandwidth for a reduction in the number of cache entries. In order to hide group membership information from routers in area 0.0.0.2, and to hide membership location information from the backbone routers, the datagram sent by S2 to group G2 is unnecessarily sent to router D (through router F), where it is then discarded in favor of the path through routers B and C.

10.4.2 Routing Calculations in Hierarchical MOSPF

In the presence of hierarchy, calculation of the path of multicast datagrams must change slightly. These changes are due to the aggregation of sources and group membership across area boundaries. The neighborhood of a source in another area cannot be determined completely, and so the source's location must be estimated using summary-LSAs. Also, the location of group members cannot always be precisely pinpointed; wildcard receivers must remain on all multicast paths regardless of destination multicast group.

Paths are calculated for each area separately. The path through area 0.0.0.2 of a multicast datagram sent by source S1 to group G1 is shown in Figure 10.5. The area border routers in area 0.0.0.2 provide estimates of the location of the source through their summary-LSAs. All routers in area 0.0.0.2 end up being on the path of the multicast datagram: Router B provides the entry of the datagram to the area, router H because there is a group G1 member on H's attached stub network, and routers D and F because they are wildcard multicast receivers in area 0.0.0.2. Router D provides an equal-cost entrance to area 0.0.0.2 for the datagram on its way to routers D and F, but this alternative path is removed by MOSPF tiebreakers.

To create the entire path throughout the MOSPF domain, the area border routers merge the shortest-path trees for the individual areas. Assuming that the routers labeled with letters later in the alphabet have larger OSPF router IDs, the resulting complete path for our example is as shown in Figure 10.6. Note that some area border routers receive datagram copies from multiple areas. In this case, MOSPF tiebreakers will again dictate which interface (if any) should accept the datagram for further forwarding, whereas datagram copies received on all other interfaces are discarded. In our example, router D receives copies from routers B and C but forwards neither.

As mentioned earlier, the farther away from a router a network change occurs, the fewer forwarding cache entries need to be recalculated. A change in an area not directly attached to the router may cause no new summary-LSAs to be flooded; in this case, the

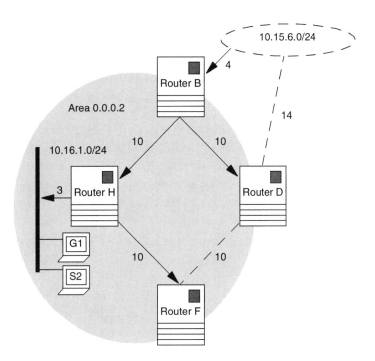

Figure 10.5 Path of datagram sent by S1 to group G1, through area 0.0.0.2.

change is completely hidden from the router, and no forwarding cache entries need be recalculated. If summary-LSAs do get updated, only those forwarding cache entries whose sources fall into the range of the summary-LSA need be redone.

Figure 10.6 again demonstrates that MOSPF hierarchical routing can produce extraneous forwarding hops. For example, routers C, D, E, and G receive copies of the datagram, only to have it be eventually discarded before reaching any group members. In these cases, MOSPF could benefit from a DVMRP-like pruning message (see Section 14.1).

10.5   Backward Compatibility: Mixing with Nonmulticast Routers

In order to be able to deploy a multicast routing capability incrementally, a multicast routing protocol must be able to deal with situations in which the multicast topology is different from the unicast topology. Some routers in a network may be capable of multicast forwarding, and others may not. This difference may be short in duration—for example, as new software is deployed in a network's routers. Or the difference may be more protracted—for example, the Internet's MBONE imposes a different multicast

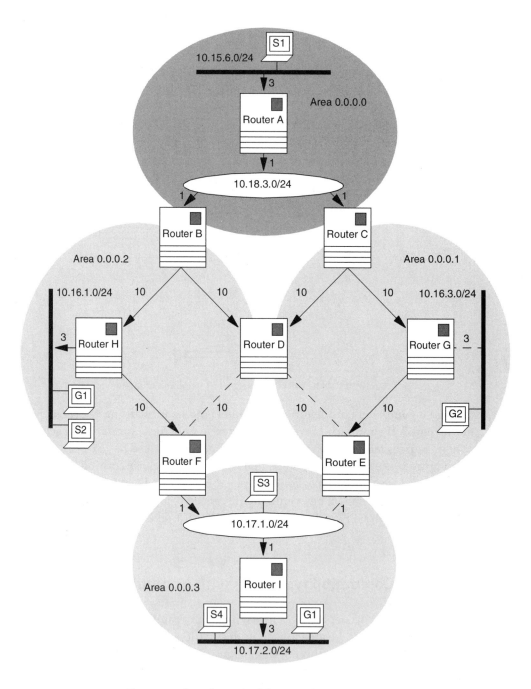

Figure 10.6 Complete path of datagram from S1 to group G1.

topology overlaying the unicast topology, a situation that has persisted since the MBONE's inception in 1992 [69].

MOSPF routers deal with differences between multicast and unicast topology by forwarding multicast datagrams around those OSPF routers not running MOSPF. MOSPF routers announce their multicast capability by setting the MC-bit in the Options field of their router-LSAs (see Chapter 7). Then, when a MOSPF router calculates the path of a multicast datagram, only those router-LSAs with MC-bit set are included in the calculation.

The advertisement of multicast sources across area boundaries piggybacks on the advertisement of unicast information across area boundaries in summary-LSAs. This behavior does not require that multicast and unicast capabilities match along area boundaries: If the MC-bit is not set in a summary-LSA, the summary-LSA is used only in unicast calculations. In this case, MOSPF uses the MC-bit to indicate whether the area border router advertising the summary-LSA is both (a) running MOSPF and (b) capable of forwarding multicast datagrams across area boundaries.

In the analogous situation of inter-AS multicast, MOSPF uses the MC-bit in AS-external-LSAs to signal differences in multicast and unicast topology along AS boundaries. This case is explained further in Section 10.6.

Restrictions

On LANs, mixing MOSPF routers with OSPF routers incapable of running MOSPF poses some problems. All such problems can be solved by making sure that a MOSPF router is elected Designated Router for the LAN, which is guaranteed when the non-MOSPF routers are assigned a Router Priority of 0 (see Section 5.2).

When using IGMP as specified in [56], the OSPF Designated Router is assigned the IGMP Querier function, responsible for sending periodic IGMP Host Membership Queries onto the LAN. The Designated Router is relieved of this function when IGMPv2 [71] is deployed, because IGMPv2 itself implements a Querier election.

However, regardless of which version of IGMP is in use, the OSPF Designated Router is responsible for originating group-membership-LSAs to report the LAN's group membership throughout the MOSPF domain. In addition, the normal OSPF rules for processing optional LSA types apply to group-membership-LSAs: Only MOSPF routers are required to store and flood group-membership-LSAs. Due to the central role that the Designated Router plays in flooding LSAs across the LAN (see Section 5.2), group-membership-LSAs will not be forwarded across the LAN unless the Designated Router is MOSPF-capable. It is this last restriction that caused the flooding of unknown LSA types to be changed in OSPF for IPv6 (see Section 3.7). In OSPF for IPv6, unknown LSA types are always flooded locally; in the case of group-membership-LSAs, this means that group-membership-LSAs would be flooded across a LAN even if the Designated Router were not MOSPF-capable.

10.6   MOSPF in the MBONE

Just as there are multiple unicast routing protocols deployed in the Internet, there
are also multiple multicast routing protocols in use. To forward datagrams between
domains using different routing protocols, information must be exchanged between the
routing protocols. In unicast routing, this information is the location of IP destinations.
In multicast routing, this information is the location of multicast sources and destination
groups.

This section describes the exchange of information between MOSPF and DVMRP,
the routing protocol deployed in the MBONE (see Section 14.2). In order to connect a
MOSPF domain to the MBONE, one or more of the routers within the MOSPF domain
must also run DVMRP. In the interaction between the two protocols, MOSPF plays the
multicast equivalent of an IGP, whereas DVMRP acts like an EGP. An example of a
MOSPF domain connected to the MBONE is shown in Figure 10.7. Routers A and D run
both MOSPF and DVMRP, leaking multicast routing information from one protocol to
the other. In addition, a BGP connection on router C provides unicast connectivity to the
Internet.

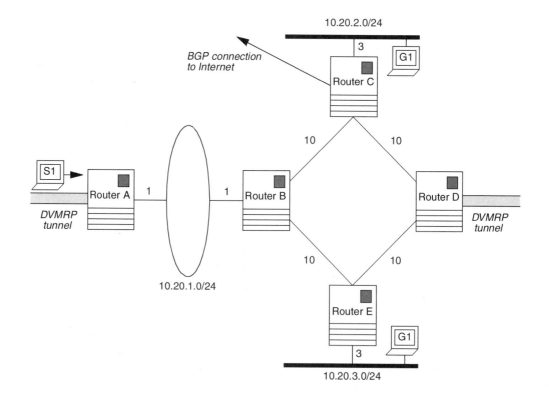

Figure 10.7 Example MOSPF domain within the MBONE.

Probably the best way to view the interaction between MOSPF and DVMRP is to think of the MOSPF domain as an extended Ethernet segment within the DVMRP routing system.

- DVMRP routers consider the group membership of their attached network segments when deciding whether to send prune messages: If none of the DVMRP router's attached network segments have group members and if all of its subordinate DVMRP routers (see Section 14.2) have sent prunes for a given source and destination group, the router itself will send matching prunes back toward the source. Similarly a router running both DVMRP and MOSPF will send prunes if (a) there are no group members in the MOSPF domain and (b) all of its subordinate DVMRP routers have sent prunes.

- DVMRP routers include the addresses of their directly attached LAN segments in DVMRP routing updates. A router running MOSPF and DVMRP will include all MOSPF intra-area and inter-area addresses in its DVMRP updates.

- In order to get DVMRP routing information across a MOSPF domain, one must exchange DVMRP routing messages between the DVMRP routers at the edge of the MOSPF domain—this is analogous to running IBGP to communicate BGP routing information across an AS (Section 13.3). DVMRP routing messages are multicast over Ethernet segments. Over a MOSPF domain, DVMRP routing messages are again multicast, this time after encapsulating within an additional IP header whose destination is set to the group address 224.0.1.21 (DVMRP over MOSPF in [212]). This can be thought of as a *DVMRP multicast tunnel*. For example, in Figure 10.7, both routers A and D would join the multicast group 224.0.1.21. Then, when router A sent a DVMRP routing update, it would encapsulate the DVMRP update within a multicast datagram sent to 224.0.1.21, which would be delivered by MOSPF routing to router D.

- When multiple DVMRP routers are attached to a LAN, the exchange of DVMRP routing updates determines which DVMRP router is responsible for forwarding multicasts onto the LAN from any given source. Similarly the DVMRP routing updates multicast over the MOSPF domain determine which DVMRP router is responsible for forwarding multicast datagrams into the MOSPF domain.

Since we are taking a MOSPF-centric view, we will speak of the advertising of MOSPF information within DVMRP as *exporting* information to DVMRP and that DVMRP information is *imported* into MOSPF.

As mentioned, MOSPF internal sources are exported to DVMRP as if they were addresses assigned to a DVMRP router's attached network segments. In Figure 10.7, both routers A and D would advertise the aggregate 10.20.0.0/16 within their DVMRP routing updates. Group information, on the other hand, is exported indirectly through the DVMRP pruning logic. If, for example, router D sends router A a prune message for source S1 and group G2, A will in turn send a prune message back toward S1, since no group G2 members are within the MOSPF domain. However, if A receives a prune for S1 and G1, A will not send a prune, due to the presence of group members on 10.20.2.0/24 and 10.20.3.0/24.

Importing DVMRP information into MOSPF is analogous to advertising multicast routing information from the OSPF backbone area into nonbackbone areas (see Section 10.4.1). Whereas inter-area source information is advertised in summary-LSAs, DVMRP sources are imported in AS-external-LSAs. The MC-bit is set in the AS-external-LSA's Options field to indicate that, besides advertising a unicast route, the advertised network is also a multicast source. Only this single bit and not a separate metric for multicast is needed, since, according to the fourth item listed, at most one DVMRP router will be importing any particular source. Of course, the multicast and unicast topologies may be quite different, and a DVMRP router may want to advertise a multicast source *without* also advertising a matching unicast route. For example, in Figure 10.7, router A may wish to advertise the multicast source S1 but may want unicast traffic destined for S1 to be forwarded to router C's Internet connection. In order to advertise a multicast-only route, router A originates an AS-external-LSA for S1 with the MC-bit set and an infinite cost.

Since only one DVMRP router will import any given source, the DVMRP routers can reduce the number of multicast sources imported into the MOSPF domain by having the DVMRP router that would have imported the most sources import a multicast default route (AS-external-LSA with destination 0.0.0.0 and MC-bit set) instead.

We saw earlier that multicast group information is not advertised from the OSPF backbone into nonbackbone areas. Similarly multicast group information learned by DVMRP is not imported into the MOSPF domain either. Instead the routers running both DVMRP and MOSPF declare themselves wildcard multicast receivers (see Section 10.4.1), performing the same function that the area border routers did in inter-area multicast routing. Labeling the DVMRP routers as wildcard multicast receivers ensures that multicast datagrams will be forwarded to the point where the DVMRP group membership information can be accessed and acted on.

Further Reading

IP multicast is based on the work of Steve Deering. He defined the interaction of hosts and routers in IP multicast in the original IGMP specification [56]. In [58] and [59], he explored various multicast routing algorithms, which led to the development of both the DVMRP ([202], [255]) and MOSPF routing protocols.

IGMP has been extended since the development of MOSPF. In IGMPv2 [71], an election algorithm for the designated Querier (the router responsible for sending periodic Host Membership Queries) is introduced, removing the need to link this function to the MOSPF Designated Router. Also, Leave Membership Reports are introduced to reduce the group leave latency. IGMPv3 [28] defines source-specific join and leave group messages that MOSPF, in its present form, cannot take advantage of.

The encapsulation of IP multicast datagrams varies according to the data-link protocol. For those data links with a multicast capability, the IP multicast destination is usually mapped in some way to a data-link multicast address. The IP multicast encapsulation for Ethernet is given in [56], FDDI in [122], 802.5 Token Ring in [203], and SMDS in [134]. IP multicast support over ATM is still under development, with the leading proposal described in [4]. Multicast encapsulations for IPv6 are different, as are the unicast encapsulations, as described in Section 1.3.

Detailed description of the MBONE and some of its applications can be found in [69] and [131]. Answers to frequently asked questions about the MBONE, including how to get connected to it and where to find the proper applications, can be found in [36].

MOSPF does not have its own Management Information Base, but instead MOSPF variables have been added to the OSPF MIB [14]. For more information on configuration and management of MOSPF, see Chapter 11, OSPF Management.

Adding MOSPF to an OSPF implementation tends to increase code size by about 30 percent. For further details on code size and other MOSPF performance statistics, see [170].

Exercises

10.1 What MOSPF-specific events would cause demand circuits' underlying data-link connections to be (re)established? How would this change if the MOSPF domain were split into areas?

10.2 Which routers originate group-membership-LSAs in Figure 10.7? Which routers are declaring themselves wildcard multicast receivers?

Part IV

Configuration and Management

In Part IV, we discuss how to configure, monitor, and debug Internet routing. Chapter 11, OSPF Management, explains how to configure and manage an OSPF network. All configurable OSPF items are contained in the OSPF MIB; we discuss the use of SNMP and this MIB. Common configuration tasks, such as the setting of interface costs, are explained. We also discuss whether, and if so how, to split an OSPF routing domain into areas. An example of a real OSPF network configuration, the Arkansas Public School Computer Network, is provided. The interaction between OSPF and BGP and RIP is described. The chapter ends with a description of OSPF's security features.

Chapter 12, Debugging Routing Problems, is a practical discussion of the techniques for debugging routing problems in a TCP/IP network. All of the common tools for analyzing IP routing difficulties are covered, including `ping`, `traceroute`, SNMP, network analyzers, and multicast traceroute. We describe how each tool is used, explain how the tool works, and discuss the tool's strengths and weaknesses.

11

OSPF Management

In this chapter, we discuss how to manage the OSPF protocol. At the macro level, a network administrator must decide how to organize an Autonomous System (AS) that runs OSPF as its routing protocol. This involves answering the following questions.

- Where are the boundaries of the AS?

- Which links should be preferred for data traffic, and which links should be avoided?

- What information learned from other ASs should be imported into the AS? Conversely how much of the AS's internal routing information should be advertised to other ASs?

- Should the OSPF AS be divided into areas? If so, where should the area boundaries be placed?

- Does the OSPF routing within the AS need to be protected from hostile attackers?

After determining the OSPF configuration for the Autonomous System, the administrator must then master the mechanics of how to configure the individual routers to run the OSPF protocol. Unfortunately this step is often vendor specific. However, the Internet standard network management framework, consisting of SNMP and its MIBs, provides a good place to start.

11.1   SNMP

The standard method for configuring and monitoring Internet protocols and devices is via the Simple Network Management Protocol (SNMP) [226]. SNMP manipulates management data within an Internet device, such as a router. This management data forms a device's Management Information Base (MIB) [144], which is organized as a tree structure, as depicted in Figure 11.1. All management data for Internet devices falls under the branch *internet (1.3.6.1)*, with the subbranch *mgmt (2)* for standardized management data, *experimental (3)* for management data currently under development, and *private (4)* for vendor-specific management data. The core set of management data for Internet protocols is called MIB-II and falls under the subbranch labeled *mib-2*.

Each Internet protocol running within the device is required to provide its own set of management data. Some of these protocol-specific MIBs are pictured in Figure 11.1: *system (1)* for generic information about Internet devices, such as system-up time; *interfaces (2)* for network interface statistics, such as a count of packets sent and received; *at (3)* for ARP; *ip (4)* for Internet Protocol network-layer data, including the routing table; and MIBs for the various IP routing protocols. These MIBs are defined in a precise language so that they can be compiled into a network management station, just like a program written in any computer language.

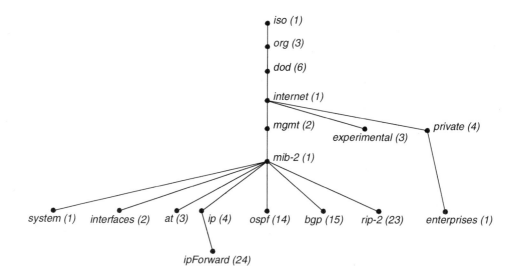

Figure 11.1 The structure of Internet management information.

Each management variable within one of these MIBs has a number of attributes. One such variable, the cost of an OSPF interface for a particular Type of Service, is shown in Figure 11.2 as it has been defined within the OSPF MIB. The variable has been assigned the textual name **ospfIfMetricValue**. The format of the variable's value is specified in the **SYNTAX** clause; MIB values are coded in basic ASN.1 [113] formats, such as integers, octet strings, and so on. In this case, the value has been defined to be a **Metric**, which has been defined earlier in the OSPF MIB to be an integer between 0 and 65,535. The **MAX-ACCESS** clause indicates whether the variable is writable for configuration purposes, readable for monitoring, or both. The variable **ospfIfMetricValue** is used for both configuration and monitoring. Variables can also specify default values in a **DEFVAL** clause, although this clause has not been provided for **ospfIfMetricValue**. The last line in the variable specification provides the location, or *object identifier,* of the variable within the global MIB. The OSPF MIB can be found at branch 1.3.6.1.2.1.14, and **ospfIfMetricValue** is subbranch 4 of **ospfIfMetricEntry**, which is itself subbranch 8.1 within the OSPF MIB. This yields an object identifier of 1.3.6.1.2.1.14.8.1.4. It is this identifier, not the textual name **ospfIfMetricValue**, that is handed to SNMP when you want to manipulate the cost of an OSPF interface.

```
ospfIfMetricValue OBJECT-TYPE
     SYNTAX    Metric
     MAX-ACCESS    read-create
     STATUS    current
     DESCRIPTION
        "The metric of using this type of service on this interface.
        The default value of the TOS 0 Metric is 10^8 / ifSpeed."
     ::= { ospfIfMetricEntry 4 }
```

Figure 11.2 Specification of variable **ospfIfMetricValue** within the OSPF MIB.

The value of a management variable can depend on context. For example, **ospfIfMetricValue** can have a separate value for each OSPF interface and also for each IP Type of Service (TOS). Within MIBs, such context dependence is captured by organizing variables in *tables*: Each row of a table specifies the value of a set of variables within a specific context.

An example is shown in Figure 11.3. The variable **ospfIfMetricTable** describes a router's OSPF interface metrics; **ospfIfMetricEntry** defines what a row of the table looks like. The **INDEX** clause indicates that there is a separate row for each interface and TOS: The interface is given by a combination of **ospfIfMetricIpAddress** (the IP address of an interface), **ospfIfMetricAddressLessIf** (for unnumbered interfaces set to the MIB-II IfIndex of the interface but otherwise set to 0), and **ospfIfMetricTOS** (for TOS). Each row within **ospfIfMetricEntry** has five variables, including the three **INDEX** variables (required by SNMP to be listed in the table's rows but otherwise uninteresting) and the value of the metric (**ospfIfMetricValue**). The last variable in the row, **ospfIfMetricStatus**, provides the SNMP standard way of deleting rows from tables: Setting **ospfIfMetricStatus** to **destroy** for a particular index deletes the OSPF metric for a particular interface and TOS combination.

```
ospfIfMetricTable OBJECT-TYPE
        SYNTAX    SEQUENCE OF ospfIfMetricEntry
        MAX-ACCESS    not-accessible
        STATUS    current
        DESCRIPTION
           "The TOS metrics for a nonvirtual interface
           identified by the interface index."
        REFERENCE
           "OSPF Version 2, Appendix C.3 Router interface
           parameters"
        ::= { ospf 8 }

    ospfIfMetricEntry OBJECT-TYPE
        SYNTAX ospfIfMetricEntry
        MAX-ACCESS    not-accessible
        STATUS    current
        DESCRIPTION
           "A particular TOS metric for a nonvirtual
           interface identified by the interface index."
        REFERENCE
           "OSPF Version 2, Appendix C.3 Router interface
           parameters"
        INDEX { ospfIfMetricIpAddress,
                ospfIfMetricAddressLessIf,
                ospfIfMetricTOS }
        ::= { ospfIfMetricTable 1 }

ospfIfMetricEntry ::=
    SEQUENCE {
        ospfIfMetricIpAddress
            IpAddress,
        ospfIfMetricAddressLessIf
            Integer32,
        ospfIfMetricTOS
            TOSType,
        ospfIfMetricValue
            Metric,
        ospfIfMetricStatus
            RowStatus
              }
```

Figure 11.3 Table specifying OSPF interface metrics.

The value of a management variable within a table row is called an *instance* of the variable. An SNMP object identifier specifies both a variable and an instance. Returning to our previous example, there is a separate instance of **ospfIfMetricValue** for each interface and TOS. The object identifier for a particular instance of **ospfIfMetricValue** is formed by concatenating 1.3.6.1.2.1.14.8.1.4 with the relevant instances. The object identifier of **ospfIfMetricValue** for interface with IP address of 10.1.1.1 and for TOS 0 is shown in Figure 11.4.

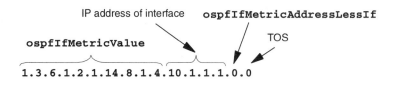

Figure 11.4 Object identifier of **ospfIfMetricValue** specifying instances.

SNMP provides three functions to access the management data: get, get-next, and set. These are separate SNMP packet types. However, programs such as Carnegie-Mellon University's SNMP tools [31] have been written to access these SNMP functions directly from the UNIX or DOS shells, which is the model we shall assume in the rest of this chapter. The SNMP get function reads the value of a particular instance of a MIB variable; for example, **get 1.3.6.1.2.1.14.8.1.4.10.1.1.1.0.0** would return the TOS 0 cost of the OSPF interface whose IP address is 10.1.1.1. The get-next function also takes an object identifier as argument but returns the value of the MIB variable instance that immediately follows the given object identifier, in lexicographic order (that is, the order that words are listed in a dictionary). This allows one to use get-next repeatedly to walk through the entire management database. Often command line get-next functions are implemented so that they issue repeated SNMP get-next queries until reaching an object identifier whose prefix is different from the one issued on the command line. This feature makes it easy to list an entire table or one of a table's columns. For example, Figure 11.5 shows how get-next can be used easily to list all of a router's OSPF interface costs by walking through the **ospfIfMetricTable**. There are three interfaces, having IP addresses 10.1.1.1, 10.2.3.7, and 10.6.1.1, with OSPF interface TOS 0 costs of 110, 10, and 200, respectively.

```
$ get-next 1.3.6.1.2.1.14.8.1.4
1.3.6.1.2.1.14.8.1.4.10.1.1.1.0.0 110
1.3.6.1.2.1.14.8.1.4.10.2.3.7.0.0 10
1.3.6.1.2.1.14.8.1.4.10.6.1.1.0.0 200
```

Figure 11.5 Walking the **ospfIfMetricTable**, using SNMP's get-next function.

The SNMP set command allows you to write a particular MIB variable instance. For example, in order to set the cost of OSPF interface 10.6.1.1 to the value 150, the command **set 1.3.6.1.2.1.14.8.1.4.10.6.1.1.0.0 150** is issued.

SNMP also has a facility allowing Internet devices to send asynchronous notification of interesting events, called SNMP *traps*, to a network management station. SNMP traps have always been controversial: Many people are concerned about the additional network load that traps can incur during unexpected network conditions. For this reason, SNMP traps are used rarely, and much of the MIB development involving traps has centered on ways to rate-limit trap generation [14].

Work began in 1993 on updating SNMP, resulting in a new version of SNMP, SNMPv2 [32], [33]. However, the differences between SNMPv2 and SNMP (now called SNMPv1) are fairly minor, and the major advantage of SNMPv2, namely, increased protocol security, failed to materialize, due to lack of consensus. The limited improvements over SNMPv1 and the large installed base of SNMPv1 devices have prevented deployment of SNMPv2. However, the updated MIB description language used by SNMPv2 [34] has gained acceptance and is now used when new Internet MIBs are developed.

As mentioned, SNMP is the standard for management of Internet devices. However, that does not mean that people always use SNMP to monitor and configure their devices. Many routers are instead managed through command line interfaces, via either TELNET or dedicated serial line connections, or via Web browsers. These other methods are especially common for configuration, due to SNMP's lack of security. Still, when you want to see how to manage a particular protocol or device, the protocol-specific or device-specific MIB is the place to start. The IETF puts a lot of its energy into creating MIBs, which almost always have all the information you want (in fact, usually more information than you want), including recommended default values for management variables.

11.2 OSPF MIB

OSPF has a large MIB [14], with 110 management variables organized into 12 tables. More than half (65) of the variables, including 3 complete tables, are read-only, meaning that they are used only for monitoring. Of the 45 configurable variables, most have default values that rarely need to be altered.

The structure of the OSPF MIB is shown in Figure 11.6. Those tables containing configurable variables are shaded. Notice that there are some gaps in the way object identifiers have been assigned to tables. An earlier version of the table used to configure area address aggregation, **ospfAreaRangeTable (ospf 5)**, is not pictured, having been replaced by **ospfAreaAggregateTable (ospf 14)**. Another collection of object identifiers, **ospfRouteGroup (ospf 13)**, does not specify management variables but instead defines object identifiers that can be used by the IP Forwarding Table MIB [11] to

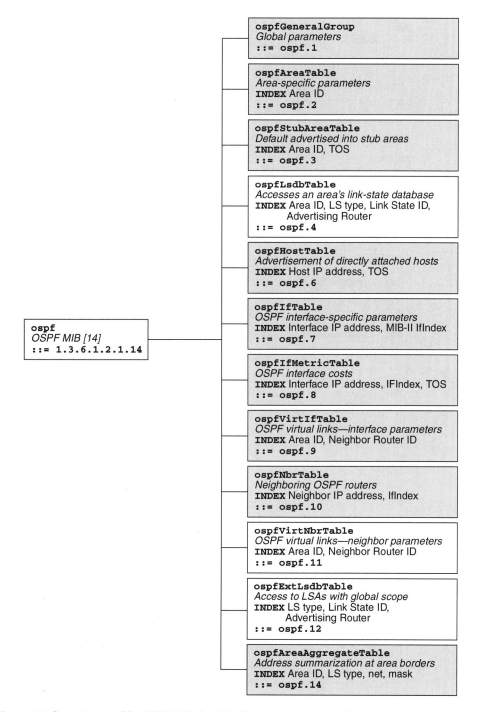

Figure 11.6 Organization of the OSPF MIB. Shaded tables contain configurable parameters, whereas unshaded tables are used only for monitoring.

indicate specific kinds of OSPF routes (intra-area, inter-area, external Type 1, and external Type 2).

When configuring an OSPF router, you end up setting variables from one or more of the following tables within the OSPF MIB:

- **ospfGeneralGroup**. This *group*, a table that has only a single row, contains the router's global OSPF parameters and statistics. The router's OSPF Router ID is set by writing **ospfRouterId**; **ospfAdminStat** turns the OSPF protocol on or off. The OSPF optional extensions of TOS routing, multicast routing (MOSPF), and Demand Circuit extensions (see Chapter 7) are enabled or disabled by writing appropriate values into **ospfTOSSupport**, **ospfMulticastExtensions**, and **ospfDemandExtensions**, respectively. The optional OSPF database-overflow logic can be enabled through setting **ospfExtLsdbLimit**, the maximum number of AS-external-LSAs that the router can hold. If more than this number of AS-external-LSAs are received, the router goes into overflow state (see Section 7.5), which is automatically left after **ospfExitOverflowInterval** seconds.

- **ospfAreaTable**. There is a separate row in this table for each of the router's attached areas, each identified by the area's OSPF Area ID. The type of OSPF area (regular, stub, or NSSA; see Sections 7.2 and 7.4) is dictated by **ospfImportAsExtern**. For stub areas, **ospfAreaSummary** controls whether a stub area's border routers will originate summary-LSAs into the stub area.

- **ospfStubAreaTable**. For each stub area or NSSA and for each separate TOS value, there can be a separate row in this table. This table configures the default routes imported into the stub area or NSSA by the area's border routers, with **ospfStubMetric** specifying the cost of the default route and **ospfStubMetricType** specifying whether the default should be a Type 1 or Type 2 external metric (NSSAs only).

- **ospfHostTable**. This table indicates which hosts are directly attached to the router: their addresses (**ospfHostIpAddress**), which OSPF area they belong to (**ospfHostAreaID**), and their advertised cost (**ospfHostMetric**). For example, a remote-access router providing dial-up access might have a configured host address for each dial port.

- **ospfIfTable**. There is a row in this table for each OSPF interface. Interfaces are identified by their IP address (**ospfIfIpAddress**) or, if the interface is unnumbered, by the physical interface's MIB-II **IfIndex** (**ospfAddressLessIf**). The OSPF area that the interface attaches to (**ospfIfAreaId**) and the type of interface (**ospfIfType**, one of broadcast, NBMA, point-to-point, or Point-to-MultiPoint) are configured, together with various timers used by OSPF's neighbor maintenance and database synchronization procedures (see Sections 4.6 and 4.7). Using this table, you also configure the authentication procedures used in packets sent and received over the interface (**ospfIfAuthType** and **ospfIfAuthKey**; see Section 11.7) and whether the attached subnet should be treated as a demand circuit (**ospfIfDemand**, see Section 7.3).

- **ospfIfMetricTable**. The cost of an interface, advertised in the router's router-LSA and used by the OSPF routing table calculation, is set by writing the appropriate instance of **ospfIfMetricValue**.

- **ospfVirtIfTable**. A router's configured virtual links are specified by the OSPF Router ID of the other end point (**ospfVirtIfNeighbor**) and the nonbackbone area that will carry the link (**ospfVirtIfAreaId**). As in the regular interface table, timers used by OSPF neighbor maintenance and database synchronization, and authentication procedures can also be configured for each virtual link.

- **ospfNbrTable**. Neighbors may have to be configured on NBMA and Point-to-MultiPoint subnets (see Sections 5.3 and 5.4). Each neighbor is identified by its IP address (**ospfNbrIpAddr**). On NBMA subnets, the Router Priority of each neighbor (**ospfNbrPriority**) must also be configured.

- **ospfAreaAggregateTable**. Each row in this table indicates a range of IP addresses (**ospfAreaAggregateNet** and **ospfAreaAggregateMask**) belonging to a given area (**ospfAreaAggregateAreaID**), which should be aggregated into a single prefix when advertised to other areas. By setting **ospfAreaAggregateEffect** accordingly, you can also hide a range of IP addresses from other areas. This table can also be used by NSSA areas when aggregating multiple Type-7-LSAs into a single AS-external-LSA at the NSSA boundary (see Section 7.4).

The other tables in the OSPF MIB are read-only, for use in monitoring the OSPF protocol.

- **ospfLsdbTable**. This table allows you to scan the link-state database, one OSPF area at a time. There is a separate row for each LSA in an area's link-state database, with entries in the row for each of the LSA's header fields (**ospfLsdbAge** for the LS Age field, **ospfLsdbChecksum** for the LS Checksum field, and so on) and an entry (**ospfLsdbAdvertisement**) allowing you to get the complete LSA represented as an octet string. Using this table, the command **get_next ospfLsdbAdvertisement** would dump the entire contents of the link-state databases for all of the router's attached areas.

- **ospfVirtNbrTable**. This table is used to monitor the state of a virtual link. For example, has the virtual link been established? Have the routers at either end synchronized their link-state databases?

- **ospfExtLsdbTable**. Similar to the **ospfLsdbTable**, this table is only for those LSAs with global flooding scope. For example, the command **get_next**

`ospfExtLsdbAdvertisement.5` (`ospfExtLsdbType == 5 ==` *AS-external-LSA*)
would dump all the AS-external-LSAs in the OSPF routing domain.

The OSPF MIB also defines a set of traps, used to provide asynchronous notification
of significant events. These traps can be turned off and on individually by writing to
`ospfSetTrap`. Just as there were separate tables for interfaces and virtual interfaces
(likewise neighbors and virtual neighbors), most of the traps have a "virtual" counterpart. There are traps to indicate interface state changes (`ospfIfStateChange` and
`ospfVirtIfStateChange`); neighbor state changes (`ospfNbrStateChange` and
`ospfVirtNbrStateChange`); configuration errors, such as mismatches in timer settings
(`ospfIfConfigError` and `ospfVirtIfConfigError`); OSPF packet authentication
failures (`ospfIfAuthFailure` and `ospfVirtIfAuthFailure`); reception of improp-
erly formatted OSPF packets (`ospfIfRxBadPacket` and `ospfVirtIfRxBadPacket`);
and retransmission of LSAs during flooding (`ospfTxRetransmit` and
`ospfVirtTxRetransmit`). There are also traps to indicate (re)origination of LSAs
(`ospfOriginateLsa`), LSAs that naturally age out and are flushed from the routing domain (`ospfMaxAgeLsa`), and LSAs that the current number of AS-external-
LSAs in the link-state database are close to or at the configured maximum
(`ospfLsdbApproachingOverflow` and `ospfLsdbOverflow`; see Section 7.5).

11.3   Configuring OSPF

We have seen that OSPF has many configuration parameters. However, that does not
necessarily mean that OSPF is difficult to configure. Most of the parameters can be left
at their default values. In a basic configuration, OSPF is as simple to configure as RIP:
You enable the OSPF protocol and specify which router interfaces you want to run OSPF
on. Some OSPF implementations will also require you to specify the OSPF area to which
each interface connects, although most implementations will default to the backbone
OSPF area (Area ID 0.0.0.0).

The one additional item that you probably always want to configure is the router's
OSPF Router ID. If that is left unspecified, most OSPF implementations will set the
Router ID to one of the router's interface IP addresses. However, this is problematic:
When that interface is deleted or, in some implementations, even if the interface is disabled, the router's Router ID is forced to change. A change in Router ID requires that the
router's OSPF software be restarted, which will cause small service disruptions as the
router's link-state database and routing table are rebuilt.

As mentioned, SNMP is the common frame of reference for configuring routers. But
not all routers are configured using SNMP. As an example, suppose that we want to
enable a basic OSPF configuration on a router with three interfaces: an Ethernet interface with an address of 10.1.2.4 (mask 255.255.255.0) and two point-to-point links with
addresses of 10.2.6.1 and 10.2.6.5, respectively. We also want to explicitly give the router

an OSPF Router ID of 10.10.0.4, which is an address that has been assigned to the router's loopback interface. To configure the router through SNMP, we would use the SNMP sets pictured in Figure 11.7.

```
set ospfRouterId.0 10.10.0.4
set ospfIfAdminStat.10.1.2.4.0 1
set ospfIfAdminStat.10.2.6.1.0 1
set ospfIfAdminStat.10.2.6.5.0 1
set ospfAdminStat.0 1
```

Figure 11.7 Basic OSPF configuration, using SNMP.

To enable the same configuration on GATED, the syntax in Figure 11.8 is used. GATED is a routing daemon for UNIX workstations; its configuration resides on a disk file that you manipulate with a text editor. In the example, we have explicitly assigned the Router ID; if we had not, GATED would instead select one of the IP interface addresses to serve as Router ID, using the following order of preference: first addresses (other than the 127.0.0.1 address) assigned to the loopback interfaces, then addresses assigned to LAN interfaces, and finally addresses assigned to point-to-point interfaces. In addition, in one of the quirks of the UNIX networking code, point-to-point interfaces are referred to by the IP address of the neighboring router (assumed to be 10.2.6.2 and 10.2.6.6 in our example).

```
routerid 10.10.10.4;
ospf yes {
  backbone {
    interface 10.1.2.4 {
      enable;
      };
    interface 10.2.6.2 {
      enable;
      }
    interface 10.2.6.6 {
      enable;
      };
  };
```

Figure 11.8 Basic OSPF configuration, GATED syntax.

To enable the basic configuration on a Cisco router, the commands in Figure 11.9 would be typed on the router console or downloaded into the router. Like GATED, the Cisco router uses one of the IP interface addresses as Router ID. However, the loopback address always takes precedence and can therefore be used to explicitly set the Router ID. In the Cisco router, each routing protocol runs as a separate process, and you must specify the process ID when enabling the protocol. The network command pictured in Figure 11.9 enables OSPF on all interfaces with prefix 10/8, attaching them to the backbone OSPF area (Area ID 0.0.0.0).

```
interface loopback 0
ip address 10.10.0.4 255.255.255.255
interface ethernet 0
ip address 10.1.2.4 255.255.255.0
interface serial 0
ip address 10.2.6.1 255.255.255.255
interface serial 1
ip address 10.2.6.5 255.255.255.255
router ospf 201
network 10.0.0.0 0.255.255.255 area 0
```

Figure 11.9 Basic OSPF configuration, Cisco router syntax.

The basic configuration is all that you are required to perform in order to get OSPF up and running. Note that we did not set the OSPF interface type (**ospfIfType**)—the router will figure this out by itself, setting the Ethernet's type to broadcast and the PPP links to point-to-point. There are, however, some additional parameters that you may want to tune eventually. The first is the link cost (**ospfIfMetricValue**), which controls the way data traffic is forwarded through your network—which links should be preferred, which should be avoided, and so on (see Section 11.3.1). If your routing domain will grow very large, you may want to split it into OSPF areas (see Section 11.3.2). Other parameters that you may want to set include the following.

- You may want to secure your OSPF routing against intruders, by enabling the authentication of OSPF packet exchanges (see Section 11.7).

- On nonbroadcast networks, such as Frame Relay, ATM, and X.25 subnets, you have to choose whether NBMA mode or Point-to-MultiPoint mode is most appropriate (see Sections 5.3 and 5.4). In addition, routers attached to nonbroadcast networks may not be able to discover their neighbors automatically, and neighboring routers may have to be configured instead (**ospfNbrTable**). If you are using NBMA mode, a certain small subset of the attached routers should be configured as eligible to become Designated Router. Neighbors need be configured only in these eligible routers, although the Router Priority of each neighbor must also be configured in this case.

- You may also be running other routing protocols in your network—RIP to your edge routers, BGP on your Internet connections, and so on. In these cases, you will want to exchange routing information between OSPF and these other protocols. These routing exchanges most often need to be configured (see Section 11.6).

11.3.1 Configuring Link Costs

Each router interface within an OSPF network is assigned a cost, ranging in value from 1 to 65,535. The cost of any path within the OSPF routing domain is then calculated as the sum of interface costs along the path. IP packets flow along the path having the least cost. When multiple shortest paths exist between the packets' source and destination, routers may split the load across the multiple paths. Thus cost represents the desirability of using the interface for data traffic; the smaller the cost, the more likely that data traffic will be transmitted out the interface. In particular, if there are multiple parallel links between a pair of OSPF routers, traffic will load share between the two links if they have equal OSPF cost; otherwise the link with the higher cost will serve as a hot standby.

All routers have defaults for OSPF cost, although default values typically vary based on manufacturer. Many set the default cost to 1, matching RIP's metric and resulting in minimum hop routing. Others set the default cost to that specified in the OSPF MIB, a value proportional to the link's transmission delay. Note that if you mix router manufacturers with different defaults, your routing will still work—that is, packets will be delivered along loop-free paths. However, the paths may very well be suboptimal, leading you to choose one default (or a whole different cost scheme) over the other.

Selecting a cost scheme is up to the routing domain's administrator. Besides the two common defaults mentioned previously, other cost schemes include the following.

- *Weighted hop count.* You may want to use small integers as costs but make some link costs higher than others to bias the routing away from pure hop count. For example, you may have the rule that one T1 hop is equal to three T3 hops, in which case you might set the cost of T1 links to 3 and leave the T3 links at cost 1.

- *Delay.* You may want to set the cost of each link to the delay that a packet would experience when transmitted over the link. This delay is typically dominated by propagation delay instead of the transmission delay used by default in the OSPF MIB.

- *Reverse engineering the link costs based on a measured or expected traffic matrix.* If you know the amount of traffic, indexed by source and destination, that your network will carry, you can attempt to set link costs to keep the traffic load on all links at acceptable levels. This is a subproblem of the network design problem, which would tell you which links to provision in the first place [20].

For more information on setting OSPF interface costs, see Chapter 8.

11.3.2 Configuring OSPF Areas

When your OSPF routing domain grows large, you may have to split the domain into OSPF areas. OSPF areas reduce the resource demands that OSPF puts on routers and links. In particular, the use of OSPF areas reduces the router CPU usage by the OSPF routing calculation, since the calculation is performed on each area separately, with a cost of $O(l * \log(n))$, where l is the number of links (that is, router interfaces) in the area, and n is the number of routers in the area. Also, it reduces the amount of memory that the router has to use for its link-state databases, since the size of each area's database is usually proportional to the number of links in the area. In those cases in which the size of the link-state database is dominated by the number of external routes imported into the OSPF domain (that is, AS-external-LSAs), routers with limited resources can be relegated to OSPF stub areas or NSSAs, which omit external routes and instead rely mostly on default routing (see Sections 6.3, 7.2, and 7.4).

Although areas can reduce resource requirements, they should not be overused. Areas reduce resource requirements by hiding information, but any time you hide information, you potentially create suboptimal data paths (see Section 6.1). Areas also complicate the task of configuring an OSPF routing domain.

Each IP subnet belongs to one, and only one, OSPF area. A router, on the other hand, may belong to multiple areas: the areas to which the router's interfaces directly connect. Each router interface is configured with the Area ID of the attached subnet (**ospfIfAreaId**). Routers belonging to multiple areas are called *area border routers*.

All other area configuration is isolated to the area border routers only.

- *Area summarization*. You can further reduce the size of link-state databases by aggregating routes at area boundaries. This is configured by writing entries in the **ospfAreaAggregateTable** of the appropriate area border routers. Certain networks can also be hidden from other areas by setting their range's **ospfAreaAggregateEffect** variable to **doNotAdvertiseMatching**.

- *Default routes*. The cost of the default route advertised by area border routers into stub areas and NSSAs must be configured by writing entries in the **ospfStubAreaTable**.

- *Virtual links*. OSPF requires that all nonbackbone areas connect directly to the backbone (Area ID 0.0.0.0) area. When the area configuration violates this rule, virtual links must be configured through certain nonbackbone areas. Virtual links are configured by writing entries in the **ospfVirtIfTable** of the area border routers at both ends of the virtual link. When and where to configure virtual links is probably the most complicated configuration task in OSPF. Virtual links are explained further in Section 6.1.2.

When designing area boundaries, one should think ahead, keeping future network growth in mind. Changing the area to which a particular network segment belongs is difficult to do in an incremental fashion. All routers connected to the segment must be reconfigured; until then, some routers on the segment will refuse the protocol packets of others, complaining of "wrong area." The safest way to perform such a transition is to allocate a second IP subnet to the segment, running OSPF on both subnets. Then, as the first subnet is undergoing transition, the second subnet's adjacencies will be used to maintain data forwarding across the segment. For more information on configuring areas, consult Chapter 8.

11.3.3 Configuring Timers

OSPF has a number of configurable timer values, which can be used to tune the neighbor discovery and maintenance procedures and the flooding process. These timers should almost always be left at their default values, which are given in Table 11.1.

Table 11.1 Default Timer Values in OSPF

Timer	Default Value (seconds)
`ospfIfTransitDelay`	1
`ospfIfRetransInterval`	5
`ospfIfHelloInterval`	10
`ospfIfRtrDeadInterval`	40
`ospfIfPollInterval`	120

An OSPF router periodically sends OSPF Hello packets out each of its interfaces at the rate of once every `ospfIfHelloInterval` seconds. On very low-speed links, you may want to increase the interval between Hello packets so as to use less link bandwidth for control packets. Hello packets also serve as a method of last resort to detect when a neighboring router has failed, although usually the failure is detected much more quickly by the data-link protocol (for example, PPP's link-quality monitoring). When no Hello packet has been received from the neighbor for `ospfRtrDeadInterval`, the neighbor is declared inoperational. To ensure that a couple of lost Hello packets do not incorrectly cause a neighbor to be declared inoperational, `ospfRtrDeadInterval` should always be several times the `ospfIfHelloInterval`. If the OSPF Hello protocol is the only mechanism for detecting failed neighbors, you may want to reduce the values of `ospfRtrDeadInterval` and `ospfIfHelloInterval` in order to detect the failure more quickly.

The `ospfIfHelloInterval` and `ospfRtrDeadInterval` variables must be set identically in all router interfaces attached to a common IP subnet. Changing these values on a subnet is similar to changing the subnet's Area ID (see Section 11.3.2); in order to avoid service interruptions, a second subnet must be configured on the link during the transition from one set of timer values to another.

On NBMA subnets (see Section 5.3), routers periodically send Hello packets to inoperational neighbors, in an attempt to detect when a neighbor comes back into service. This polling is performed once every `ospfIfPollInterval` seconds, which is typically larger than `ospfIfHelloInterval` in order to avoid wasting network bandwidth.

The time it takes to transmit an LSA to neighbors on the interface is represented by `ospfIfTransitDelay`. This value must be greater than 0, and is added to the LS Age field of all LSAs flooded out the interface. This value should not be set to unreasonably large values (for example, a value near 900 seconds), or the OSPF flooding process will fail. The variable `ospfIfRetransInterval` is the length of time before unacknowledged LSAs (and also Database Description packets and Link State Request packets) will be retransmitted to the neighbor. This value should be larger than the round-trip time to the neighbor and back, or needless retransmissions will ensue. The variable `ospfIfRetransInterval` may need to be increased on low-speed and/or satellite links.

11.4   An Example: The Arkansas Public School Computer Network

In this section, we illustrate the configuration of an OSPF routing domain, using the Arkansas Public School Computer Network (APSCN) as an example. The APSCN, which interconnects all the public schools in the state of Arkansas, is used for administrative purposes, such as collection of financial and student data, using TELNET-based applications. APSCN also provides Internet connections for all of the Arkansas school districts. Using the Internet, Arkansas students can interact with other students around the world. For example, students participate in environmental surveys in order to study worldwide weather patterns.

APSCN is an IP network that runs OSPF as its routing protocol. The configuration of APSCN's OSPF routing is pictured in Figure 11.10. To date, 778 routers are running OSPF, organized into 20 OSPF areas (one backbone area and 19 nonbackbone areas). The backbone OSPF area consists of 4 hub routers (labeled H1–H4) connected by an Ethernet segment. Hub router H4 is also attached to a Token Ring segment that provides a connection to an Internet Service Provider. H4 has a static default route pointing at the ISP's router. H4 also imports this static default into the OSPF routing domain in an AS-external-LSA with a Type 2 external metric of 1.

Each hub router attaches to 4–5 nonbackbone OSPF areas. Each of these areas has 30–70 routers. All of the areas have a similar topology, pictured in the bottom half of Figure 11.10. Each area connects a number of "district routers" (labeled D1–D7) with local Ethernet segments into a single regional or cooperative site. A minicomputer at the cooperative site (labeled S1) collects administrative data entered by the districts. Each district is also connected to the hub router, which provides Internet connectivity and

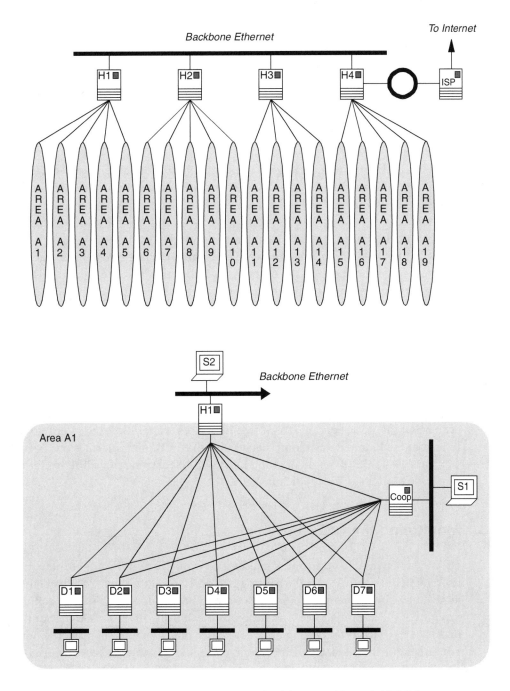

Figure 11.10 The Arkansas Public School Computer Network (APSCN).

backup servers for data collection (labeled S2). Interconnection of the district, cooperative, and hub sites is provided by Frame Relay PVCs.

The collection of PVCs in a single area is configured as a single IP subnet, using the OSPF Point-to-MultiPoint subnet support. Each router has a single OSPF Point-to-MultiPoint interface to the subnet, with a cost of 1. As a result, data traffic is forwarded over the path consisting of the fewest number of PVC hops; a district router forwards Internet traffic directly to its hub router and administrative traffic directly to its cooperative router. All OSPF timer values have been left set to their default values (Table 11.1).

APSCN discovered that it was taking too long for its routers to discover Point-to-MultiPoint neighbors using Inverse ARP. To speed up neighbor discovery, neighbors are configured but only in the downstream end of each neighbor pair. District routers have the identity of their cooperative and hub routers configured, and the cooperative routers have the identity of their hub router configured.

All of APSCN's IP addresses are taken from two Class B networks. Each area is assigned pieces from one or the other Class B address, with the area's hub router aggregating these pieces into a single route for advertisement into the backbone and other areas. For example, in one area, there are 31 LAN segments, each of which has been assigned a prefix ranging in size from a /28 to a /24. At the area border, the hub router aggregates all 31 prefixes into a single advertisement for a prefix of length 20 bits (a /20). This procedure reduces the size of the routing table within APSCN's routers. Routers at the district and cooperative levels have routing tables of 300 entries, whereas the hub routers have routing tables of 700 entries.

Hub routers can have as many as five separate OSPF Point-to-MultiPoint interfaces, each belonging to a separate area. These interfaces are multiplexed over two separate T1 links into the Frame Relay cloud. Each Point-to-MultiPoint interface on the hub router supports 30–70 OSPF neighbors (and hence OSPF adjacencies); a hub router may therefore have more than 200 OSPF adjacencies.

11.5   Monitoring the OSPF Protocol

Usually a network administrator does not continually monitor the routing protocols used in the network. When the routing protocols are doing their job correctly, they are almost invisible. However, sometimes routing breaks down. This is probably first brought to the administrator's attention by a call from an irate customer or maybe because of red icons appearing on the network management console. The network administrator then isolates the problem, using such diagnostic tools as `ping` and `traceroute` (see Chapter 12, Debugging Routing Problems). The administrator may determine that the outage is due to a physical problem, such as a dead telephone circuit. However, if no physical problems are found, the administrator has to start looking at the routing protocols.

Synchronization Problems

The first thing to determine when diagnosing an OSPF routing system is whether the routers' link-state databases are synchronized. If they are not, OSPF will not function properly. It is difficult to compare two routers' link-state databases one LSA at a time; there can be thousands of LSAs in the database, and the database changes often. But the OSPF MIB provides a database checksum (**ospfAreaLsaCksumSum** for an area's link-state database and **ospfExternLsaCksumSum** for AS-external-LSAs) that lets you compare router databases by checking a single number. Using these variables, it is a simple task to write an SNMP application that displays, in a single window, the database checksums of all routers, allowing you to verify synchronization networkwide at a single glance (see Section 3.4). This assumes that you still have SNMP connectivity to your routers; if not, you will need to look at the management variables via more cumbersome out-of-band management schemes, such as dial-up modems connected to the router consoles.

   If the databases are not synchronized, you probably want to isolate the problem further. Look at the **ospfNbrTable** in one of the routers that is not synchronized with its neighbors. You will probably find that the router (or its neighbor or both) is continually trying to retransmit LSAs to the neighbor, detected by **ospfNbrLsRetransQLen** remaining nonzero. Continual retransmissions can be due to MTU mismatches between the two routers or to bugs in the routers' OSPF software. If possible, you should obtain copies of the LSAs being retransmitted, so you can send the information to your router vendor(s) for later analysis. This could be done by capturing the transmitted Link State Update packets on a network analyzer. Even if there are no retransmissions, comparing the two routers' link-state databases one LSA at a time (**ospfLsdbTable** and **ospfExtLsdbTable**) can provide valuable information, possibly indicating bugs in the initial database synchronization (see Section 4.7.1). In any case, restarting the associated router interface (setting **ospfIfAdminStat** to **disabled**, then back to **enabled**) will most likely restore synchronization by forcing the two routers to undergo initial database synchronization again.

Checking Database Contents

If databases are synchronized, you have to start looking at the OSPF database to see that the required links (or inter-area routes or external routes) are being advertised. This requires looking at the contents of individual LSAs, something that most OSPF implementations help you to do by intelligently formatting the LSAs' displays. The nice thing is that this examination can be done at any router—they all have the same database. In fact, I have sometimes debugged networks by attaching special routers whose OSPF implementations are instrumented with sophisticated searching and event-monitoring capabilities.

OSPF requires that initial database synchronization be performed over a link (that is, an adjacency form) before the link can be included in the database (see Section 4.7). You can tell that a router is having difficulty establishing adjacencies with some of its neighbors by looking at the router's **ospfNbrState** variables; values consistently other than **twoWay** and **full** indicate problems such as

- *Physical problems.* If the link's error rate is too large, the routers attached to the link disagree on the link's MTU, or a broadcast link's multicast services fail, an adjacency may fail to form. For example, if a given neighbor's **ospfNbrState** reads consistently as **init**, the router can receive from, but not transmit packets to, the neighbor (that is, it is a one-way link).

- *Configuration problems.* If routers attached to the link disagree on the link's Area ID (see Section 11.3.2), the link's Hello protocol timers (Section 11.3.3), or the link's authentication type or keys (Section 11.7), adjacencies will fail to form.

- *Implementation bugs.* Problems in vendor implementations may prevent adjacencies from forming.

Other Issues

If databases are synchronized and their contents are correct, a router has incorrectly run the routing calculation or has failed to rerun the calculation when LSAs have changed. The guilty router can be found via **traceroute**. Then, by changing the cost of one of that router's interfaces, you can force the router to rerun its routing calculation and, ideally, fix the problem.

Network performance problems may also be detected when monitoring OSPF routers. For example, if **ospfSpfRuns** increases too quickly, a router may be performing routing calculations (and therefore consuming CPU cycles) unnecessarily. Or particular LSAs that change very often may indicate flapping links (links that go up and down very frequently). Very long retransmission queue lengths on a link (**ospfNbrLsRetransQLen**) may indicate that the speed of the link is too low for its combined data and control traffic demands.

If you enable SNMP traps on your network, some of the preceding information may be reported automatically by your routers. For example, a router sends an **ospfNbrStateChange** trap when an attempt to form an adjacency with a neighbor fails, an **ospfIfConfigError** trap when certain misconfigurations are detected, and an **ospfTxRetransmit** trap to indicate that an LSA is being retransmitted. However, many administrators do not like SNMP traps, for fear that the traps themselves will consume too much network bandwidth. Another possibility for asynchronous notification of events is through the logging facilities (for example, UNIX **syslog** or printing events to the router console) that many routers provide.

11.6   Interactions with Other Routing Protocols

As we describe in Section 13.7, there are few rules about the interaction of TCP/IP routing protocols. However, the interaction between OSPF and BGP has been described in an RFC, and although not formally documented, there are several simple possibilities when running OSPF and RIP simultaneously. These interactions are described next.

11.6.1 OSPF/BGP Interaction

The interaction between the BGP and OSPF protocols is specified in [252], which also specifies the interaction between IDRP (Inter-Domain Routing Protocol) and OSPF. IDRP is the ISO-customized version of BGP that was expected at one time to replace BGP in the Internet, but so far this replacement has not occurred. The document is written for implementors, specifying required controls on the exchange of routing information between BGP and OSPF.

The assumed environment is an AS running OSPF and exchanging BGP routes with other ASs. An example is shown in Figure 11.11. According to [252], no routes should be exchanged by default between BGP and OSPF; however, the network administrator must be able to configure the exact set of destination prefixes readvertised from OSPF to BGP (and vice versa). When readvertising an OSPF-learned prefix into BGP, you must be able to configure the BGP multiexit discriminator (sort of the BGP metric). When readvertising a BGP-learned prefix into OSPF, you must be able to configure whether it is advertised as a Type 1 or 2 external metric and the OSPF external cost.

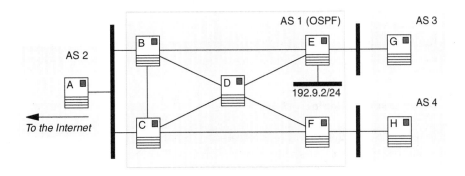

Figure 11.11 A sample BGP/OSPF environment.

Those were the generic rules, which could also be paraphrased as, "You have to be able to configure everything." However, the document goes on to describe some more useful things that you might want to do. When readvertising OSPF-learned routes into

BGP, you might just want to specify, "Readvertise all internal, that is, intra-area and inter-area, OSPF routes." In addition, you might want to readvertise all OSPF external routes with a particular external route tag (Section 6.2), or with tags matching a particular pattern.

Conversely the document notes that when readvertising BGP information into OSPF, instead of readvertising specific routes, you may want to conditionally advertise a default route into the OSPF domain. For example, in Figure 11.11, suppose that the core of the Internet is reached through AS 2. When router C exchanges BGP information with router A from AS 2, router C can tell that AS 2 is connected to the Internet core by the presence of a particular destination and with a particular AS path, received in BGP updates from router A. If, and only if, this destination is received will router C advertise a default route into AS 1's OSPF system. The origin of this behavior goes all the way back to the Fuzzball routers in the original NSFNET [161], which used the presence of network 10 (the ARPANET's network number, which at that time was the Internet core) in routing updates as an indication of default route. The document also declares that each AS boundary router is responsible for readvertising the information learned from its external BGP peers; readvertising information learned via IBGP into OSPF is forbidden.

As explained in the document, both BGP and OSPF allow you to advertise "third-party information." In BGP, this is called the "BGP next hop." In OSPF, this is called the "forwarding address" (Section 6.2). As an example, suppose that routers A and C in Figure 11.11 are BGP peers but that routers A and B are not. The internal OSPF network 192.9.2/24 would be readvertised in C's BGP updates to A, using router B as BGP next hop. This avoids an extra hop for data traffic entering the OSPF system destined for 192.9.2/24. Conversely BGP information learned from A would be readvertised by C into the OSPF system using A as forwarding address, avoiding extra hops for data traffic sourced by 192.9.2/24 and exiting the OSPF system toward the Internet core.

However, the main part of the document is a description of how to use OSPF to transport BGP information across the OSPF routing domain, removing the necessity of running IBGP in some circumstances. This is the subject of the next section.

Using OSPF to Replace IBGP

In its routing updates, BGP advertises an AS path with each destination. The AS path lists the sequence of ASs that must be traversed before reaching the destination—in essence, a source route. The AS path is used first for loop prevention. On receiving a BGP update, a router rejects all destinations with the router's own AS in the AS path; to accept any destination would form a routing loop. The AS path is also used to make policy decisions. Typically network administrators accept or reject updates based on the presence of certain ASs (or patterns of ASs) in the AS path.

It is important to maintain this AS path information as BGP updates are advertised from one BGP router to another. This is why you cannot in general readvertise BGP information into your IGP at one side of your AS and then readvertise the IGP information back into BGP at the other side: The IGP cannot carry full path information. For this reason, IBGP was invented. You run IBGP internal to your AS to communicate AS paths, in addition to your IGP.

However, OSPF associates a 32-bit external route tag with each destination. This tag can be used to carry additional information across an OSPF AS. In particular, there is enough information to carry the BGP origin (IGP or EGP; see Section 13.3) and an AS path of length 1 within the OSPF Tag field. The formats used in the Tag field for this purpose are defined in [252]. In particular, use of the OSPF Tag field in this way allows you to get rid of IBGP in networks such as the one in Figure 11.11. ASs 3 and 4 are stubs, connected only through the Internet through AS 1. Their routing information can be readvertised into AS 1's OSPF routing and tagged with AS 3 or 4, respectively. When readvertised back into BGP by router C, the proper AS path (terminating at either AS 3 or 4) can then be reconstructed. Similarly router C can advertise a default route into the OSPF AS, which can then be readvertised by BGP into ASs 3 and 4.

Sometimes a destination will be advertised both in OSPF AS-external-LSAs and in IBGP updates. In this case, it is the OSPF-external-LSA that will dictate the path that data traffic will take to the destination. In order to find the IBGP information (that is, the AS path) that matches the route indicated by the AS-external-LSA, [252] requires that routers running both BGP and OSPF set their BGP Identifier and OSPF Router ID to the same value. In a related issue, if OSPF's multipath logic chooses multiple exits from the AS toward the destination, the AS paths associated with these exits must be combined to form an *AS set* (as in BGP aggregation, see Section 13.3) before the destination is advertised to an external BGP peer. Failure to do so can result in routing loops, as described in the appendix to [252].

By using the external-attributes-LSA (Section 7.6), you can carry the entire AS path in OSPF LSAs, in theory replacing IBGP regardless of AS path length. However, this solution has never been deployed.

11.6.2 OSPF/RIP Interaction

In this section, we discuss interactions between RIP and OSPF. The original definition of an Autonomous System was a collection of routers, all running a common IGP. However, over the years, this definition has been liberalized to be "a set of routers all under a common administration." It is now quite common to run both OSPF and RIP in a single AS. Also, as ASs gradually transition from RIP to OSPF, the interactions between the two protocols must be addressed.

The two types of OSPF external metrics, Type 1 external metrics and Type 2 externals, allow for two entirely different strategies, neither requiring metric translation or hand-configured routing filters. We illustrate these two methods by using the network in Figure 11.11, which you should now think of as a central OSPF routing domain (region 1) gluing together three isolated regions (2, 3, and 4) running RIP.

In the first method, we try to make the combined OSPF and RIP AS look like a coherent whole, attempting a seamless integration of RIP and OSPF and calculating paths based on least-hop count. The OSPF metric of each interface is assigned to be 1. When a RIP route of cost x is learned at the edge of the OSPF routing domain, it is re-advertised (or imported) into the OSPF domain as a Type 1 external route of cost x. At the other side of the AS, n hops away from the OSPF router that imported the original RIP route, the route is readvertised into RIP with a cost of $x + n$. This method does not quite give you least-hop routing, because OSPF insists on keeping its routing domain *convex:* The path between any two OSPF routers is forced to remain within the OSPF routing domain, even if there is a shorter hop-count path that exits and reenters the OSPF domain (that is, OSPF→RIP→OSPF). Convexity is a useful property when deploying new features in the OSPF routing domain and is a requirement for deployment of so-called protocol-independent multicast schemes, such as PIM (see Sections 14.4 and 14.5).

The disadvantage of this scheme is, of course, the hop-count metric. Hop count is not very descriptive (see Section 11.3.1), and RIP limits the diameter of the resulting AS to 16 (Section 13.1).

In the second method, we treat the entire OSPF routing domain as a single RIP hop. This method allows you to use a different routing metric, say, delay, inside the OSPF routing domain. And it allows you to circumvent RIP's diameter-16 limitation, something that could previously be done only with risky metric translation. This method employs OSPF Type 2 external metrics. When a RIP route of cost x is learned at one side of the OSPF routing domain, it is readvertised into OSPF as an AS external Type 2 route of cost x. Then, at the other side of the RIP domain, it is readvertised back into RIP with a cost of $x + 1$. Another way to think about this is to consider the OSPF routing domain as "one big router" within the collection of RIP routers.

11.7   OSPF Security

The idea behind OSPF's security mechanisms is to prevent the OSPF routing domain from being attacked by unauthorized routers. For example, a misconfigured router or a router operated by parties with malicious intent may try to join the OSPF routing domain and advertise false information in its OSPF LSAs. Or someone may gain physical access to one of the network segments and intentionally modify OSPF routing information as it flows across the segment. Or that same party may record OSPF protocol packets and replay them at a later time when those same packets would disrupt established OSPF conversations. OSPF's cryptographic authentication is designed to prevent these kinds of attacks.

11.7.1 OSPF Cryptographic Authentication

The idea behind OSPF's cryptographic authentication is simple. All OSPF routers connected to a common network segment share a secret key. When transmitting an OSPF packet onto the segment, an OSPF router signs the packet using the key. This signing is performed in such a way that, if the packet is intercepted by a hostile party, the key cannot be recovered. However, on receiving the packet, legitimate routers easily can determine whether the signature is valid, and a valid signature implies both that the sending router is trusted (that is, the sending router has the key) and that the OSPF packet has not been altered.

Figure 11.12 shows the packet-signing process. An OSPF packet has been built, both header and body, and is ready to be sent onto a given network segment. The sending router picks the primary key for the attached network segment. This key is identified by an 8-bit Key ID and specifies a cryptographic hash algorithm and a shared secret. (Key IDs have only per segment scope; a key with Key ID of 5 on segment 10.1.1.0/24 is different from the key with Key ID of 5 on segment 10.1.2.0/24). The Key ID is then inserted into the OSPF packet header. The cryptographic hash function will produce a hash value of some fixed length; the length of the hash in bytes is also inserted in the OSPF header. Finally, a 32-bit cryptographic sequence number is inserted into the OSPF header for replay protection. The sequence number in the current packet must always be greater than or equal to the sequence number used in the previous packet sent out onto the segment; using a value such as "seconds since the router was booted" is sufficient.

The secret is then appended to the packet, and the cryptographic hash algorithm is run, using the combination packet and secret as input. The hash algorithm produces an output hash of fixed length, which is then written over the secret at the end of the packet. The packet and appended hash are then transmitted onto the network segment.

In particular, Figure 11.12 shows this process when a key with Key ID of 5, using MD5 as the hash algorithm. Following the procedure specified in [216], a 16-byte secret is appended to the OSPF packets and then is overwritten by the 16-byte MD5 cryptographic hash (or message signature).

MD5 is the only cryptographic hash algorithm that is completely specified by the OSPF specification, although other cryptographic hash algorithms may be used. A good cryptographic hash has the following one-way property: It is easy to find the hash for any particular input but difficult to find two inputs that hash to the same value. For OSPF's application of hash functions, this means that it is difficult for an attacker to modify the OSPF packet without the receiver's detecting the modification (see Section 11.7.2). In addition, since OSPF's hash includes a secret key in its input, it is hoped that a good hash function will prevent an attacker from generating a false packet: Not knowing the secret key, the attacker cannot figure out the correct hash value to append to the false packet.

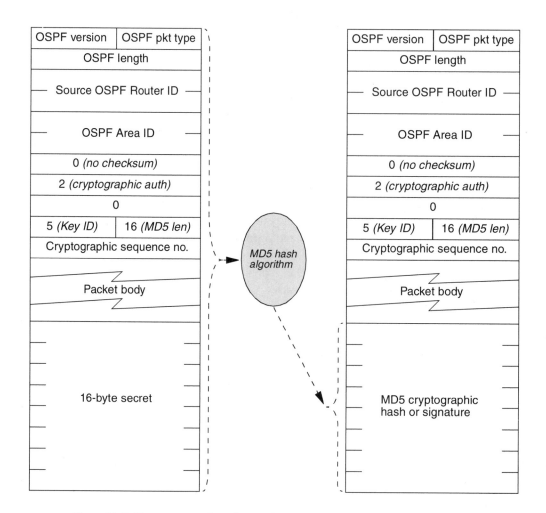

Figure 11.12 Message generation when performing OSPF cryptographic authentication.

Unfortunately it is very difficult to prove the security of various algorithms. In addition, although some algorithms may be secure, the way in which they are used (called a *security protocol*) may be insecure. MD5 has been popular in the Internet community due to the relative speed of generating MD5 hashes. However, some progress has been made in attacking MD5 [225], and so other hash algorithms, such as SHA [182], may be more appropriate. In addition, the security of the security protocol, namely, simply appending the secret to the packet before hashing, has been called into doubt [121], leading to the development of the HMAC construction [185].

11.7.2 Message Verification

An OSPF router running cryptographic authentication on one of its interfaces verifies all packets received on the interface. Verification proceeds as follows. The OSPF header and packet contents have been transmitted in the clear. By looking at the Key ID in the OSPF header, the receiving router knows which key has been used to generate the hash (multiple keys are used when transitioning from one key to another; see Section 11.7.3). To verify that the sending router really does know the key, the receiving router stores the received hash and then regenerates the hash, using its own secret key. If the regenerated hash does not match the received hash, the receiving router rejects the packet as being invalid.

The receiving router now knows that the received packet was generated by a router that has the secret key. However, the packet could have been generated a while ago and then resent later by an attacker to confuse the routing: a replay attack. To guard against this attack, the receiving router looks at the cryptographic sequence number in the OSPF header. As long as this number is greater than or equal to the last sequence number received from the sending router, the received packet is accepted as being both valid and up to date.

Note in Figure 11.12 that the OSPF packet checksum is not calculated when cryptographic authentication is in use, because the checksum is redundant in this case. The cryptographic hash is already guaranteeing that the packet has not been corrupted (either unintentionally, which is what a checksum is designed to detect, or maliciously).

OSPF cryptographic authentication ensures that received packets have been generated by trusted routers, have not been modified, and are up to date. However, since packets are transmitted in the clear, OSPF cryptographic authentication does not provide other typical security functions, such as confidentiality. For example, anyone who gains physical access to any single network segment can collect all OSPF packets transmitted and can build a complete network map of the OSPF routing domain. Encryption of OSPF data must be employed to prevent intruders from gaining this kind of data (see Section 11.7.4).

11.7.3 Key Management

The security of OSPF's cryptographic authentication depends on the following: All of the trusted routers must know the secret key, but this same key must be kept hidden from any attacker. How this property is accomplished falls under the general category of *key management*. First, the key must be chosen in a random fashion. Then the key must be distributed to the trusted routers, without disclosing the key to others. Also, the key must be stored in the routers so that it can be accessed after a router restart but so that it cannot be retrieved by an unauthorized party. All of these issues are difficult to solve, and none are addressed directly by the OSPF specification.

It is assumed that the distribution of keys for OSPF's cryptographic authentication will be done either manually, through a protocol such as Diffie-Hellman, which uses public-key cryptography [66], or through the standard key-management mechanisms being developed by the Internet Engineering Task Force [155].

The one thing that the OSPF specification does address is the changing of keys. The more messages that an attacker sees signed with a particular key, the more likely it is that the attacker will be able to "break the key." (One commonly thinks that the attacker needs to discover the secret key, but it may be possible for the attacker to learn enough to modify and/or originate false messages, without ever learning the key.) So in order to maintain security, you want to change keys every so often. You cannot change all routers' keys simultaneously. Therefore to prevent routing disruption while keys are being changed, OSPF allows for multiple keys to be active at once, identified by Key ID. The switchover to a new key then goes as follows: The new key is installed router by router, leaving the old key in place. As soon as all routers have the new key, the old key can then be deactivated.

11.7.4 Stronger Security

Stronger security has been proposed in *OSPF with Digital Signatures* [179] and [249], along the lines of previous link-state protocol security designs described in [190] and [236]. In this proposal, in addition to the authentication of packet exchanges using algorithms such as OSPF cryptographic authentication, OSPF LSAs carry signatures so that routers can verify the LSAs' integrity as the LSAs are flooded through the OSPF routing domain.

What does this additional security gain you? The OSPF cryptographic authentication of Section 11.7.1 already protects against attackers that gain access to a network segment—these attackers can neither disrupt OSPF protocol exchanges nor impersonate OSPF routers. However, the addition of signatures to LSAs even prevents errors in trusted routers from corrupting LSAs [261]. For example, the OSPF specification says that only the originator of the LSA can flush it from the routing domain. With the addition of signatures to LSAs, when a router receives the directive to flush an LSA (that is, an LSA with Age set to MaxAge), the router can tell whether it was the originator or another router that is attempting to flush the LSA and can ignore the latter. Another example that happened in the ARPANET network is the following: A router became confused about its Router ID and started originating LSAs claiming to be a different router. With the addition of signatures to LSAs, this failure is also detected. Signing of LSAs even allows the certification authority to indicate which network addresses a given router is allowed to advertise (see [179], [261]).

OSPF with Digital Signatures employs public-key cryptography. Each router has a private key and then obtains a certificate for the corresponding public key from a certification authority (see [225] for an explanation of key certificates). The router's public key is then distributed, together with its certificate, throughout the routing domain, using standard OSPF flooding mechanisms. When a router wishes to originate an LSA, it signs the LSA, using the router's private key and the RSA algorithm [224]. As the LSA is flooded, the other routers can verify the LSA's integrity by using the originating router's public key.

As with OSPF cryptographic authentication, OSPF with Digital Signatures protects the routing via authentication. But it does not provide additional security functions, such as confidentiality.

Further Reading

The Simple Book [218] by Marshall Rose is an excellent introduction to SNMP and the management of TCP/IP networks. Schneier's book *Applied Cryptography* [225] is an excellent resource for communications security and authentication issues, including detailed explanations of cryptographic hash functions, public-key cryptography, and key management. A good explanation of security threats to routing protocols is [261]. A companion paper [253] describes a security attack to OSPF that exploits a common bug in OSPF implementations.

Exercises

11.1 Suppose that one of the routers in Figure 5.3 has its **HelloInterval** misconfigured. How would you tell which router is misconfigured: by look- ing at **ospfLsdbTable**? **ospfNbrTable**? OSPF traps?

11.2 Suppose in Figure 11.11 that routers D and F are continually reoriginating their router-LSA. What is going on?

11.3 Suppose that router C in Figure 11.11 is readvertising more BGP information into OSPF than simply a default route but that some of these AS-external-LSAs are continually getting reoriginated. What is going on?

11.4 Describe a scenario in which the replay of old OSPF packets could disrupt current OSPF routing exchanges.

11.5 Specify in detail how SHA and HMAC would be used in OSPF cryptographic authentication.

12

Debugging Routing Problems

Network administrators can be assured that their routing will break every once in a while. Internet routing is not yet a science—many parts of the Internet have been glued together in a hodge-podge fashion. And sometimes the glue comes loose. Fortunately a number of tools are available to help you debug the situation.

In this chapter, we survey the available tools—what they do, how they work, and their strengths and weaknesses. In addition to being used by network administrators, some of these tools may be used by users of the network to diagnose routing problems before reporting them to their ISPs. For example, the first two tools that we examine, **ping** and **traceroute**, are often performed by network users.

The tools in this chapter are specifically for diagnosing IP connectivity at the network layer. Can an IP packet be forwarded from one place to another, and if so, what is the path that the packet is currently taking? If not, what is the network problem that is preventing the forwarding of the packet? Different tools may be necessary to diagnose connectivity at the application layer, such as problems with electronic mail delivery.

When IP connectivity has deliberately been hampered through the deployment of firewalls (Section 1.2), some or all of the tools described in this chapter may fail. To see whether a given tool will work through your firewall, you have to read the "how it works" section for the tool and then consult the documentation provided with your firewall to see whether the firewall will permit the necessary packets to pass through.

All of the tools mentioned in this chapter are for debugging IPv4 routing. However, since the routing architecture of IPv6 is so similar to IPv4 (Section 1.3), it is assumed that similar tools will eventually be available to debug IPv6 routing.

12.1 War Stories

Most routing problems are of the form: I can't get there from here. These are usually pretty easy to pinpoint. A `traceroute` (see Section 12.5) will usually tell you which router is at fault. However, finding out what exactly is wrong with that router is sometimes difficult.

Everyone has a war story to tell. People who are involved in day-to-day operations of Internet Service Providers can tell many of them. I've never been a network operator, but as a developer of router software, I've seen quite a few problems over the years. Here are some examples.

1. *"I loaded new software and lost my Internet connection."* The router that had been reloaded had a point-to-point link to our Internet Service Provider. Everything seemed all right, but the router never populated its routing table with the correct number of entries. Finally, I turned on the router's logging messages and noticed that the router on the other end of the connection was sending routing packets that exceeded my router's MTU. Apparently the point-to-point link's MTU had been changed in the new release.

    Note 1: I happened to be running OSPF over the point-to-point link, which has a tendency to send maximum-sized packets when initializing routing conversations. This is a feature. If the routing had come up, more subtle application problems would have appeared because of the MTU mismatch.

    Note 2: Had I been using a better data-link protocol, the MTU mismatches would not have happened. For example, the PPP data-link protocol [232] negotiates the MTU of the point-to-point link.

• *"The whole subnet loses its Internet connectivity."* Someone had brought up a host that had the same IP address as the subnet's default router. This was not so much a routing problem as an ARP problem. All hosts on the subnet ended up with their ARP caches pointing at the host instead of to the default router.

• *"One of my networks becomes unreachable from the outside world."* Unfortunately that network happens to have my mail server on it, so we're not getting our electronic mail anymore. I could TELNET out to the Internet from another one of my networks, and when I did a `traceroute` back to the network having the problem, the `traceroute` goes all the way to the destination. But it goes to another customer of my provider, not to me! Obviously someone has hijacked one of my network numbers. I call up my provider to complain, and the problem is soon fixed. Undoubtedly my provider started filtering the routing advertisements that it was getting from that customer (see Section 13.7).

- *"My MBONE feed stops, and the router connecting us to the MBONE is continuously crashing."* I can tell from the router's crash dump that the MBONE routing table is much bigger all of a sudden. Soon that is confirmed by messages on the MBONE mailing list. The size of the MBONE's routing updates has grown dramatically, and the MBONE is pretty much unusable. This problem turns out to be a difficult one to solve—there were not many tools for debugging multicast routing at the time, and the instability of the MBONE routers made it difficult to get any data from them. Finally, people tracked down the source of the large updates (an experimental PIM-to-DVMRP translator) by dumping the **mrouted** routing tables and following the bogus routing table entries hop by hop back to their source.

12.2 Finding Tools for Debugging Routing Problems

The remainder of this chapter covers useful routing debugging tools. For each tool, we explain how to use it, how it works, and its strong and weak points.

Most of these tools are publicly available over the Internet. The most common way to find them is to use the search engine in your Web browser. Search engines predating the Web, such as Archie, may give more concise answers when looking specifically for software, although the Archie database is probably not as up to date as the more popular Web search engines. For example, using Archie, I found many sites supplying **ping** software; some of those sites are listed in Figure 12.1. For people who like to do everything from within their Web browsers, Archie servers with HTML interfaces can easily be found.

12.3 Tool Interpretation

IP routing deals with IP addresses, and that is why most of the examples in this chapter display IP addresses as the output of the various debugging tools. However, when you are trying to track down the human who can fix the routing problem you're seeing, a domain name is probably more useful than an IP address. For example, when a **traceroute** (Section 12.5) shows that your packets are being thrown away by the router with address 38.1.3.4, you'd rather know that the router's domain name is **sw.sc.psi.net**. That way, you could check the Web site **www.psi.net** for contact and outage information.

Fortunately most debugging tools do output domain names by default. The tools produce domain names by performing reverse domain name lookups on the IP addresses that they discover. (The Domain Name System, or DNS, was originally

```
archie> find ping
# Search type: sub, Domain: northamerica.
# Your queue position: 1
# Estimated time for completion: 5 seconds.
working... =

Host ftp.ripe.net     (193.0.0.195)
Last updated 02:49 23 Apr 1996

    Location: /tools
       FILE      -r--r--r--    54140 bytes  07:12 15 Mar 1996  ping.tar.Z

Host qiclab.scn.rain.com    (204.188.34.97)
Last updated 02:58 15 Apr 1996

    Location: /pub/network
       FILE      -rw-rw-r--    37517 bytes  02:18  4 Dec 1995  ping.tar.Z

Host ftp.cerf.net    (192.102.249.9)
Last updated 02:56 19 Apr 1996

    Location: /pub/software/unix/networking
       FILE      -rw-r--r--    36444 bytes  20:00 13 Apr 1995  ping.tar.Z

Host ftp.uunet.ca    (142.77.1.254)
Last updated 02:56 19 Apr 1996

    Location: /pub/software/Unix/utils
       FILE      -rw-r--r--     9087 bytes  20:00  1 May 1992  ping.tar.Z
```

Figure 12.1 Sample of sites supplying **ping** software.

designed to map ASCII domain names into IP addresses; the reverse mapping was introduced later, using the IN-ADDR domain of the DNS [163].) There are times, however, when you might want to skip the reverse domain name lookup—for one thing, this makes the tools run faster. For UNIX-based tools, the **-n** command line option usually turns off reverse domain name lookups in favor of the raw IP addresses. This is how many of the figures in this chapter were produced.

Many operating systems supply an application that performs DNS lookups. For example, on UNIX, you can use the command **nslookup**. After typing the **nslookup** command in a UNIX shell, you obtain a prompt. If you enter an ASCII domain name at the prompt, **nslookup** prints the corresponding IP address; if you enter an IP address, the domain name resulting from the reverse lookup will be printed.

On many operating systems, you can get contact information for a domain name by using the **whois** command, an implementation of the whois protocol [92], which looks up records in the Network Information Center (NIC) database. For example, the command **whois mci.net** on a UNIX workstation will produce the contact information for MCI Internet Services. The protocol can also be used to find the contact information for a particular AS number. For example, **whois "as 1"** produces the contact information for the owner of AS 1: BBN Planet. Whois can also be used to look up information on IP addresses, people, and so on; the command **whois help** gives details on the correct syntax for these types of queries.

12.4 The ping Tool

You can use **ping** to verify connectivity between your host and a given Internet destination. Simply type **ping** *destination_host* (specified as either a domain name or an IP address), and **ping** sends a packet (called a **ping** packet) to the destination and tells you whether the destination responds. An example is shown in Figure 12.2.

```
$ ping -s -n 198.49.45.10
PING 198.49.45.10 (198.49.45.10): 56 data bytes
64 bytes from 198.49.45.10: icmp_seq=0. time=63. ms
64 bytes from 198.49.45.10: icmp_seq=1. time=60. ms
64 bytes from 198.49.45.10: icmp_seq=2. time=139. ms
64 bytes from 198.49.45.10: icmp_seq=3. time=77. ms
64 bytes from 198.49.45.10: icmp_seq=4. time=74. ms
64 bytes from 198.49.45.10: icmp_seq=5. time=66. ms
64 bytes from 198.49.45.10: icmp_seq=6. time=86. ms
64 bytes from 198.49.45.10: icmp_seq=7. time=69. ms
64 bytes from 198.49.45.10: icmp_seq=8. time=107. ms
^C
----198.49.45.10 PING Statistics----
9 packets transmitted, 9 packets received, 0% packet loss
round-trip (ms)   min/avg/max = 60/82/139
```

Figure 12.2 Sample output of **ping**.

If the destination does not respond but an ICMP error response is received instead, the ICMP error code is displayed. This may help pinpoint the problem. An ICMP TTL Exceeded error code indicates a probable routing loop, whereas an ICMP Destination Unreachable may identify an intermediate router with an incomplete routing table.

You can also specify an IP multicast group as the *destination_host*, if you have a multicast-capable host. In this case, every **ping** packet will elicit multiple responses, one from each member of the multicast group, as shown in Figure 12.3. This allows you to find all the members of a particular multicast group. Similarly using a broadcast address as destination in the **ping** command allows you to see all the IP hosts attached to a given IP subnet.

```
$ ping -s -n 224.3.2.17
PING 224.3.2.17 (224.3.2.17): 56 data bytes
64 bytes from 194.43.2.17: icmp_seq=0. time=1. ms
64 bytes from 18.10.16.22: icmp_seq=0. time=69. ms
64 bytes from 128.69.22.10: icmp_seq=0. time=106. ms
64 bytes from 194.43.2.17: icmp_seq=1. time=1. ms
64 bytes from 18.10.16.22: icmp_seq=1. time=88. ms
64 bytes from 128.69.22.10: icmp_seq=1. time=144. ms
64 bytes from 194.43.2.17: icmp_seq=2. time=2. ms
64 bytes from 18.10.16.22: icmp_seq=2. time=67. ms
64 bytes from 128.69.22.10: icmp_seq=2. time=114. ms
64 bytes from 194.43.2.17: icmp_seq=3. time=1. ms
64 bytes from 18.10.16.22: icmp_seq=3. time=58. ms
64 bytes from 128.69.22.10: icmp_seq=3. time=157. ms
^C
----224.3.2.17 PING Statistics----
4 packets transmitted, 12 packets received, 3.0 times amplification
round-trip (ms)  min/avg/max = 1/67/157
```

Figure 12.3 Sending **ping** to a multicast address.

If you look around, you will find an infinite number of variations on the basic **ping** program. Some **ping** programs, like the one in Figure 12.2, can be used to indicate the quality of the connection between your host and the destination. These programs send a continuous stream of packets, telling you how long it takes to receive the responses (thereby giving you round-trip delay) and what percentage of packets are responded to (giving you an idea of packet-loss rates).

Other common options in **ping** programs include the ability to specify

- The number of packets to send and the rate at which to send them.

- The size of packets sent.

- The data contents of the **ping** packet. This may allow you to uncover data-sensitivity problems in certain network paths. Also, the **ping** program may allow you to randomly vary the size and contents of the **ping** packet.

- One or more intermediate hops through which the **ping** packets should go on the way to the destination. This is useful in several situations. Instead of debugging connectivity between your own host and a destination, you may want to debug connectivity between two remote hosts. In this case, use **ping** with one remote host as intermediate hop and the other as *destination_host*. Also, you may encounter routing problems such that you cannot reach a destination *Y* but you can reach *X* and they can then reach *Y*. This can be determined by pinging *Y* with an intermediate hop of *X*, after a simple **ping** of *Y* fails.

- The ability to report the path the **ping** packet takes through the Internet.

How It Works

The **ping** tool is implemented using ICMP (see Section 1.2 and [194]). The **ping** packets are ICMP Echo Requests (ICMP type 8). Any host or router receiving an ICMP Echo Request addressed to one of its IP addresses responds with an ICMP Echo Reply (ICMP type 0). As with other kinds of IP packets, if a host or router is unable to deliver the ICMP Echo Request to the addressed destination, an ICMP error message is returned.

ICMP Echo Requests contain a Sequence Number field that enables you to match received ICMP Echo Replies to the proper Echo Request, when a sequence of pings is being transmitted. The data portion of the ICMP Echo Request must be returned unchanged in the Echo Reply. This enables the **ping** program to store such things as timestamps in the packet, for later calculation of round-trip delays.

Forcing **ping** packets through one or more intermediate hops is done by inserting an IP loose-source route option in the ICMP Echo Request's IP header. Recording the path a **ping** packet takes is done through the inclusion of an IP record-route option. Because of size limitation in the IP packet header (60 bytes), a maximum of nine hops can be recorded.

Strong Points

Support for **ping** is ubiquitous. All sorts of machines have IP in them these days—networked printers, disk arrays, in-circuit emulators, and so on. Since ICMP support is also required of all IP implementations, these devices all reply to **ping**. In fact, using **ping** on the device is always one of the first things you do after installation to see that the device has been properly configured. Available on virtually every operating system, **ping** programs support a variety of useful options.

If you are new to network programming, modifying a **ping** program to meet your special needs is a good place to start. Also, **ping** is the one tool that remains essentially unchanged when debugging multicast routing problems.

When you are having intermittent routing problems, using **ping** to test connection quality can uncover patterns that lead to the cause of the problem. For example, at one time, connections through a particular ISP were suffering performance problems. A continuous **ping** to destinations whose paths traversed the provider showed that **ping** times increased dramatically every 90 seconds. This was found to be an architectural constant in the routing protocol employed by the ISP and uncovered problems in the routing protocol's implementation provided by the ISP's router vendor (see [78]).

Weak Points

If the destination is unreachable, **ping** returns only limited information: received ICMP errors. In trying to pinpoint where the routing problem is, you are reduced to pinging intermediate destinations. However, you may not be able to determine the intermediate hops. Even if you can, each of them may be reachable while your destination still may not be (see the earlier discussion of intermediate hops).

When **ping** to a destination succeeds, it cannot be relied on to give you the route your data packets are taking, as **ping**'s record-route feature is limited to nine hops. In addition, you have the common problem that the act of measurement changes the system's behavior (see [97]): Using IP options forces the ICMP Echo packet off the main forwarding path in many vendors' routers, possibly changing the path the packet will take.

All these problems are solved by the **traceroute** diagnostic. This tool is covered in the next section.

12.5   The **traceroute** Tool

The **traceroute** program is usually the best tool for diagnosing routing problems. Originally developed on UNIX systems, it is now available on many other host and router platforms as well. Given a destination (domain name or IP address, as usual), **traceroute** traces the routers on the path to the destination, stopping when the destination is reached, an ICMP Destination Unreachable is received, or the maximum number of router hops has been exceeded (the default is 30, but it can be overridden with the **-m** option). The **traceroute** program was written by Van Jacobson at Lawrence Berkeley Laboratories. An excellent UNIX man page is available describing **traceroute**'s usage and options [247].

The **traceroute** program probes each successive hop along the path to the destination. By default, each hop is probed three times (this can be changed with the **-q** option). The results of the probes for a given hop are printed on a single line, with the hop number, the router at that hop (printed as a domain name or as an IP address if the **-n** option is given), and the round-trip delay encountered by each of the probes.

Figure 12.4 shows a sample **traceroute**. The output shows the path to 128.9.0.32, going through routers 132.236.200.1, 132.236.230.1, and so on.

Two other options are commonly available in **traceroute** tools.

- You can trace the route between two remote hosts by using the **-g** option. For example, to trace the route between 128.9.0.32 and 198.49.45.10, you can give the command **traceroute -g 128.9.0.32 198.49.45.10** from any Internet host.

- You can trace paths for traffic of differing IP Type of Service (TOS; see Section 1.2) by using the **-t** option.

When a **traceroute** probe fails for a given hop, instead of a round-trip time, an indication of the failure is displayed. Table 12.1 lists the most common failure indications.

```
% traceroute -n ftp.isi.edu
traceroute to venera.ISI.EDU (128.9.0.32), 30 hops max, 40 byte packets
  1   132.236.200.1   1.535 ms    1.388 ms    1.331 ms
  2   132.236.230.1   2.71 ms     2.746 ms    2.823 ms
  3   132.236.100.10  4.552 ms    4.711 ms    4.185 ms
  4   169.130.61.9    5.504 ms    4.907 ms    5.63 ms
  5   169.130.1.41    6.987 ms    6.348 ms    7.449 ms
  6   169.130.30.2    6.623 ms    6.816 ms    6.427 ms
  7   169.130.1.94    16.885 ms   17.226 ms   17.41 ms
  8   144.228.20.8    17.482 ms   18.624 ms   17.489 ms
  9   144.228.10.42   142.41 ms   19.593 ms   197.452 ms
 10   192.41.177.180  21.515 ms   21.618 ms   20.867 ms
 11   204.70.74.117   22.082 ms   20.125 ms   21.919 ms
 12   204.70.74.65    22.609 ms   21.164 ms   24.833 ms
 13   204.70.4.161    90.883 ms   90.757 ms   90.151 ms
 14   204.70.2.130    92.739 ms   92.522 ms   91.673 ms
 15   204.70.48.6     95.613 ms   95.085 ms   95.193 ms
 16   204.102.78.1    95.317 ms   94.065 ms   96.339 ms
 17   128.9.16.1      100.846 ms  98.017 ms   98.266 ms
 18   128.9.0.32      95.757 ms   96.377 ms   101.955 ms
```

Figure 12.4 Sample output of **traceroute**.

Table 12.1 Common Failure Indications of **traceroute**

Failure Indication	Meaning
*	No response was received. The default period to wait for a response is 3 seconds and can be changed with the **-w** option.
!H	An ICMP Host Unreachable indication was received in response to the query.
!N	An ICMP Net Unreachable was received in response. These should be less and less likely, as ICMP Host Unreachables are now preferred [12].
!	Response from the final destination has TTL set to 1 or less. This likely indicates a TCP/IP bug common in networking stacks derived from BSD UNIX 4.2 and 4.3 networking code. In this bug, ICMP errors are sent using the IP TTL from the packet causing the error. When this bug is encountered, **traceroute** has to probe twice the number of hops in order to get an answer from the destination.
An IP address or domain name	Identifies a responder to the probe packet different from the previous response. This means that over the multiple probes for the nth hop, the identity of the nth hop has changed. This can be caused by routing changes or by routers' doing multipath routing (see Section 1.2).

The **traceroute** program fails when the ultimate destination is not reached. Such failures commonly end with the reception of an ICMP Host or Net Unreachable or with probe failures until the maximum hop count is received, as shown in Figure 12.5.

```
% traceroute -n 132.236.199.65
 1   153.161.10.254   5 ms   5 ms   4 ms
 2   153.161.40.240   6 ms   9 ms   4 ms
 3   153.161.1.1   8 ms   7 ms   7 ms
 4   38.1.22.15   670 ms   657 ms   699 ms
 5   38.1.3.4   677 ms   600 ms   179 ms
 6   149.20.64.1   204 ms   130 ms   256 ms
 7   * * *
 8   * * *
 9   * * *
10   * * *
11   * * *
12   * *
```

Figure 12.5 Sample output of **traceroute**, showing probe failures.

Another common failure is the repetition of one or more router hops, which indicates a routing loop. For more examples of **traceroute** problem diagnosis, see the **traceroute** UNIX man page [247].

You can find *traceroute gateways* on the Web by typing **traceroute** into your favorite Web search engine. These gateways are servers on which you are allowed to execute the **traceroute** command remotely. You enter the **traceroute** command options on a Web form, and the results are displayed in your Web browser. The result is the path that packets would take from the server to your machine or from the server to any other destination you specify. You can also use the **traceroute** gateway to trace the path of your host to any destination, by using the **-g** option to **traceroute**. This option is useful if you do not have **traceroute** installed on your host.

Van Jacobson has recently extended **traceroute**, creating a more sophisticated tool called **pathchar** [118]. In addition to finding the path to a given destination, the **pathchar** tool analyzes the path's performance by estimating the bandwidth, propagation delay, packet loss, and queuing delay of each link in the path.

How It Works

A **traceroute** probe is a UDP packet addressed to the destination host and specifying an (ideally) unused UDP port. A base UDP port of 33434 is used but can be overridden with the **-p** option. The **traceroute** program first sends a set of probes with IP TTL set to 1, then sends a set with IP TTL set to 2, and so on. The nth set of probes is sent with IP TTL set to n and a UDP port set to the base UDP port plus n. These should elicit either an ICMP TTL Exceeded from the nth hop router or an ICMP Port Unreachable from the destination host. Tracing the path between two remote hosts is done by inserting an IP loose-source route option in the UDP probe's IP header.

The size of the UDP packets used by **traceroute** is so small (38 bytes) that IP fragmentation problems should not be encountered. However, the size of the probes can be changed on invocation by specifying the probe size in bytes after the destination host.

In order to estimate the performance of each hop in the path, the **pathchar** tool sends UDP packets of varying sizes for each IP TTL value. By examining the different response times to these variable-sized probes, link characteristics, such as bandwidth, propagation delay, and queuing delay, can be deduced after some rather complicated mathematics [117].

Strong Points

The **traceroute** program is the most powerful tool for diagnosing routing problems. It depends only on something that is required in the main forwarding path of all IP routers and hosts—TTL processing.

Also, **traceroute** is quite robust. For example, it cleverly flags implementation bugs, such as the BSD UNIX 4.3 TCP/IP bug that makes destination hosts look twice as far away as they in fact are (see the ! failure indication in Table 12.1). As another example, incrementing the UDP port on each hop may circumvent port collisions at the destination host (with the side effect of insertion of phantom hops).

Weak Points

Even though TTL processing is required in the main path of every IP router and host, it may still be broken, with the router/host remaining more or less functional. For example, a common error is to forward packets after decrementing the TTL to 0 instead of responding with an ICMP TTL Exceeded. Routers exhibiting this error will be omitted from the **traceroute** path, with the next-hop router instead appearing twice.

Some routers may not send ICMP errors or may not send ICMP TTL Exceeded messages. These routers will also not show up in a **traceroute**. Other routers may rate-limit the number of ICMP messages that they generate; these routers appear in **traceroute** output only intermittently.

Some routers do not put large enough TTLs in their ICMP error responses, and so the ICMP responses do not get back to the **traceroute**-executing host. The BSD UNIX 4.3 bug described in Table 12.1 is in this category—the TTL in the ICMP error response is set to the remaining TTL in the offending packet.

A **traceroute** can be difficult to interpret when routers are doing multipath, since there is then no good way to associate consecutive hops. Also, **traceroute** does not work for IP multicast, because ICMP errors, and in particular ICMP TTL Exceeded and ICMP Port Unreachables, are not returned in response to IP multicast datagrams. Instead a totally separate mechanism for multicast, called multicast traceroute, or **mtrace**, has been developed (see Section 12.11).

12.6   SNMP MIBs

SNMP [226] is the standard protocol used to monitor and control Internet devices. In SNMP, management data within an Internet device is organized into various *Management Information Bases* (MIBs) [144]. There is no shortage of MIBs. MIBs exist for Ethernet interfaces, printers, uninterruptible power supplies, and you name it. In the desire for a more manageable Internet, the IETF has mandated the creation of a MIB for each of its standard protocols. Also, many vendors have created large proprietary MIBs for the management of their own products.

One way to debug routing problems is to dump routing tables and examine routing protocol state through SNMP. The following routing-related MIBs can be used for this purpose.

- *MIB-II, documented in RFC 1213 [143].* This is the granddaddy of all Internet MIBs and is the one that you can almost be assured that any Internet device implements. This MIB contains IP and ICMP statistics, such as packets received and packets forwarded. It also contains ARP mappings, which can be used to indicate which neighboring IP hosts and routers the device is talking to—this has been used for automatic network map discovery in some network management products. MIB-II also contains a routing table, although one that has been superseded by later MIBs. However, in the name of backward compatibility, MIBs or pieces of MIBs never go away even when superseded. So there are plenty of implementations of MIB-II routing tables still out there.

- *The IP Forwarding MIB, documented in RFC 1354 [10].* This provides a way to dump a device's IP routing table. It improves on the routing table in MIB-II by allowing multiple routes per IP destination. Also, a separate set of paths can be represented for each Internet Type of Service (TOS). However, this routing table does not allow representation of all routes possible in CIDR routing and so has also been superseded.

- *The recently revised IP Forwarding MIB.* The resulting RFC 2096 [11] replaces RFC 1354. This MIB now can express CIDR routes; two routing entries, both having the same network address by differing masks, can now be distinguished.

- *The OSPF MIB, documented in RFC 1850 [14].* This is a large MIB, with more than 100 variables. You can use this MIB to examine the OSPF link-state database; general OSPF statistics, such as the number of routing calculations performed; and the state of OSPF areas, interfaces, and neighbors. This MIB can also be used to monitor and configure the OSPF extensions, including MOSPF.

- *The BGP MIB, documented in RFC 1657 [262].* This MIB contains a BGP router's AS number, the state of its BGP peers, and the BGP routing information that has been received from each of the peers.

- *The RIPv2 MIB, documented in RFC 1724 [150].* This MIB provides RIP statistics, monitoring and configuration data for each RIP interface, and (optionally) information about each RIP neighbor.

- *A MIB developed for DVMRP [243].* This MIB allows the monitoring of the DVMRP protocol via SNMP. The contents of the DVMRP routing table can be examined, along with information about DVMRP physical interfaces, tunnels, and neighbors. The administrative boundaries of the DVMRP routing domain can also be examined.

- *An experimental MIB for IGMP [141].* This MIB allows you to monitor the state of IGMP within a multicast router. Two tables are provided. The first table shows interfaces on which the router is sending Host Membership Queries and at what rate. The second table shows the group membership of the attached network segments, including the last reporting host and the time of the report.

- *An experimental multicast forwarding MIB [142].* This MIB is the multicast analog of the IP Forwarding MIB. For each [source net, multicast group] combination, this MIB shows the interface on which matching datagrams should be received and the set of interfaces out which the datagram should be forwarded.

How It Works

SNMP is a query-response protocol. SNMP packets are encoded in a dialect of ASN.1 [113]. There are five separate SNMP packet types: GetRequest, GetNextRequest, GetResponse, SetRequest, and Trap. Requests for specific management data are accomplished with GetRequest, with the answers returned by GetResponse. A MIB can be linearly searched using GetNextRequest (for example, this is how you would dump a routing table using SNMP; see Figure 12.6), and SetRequest is used to configure devices; both of these packet types also elicit GetResponses. Traps are unsolicited messages sent by Internet devices as a result of an event (for example, a router interface going out of service). Traps are somewhat controversial within the SNMP community and are used sparingly.

Management data in an Internet device are represented as variables. Variables have ASCII names, such as `ipCidrRouteIfIndex`, and Object Identifiers, or OIDs, such as 1.3.6.1.2.1.4.24.4.1.5. OIDs and their values are also coded in ASN.1. When multiple instances of data exist within a device—for example, separate routes in a routing table—they are identified by a combination of OID and instance (see Figure 12.6). Instances can be thought of as indexes into a table of entries.

Variables are organized into groups and tables, which in turn are collected into Management Information Bases, or MIBs. The collection of MIBs is further organized into a tree structure, which is reflected in the variables' OIDs (see Figure 11.1). MIBs are

```
$ get-next ipCidrRouteIfIndex
1.3.6.1.2.1.4.24.4.1.5.0.0.0.0.0.0.0.0.0.128.1.1.3 1
1.3.6.1.2.1.4.24.4.1.5.128.1.1.0.255.255.255.0.0.128.1.1.10 1
1.3.6.1.2.1.4.24.4.1.5.128.1.3.0.255.255.255.0.0.128.1.3.10 2
1.3.6.1.2.1.4.24.4.1.5.128.41.0.0.255.255.0.0.0.128.1.1.4 1
1.3.6.1.2.1.4.24.4.1.5.128.41.10.0.255.255.255.0.0.128.1.1.254 1
1.3.6.1.2.1.4.24.4.1.5.128.41.12.0.255.255.255.0.0.128.1.1.254 1
1.3.6.1.2.1.4.24.4.1.5.192.67.0.0.255.255.140.0.0.128.1.1.4 1
1.3.6.1.2.1.4.24.4.1.5.192.67.1.0.255.255.255.0.0.128.1.3.254 2
1.3.6.1.2.1.4.24.4.1.5.192.67.2.0.255.255.255.0.0.128.1.3.254 2
1.3.6.1.2.1.4.24.4.1.5.193.28.84.0.255.255.255.0.0.128.1.3.1 2
```

Figure 12.6 Dumping a routing table using SNMP's get-next function; **ipCidrRouteIfIndex** gives the outgoing interface for the entry; the next hop is one of the indexes.

documented using a specific syntax that allows them to be converted by MIB compilers into formats easily processed by network management applications.

For more information on SNMP and the structure of MIBs, see Section 11.1.

Strong Points

The IETF mandates that MIBs be developed for each standard Internet protocol. As a result, many MIBs have been defined, potentially making a great deal of data accessible via SNMP.

SNMP provides a vendor-independent way to get data out of an Internet device. For example, no matter how a vendor has organized its routing table internally, if the IP forwarding MIB has been implemented, the routing table can be dumped in a standard manner.

At this point, almost all Internet devices support SNMP. Although support for specific MIBs varies, almost all devices include an implementation of MIB-II. Many public-domain SNMP tools also are available.

Weak Points

Vendor support for MIBs beyond MIB-II is spotty. Although the IETF can mandate that MIBs be developed for all protocols, it cannot force vendors to implement the MIBs. For example, a poll of OSPF implementations indicated that only a third of them supported the OSPF MIB.

On the other hand, when MIBs are implemented, they often contain so much data that it can be difficult to find the piece of information you are looking for. Browsing a MIB can be frustrating, due to the cryptic nature of variable names and OIDs. Both of these problems can be solved via the implementation of MIB-based tools, as described in Section 12.7.

Operations, such as dumping a routing table via SNMP, can be very slow and cumbersome, due to the fact that an SNMP packet exchange is required for each routing table entry. This issue has been addressed by SNMPv2, which, however, is not yet implemented in most Internet devices.

Neither SNMP nor SNMPv2 has very strong security provisions. For that reason, vendors do not always implement SNMP SetRequests in their products. Even if SetRequests are implemented, network administrators often disable the SetRequests in order to plug an obvious security hole. In fact, for security reasons, administrators often block SNMP read access to part or all of an Internet device's management information base. These limitations to SNMP read and write access can limit the usefulness of SNMP as a debugging tool, especially when you are trying to debug a device that is owned and managed by someone else.

Routing diagnostic information collected from a device using SNMP may not reflect the true behavior of the device. Processing of SNMP GetRequests and GetNextRequests is a separate code path from the device's forwarding and routing protocol processing and therefore is subject to measurement errors. In particular, GetNextRequest is difficult to interpret and implement for some tables when multiple indexes are involved, and so MIB walks (of which a routing table dump is a portion) are sometimes wrong.

SNMP only works when the management station can communicate with the Internet device. If a routing problem prevents the management station from sending packets to the device, SNMP cannot be used to debug problems within the device.

12.7   MIB-Based Tools

A multitude of SNMP-based tools exist. These tools automate the process of getting SNMP data out of Internet devices, organizing and displaying the returned data in a form that is better suited for human consumption.

Network management stations fall into this category. Typically they are window-based applications running on PC or UNIX platforms; they monitor devices using standard MIBs, such as MIB-II. Often a network map is part of the user interface, with the color of map components reflecting their current status (such as green for OK and red for out of service). These applications also often include MIB browsers, which allow you to search through MIBs, based on the variables' ASCII names (instead of their more obscure ASN.1 representations). MIB compilers are also often included, allowing you to add additional MIBs to the browser. Standard dialog boxes may display information, such as interface statistics, in an easy-to-understand manner, although display of routing-related data is usually restricted to a dump of the device's routing table.

MIB-based tools can be built fairly easily to accomplish specific tasks. A couple of examples follow.

- At the 1991 INTEROP, an OSPF demonstration was given. The INTEROP backbone network consisted of OSPF routers from 11 vendors, providing complete connectivity between show booths and between the show and the Internet (see Section 3.4 for more details). The state of the backbone was monitored from a UNIX network management station. An additional dialog box in the NMS application was created for the demo, which displayed the OSPF link-state database checksum (OSPF MIB variable **ospfAreaLsaCksumSum**, see Section 11.5) for all OSPF routers in the network simultaneously. This display gave a quick indication of whether OSPF databases were synchronized.

- A UNIX program called **ospfquery** [204] has been written by Tom Pusateri. This program organizes the information in the OSPF MIB into easy-to-read screens, with command line options to show OSPF interfaces, neighbors, and the link-state database (see Figure 12.7). In addition, **ospfquery** dumps and displays RFC 1354's IP Forwarding MIB in a tabular form.

```
% ospfquery -n

Router Id          Nbr IP Addr      State     Pri Events    RetransQLen
------------------------------------------------------------------------
128.111.100.1     128.111.100.1     2 Way     1    2         0
128.111.100.3     128.111.100.3     2 Way     1    2         0
128.111.100.4     128.111.100.4     2 Way     1    2         0
128.111.100.5     128.111.100.5     2 Way     1    4         0
192.107.120.1     128.111.100.10    2 Way     1    20        0
192.107.120.2     128.111.100.11    2 Way     1    22        0
128.111.100.20    128.111.100.20    2 Way     1    4         0
128.111.100.30    128.111.100.30    2 Way     1    2         0
128.111.100.40    128.111.100.40    2 Way     1    2         0
128.111.100.50    128.111.100.50    2 Way     1    4         0
128.111.100.60    128.111.100.60    2 Way     1    2         0
128.111.100.70    128.111.100.70    2 Way     1    4         0
128.111.100.80    128.111.100.80    Full      1    6         0
128.111.100.94    128.111.100.94    Full      1    6         0
```

Figure 12.7 Examination of OSPF neighbor status, using the **ospfquery** program (excerpted from the **ospfquery** UNIX man page).

How They Work

MIB tools for specific tasks can be built fairly easily, using publicly available SNMP programs such as CMU's SNMP toolkit, combining them with user interface and scripting libraries, such as Tk/Tcl. On the other hand, general-purpose SNMP network management stations can be significant development tasks, typically using commercial databases and interfaces to other management protocol stacks.

Strong Points

The main advantage of SNMP tools is their vendor independence. SNMP tools can provide nice graphical configuration and monitoring tools for specific applications, which can be used with any device that implements standard SNMP MIBs.

Weak Points

SNMP tools inherit some of SNMP's problems: Many SNMP MIBs are not widely implemented; write and even sometimes read access to MIBs may be restricted due to security concerns; SNMP data can suffer from measurement errors; and SNMP GetNextRequest is sometimes incorrectly implemented. Also, dumping large volumes of data, such as large routing tables via SNMP, can be extremely slow.

12.8 Network Analyzers

Network analyzers are tools that collect packets as they are transmitted on one or more network segments. These tools are used to troubleshoot and monitor networks, as well as while developing and debugging protocols.

Network analyzers usually display a summary of packets in real time. For example, a single line may be printed for each packet, displaying IP source and destination addresses, IP protocol number, and the time the packet was received (Figure 12.8). Complete packet contents may be saved to memory or disk, allowing later examination in more detail. Often an analyzer understands how to decode packets of a given protocol into fields to make analysis of packet contents easier. Sometimes an analyzer will allow you to write your own parsing routines for your favorite protocol. For example, I wrote OSPF parsing routines for the Network General Sniffer to help initial debugging of the OSPF protocol.

Analyzers usually allow you to specify filters for packet collection and/or display, allowing you to restrict your view to only those packets you are interested in.

Some analyzers will allow you to construct packets for transmission onto the segment or to play back collected packets. The latter capability can be very useful when trying to reconstruct a failure.

Some analyzers can perform in a distributed fashion. Collection points can be established on multiple remote segments, with the gathered packet sent to a central location for correlation and display.

Some analyzers can also perform more intelligent functions, verifying checksums, checking for common errors (such as illegal broadcast addresses), or associating all packets belonging to a given TCP connection.

```
SUMMARY  Delta T  Destination  Source         Summary
   21    2.2732   01005E000005 Wllflt00347D   OSPF Hello
   24    0.5571   Wllflt00347D ACC    410413  OSPF Database Description
   25    0.3976   ACC    410413 Wllflt00347D  OSPF Database Description
   26    0.3114   01005E000005 WstDig627A18   OSPF Hello
   29    5.4289   Wllflt00347D ACC    410413  OSPF Database Description
   30    0.0047   ACC    410413 Wllflt00347D  OSPF Database Description
   31    0.1538   Wllflt00347D ACC    410413  OSPF Database Description
   32    0.1673   ACC    410413 Wllflt00347D  OSPF Database Description
   33    0.2269   01005E000005 BridgeA00E44   OSPF Hello
   36    0.7030   BridgeA00E44 ACC    410413  OSPF Database Description
   37    0.0031   ACC    410413 BridgeA00E44  OSPF Database Description
   38    0.0011   ACC    410413 BridgeA00E44  OSPF Database Description
   39    0.1561   BridgeA00E44 ACC    410413  OSPF Database Description
   40    0.0017   ACC    410413 BridgeA00E44  OSPF Database Description
   41    0.0039   01005E000005 BridgeA00E44   OSPF Link State Update
   42    0.1474   01005E000006 WstDig627A18   OSPF Link State Ack


- - - - - - - - - - - - - - - Frame 42 - - - - - - - - - - - - - - - - - -


SUMMARY  Delta T  Destination  Source         Summary
   42    0.1474   01005E000006 WstDig627A18   OSPF Link State Ack

OSPF:  ----- OSPF Header -----
OSPF:
OSPF:  Version = 2
OSPF:  Type = 5
OSPF:  Length = 64
OSPF:  Source Router ID = 10.0.0.5
OSPF:  Area ID = 0.0.0.0
OSPF:  Checksum = 0x971e
OSPF:  Authentication type = 1
OSPF:  Authentication data = 4152454130303030
OSPF:
OSPF:  ----- OSPF Link State Acknowledgment Packet -----
OSPF:
OSPF:  2 acknowlegment(s) follow.
OSPF:  Each displayed as (type,id,adv,seq,xsum,age).
OSPF:
OSPF:  (1,2.160.14.67,2.160.14.67,0x800000bb,0x455,1)
OSPF:  (2,10.0.0.2,2.160.14.67,0x8000000b,0x160e,1)
```

Figure 12.8 Example of a packet trace from a Network General Sniffer.

Network analyzers can be implemented as dedicated platforms or as add-on software for existing hosts. Many network analyzers are available, some commercially and some in the public domain. A small sample of the available analyzers follows.

- *The* **tcpdump** *program.* Freely available for UNIX systems, this program collects packets seen on one of the UNIX system's attached network segments, printing the headers of those packets matching a Boolean expression given on the program command line. The program understands the format of ARP, TCP, and UDP packets and has been extended to understand the format of most routing protocols' packets.

- *The* **etherfind** *program.* Available on SunOS 4.x, this program allows collection of specified packets, displaying one collected packet per line of program output. A better analyzer, called **snoop**, is available in SunOS 5.x (also called Solaris 2.x).

- *LANwatch.* This add-on software turns a DOS platform into a network analyzer. It features real-time display of captured packets, flexible filtering, and an examine mode to display packet contents in more detail. LANwatch is available commercially from FTP Software.

- *Network General Sniffer.* This self-contained, portable analyzer is available in standalone or distributed configurations. Besides the usual analyzer functions, it supports LAN diagnostics and traffic generation and allows people to write their own protocol interpreters. It is available commercially from Network General.

How They Work

Most network analyzers are implemented as either dedicated platforms or software add-ons to existing hosts (such as PCs or UNIX workstations). By putting one or more of their LAN interfaces into promiscuous mode, they can receive all packets being transmitted on the attached network segment. Network analyzers for point-to-point media (such as synchronous serial lines) are generally implemented with pass-through or Y cables that allow the monitor to receive all transmitted packets in a transparent fashion.

Any host or router implementing the variables in RFC 1757's Remote Network Monitoring (RMON) [256] MIB can also be used to capture and store packets for later analysis. Network management stations or other MIB-based tools can then be used to implement the display and filtering functions of a typical network analyzer.

Strong Points

For debugging complex protocol interactions, network analyzers are invaluable. We held numerous bake-offs during the development of the OSPF protocol; all the various implementors got together for several days of testing. When two implementations were not interoperating, we invariably used a network analyzer to capture the packets that were being sent. This technique uncovered numerous implementation bugs, as well as a few protocol bugs. After a bake-off, I often went home with a large collection of packet traces that I used later to analyze OSPF protocol performance.

Network analyzers are used extensively in any multivendor testing situation. For example, the INTEROP ShowNet is typically constructed so that a network analyzer can be patched onto any given network segment. Typical complaints, such as "Booth 24 is not getting routing advertisements," are quickly resolved by the Network Operations Center.

Watching protocol exchanges with a network analyzer is a terrific way to learn how a protocol works. This is the reason that we have included many network analyzer traces in this book.

Weak Points

Network analyzers require physical access to the network segment being monitored. Either a dedicated piece of hardware must be attached to the segment, or software must be added to one of the segment's existing hosts. Alternatively if a router or host implements the variables in the RMON MIB, it can be used for packet collection. A chicken-and-egg situation often arises. You do not monitor a segment until a problem occurs, and then you may have missed the problem's root cause. This has happened to me numerous times during interoperability tests.

Most software-only analyzers are incapable of collecting all packets when the network segment is fully utilized. Dedicated platforms usually can collect at full speed but are often quite expensive.

Network analyzers are generally passive. You can see everything that is currently happening on a segment, but you cannot test the reaction of devices to situations of your own choosing.

Network analyzers are good at breaking packets into their component fields and at doing simple calculations, such as checksum verifications, but that is usually where the analyzers' intelligence ends. Problem diagnosis of a packet trace is usually left to a human being who has good knowledge of the protocol being debugged.

The use of network analyzers invokes privacy and security concerns. Since they capture all traffic transmitted on a given network segment, analyzers can be misused to capture sensitive data, such as user passwords. This is the reason that network analyzers on UNIX systems generally require root access.

12.9 Protocol-Specific Tools

Certain routing protocols have built-in diagnostics, allowing tools to be written to debug protocol, implementation, and configuration problems. A few such tools follow.

- The **ripquery** program [51], written by Jeff Honig, enables you to see part or all of a RIP router's routing table. In addition, you can see the RIP packets that the RIP routing is currently sending. Example output from the **ripquery** program is shown in Figure 12.9.

```
$ ripquery -1 -n
504 bytes from 129.101.10.10 version 1:
129.101.12.0      metric  3
129.101.13.0      metric  3
129.101.8.0       metric  2
129.101.10.0      metric  1
129.101.17.0      metric  4
129.101.4.0       metric  2
129.101.5.0       metric  2
129.101.6.0       metric  2
129.101.7.0       metric  2
129.101.30.0      metric  6
129.101.37.0      metric  3
129.101.20.0      metric  3
129.101.27.0      metric  4
129.101.22.0      metric  1
129.101.19.0      metric  5
129.101.40.0      metric  2
129.101.47.0      metric  2
129.101.42.0      metric  2
129.101.36.0      metric  1
129.101.39.0      metric  4
129.101.32.0      metric  3
129.101.35.0      metric  3
129.101.60.0      metric  2
129.101.52.0      metric  2
129.101.49.0      metric  2
```

Figure 12.9 Sample output from the **ripquery** program.

- The **ospf_monitor** program [50], written by Rob Coltun and Jeff Honig, can display an OSPF router's link-state database and routing table, along with OSPF statistics and errors and information about OSPF interfaces and neighbors.

- The **mrinfo** program [116], written by Van Jacobson, allows you to query the state of a DVMRP router. A description of the router is printed, including its DVMRP revision level and its capabilities (such as whether it implements pruning or responds to multicast traceroute). A list of the router's DVMRP interfaces is then given. The type of interface is listed (for example, whether a tunnel and, if so, whether it is source routed or encapsulated), along with the interface metric, the TTL threshold, a list of neighbors, and whether the interface has been elected the Querier.

- The nature of OSPF's synchronized link-state database allows you to monitor an OSPF routing domain by attaching an instrumented OSPF implementation to any network segment in the domain. With an OSPF implementation modified to note rate of database change and database anomalies, such as one-way links, you can easily locate flapping links, duplicate OSPF router IDs, and so on. The OSPF implementation contained in the companion to this book (*OSPF Complete Implementation*) can be used for this purpose. Another thing that you can do is calculate the routing table of any OSPF router in the routing domain from the instrumented implementation.

How They Work

Typically the tools are enabled by the routing protocol designers' and implementors' adding monitoring request and response packets to the various protocols.

The **ripquery** program utilizes RIP's request, response, and poll commands. Each RIP packet has a Command field. RIP request packets (Command = 1) sent to a RIP router elicit RIP responses. The RIP response contains all the router's RIP routing table, unless specific RIP routes have been indicated in the body of the request. This RIP request/response procedure was not designed for diagnostic purposes; its purpose is to enable a RIP router to get a download of its neighbor's routing table quickly on restart. As a result, there is one possible undesirable behavior of request/response. When the entire table is requested, the response packet has the RIP split horizon (or split horizon with poison reverse) applied to it, possibly obscuring some of the routing information. For this reason, certain RIP implementations (such as the UNIX **gated** and **routed** daemons) added the poll command, which has equivalent semantics but is used only for monitoring and thus avoids the split-horizon rules.

The **ospf_monitor** program works in a similar fashion. The **gated** OSPF implementation added a new OSPF packet type to be used in querying the **gated** OSPF for operational information.

The **mrinfo** program uses the DVMRP ASKNEIGHBORS2 and NEIGHBORS2 packets, the "2" having been appended to replace an earlier pair of monitoring packets. When a DVMRP router receives an ASKNEIGHBORS packet, it responds with a NEIGHBORS2 packet describing the router, its interfaces, and neighbors. This same procedure is utilized by the **map_mbone** program, which, when given a seed router, can map an entire DVMRP routing system (such as the MBONE).

Strong Points

These tools have generally been designed by the protocol designers and implementors specifically for protocol debugging. As such, the tools are generally efficient and provide concise, accurate troubleshooting information.

Weak Points

Many routing protocols do not have built-in diagnostic capabilities. If not included from the very start, it is often difficult to retrofit diagnostics after the protocol has been widely deployed. Also, if a diagnostic capability is not necessary for a protocol's operation (for example, the RIP poll command), it is likely that the diagnostic will not be supported by all implementations.

Many people in the SNMP community believe that SNMP should be used to monitor protocols rather than building protocol-specific monitoring support.

12.10 Product-Specific Monitoring and Tracing

Most TCP/IP hosts and routers have product-specific monitoring and debugging tools built into their TCP/IP implementations. Normally these tools are accessed through a terminal interface, either local or remote through TELNET or a Web server. Sometimes the tools can also be accessed through a proprietary MIB. These tools can be used to examine in real time routing state and data. In addition, many products have tracing capabilities so that a log of significant events can be made to a terminal or a local disk, via SNMP traps, or sometimes even through the UNIX **syslog** facility.

For example, most routers have built-in tools to

- Dump the routing table. Although this can also be done through SNMP, it is often faster and more reliable to do this via a product's terminal interface.

- Dump the ARP table. This can tell you which hosts and routers are currently active on attached network segments.

- Query the router as to how it would route to a given destination.

- Enable tracing of specific protocol events, such as all BGP packets received and transmitted.

Monitoring commands and tracing facilities have been built into most OSPF implementations, including the one contained in the companion to this book (*OSPF Complete*

Implementation). As an example, we include monitoring information taken from a large operational OSPF network, the Arkansas Public School Computer Network, which is discussed in more detail in Section 11.4. Commands executed on the command line interface of that network's routers allow the network managers to examine OSPF's routing table, link-state database (Figure 12.10), and the state of OSPF's database synchronization procedures. In addition, OSPF protocol activity can be traced by examining logging messages (printed either locally on a router's console or remotely on a network management station via the TELNET protocol), as shown in Figure 12.11.

How They Work

These product-specific tools have usually been designed by the original product developers for initial debugging and then later for remote problem diagnosis.

Strong Points

These commands often provide exactly what the product developers want to see, should you end up asking their help in debugging a problem. Developers often include a lot of interesting information in these commands and in a concise manner; they are motivated to be able to debug their product remotely, lest they be woken up in the middle of the night and told to take the first plane to Omaha in the morning.

Weak Points

These tools are often cryptic and poorly documented, if documented at all. Sometimes these tools are removed from a product when it ships or are made inaccessible to the customer.

12.11 Multicast Traceroute

Multicast traceroute, implemented as the **mtrace** utility for UNIX systems, is the IP multicast analog to the unicast **traceroute** utility (see Section 12.5). This tool allows you to trace the path of a multicast datagram with a given group destination as it travels from a given source to a specific group member (indicated by the group member's unicast IP address). As with unicast traceroute, you can trace the path until either (a) a router on the path fails to answer or (b) an error indication is returned. This information lets you pinpoint the precise router that is having a problem when multicast datagrams are for some reason not getting delivered.

However, unlike in unicast traceroute, the path is traced backward, from the specific group member back to the source. The reason is that in the forward direction, the

```
OSPF>database
For which area [170.176.0.0]?

Type LS destination      LS originator     Seqno      Age   Xsum
   1  165.29.1.6          165.29.1.6        0x80001A89  219  0xDD01
   1  165.29.50.33        165.29.50.33      0x8000DB80  611  0xDD81
   1  170.211.176.3       170.211.176.3     0x800015BF  239  0x6417
   1  170.211.176.4       170.211.176.4     0x8000285B 1253  0xD079
   1  170.211.176.6       170.211.176.6     0x80000E22 1084  0xBC9D
   1  170.211.176.7       170.211.176.7     0x8000000A  611  0x14E1
   1  170.211.176.8       170.211.176.8     0x800017D4 1317  0x73DF
   1  170.211.176.9       170.211.176.9     0x80000E4C  192  0x5A02
   1  170.211.176.10      170.211.176.10    0x80003446  811  0xDCB9
   1  170.211.176.11      170.211.176.11    0x800017E7 1566  0x365A
   1  170.211.176.12      170.211.176.12    0x800017E1 1593  0xBF12
   1  170.211.176.13      170.211.176.13    0x80003C43 1411  0xB86C
   1  170.211.176.14      170.211.176.14    0x800036C0 1240  0x524
   1  170.211.176.17      170.211.176.17    0x80002AF3  951  0x14A4
   1  170.211.176.24      170.211.176.24    0x800019B5 1166  0x94DD
   1  170.211.176.25      170.211.176.25    0x800026E6 1238  0xF747
   1  170.211.177.129     170.211.177.129   0x80004643   52  0xC356
   1  170.211.180.5       170.211.180.5     0x800031BC 1121  0x2117
   1  170.211.180.225     170.211.180.225   0x800014EA 1256  0xE25F
   1  170.211.181.5       170.211.181.5     0x800017D6 1081  0xA091
   1  170.211.183.193     170.211.183.193   0x80003D61  474  0x8982
   1  170.211.184.129     170.211.184.129   0x800023C0 1095  0x6146
   1  170.211.185.5       170.211.185.5     0x80004D73 1576  0xAD7C
   1  170.211.185.129     170.211.185.129   0x80000FDA  461  0x8807
                              etc.
   1  170.211.189.129     170.211.189.129   0x800003DC 1116  0xF907
   1  170.211.189.161     170.211.189.161   0x80000167  265  0x3302
   1  170.211.190.5       170.211.190.5     0x800009C3 1027  0x56C3
   1  170.211.191.193     170.211.191.193   0x800003E7  213  0x7103
   1  170.211.191.225     170.211.191.225   0x800003DF 1181  0x350A
   3  165.29.1.0          165.29.1.6        0x80004D4D 1794  0x81D2
   3  165.29.1.64         165.29.1.6        0x800008C0 1794  0xE7FD
                              etc.
   4  170.211.160.1       165.29.1.6        0x800008BF  545  0x6149
   4  170.211.208.14      165.29.1.6        0x8000006A  919  0x9930
   4  198.247.208.252     165.29.1.6        0x800007D7  451  0x35F0

                # advertisements:        258
                Checksum total:          0x83B4C2
```

Figure 12.10 Dumping the OSPF link-state database through a terminal interface.

```
OSPF.010: Received packet type 1 from 165.29.1.65
OSPF.010: Received packet type 1 from 165.29.16.26
OSPF.010: Received packet type 1 from 170.211.96.3
OSPF.010: Received packet type 1 from 170.211.176.30
OSPF.010: Received packet type 4 from 165.29.16.52
OSPF.034: LS ack sent direct to 165.29.16.52
OSPF.011: Sending unicast type 5 dst 165.29.16.52
OSPF.010: Received packet type 4 from 165.29.16.40
OSPF.034: LS ack sent direct to 165.29.16.40
OSPF.011: Sending unicast type 5 dst 165.29.16.40
OSPF.010: Received packet type 4 from 165.29.16.40
OSPF.030: from 165.29.16.40, new adv: (1,165.29.16.40,165.29.16.40)
OSPF.012: Sending mcast type 4, dst 224.0.0.5 net 5 ifc FR/3
                            etc.
```

Figure 12.11 Implementation-specific tracing of OSPF events.

multicast delivery tree has many branches, and it is in general difficult to find the exact branch leading to any particular group member.

Even when multicast routing is working, **mtrace** can be used to find problems that are affecting the delivery of multicast datagrams. The program indicates how large the source must set a datagram's IP TTL field in order for the datagram to be delivered successfully to the destination group member. In IP multicast, TTL has additional semantics over and above simple hop count: TTL thresholds are configured at administrative boundaries to restrict the scope of multicast traffic (see Section 9.4). TTL information coming from **mtrace** can help discover configuration errors in these thresholds. In addition, **mtrace** collects packet statistics, allowing you to detect congestion along the multicast path.

Although you can specify the source, multicast group, and specific group member for your trace, you need specify only the source. By default, the multicast group is set to the MBONE's audio channel (224.2.0.1), and the group member is set to the host on which you are executing **mtrace**. In other words, **mtrace** by default indicates how packets on the MBONE audio channel will be delivered from a specified speaker to you.

Also, **mtrace** prints a separate line for each multicast router encountered on the way from the multicast group member back to the multicast datagram source. Each line includes

- The DNS name and/or IP address of the multicast router.

- The multicast routing protocol being used by the multicast router.

- The minimum TTL required in the multicast datagram for it to be forwarded by the multicast router.

A router along the path may also report an error, which causes matching multicast datagrams not to be forwarded. Example of such errors reported by **mtrace** include the following.

- The multicast router does not know how to forward multicast datagrams from the given source.

- The multicast router's outgoing interface for this datagram does not match the incoming interface for the next multicast router on the way to the destination group member.

- The multicast router has pruned the multicast group.

- The multicast group is subject to administrative scoping at this router (see Section 9.4).

The syntax and output of the **mtrace** program parallels that of **traceroute**. Also like **traceroute**, **mtrace** has a very good UNIX man page that describes how to use the program in various scenarios. Figure 12.12 displays an example of **mtrace** output. In this example, the path of a multicast datagram addressed to group 224.2.0.1 is traced backward from one of the group's members, a host with a unicast address of 206.34.99.38, to the datagram's source (which defaults to the host that the **mtrace** command is executed on, in this case, the host 132.236.199.65).

```
# mtrace -l -n 206.34.99.38 224.2.0.1
Mtrace from 132.236.199.65 to 206.34.99.38 via group 224.2.0.1
Querying full reverse path...
  0  206.34.99.38
 -1  199.94.205.14  DVMRP thresh^ 1  2 ms
 -2  4.0.2.22  DVMRP  thresh^ 1  3 ms
 -3  144.228.180.10  DVMRP  thresh^ 1  4 ms
 -4  144.228.60.11  DVMRP  thresh^ 1  6 ms
 -5  169.130.1.121  DVMRP  thresh^ 1  14 ms
 -6  169.130.61.9  DVMRP thresh^ 1  16 ms
 -7  132.236.100.10  DVMRP  thresh^ 1  17 ms
 -8  132.236.232.65  DVMRP  thresh^ 1  22 ms
 -9  132.236.232.139  DVMRP  thresh^ 1  30 ms
-10 132.236.199.65
Round trip time 49 ms
```

Figure 12.12 Sample **mtrace** output.

How It Works

Two additional IGMP packet types, 0x1F for traceroute request and 0x1E for traceroute response, were created in order to implement **mtrace**. The processing of these new

IGMP types has been documented by the IETF's Inter-Domain Multicast Routing Working Group (see [72]).

When **mtrace** is executed, a traceroute request packet is sent to the last-hop router on the path of a multicast datagram from multicast source to destination group member. The traceroute request packet is then forwarded hop by hop toward the multicast source. The multicast router at each hop reports a set of data, such as the IP addresses of the incoming and outgoing interfaces that the multicast datagram would traverse, the multicast routing protocol responsible for the incoming interface, the minimum TTL that the datagram would have to contain in order to be forwarded, and various statistics, such as the number of matching multicast datagrams that have been forwarded by the router. Forwarding of the traceroute request packet stops when (a) a maximum number of hops, specified by the **mtrace** program, has been reached; (b) the reported data has filled the traceroute request packet; (c) the first-hop router along the multicast datagram's path is reached; (d) a router is reached that does not know the route back to the multicast datagram's source; or (e) a router that does not understand traceroute requests is encountered. In all but the last case, the traceroute request is converted to a traceroute response and is then sent back to the host executing the **mtrace**.

When a router that does not understand traceroute requests is encountered, **mtrace** gets no response. In this case, **mtrace** starts an *expanding-length search*, sending a sequence of traceroute request packets to the last-hop router, first with maximum hop count of 1, then with 2, and so on. In this way, the path from the last-hop router back to the traceroute-ignorant multicast router is discovered.

The identity of the last-hop router may be specified by using the **-g** option on the **mtrace** command line. If the identity of the last-hop router is unknown, **mtrace** attempts to discover it by multicasting the traceroute request to the same group whose datagrams are being traced. This should reach the last-hop router, assuming that (a) the TTL in the traceroute request is high enough (settable by **mtrace**'s **-t** option); (b) the "destination group member" is truly a member of the group; and (c) multicast routing is working between the host executing **mtrace** and the destination group member (which are often the same host).

Tracing a multicast datagram's path using traceroute request packets is very similar to how you would trace the path using SNMP and the multicast forwarding MIB. However, traceroute requests use fewer packets and enable you to discover the last-hop router (which you could do with the multicast forwarding MIB unless you multicasted SNMP requests!).

Strong Points

The **mtrace** program is definitely the best way to track down multicast routing problems. It allows you to trace partial paths efficiently, locating the problematic multicast router. The program discovers not only inconsistencies in multicast forwarding between routers but also configuration and congestion problems. The only other tools available for debugging multicast routing are **ping** and the multicast forwarding MIB.

There is wide deployment of routers that understand multicast traceroute on the MBONE. This functionality was first released in **mrouted** 3.3.

As with the unicast traceroute utility, the implementors of **mtrace** have thought about many contingencies, enabling useful information to be returned in the face of a wide variety of failures. As one example, they allow the traceroute response packet to be returned as a multicast instead of being unicast to the host running **mtrace**, for those situations in which multicast connectivity exists but unicast does not!

Weak Points

Unlike unicast traceroute, a separate mechanism (IGMP traceroute request and response packet types) had to be developed for multicast traceroute, rather than just using required features of the data forwarding in all multicast routers. This means that, just like SNMP solutions, multicast traceroute may be subject to measurement errors.

If the last-hop multicast router does not understand traceroute request packets or is grossly malfunctioning, **mtrace** cannot gain any information at all. Similarly **mtrace** may not be able to discover the identity of the last-hop router in some cases. Examples of such cases are when the traceroute destination is not really a group member or when there is no multicast connectivity between the host executing **mtrace** and the traceroute destination.

Further Reading

The *Network Management Tool Catalog* [68] provides a good, although somewhat dated, list of tools for network monitoring and control, including analyzers, SNMP programming libraries, and debugging and mapping tools. Pointers to a more up-to-date online version of the tool catalog are also provided.

Marshall Rose's *The Simple Book* [218] is the best introduction to SNMP. We examine SNMP and its MIBs in more detail in Chapter 11.

The Tk/TCL toolkit [187] allows you to quickly code applications such as those described in Section 12.9. Perl [260] is another scripting language popular with application developers. Both packages are freely available on the Internet.

The MBONE—its applications, design, and management tools—is described further in [36], [69], and [131]. The **mtrace** man page [37] provides the best description on how to use multicast traceroute to track down problems in multicast routing, just as the **traceroute** man page [247] is a good resource for unicast routing debugging.

The **gated** routing daemon can turn a UNIX workstation into a TCP/IP router. Unlike the **routed** program, which runs only RIP, **gated** contains an implementation of most IP unicast and multicast protocols. It is also used as a platform to experiment with new routing protocols and has been incorporated into many commercial routers as well. See [83] for detailed documentation on **gated** configuration and internals. The Routing Server created as part of the NSF-funded Routing Arbiter project [223], used at some exchange points to simplify the administration of BGP peering, is also built on top of **gated**.

Exercises

12.1 Find the number of routers your packets traverse on the way to the Internic's RFC depository (**ds.internic.net**). Which ISPs and backbone service providers do you end up using?

12.2 Modify the **ping** program so that it returns whether the destination is reachable and, if so, the number of hops to the destination, assuming a symmetric path.

12.3 Use SNMP to dump an IP routing table. First, use a command line tool (such as the publicly available CMU SNMP tools), and then write your own MIB-based tool.

12.4 Write a program to receive and display all RIP packets broadcast on your local network segment.

12.5 Write a program to find all DVMRP routers within n hops of a given DVMRP router, where n is specified by the user.

Part V

Routing Protocol Comparisons

In Part V, we survey the routing protocols, both unicast and multicast, in use in the Internet. Chapter 13, Unicast Routing Protocols, compares and contrasts the unicast routing protocols in use in today's Internet: RIP, OSPF, BGP, IGRP, and Integrated IS-IS. Each protocol is explained in terms of the basic functions that every IP routing protocol provides: neighbor discovery, distribution of routing data, routing calculations, aggregation, policy controls, and so on. We end with a discussion of how routing information is exchanged between routing protocols.

Chapter 14, Multicast Routing Protocols, examines the multicast routing protocols that have been developed for the Internet: DVMRP, MOSPF, PIM Dense, PIM Sparse, and CBT. Before getting into the details of the specific protocols, we describe the operation of broadcast-and-prune protocols.

13

Unicast Routing Protocols

In this chapter, we compare and contrast the routing protocols in use in today's Internet: RIP, OSPF, BGP, IGRP, and Integrated IS-IS. As we have seen, routing protocols can be categorized into IGPs and EGPs. (By the way, many TCP/IP routing protocols contain the word *gateway*. This was the original term for what we now call a router, a network-layer switching device. Today the word gateway is used for devices that switch at higher levels of the OSI reference model: mail gateways, application-level gateways, and so on.) Internet routing protocols can also be classified according to the basic routing technology they employ: Distance Vector or link-state (Table 13.1).

Table 13.1 Classification of TCP/IP Routing Protocols. (Boldface type indicates protocols in use in the Internet.)

Protocol Type	Distance Vector	Link State
IGPs	GGP Hello **RIP** **IGRP**	**OSPF** **Integrated IS-IS**
EGPs	EGP **BGP**	IDPR

In the sections that follow, we will describe each of the Internet's routing protocols. Each routing protocol has to perform a basic set of activities. For example, a router has to be able to detect its neighboring routers. It also has to have a reliable way of collecting routing data and of turning this data into routing table entries. In order to better understand how the protocols work and to compare and contrast them, we will describe each protocol in terms of the following categories.

- *Type.* Is the protocol an EGP or an IGP; does it employ Distance Vector or link-state routing technology?

- *Encapsulation.* Does the routing protocol run directly over IP, over one of the Internet transport protocols (TCP or UDP), or directly over the data-link layer?

- *Path characteristics.* What do the "best" paths selected by the protocol look like? For example, RIP always selects paths that go through a minimum number of routers. Other protocols can select minimum-delay paths or minimize other metrics. Still other protocols do not include a metric but allow the network administrator to indicate path preferences.

- *Neighbor discovery and maintenance.* How does a router running the protocol discover the routers (called neighbors, or peers) with which it is to exchange routing information? How does the router discover failures in these neighbors so that it can route traffic around them when necessary?

- *Routing data distribution.* What is the raw routing data that is distributed between routers running the protocol, and how is this distribution performed?

- *Route deletion.* When a destination prefix becomes unreachable, how is this information propagated by the routing protocol?

- *Routing table calculation.* How does the router calculate routing table entries from the raw routing data received from its neighbors?

- *Robustness/reliability.* How does the protocol ensure that routing data is transmitted reliably between routers? In what other ways does the protocol try to ensure that transmission errors and hardware or software errors within the routers do not permanently impair routing?

- *Aggregation.* How does the protocol combine routing information for a collection of prefixes, producing a routing advertisement for a single, smaller prefix?

- *Policy controls.* In what ways can the network administrator bias the paths calculated by the protocol? For example, an ISP may wish to ensure that traffic going between two of its customers never leaves the ISP's network. Or, the network administrator may not wish to route traffic to prefixes originating from a particular AS number.

- *Security.* How does the protocol guard against intruders trying to disrupt protocol exchanges and/or corrupt routing data?

13.1 RIP

The development of TCP/IP and the Internet was strongly influenced by the University of California at Berkeley's BSD UNIX project. BSD UNIX was the first widely deployed TCP/IP host implementation and still serves as the reference implementation for TCP/IP developers [264]. The work done in BSD UNIX on TCP congestion control has been one of the major factors enabling the Internet to grow to its present size. And BSD UNIX provided the Internet with its first widespread routing protocol implementation, which is still probably the most common routing protocol in use in today's Internet: the *Routing Information Protocol* (RIP) [95]. RIP also is run commonly by TCP/IP hosts as a router discovery mechanism and as a way to find the best router to use for a given destination (Section 1.2). The `routed` program, an implementation of RIP, is shipped with all UNIX systems.

TCP/IP's RIP is an adaptation of the XNS Routing Information Protocol [265]. Leaving the protocol mechanisms largely unchanged, the BSD networking developers made RIP multiprotocol by advertising UNIX `sockaddr` structures within RIP routing updates. This allowed RIP to be used not only as a TCP/IP routing protocol but also for other network stacks, such as OSI.

TCP/IP's RIP is the classic Distance Vector protocol (Section 2.3) and is used as an IGP within the Internet. As such, RIP employs a distributed computation scheme: RIP routers cooperate by sending routing updates to their neighbors. These updates cause their neighbors to change their routing tables incrementally and to send new updates in response, causing further routing table changes. Eventually this process causes all the routers' routing tables to converge to stable values (see Figure 13.1).

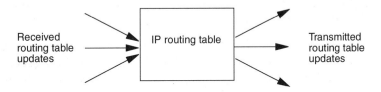

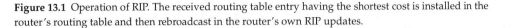

Figure 13.1 Operation of RIP. The received routing table entry having the shortest cost is installed in the router's routing table and then rebroadcast in the router's own RIP updates.

RIP depended on the original division of TCP/IP addresses into Class A, B, and C networks, allowing any of these networks to be split into physically contiguous, fixed-sized subnets. In order to support CIDR, a new version of RIP was developed, RIPv2. The original RIP protocol, also now called RIPv1, has the following properties.

- *Type:* RIP is a Distance Vector IGP.

- *Encapsulation:* RIP runs over UDP, using UDP port 520.

- *Path characteristics:* RIP routes are based solely on hop count. To get to a particular destination, RIP routers choose the path that goes through the minimum number of routers. The maximum hop count supported by RIP is 15; destinations 16 hops or farther away are considered unreachable.

- *Neighbor discovery and maintenance:* RIP has no neighbor discovery and maintenance procedures separate from route distribution. In particular, RIP has no way to discover one-way links.

- *Routing data distribution:* RIP routers broadcast RIP updates to their neighbors. RIP updates list a collection of destination prefixes, together with their metrics (Figure 13.2). On receiving a RIP update from a neighbor, a RIP router decides whether to update its routing table. However, unlike OSPF, with its link-state database, and BGP, with its RIB-In, a RIP router keeps only the current best route, which is stored directly in the router's routing table. RIP routing updates are limited to a size of 512 bytes. Each prefix entry within a RIP routing update consumes 20 bytes, limiting the number of prefixes per routing update to 25. To advertise a larger number of prefixes, multiple RIP updates are sent.

- *Response to changes:* When a routing table in a RIP router changes, the RIP router usually will broadcast updates for the new prefix immediately, before waiting for the normal 30-second timer. These updates, called triggered updates, are caused by (a) one of the router's interfaces becoming operational, in which case the router starts advertising the attached prefix with a cost of 1; (b) one of the router's interfaces going inoperational, in which case the router advertises the prefix as unreachable by assigning the prefix a metric of 16; (c) a RIP update from a neighbor has modified the routing table; or (d) a routing table entry has timed out (more on this later). Triggered updates advertise only those prefixes whose cost has changed.

- *Routing table calculation:* Prefixes belonging to directly connected network segments are always installed in the routing table with a cost of 1. The next hop for other prefixes is set equal to the RIP router advertising the smallest metric N, with the routing table cost for the prefix set to $N + 1$.

- *Robustness/reliability:* A RIP router broadcasts its complete routing table every 30 seconds. If for some reason a neighbor fails to receive one of the router's RIP update packets—for example, the packet is damaged by transmission errors or dropped due to congestion—the neighbor will probably just receive an identical update 30 seconds later.

- *Aggregation:* RIP aggregates routing information at the boundary of a subnetted network (the collected subnets of a Class A, B, or C network). Inside the subnetted network, individual subnets are advertised separately. Outside the subnetted network, the entire subnetted network is advertised as a single prefix having a cost of 1. For example, if RIP were running in Figure 1.5, routers G–J would exchange information about the four subnets of 128.1/16, but G advertises only the single prefix 128.1/16 to the routers C and D.

- *Policy controls:* Although not formally part of the RIP specification, most RIP implementations allow the implementation of routing policies through the configuration of routing filters. By configuring routing filters, a network administrator can control which subnets a RIP router will accept and which subnets a RIP router will advertise, usually on a per neighbor basis.

- *Security:* RIPv1 has no provisions for security.

When a RIP router first comes up, it need not wait for 30 seconds before getting RIP updates from its neighbors. The RIP router can instead broadcast *RIP request packets*, asking its neighbors to immediately send their updates.

Figure 13.2 shows a packet trace of a router, 192.148.30.22, broadcasting its RIP updates. Since the router's routing table has 355 entries, 15 consecutive RIP packets must be sent back to back. RIP's strategy of broadcasting the entire routing table every 30 seconds is a simple, fairly robust scheme for reliably delivering routing information. However, as this trace shows, the scheme also has its problems. First, it can take a lot of consecutive update packets to transmit even a moderate-sized table: 1,000 entries would take 40 packets, utilizing an average bandwidth of 5.4 Kbits/sec (in comparison, OSPF would use only 142 bits/sec). Also, many routers cannot process a large number of back-to-back routing updates. In these situations, the receiving router usually drops the same part of the back-to-back packet sequence every time, resulting in the inability to receive certain prefixes.

Since a RIP router expects to receive routing updates continually confirming its choice of next hop, it eventually gives up on the next-hop router if updates cease to be received. After not hearing from the next hop for 90 seconds, the router will move the next hop to any neighboring router that advertises a path of equal cost. After not hearing from the next hop for 180 seconds, the routing table entry will simply be declared unreachable.

RIP routers usually implement some of the standard mechanisms for improving convergence of a Distance Vector algorithm (Section 2.3). These include triggered updates, split horizon, and infinite split horizon.

RIPv2

In order to support CIDR, a new version of RIP was designed, called RIPv2 [149]. By adding a mask field to each route, RIPv2 can advertise CIDR prefixes. All RIP mechanisms and convergence behaviors are maintained in RIPv2. But additional fields besides the mask are advertised with each route: a 16-bit *route tag*, used to group routes together for policy reasons; and a *next-hop* field, used to eliminate extra forwarding hops at the edge of a RIP routing domain (see the documentation of the equivalent OSPF functions,

```
SUMMARY  Delta T  Destination      Source       Summary
   212   9.9839  255.255.255.255 192.148.30.22  RIP R Routing entries=25
   213   0.0005  255.255.255.255 192.148.30.22  RIP R Routing entries=25
   214   0.0005  255.255.255.255 192.148.30.22  RIP R Routing entries=25
   215   0.0005  255.255.255.255 192.148.30.22  RIP R Routing entries=25
   216   0.0005  255.255.255.255 192.148.30.22  RIP R Routing entries=25
   217   0.0244  255.255.255.255 192.148.30.22  RIP R Routing entries=25
   218   0.0001  255.255.255.255 192.148.30.22  RIP R Routing entries=25
   219   0.0001  255.255.255.255 192.148.30.22  RIP R Routing entries=25
   220   0.0001  255.255.255.255 192.148.30.22  RIP R Routing entries=25
   221   0.0001  255.255.255.255 192.148.30.22  RIP R Routing entries=25
   222   0.0001  255.255.255.255 192.148.30.22  RIP R Routing entries=25
   223   0.0001  255.255.255.255 192.148.30.22  RIP R Routing entries=25
   224   0.0001  255.255.255.255 192.148.30.22  RIP R Routing entries=25
   225   0.0001  255.255.255.255 192.148.30.22  RIP R Routing entries=25
   226   0.0001  255.255.255.255 192.148.30.22  RIP R Routing entries=5
- - - - - - - - - - - - - - - Frame 226 - - - - - - - - - - - - - - - - - - -
RIP:  ----- RIP Header -----
RIP:
RIP:  Command = 2 (Response)
RIP:  Version = 1
RIP:  Unused  = 0
RIP:
RIP:  Routing data frame 1
RIP:     Address family identifier = 2 (IP)
RIP:     IP Address = [192.176.149.0]
RIP:     Metric    = 2
RIP:
RIP:  Routing data frame 2
RIP:     Address family identifier = 2 (IP)
RIP:     IP Address = [207.147.171.0]
RIP:     Metric    = 10
RIP:
RIP:  Routing data frame 3
RIP:     Address family identifier = 2 (IP)
RIP:     IP Address = [192.176.150.0]
RIP:     Metric    = 2
RIP:
RIP:  Routing data frame 4
RIP:     Address family identifier = 2 (IP)
RIP:     IP Address = [192.176.151.0]
RIP:     Metric    = 2
RIP:
RIP:  Routing data frame 5
RIP:     Address family identifier = 2 (IP)
RIP:     IP Address = [207.147.173.0]
RIP:     Metric    = 10
```

Figure 13.2 A trace of RIP routing update behavior.

OSPF's external route tag and forwarding address, in Section 11.6). RIPv2 also allows received RIP updates to be authenticated by including authentication information within the RIP updates [13]. RIPv2 routing updates are multicast to the address 224.0.0.9, although all RIPv2 routers can be configured to revert to broadcast in order to interoperate with RIPv1 routers.

RIP has also been modified to carry IPv6 addresses, resulting in the RIPng routing protocol for IPv6 [151].

13.2 OSPF

The *Open Shortest Path First* (OSPF) protocol is a link-state IGP designed expressly for the Internet. OSPF was originally built as a RIP replacement, designed to provide quick convergence with only a small amount of routing control traffic, even in ASs with a large number of routers. The original proving grounds for OSPF were some of the second-level networks of the T1 NSFNET, the so-called *NSF regional networks* [168]. OSPF is now the recommended IGP for the Internet [85]. This is a recommendation made by the *Internet Engineering Task Force* (IETF). It is impossible to legislate protocol usage in the Internet, so the recommendation simply encourages all makers of Internet routers to implement the OSPF protocol.

As a link-state protocol, the core of OSPF consists of creating and maintaining a distributed replicated database, called the *link-state database*. As long as every OSPF router has an identical link-state database, OSPF calculates loop-free paths; most of the protocol machinery within OSPF is dedicated to keeping the database synchronized between routers. Figure 13.3 shows how OSPF operates.

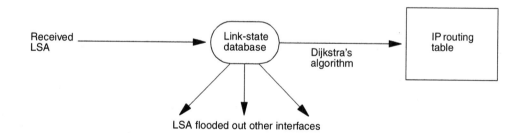

Figure 13.3 Operation of the OSPF protocol. OSPF LSAs received on one interface are installed in the link-state database and flooded out the router's other interfaces. From the link-state database, an OSPF router calculates its routing table, using Dijkstra's Shortest Path First (SPF) algorithm.

A router running OSPF discovers its neighboring OSPF routers by multicasting *OSPF Hello packets* onto its directly connected network segments. After discovering a neighboring router, the router synchronizes link-state databases with the neighbor. Only then does the router advertise the connection to the neighbor in a *link-state advertisement* (LSA, the name OSPF uses for individual pieces of the link-state database). The router then starts the distribution of the LSA to all other routers through OSPF's *reliable flooding* mechanism. Once the other routers receive this LSA, they rerun their routing calculations, which consist of Dijkstra's SPF algorithm performed on the link-state database. The output of the calculation is the new set of best-cost paths to the network's destinations. Some of these new paths will probably utilize the just established connection from the LSA's originating router to its new neighbor.

A two-level routing hierarchy can be implemented in an OSPF domain by dividing the routing domain into regions called *OSPF areas*. Routing information from other protocols can be imported into the OSPF domain and readvertised by OSPF routers as *external routing information*.

- *Type:* OSPF is a link-state IGP.

- *Encapsulation:* OSPF runs directly over the Internet Protocol as IP protocol 89. OSPF Hello packets, which are used to discover and maintain neighbor relationships, are multicast to the IP multicast address 224.0.0.5. OSPF's reliable flooding uses a combination of multicasting to 224.0.0.5, 224.0.0.6, and unicasting.

- *Path characteristics:* The network administrator of an OSPF routing domain assigns a cost to the output side of each router interface. The cost of a path is then the sum of all output interfaces contained by the path—paths are unidirectional. OSPF selects the path(s) with the lowest cost; therefore the higher an interface's cost, the fewer packets the interface will be asked to transmit. The network administrator has complete control over the units and semantics of interface cost. For example, if each interface is assigned a cost of 1, OSPF finds minimum-hop paths (just like RIP). If, instead, each interface is assigned a cost of the length in kilometers of the underlying physical circuit, OSPF will calculate paths having minimum static delay. The cost of an output interface must be between 1 and 65,535 inclusive. There are no limits on path cost.

- *Neighbor discovery and maintenance:* An OSPF router discovers a neighbor when it receives the neighbor's OSPF Hello packet. The neighbor multicasts these Hello packets periodically; if the router fails to receive Hellos from the neighbor, the router will in time report as down the connection to the neighbor. The rate of sending Hellos and the length of time before declaring the neighbor unreachable are configurable per network segment.

- *Routing data distribution:* OSPF LSAs are distributed throughout the OSPF routing domain via a reliable flooding mechanism. The router originating the LSA begins the flood by sending the LSA to its neighbors. Any other router will, when receiving the LSA, acknowledge receipt of the LSA and then compare the LSA to the contents of its present database. If the received LSA is more recent, the receiving router will send the LSA out all interfaces other than the one on which the LSA was received. In order to make this flood reliable, after having sent the LSA out an interface, the router will retransmit the LSA until it is acknowledged.

- *Response to changes:* Changes to a router's local environment—for example, one of the router's interfaces is no longer operational or its cost changes, cause the router to modify one of its existing LSAs and reflood, to originate a new LSA and flood, or to begin flushing one of its LSAs from the routing domain. All LSAs include the age in seconds since they were originated, called the *LS Age field*. Setting the LS Age field to a value that is not normally attained, 3,600 seconds, or 1 hour, and then reflooding the LSA, is an instruction to the other routers to delete the LSA rather than to insert it into their databases.

- *Routing table calculation:* Using the link-state database as input, an OSPF router uses Dijkstra's Shortest Path First algorithm to calculate the shortest paths to all prefixes within the network.

- *Robustness/reliability:* Flooding is made reliable by requiring that all transmitted LSAs be acknowledged explicitly. In addition, OSPF requires that all LSAs be reoriginated at 30-minute intervals, even if their contents have not changed. In this way, even if an LSA has been damaged or deleted mistakenly from a router's database, the LSA will eventually be replaced and correct routing restored without human intervention.

    OSPF also has additional robustness features. First, all LSAs have checksums that are permanently attached to the LSA. The checksum allows LSA data corruption, either during flooding or while held in a router's link-state database, to be detected. Second, to protect against flooding loops, the LSA's LS Age field also functions as a TTL field. By incrementing LS Age at least 1 every flooding hop, a looping LSA will eventually be discarded when its LS Age reaches 3,600. Third, to prevent black holes due to one-way links, links are not included in the OSPF link-state database until they are known to be bidirectional. Fourth, to prevent routing loops due to unsynchronized databases, links are not advertised in LSAs (and hence are not used for data traffic) until the routers at each end of the link have synchronized their databases.

- *Aggregation:* Routes can be aggregated at area borders, under configuration control of the network administrator. By configuring a prefix as an OSPF *area address range*, all addresses within the area that match the prefix will be advertised as a single route outside the area.

- *Policy controls:* Configuration of area borders can also implement rudimentary routing policies. If possible, OSPF always chooses paths that stay within a single area. OSPF also prefers intra-AS paths over paths that leave the Autonomous System. Routing filters may also be configured at area borders—area address ranges can be configured as *no advertise*, keeping information about certain network segments local to a given area. An *external route tag* may also be attached to each external route imported into the OSPF routing domain. This allows external routes to be grouped together, simplifying the configuration of redistribution into other protocols (Section 13.7).

* *Security:* An OSPF router can authenticate received OSPF packets by requiring the sender to append keyed message digests to the OSPF packet. Stronger security has been proposed for OSPF by attaching digital signatures to OSPF LSAs.

Routing data distribution works slightly differently on LANs and other network segments having more than two routers attached (which OSPF calls *multiaccess networks*). On each multiaccess network, a special router, called the *Designated Router* (DR), is elected in order to cut down on the number of acknowledgments. Routers other than the DR require only an acknowledgment from the DR when flooding LSAs onto the multiaccess network; the DR ensures that acknowledgments have been seen from all other routers attached to the segment.

OSPF keeps the size of its LSAs small and types the LSAs according to function. The *router-LSA* advertises the state of all of a router's interfaces, the *network-LSA* advertises all routers attached to a multiaccess network segment, *summary-LSAs* advertise routing information across area boundaries, and each external route is imported into OSPF in a separate *AS-external-LSA*. It is not unusual for a single OSPF router to originate hundreds of LSAs; the link-state database may consist of many thousands.

The packet trace in Figure 13.4 shows the beginning of an OSPF protocol exchange between two neighboring routers, routers A and B. After the second Hello from router A indicates bidirectional connectivity, the two routers start describing the current contents of their link-state databases by exchanging *OSPF Database Description packets*. When router B notices that some of its LSAs are out of date or that it is missing other LSAs, it requests the LSAs from router A in *OSPF Link State Request packets*. Router A then floods the requested LSAs to router B in *OSPF Link State Update packets*, just as if it were flooding newly received LSAs.

OSPF was designed with variable-length subnet masks in mind and always advertises the prefix mask instead of depending on Class A, B, and C network divisions. However, OSPF did require a bug fix when CIDR was deployed (see Section 3.7). A new version of the OSPF protocol has been designed as an IPv6 routing protocol (Section 3.7).

13.3 BGP

The Border Gateway Protocol (BGP) [208] is a Distance Vector EGP. BGP is the workhorse of the Internet; routing information is exchanged between the Internet's ISPs using BGP. Each ISP expends a considerable amount of its people resources managing

```
SUMMARY   Time      Destination   Source       Summary
    21    2.2391    01005E000005  Router A      OSPF Hello
    23    4.3046    01005E000005  Router B      OSPF Hello
    29   12.2715    01005E000005  Router A      OSPF Hello
    35   12.2832    Router A      Router B      OSPF Database Description
    36   12.2866    Router B      Router A      OSPF Database Description
    37   12.2878    Router B      Router A      OSPF Database Description
    38   12.4461    Router A      Router B      OSPF Database Description
    39   12.4479    Router B      Router A      OSPF Database Description
    41   12.5994    Router A      Router B      OSPF Link State Request
    42   12.6030    Router B      Router A      OSPF Link State Update


- - - - - - - - - - - - - - - Frame 42 - - - - - - - - - - - - - - - - -

OSPF:  ----- OSPF Header -----
OSPF:
OSPF:  Version = 2
OSPF:  Type = 4
OSPF:  Length = 504
OSPF:  Source Router ID = 2.160.14.67 (Router A)
OSPF:  Area ID = 0.0.0.0
OSPF:  Checksum = 0x19c1
OSPF:  Authentication type = 1
OSPF:  Authentication data = 4152454130303030
OSPF:
OSPF:  ----- OSPF Link State Update Packet -----
OSPF:
OSPF:  11 link state advertisement(s) follow.
OSPF:  Each displayed as (type,id,adv,seq,xsum,age).
OSPF:
OSPF:  (1,11.3.0.10,11.3.0.10,0x8000001b,0x1957,1032)
OSPF:  (1,2.160.60.7,2.160.60.7,0x80000038,0x3cc6,81)
OSPF:  (1,11.3.0.3,11.3.0.3,0x80000019,0xaefd,112)
OSPF:  (1,6.6.6.6,6.6.6.6,0x80000048,0x8914,456)
OSPF:  (1,128.185.200.1,128.185.200.1,0x80000008,0x30e2,457)
OSPF:  (1,10.0.0.5,10.0.0.5,0x80000070,0xa6df,462)
OSPF:  (1,4.4.4.4,4.4.4.4,0x80000044,0xf8bb,471)
OSPF:  (2,15.2.1.9,2.160.60.7,0x80000003,0xe770,1031)
OSPF:  (2,10.0.0.6,6.6.6.6,0x80000005,0x3dbf,371)
OSPF:  (2,10.0.0.4,4.4.4.4,0x8000000a,0xf43c,471)
OSPF:  (5,0.0.0.0,128.185.200.1,0x80000001,0x17b6,703)
```

Figure 13.4 Packet trace showing the beginning of an OSPF protocol exchange.

its BGP routing—deciding which other ISPs to peer with, maintaining the access lists of prefixes that can be received from and sent to each peer, and debugging the inevitable routing problems as they occur. Although BGP is the routing protocol that keeps the Internet running, it is used hardly at all in private TCP/IP networks. These networks typically run an IGP, such as OSPF; if they run BGP at all, they do so in only the single router that connects their network to the Internet. Figure 13.5 shows how BGP operates.

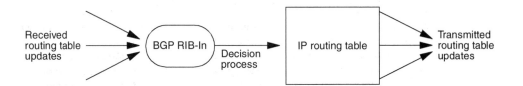

Figure 13.5 Operation of BGP. Received BGP updates are stored in the BGP router's RIB-In. For each prefix, the best route from the RIB-In is installed in the routing table and then advertised to the router's BGP peers.

The routers with which a BGP router X exchanges BGP information are called X's *BGP peers*. A BGP router's peers are configured by a network operator. To begin the exchange of BGP routing information with a peer, the BGP router sends a *BGP Open* message to the peer. If the peer also wishes to exchange BGP routing information, it responds with its own BGP Open message. At this point, the two routers exchange routing tables by transferring a collection of *BGP Update* messages. Each update message contains a list of prefixes and their *BGP path attributes*—attributes being the equivalent of other routing protocols' metrics, which we discuss further later. After this initial exchange of routing tables, only changes are transmitted, again in BGP Updates. If changes are infrequent, the peers exchange *BGP Keepalives* to keep the BGP session established. Receipt of a *BGP Notification* message informs the router that the BGP session has been terminated, either because of an error or by intentional action by the network operator. When a session with a peer is terminated, all information learned from the peer is deleted from the router's routing table.

BGP differs from a standard Distance Vector protocol in two significant ways. First, rather than continually resending their routing tables, after the first exchange of routing tables, two BGP routers send each other only changes. Transmission of routing updates must then be made reliable, which in BGP is accomplished by running over TCP. In standard Distance Vector protocols, such as RIP, if the best route disappears, the RIP router will know that it will be notified of all possible alternatives within the next 30 seconds. In contrast, since a BGP router's peers transmit only changes, a BGP router must store any alternative routes that it receives in order to recover from failures of the primary route. BGP stores these alternative routes in a database called the *RIB-In* (*Routing Information Base-Inbound*). The size of the RIB-In can be many times the size of the router's routing table.

Second, unlike standard Distance Vector algorithms, BGP always selects loop-free paths. To maintain loop-free routing a BGP router employs a simple mechanism: When advertising a prefix, the complete path to the prefix is included. Since the purpose of the BGP protocol is to exchange routing information between Autonomous Systems, this complete path consists of the sequence of ASs (called the *AS path*) that are traversed as data traffic is forwarded from the advertising router to the destination prefix. A router then avoids loops by never accepting an advertised prefix if the associated path already includes the router's own AS number.

Let's demonstrate this behavior by using the AS configuration of Figure 13.6 as an example. If the prefix 200.19.8.0/24 belongs to AS 3, it would be advertised in BGP updates from router A to router G (and from B to F and from B to I) with the AS path [AS 1, AS 2, AS 3]. If now the link between routers C and D fails, a standard Distance Vector protocol could form a loop between routers C–A–G–H–I–B–C, until counting to infinity removes the prefix from the routers' routing tables. However, BGP prevents the loop because the advertisement for 200.19.8.0/24 from router I to B would carry the AS path [AS 5, AS 4, AS 1, AS 2, AS 3], which B would reject after seeing its own AS, AS 1, already in the path to the destination prefix.

Also unlike standard Distance Vector algorithms, BGP updates do not include a metric for each prefix. Since BGP routing updates can be thought of as providing a list of paths instead of a list of distances, BGP is sometimes referred to as a *Path Vector* protocol.

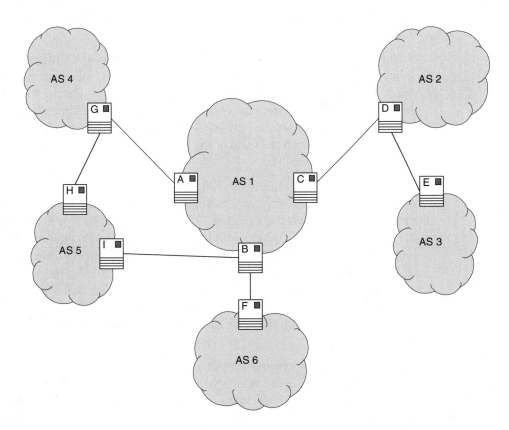

Figure 13.6 Sample Autonomous System configuration.

- *Type:* BGP is a Distance Vector EGP.

- *Encapsulation:* BGP runs over TCP, using TCP port number 179. Running over TCP ensures the reliable, sequenced delivery of BGP routing messages between BGP peers. Although BGP information is carried within TCP's reliable byte stream, BGP information is still packetized. Each BGP packet has a 19-byte header, with the maximum BGP packet size 4,096 bytes.

- *Path characteristics:* As seen earlier, BGP ensures that BGP routers find loop-free paths. However, the exact form that these paths take is determined by the routing policies configured by the network administrators. Unlike the other routing protocols considered in this chapter, BGP has no metric that it is trying to minimize. Instead, when a BGP router receives a number of paths to any particular destination, it chooses the most preferable path, based on configured policies. A common policy is to choose the path consisting of the fewest number of ASs. Another common policy is to allow the network administrator to associate a weight with each AS. The weight is a positive integer, with ASs of smaller weight preferred. Each path is then assigned a weight equal to the sum of the weights of its constituent ASs, with the paths having the smallest weight inserted into the routing table.

- *Neighbor discovery and maintenance:* A BGP router's peers are configured instead of being learned dynamically. When a BGP session is established between two peers, they exchange BGP Open messages and Keepalives. During the exchange of Open messages, the peers negotiate a *Hold Time.* If Hold Time is nonzero, no more than Hold Time seconds can elapse between BGP messages (Keepalives or Updates) received from the peer, or the peer will be declared unreachable and the BGP session terminated.

- *Routing data distribution:* As in any Distance Vector protocol, BGP routers exchange routing tables in their routing updates. Each BGP Update message a router sends has two parts (Figure 13.7). The first part lists prefixes that the BGP router has deleted from its routing table; BGP calls these *withdrawn* routes. Next comes a list of prefixes all having common BGP path attributes. BGP calls these prefixes *Network Layer Reachability Information* (NLRI); the path attributes include the AS path discussed earlier and other BGP path attributes discussed later. Unlike the other routing protocols in this chapter, BGP Update messages are always sent directly to a peer; they are never broadcast or multicast.

- *Response to changes:* As in any Distance Vector protocol, changes to the routing table in one BGP router invoke a distributed recalculation, with the router sending the changed parts of its routing table in BGP Update messages, which in turn cause its peers to recalculate their routing tables and to send Update messages, and so on. However, advertising the AS path with each prefix prevents

```
SUMMARY     Delta T Destination      Source            Summary
43          0.0011  [200.8.2.2]      [200.8.2.1]       BGP Open
44          0.0120  [200.8.2.1]      [200.8.2.2]       BGP Open
45          0.0024  [200.8.2.2]      [200.8.2.1]       BGP KeepAlive
46          0.0031  [200.8.2.1]      [200.8.2.2]       BGP KeepAlive
47          0.0494  [200.8.2.2]      [200.8.2.1]       BGP Update


- - - - - - - - - - - - - Frame 47 - - - - - - - - - - - - - -


BGP:  ----- BGP Message -----
BGP:
BGP:  16 byte Marker  (all 1's)
BGP:  Length       = 64
BGP:  BGP type     = 2 (Update)
BGP:
BGP:  Unfeasible Routes Length   = 0
BGP:     No Withdrawn Routes in this Update
BGP:  Path Attribute Length    = 18 bytes
BGP:  Attribute Flags = 0x04 (Well-known, Transitive)
BGP:  Attribute type code      = 1 (Origin)
BGP:  Attribute Data Length    = 1
BGP:  Origin type              = 0 (IGP)
BGP:  Attribute Flags = 0x04 (Well-known, Transitive)
BGP:  Attribute type code      = 2 (AS Path)
BGP:  Attribute Data Length    = 4
BGP:  AS Identifier            = 1367
BGP:  AS Identifier            = 12
BGP:  Attribute Flags = 0x04 (Well-known, Transitive)
BGP:  Attribute type code      = 3 (Next Hop)
BGP:  Attribute Data Length    = 4
BGP:  Next Hop                 = [200.8.2.1]
BGP:
BGP:  Network Layer Reachability Information:
BGP:    121.0.0.0/8
BGP:    122.0.0.0/8
BGP:    123.0.0.0/8
BGP:    136.35.0.0/16
BGP:    136.36.0.0/16
BGP:    136.37.0.0/16
BGP:    220.25.60.0/24
BGP:    220.25.61.0/24
```

Figure 13.7 Beginning of a BGP routing session.

common Distance Vector convergence problems, such as counting to infinity (Section 13.1). To keep a prefix's AS path up to date, a BGP router prepends its own AS number to the prefix's existing AS path before transmitting the prefix in an Update message to a peer. In our example, if router G accepts and installs into its routing table the update for 200.19.8.0/24 received from A having AS path [AS 1, AS 2, AS 3], it transmits the prefix to H with the prepended AS path of [AS 4, AS 1, AS 2, AS 3].

- *Routing table calculation:* The process of calculating routing table entries from the RIB-In is called the *Decision Process*. Based on configured policy information, a preferred path for each prefix is installed in the routing table. The Decision Process is invoked when the RIB-In changes—when new BGP updates are received, or a BGP session with a neighbor terminates, causing all data received from that neighbor to be deleted from the RIB-In. The Decision Process also must be invoked on policy changes, as these changes may well affect which of the RIB-In's paths are preferred.

- *Robustness/reliability:* Unlike the operation of the other protocols in this chapter, a BGP router does not refresh its routing information, instead sending updates only when changes occur. Since BGP runs over TCP, BGP Updates are delivered reliably, in order, and free from corruption. However, implementation or router hardware errors resulting in the corruption and/or deletion of parts of the BGP RIB-In are not rectified until BGP sessions are restarted—a manual process.

- *Aggregation:* A network operator can configure a BGP router so that it aggregates routing information. Aggregating multiple routes into a single prefix poses a problem: What path should be advertised for the aggregate? For example, suppose that in Figure 13.6, AS 1 is handing out pieces of two CIDR address blocks, 192.9.0.0/18 and 200.16.64.0/18, to its customers ASs 2–5. Router B is then configured to aggregate the BGP information received from ASs 2–5 into these two CIDR blocks before sending BGP updates to router F. But if the relevant part of router B's routing table is as pictured in Table 13.2, there is no accurate AS path that can be used for either block. To solve this problem, BGP introduces the concept of an *AS set*. Whereas an AS path (also called an *AS sequence*) indicates the exact sequence of ASs encountered on the way to the destination, an AS set indicates only the ASs that may be encountered somewhere along the path. AS sequences and AS sets can be concatenated within a BGP path attribute. Using brackets to indicate AS sequences and braces to indicate AS sets, router B would advertise 192.9.0.0/18 with an AS path attribute of [AS 1, AS 2]{AS 3} and 200.16.64.0/18 with an AS path of [AS 1]{AS 2, AS 3, AS 4, AS 5} in its BGP updates to F.

- *Policy controls:* BGP provides more opportunity for policy-based controls than do the other routing protocols in this chapter, combining the routing filters commonly deployed in Distance Vector protocols with the additional information provided by the AS path. BGP routers usually can be configured to accept a given set of prefixes, but only if they originated ultimately from a given AS. Alternatively, BGP routers usually can be configured to accept a different set of

Table 13.2 Aggregation Example Requiring AS Sets

Prefix	AS path
192.9.3.0/24	[AS 2, AS 3]
192.9.17.0/24	[AS 2]
200.16.67.0/24	[AS 4]
200.16.68.0/24	[AS 4]
200.16.75.0/24	[AS 5]
200.16.80.0/24	[AS 2, AS 3]
200.16.92.0/24	[AS 2]

prefixes, but only if the paths to the prefixes go through a particular provider. Sometimes these routing policies can even be configured automatically. ISPs maintain databases, such as the RIPE database [215], that describe which prefixes belong to which providers, together with other information on BGP peerings between ISPs. People have then written tools that convert these databases into automatically generated BGP router configuration files.

- *Security:* The first 16 bytes of a BGP message are reserved for authentication purposes. MD5-based authentication algorithms have been designed for BGP, similar to those used for RIPv2 and OSPF (Section 11.7.1). However, for BGP, this kind of authentication alone cannot prevent simple denial of service attacks, such as inserting TCP Resets to break the BGP routers' underlying TCP session. Preventing these attacks would require the deployment of additional security mechanisms at the IP and/or TCP level.

Figure 13.7 shows the beginning of a BGP session between the two routers 200.8.2.1 and 200.8.2.2. After exchanging Open messages and Keepalives, the two routers send each other a full set of routing updates, starting with the BGP Update message sent by 200.8.2.1. This update advertises eight prefixes, all having the AS path [AS 1367, AS 12], and a next hop of 200.8.2.1 (the advertising router itself). The setting of the *Origin* attribute to IGP in the update indicates that the eight prefixes belong to AS 12.

The other routing protocols in this chapter rely on an objective metric to converge eventually on loop-free paths. The fact that BGP does not have a true routing metric and instead allows routers to pick their routes based on configured policies can lead to problems—grossly inconsistent policies can lead to routing oscillations and/or unreachable destinations. For example, suppose in that Figure 13.6, router G has been configured to prefer sending traffic through AS 5 on its way to AS 1 and that similarly, router H has been configured to prefer using AS 4 as transit. G and H will initially find direct routes to the prefixes in AS 1, but after exchanging BGP Updates, they will prefer each other briefly, until they each realize that a loop is formed and go back to their direct routes. This process could then repeat indefinitely.

BGP has undergone a number of revisions since it was first published in 1989 [137]. Currently version 4, referred to as BGP-4, is deployed in the Internet. Previous versions, BGP-2 and BGP-3, were also deployed in the Internet; BGP-4 is the first BGP version capable of advertising CIDR prefixes.

BGP was also modified to create the OSI *Inter-Domain Routing Protocol* (IDRP). There are three main differences between IDRP and BGP. First, although IDRP was created to advertise OSI addresses, it can also advertise routes for other protocol suites at the same time (similar to Integrated IS-IS; see Section 13.5). Second, a reliable transport for routing updates was built directly into IDRP rather than relying on an external protocol such as TCP. Finally, IDRP implements another level of routing hierarchy by allowing the organization of ASs into clusters; similar support was introduced into BGP under the term *BGP confederations*. IDRP is considerably more complicated than BGP and has never seen any significant deployment.

The EGP used by IPv6 will undoubtedly be some form of BGP/IDRP. To date, the exact details of the resulting protocol are somewhat up in the air. The original intention of the IPv6 designers was to use IDRP, because it already supported the addressing flexibility to express IPv6 addresses. However, lately more effort has gone into developing multiprotocol extensions to BGP-4 [124] that can be used to carry IPv6 routing information.

IBGP

BGP information must be propagated across ASs. For example, in Figure 13.6, when router C learns BGP routing information from the neighboring AS 2, this information must somehow be conveyed to routers A and B so that it can be readvertised to ASs 4 and 6, respectively. In its original design, BGP accomplished this propagation by establishing BGP peering sessions between the routers of AS 1: A, B, and C. These sessions between routers belonging to the same Autonomous System are called *Internal BGP* (IBGP) sessions; BGP sessions between routers belonging to different Autonomous Systems are called *External BGP* (EBGP) sessions. Since IBGP routing exchanges are not protected against looping by the AS path mechanism, within each Autonomous System, every BGP router had to peer directly with every other BGP router. This situation is called *full-mesh IBGP*.

Because IBGP routing is not protected by AS path, policy inconsistencies between IBGP peers are potentially more serious than between EBGP peers, possibly resulting in routing loops. These problems have been seen in some networks, with the default IBGP preferences specified in the BGP specification and implemented by the two most common BGP implementations (Cisco and GATED) known to be at odds.

Full-mesh IBGP can strain the capacity of a BGP router. The more peers (IBGP or EBGP) a BGP router has, the greater the number of transport connections and the larger the Routing Information Base. Ever since BGP was devised, people have been working on ways to avoid the full-mesh IBGP requirement. Several proposals have since emerged, with two of them, BGP route reflection and BGP confederations, seeing significant deployment in today's Internet.

In both BGP route reflection and BGP confederations, the AS is divided into regions, or clusters. BGP routers internal to each region then need establish IBGP sessions only with routers in their own region, with routers on the region boundaries establishing IBGP sessions with routers in other regions. Figure 13.8 shows a division of AS 1 into three such regions, with each region containing three IBGP speakers.

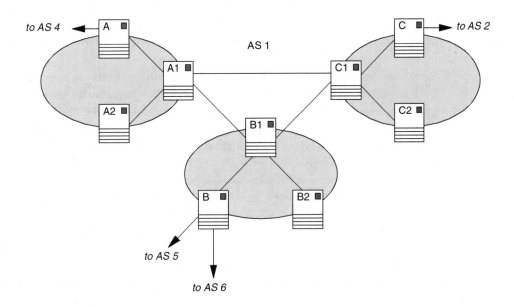

Figure 13.8 Partitioning AS 1 to avoid a full IBGP mesh.

In BGP route reflection [17], one router in each region is designated the *Route Reflector* (RR). Each other router in the region (collectively called the Route Reflector's *client peers*) establishes a single IBGP session to the Route Reflector. When the Route Reflector receives an IBGP update from one of its client peers, the Route Reflector forwards (or reflects) the update to its other clients and also to its peers in other regions. In Figure 13.8, A1 would be designated the Route Reflector for the leftmost region; IBGP updates received from A2 would be reflected by A1 to router A and also sent to the Route Reflectors in the two other regions (routers B1 and C1). The various Route Reflectors (routers A1, B1, and C1 in our example) are connected together in a full

IBGP mesh, and so, when properly configured, IBGP route reflection resists routing loops. IBGP route reflection also employs two mechanisms to prevent loops in the case of misconfiguration. To prevent loops within a region, the Route Reflector inserts its client's BGP Identifier into the ORIGINATOR_ID attribute when reflecting the client's routes. The Route Reflector then knows never to reflect these labeled routes back to the originating client. To prevent loops between regions, each region is assigned a cluster ID. When advertising IBGP updates to another region, the Route Reflector prepends its cluster ID to a new BGP path attribute called the CLUSTER_LIST, which in turn prevents intercluster loops, just as the BGP AS path prevents inter-AS loops.

In *BGP confederations* [248], the regions are called *confederations*. Within a single confederation, full-mesh IBGP is performed. To prevent interconfederation loops, each confederation is assigned a *confederation ID*. A BGP router then prevents loops by prepending its confederation's ID to the AS path attribute when sending IBGP updates to other confederations. To keep the division into confederations from being visible outside the AS, confederation IDs are later stripped from the AS path attribute at the AS boundary.

BGP Route Servers [94] are another proposed alternative, similar in many respects to BGP route reflection. In this proposal, regions are called *clusters*. Each cluster is assigned a Route Server, to which all other IBGP speakers in the cluster (called the Route Server's clients) establish IBGP sessions. An IBGP update received by a Route Server from a client is sent to the other clients in the cluster and to the Route Server's IBGP neighbors in other clusters. To avoid looping within a cluster, each client inserts its BGP Identifier into an ADVERTISER path attribute in updates sent to the Route Server. To prevent intercluster loops, cluster IDs are accumulated within an RCID path attribute similar in function to BGP's AS path.

One last alternative is to use the AS's Interior Gateway Protocol to propagate BGP information across the AS. The BGP-OSPF interaction document (Section 11.6.1) shows how to use OSPF to propagate BGP routes for prefixes belonging to neighbor ASs—that is, prefixes whose BGP AS path is of length 1. To propagate BGP information for prefixes having longer AS paths, a special OSPF LSA, called the external-attribute-LSA (Section 7.6) was designed but has never been deployed in a production network.

BGP Path Attributes

Each Update message contains a collection of path attributes and a list of prefixes sharing the attributes. BGP attributes employ type-length-value (TLV) encoding. The current list of BGP attribute types is given in [153] and is reproduced in Table 13.3. Some BGP attributes, such as the AS path, must be present in every Update message—these are called *mandatory* attributes. Another category of attributes, the *transitive* attributes, are carried unaltered from one BGP speaker to the next.

Table 13.3 BGP Path Attributes

Type Code	BGP Attribute	Category
1	ORIGIN	Mandatory
2	AS_PATH	Mandatory
3	NEXT_HOP	Mandatory
4	MULTI_EXIT_DISC	
5	LOCAL_PREF	
6	ATOMIC_AGGREGATE	
7	AGGREGATOR	Transitive
8	COMMUNITY	Transitive
9	ORIGINATOR_ID	
10	CLUSTER_LIST	
11	DPA	Transitive
12	ADVERTISER	
13	RCID_PATH	

As described earlier, the AS_PATH attribute is used to prevent BGP routing loops and also allows BGP to support certain routing policy configurations. The ORIGIN attribute indicates whether the AS path is complete. If the ORIGIN is set to IGP, the AS path is complete; otherwise (ORIGIN set to INCOMPLETE or EGP) the AS path may be only a subset of the ASs encountered on the way to the destinations. Most BGP routers can be configured to make policy decisions based on the ORIGIN attribute, although the main use of this attribute was to mark those routes that were learned by the (now historical) EGP protocol during the EGP-to-BGP transition.

The NEXT_HOP attribute can be used by a BGP router to indicate that data should be forwarded to an IP router other than the BGP router itself. Sometimes called third-party routing information, a similar field was present in the EGP protocol's routing updates, and there are similar concepts in other protocols, such as OSPF's forwarding address. NEXT_HOP eliminates extra forwarding hops in some situations (see Section 11.6.1).

MULTI_EXIT_DISC, LOCAL_PREF, and DPA are all metrics of a sort. When two neighboring ASs are connected at multiple points, one AS can use MULTI_EXIT_DISC (multiple exit discriminator) to inform the other AS which is the better entry point; the entry with the lower MULTI_EXIT_DISC value should generally be favored. A BGP router uses LOCAL_PREF (local preference) to tell its IBGP neighbors whether it should be a preferred exit point from the AS; BGP routers advertising higher LOCAL_PREF values are usually chosen as exits. The DPA (destination preference attribute [40]) can be used by a router to bias the routing of its BGP neighbors. DPA has been proposed as a mechanism to encourage symmetric routing (that is, traffic going from A to B takes the same path as traffic from B to A) in the Internet, although DPA has not been widely deployed. All these three metrics are advisory. Any BGP router can be configured to ignore them in favor of other routing policies.

When it combines a collection of routes into a single aggregate, the BGP router advertises the aggregate route with an AGGREGATOR attribute containing the router's AS number and IP address. This attribute is for information purposes only. Another attribute, ATOMIC_AGGREGATE, was intended to prevent certain advertised aggregates from being later deaggregated (that is, overridden by more specific prefixes) by a router's BGP peers; however, both the specification and implementation of this attribute seem to be minimal.

The COMMUNITY attribute [39] is used to group a collection of prefixes so that they can be treated as a single unit by configured BGP policies. A few standard communities are specified, such as the NO_EXPORT community—prefixes tagged with NO_EXPORT will not be advertised out of their Autonomous System. Other communities can be established by each AS. For example, an ISP might want to create a separate community for each of its customers. Using communities in this way would allow a policy, such as "Advertise the prefixes of customers A, B, and C to this peer only," to be configured without explicitly itemizing the prefixes that belong to A, B, and C. Although labeled as transitive, the COMMUNITY attribute is commonly stripped at AS boundaries. The COMMUNITY attribute is similar in function to OSPF's external route tag (Section 3.2).

The remaining attributes implement loop prevention in the various alternatives to full-mesh IBGP. ORIGINATOR_ID and CLUSTER_LIST are used by BGP route reflection [17], and ADVERTISER and RCID_PATH are used by the BGP Route Server proposal [94].

BGP Operational Issues

The BGP routers at an Autonomous System's boundary may have much larger routing tables than the routers interior to the AS. The question is, How do the routers internal to the AS get enough routing information to participate in loop-free forwarding? If the AS does not provide transit services (that is, all traffic entering or leaving the AS has either a local source or a local destination) the answer is easy: Just have the BGP routers import a default route into the IGP.

Transit ASs have two alternatives for getting routing information into their interior routers. First, they can leak enough BGP information into the IGP so that, combined with a default route, the interior routers can make good forwarding decisions (Section 13.7). This brings up the subject of *IGP synchronization*. If the interior routers are learning BGP information through the IGP, the BGP routers on the other side of the AS should not readvertise these routes to their EBGP peers until the appropriate IGP routes have been installed. This is the general principle that a route should not be advertised unless it is being used for forwarding. For example, in Figure 13.6, router A would not readvertise AS 3's networks to router G until these routes appear in AS 1's IGP routing.

Using these mechanisms, the default-free ASs at the core of the Internet would have to leak the whole Internet routing table into their IGPs, which they are usually loathe to do. Instead they typically run IBGP between all their routers—commonly called *Universal IBGP*. In these ASs, the IGP is relegated to the role of resolving BGP NEXT_HOP addresses. (Another alternative, which is to tunnel traffic between the BGP routers, would work, although it has not been deployed, to my knowledge.)

The size of the routing tables in the Internet's core routers is always a concern. To keep the routing tables small and to encourage aggregation, some of the backbone providers refuse to accept BGP updates for prefixes longer than a certain length. To date, the current limit is 18 bits, although addresses assigned before the advent of CIDR (for example, Class C networks falling into 192/8) are usually excluded from this limit.

BGP routing within the Internet has shown considerable instability, with a number of unexpected and pathological behaviors uncovered by studies (such as [132]) of BGP traffic patterns. To reduce the amount of BGP routing oscillations, some BGP implementations perform *route dampening* [254], whereby a BGP router seeing a prefix that is flapping (that is, is withdrawn and then reappears) will wait an interval before readvertising the prefix; the more often the prefix flaps, the longer the router will wait before readvertising.

When configuring BGP routing policies or when debugging BGP routing problems, you often want to find the ISP (and the people contacts) associated with a particular AS number. For example, you may suddenly find that the routing table size in your routers has doubled, with all new routes originating from a particular AS number. The Internic keeps a list of AS number assignments [7]. Contact information for a particular AS can also be obtained by using the command **whois -h rs.internic.net "as** *as-number***"**. The ISP community has developed other tools to analyze BGP routing, such as ASExplorer [6]. This tool can display the routes that are currently flapping in the Internet's BGP system, the nets that are currently being announced by any given AS, contact information for the AS, and so on.

13.4   IGRP

The *Inter-Gateway Routing Protocol* (IGRP) [96] is Cisco Systems' proprietary routing protocol. IGRP is a Distance Vector IGP and is deployed in many Internet sites that use Cisco routers. Cisco has also used IGRP to route other protocol stacks, such as OSI.

IGRP is very similar to RIP. The main difference between the two protocols is their choice of metrics. Instead of using hop count, an IGRP router advertises six separate pieces of information with each destination: (a) the static delay that packets will incur, (b) the amount of bandwidth provided by the path to the destination, (c) the current traffic load on the path, (d) the path's error rate, (e) the path's MTU, and (f) the number of router hops to the destination. If it sees a routing advertisement from one of its neighbors, an IGRP router combines the first four of these factors into a single composite metric that is inversely proportional to available bandwidth and proportional to both delay and error rate (for the exact equation, see [96]). If an IGRP router sees the same destination being advertised by multiple neighboring routers, it chooses the path going through the router that advertises the smallest composite metric. IGRP's composite metric allows better path discrimination than RIP's hop count. For example, RIP cannot discriminate between a 9,600-baud line and a T1 line, whereas IGRP's composite metric can.

IGRP's hop-count metric is used to terminate the counting-to-infinity behavior experienced by IGRP and most Distance Vector protocols. When the number of hops to a destination exceeds a configured value (set to 100 by default and not to exceed 255), the destination is considered unreachable.

IGRP is more aggressive than most routing protocols in trying to spread out traffic for a single destination over multiple links (also called load sharing). Not only can traffic be spread across equal-cost paths (as is done in the OSPF and IS-IS protocols) but also, with care, an IGRP router can be configured to load share over paths of relatively similar costs.

- *Type:* IGRP is a Distance Vector IGP.

- *Encapsulation:* IGRP runs directly over the Internet Protocol, as IP protocol 88.

- *Path characteristics:* An IGRP router selects the path with the smallest composite metric. For example, if two paths are otherwise equivalent, the path with the smaller static delay is chosen. Or, if two paths differ only in their available bandwidth, the one having the higher available bandwidth is chosen.

- *Neighbor discovery and maintenance:* IGRP has no neighbor discovery or maintenance procedures aside from the exchange of routing updates.

- *Routing data distribution:* An IGRP router broadcasts its routing table to its neighbors every 90 seconds. For each destination, the IGRP router advertises six properties of the path that the router is currently using to that destination: the path's static delay, provisioned bandwidth, current load, error rate, MTU, and hop count.

- *Response to changes:* When its routing table changes, an IGRP router sends triggered updates rather than waiting for the next 90-second epoch. However, unlike RIP, each triggered update in IGRP advertises the full routing table.

- *Routing table calculation:* When an update for a destination is received from a neighbor, the path's properties are modified to take into account the delay, bandwidth, and error characteristics of the link to the neighbor. When an IGRP router receives updates for the same destination from two or more neighbors, the (modified) path having the smallest composite metric is installed into the routing table and is then broadcast in the router's own IGRP updates.

- *Robustness/reliability:* To ensure that routing updates are delivered, an IGRP router sends a complete set of routing updates (describing the entire routing table) every 90 seconds. If the receiving IGRP router goes 270 seconds without receiving an update for a given destination, the router deems the destination unreachable.

- *Aggregation:* Like RIP, IGRP automatically aggregates routing information at the boundary of a subnetted network. In the updated version of IGRP for CIDR addressing, called EIGRP, an EIGRP router can be configured to aggregate routes into any CIDR prefix (similar to the address aggregation that may occur at OSPF area borders; see Section 6.1).

- *Policy controls:* Routing policies are implemented by configuring routing filters, which tell the IGRP routers which routes they are allowed to receive and which routes they are allowed to advertise. However, Cisco recommends that route filtering be performed mostly at the edge of an IGRP routing domain. For example, if two sets of routers did not want to exchange complete routing information, they could be broken into two separate routing domains; one or more routers participating in both IGRP routing domains would control which routes were advertised from one domain to the other (see Section 13.7).

- *Security:* IGRP has no provisions to protect its routing protocol exchanges and data from security attacks.

To improve on the basic Distance Vector convergence properties, IGRP employs some of the same stabilizing mechanisms that are used by RIP. These mechanisms are triggered updates, split horizon, and hold down (Section 13.1).

Unlike the other routing protocols in this chapter, which express a default route as the prefix 0.0.0.0/0, IGRP allows the network administrator to say, "The default path should follow the same path as packets to network X." For example, network X could belong to your service provider. Hello, the original NSFNET's routing protocol, had similar logic, with the default path following network 10, the ARPANET's network number.

Also like RIP, IGRP is not a "classless" routing protocol, assuming instead that the TCP routing domain consists of Class A, B, and C networks, possibly divided into fixed-sized subnets. In order to support CIDR addressing and also to improve the convergence properties of IGRP, Cisco developed *Enhanced IGRP* (EIGRP) [43].

EIGRP

EIGRP not only is capable of advertising CIDR prefixes but also contains significant changes in protocol mechanism and has improved convergence properties. EIGRP is still a Distance Vector protocol, but by implementing the *Distributed Update ALgorithm* (DUAL) of [82], it maintains loop-free paths even while the network changes, avoiding counting to infinity. As with previous proposals for loop-free Distance Vector protocols, DUAL maintains loop-free paths by synchronizing the distributed routing calculations across routers. This synchronization significantly complicates the basic Distance Vector algorithm.

- Hello messages are added to monitor the reachability of neighbors.

- A reliable transport mechanism is added to ensure the reliable and sequenced delivery of EIGRP messages between neighboring routers.

- Instead of just keeping the best route, alternate loop-free routes must also be stored by the EIGRP router. If the best route has a cost of X, the alternate routes are those that are advertised by neighboring routers as having a cost less than X. If the neighbor advertising the best route fails, one of the alternate routes is placed into the routing table.

- If the neighbor advertising the best route fails and there are no alternate paths, the EIGRP router begins a new distributed calculation for a loop-free route to the destination by contacting its neighbors. A neighbor having a loop-free route responds with the route; otherwise the neighbor contacts its neighbors. In essence, requests for recalculation flood through the network until a new loop-free route is returned. During this recalculation, the destination remains unreachable, similar to a hold-down operation.

13.5   Integrated IS-IS

Integrated IS-IS is an adaptation of the standard OSI connectionless data routing protocol, IS-IS, to be used for IP routing. Integrated IS-IS is also sometimes called Dual IS-IS. The basic protocol mechanisms for Integrated IS-IS, including the data-link encapsulation, are defined in the IS-IS specification (ISO document 10589 [112]). The Internet's RFC 1195 [30] then defines how IP routing data is carried by the protocol and the required calculations to produce an IP routing table from this data. The resulting protocol can perform routing for the IP and OSI protocol stacks simultaneously; hence the term *integrated*. (The creators of Integrated IS-IS coined the term *Ships in the Night*, or *SIN* for short, for the alternative of running separate routing protocols for each protocol stack.)

Integrated IS-IS is not widely deployed in the Internet but is run in a handful of large ISPs employing Cisco routers. Integrated IS-IS is a link-state IGP that resembles OSPF in many ways.

The OSI terminology used in IS-IS is a little difficult to follow for people who are familiar only with TCP/IP. Routers are called *Intermediate Systems* (ISs); hence the name IS-IS for the standard protocol spoken between ISs. The packets used by the routing protocol are called *Protocol Data Units* (PDUs).

The individual pieces of the IS-IS link-state database are called *link-state PDUs* (LSPs). LSPs are distributed throughout the IS-IS routing domain by a reliable flooding algorithm similar to OSPF's. IS-IS again uses the Dijkstra algorithm to calculate the router's routing table from the collected LSPs. However, by restricting the maximum path length to 1,024, IS-IS improves the performance of the standard Dijkstra.

Routing domains running Integrated IS-IS can be organized into a two-level hierarchy by splitting the routing domain into IS-IS *areas*.

- *Encapsulation:* Integrated IS-IS runs directly over the data-link layer. For example, when run over Ethernet, IP and Integrated IS-IS use separate Ethernet type codes; when run over an ATM subnet, an encapsulation (such as LLC/SNAP [133]) that can distinguish IP traffic from IS-IS control traffic must be used.

- *Path characteristics:* A value between 1 and 32 is configured for each network segment, called *circuit* by IS-IS. The cost of a path is then the sum of the path's constituent circuit costs. IS-IS selects the least-cost path(s). Path cost cannot exceed 1,024, or the path is deemed unusable.

- *Neighbor discovery and maintenance:* Neighboring ISs are discovered through the periodic transmission and reception of *IS-IS Hello PDUs* (IIH PDUs). Each IIH PDU specifies a Hold Time: the number of seconds that the neighbor should maintain reachability to the sending IS without receiving further IIH PDUs. The Hold timer is set so that even if some IIH PDUs are dropped, the neighbor connection remains active.

- *Routing data distribution:* An IS describes its local environment, for example, its attached circuits and their costs, IP prefixes, and so on, in at least 1 and not more than 256 LSPs. These LSPs are then reliably flooded throughout the IS-IS domain. The format of LSPs is rather free-form and easily extendable, with each LSP containing a sequence of TLV (type-length-value) encoded data items. A special LSP, called the *pseudonode LSP*, lists all of the ISs attached to a particular circuit (the equivalent of OSPF's network-LSA). The collection of LSPs generated by all IS-IS routers forms the link-state database.

- *Response to changes:* Changes in the local environment of an IS cause it to update one of its LSPs, originate a new LSP, or purge an LSP from the IS-IS routing domain. Purging an LSP works as follows. Each LSP has a *Lifetime* field, the number of seconds remaining before the LSP is considered to be defunct. In order to purge an LSP from all ISs' link-state databases, the IS sets the LSP's Lifetime to 0 and refloods the LSP.

- *Routing table calculation:* IS-IS performs a Dijkstra calculation on the collection of LSPs, producing the routing table. The Dijkstra algorithm is made more efficient by limiting the path cost to values less than 1,024.

- *Robustness/reliability:* In case LSPs are damaged or mistakenly discarded by an IS, each IS reoriginates its own LSPs every 15 minutes, whether or not the contents have changed. IS-IS also protects against flooding loops by decrementing an LSP's Lifetime by at least 1 at each flooding hop, and an LSP checksum field detects LSP corruption during flooding or when held in the link-state database of an IS. IS-IS also ensures that a link is bidirectional before using the link in the Dijkstra calculation.

- *Aggregation:* In Integrated IS-IS, routing information can be aggregated at area boundaries before being advertised into the Level 2 subdomain.

- *Policy controls:* As with OSPF, area boundaries can be configured to implement certain policies. Data traffic stays within a single area if at all possible; if not, paths internal to the IS-IS routing domain are preferred over those that exit and reenter the domain.

- *Security:* The PDUs of Integrated IS-IS may be authenticated. Only trivial authentication, a clear password such as that used by the TELNET application, has been completely defined for the protocol.

Because an IS can originate only a relatively small number (namely, 256) of LSPs, ISs typically create large LSPs containing a mixture of data: interface costs, area information, external routing information, and so on. However, since IS-IS runs over the data-link layer and does not have access to the fragmentation services of the network layer, care must be taken so that the size of any LSP does not exceed the MTU of any segment within the IS-IS domain.

An IS describes a collection of LSPs, using *Sequence Number PDUs*. Partial Sequence Number PDUs are used to acknowledge receipt of LSPs during the IS-IS reliable-flooding algorithm. Immediately after an IS discovers a neighboring IS, the two ISs synchronize link-state databases. Synchronization is performed by each IS sending a full summary of its link state-database, using *Complete Sequence Number PDUs* (CSNPs). After receiving the full set of Complete Sequence Number PDUs from the neighbor, an IS floods to its neighbor the LSPs that the neighbor is missing.

To simplify flooding over LANs, IS-IS elects a *Designated Intermediate System* for each LAN, similar to OSPF's Designated Router. However, unlike OSPF, IS-IS does not explicitly acknowledge LSPs flooded over the LAN. Instead flooding reliability is achieved by having the Designated Intermediate System multicast a complete set of Complete Sequence Number PDUs onto the LAN every 10 seconds; in essence, the Designated Router is continually performing the full database synchronization with the other ISs on the LAN.

IS-IS is a little more laissez faire about database synchronization than is OSPF. For example, unlike OSPF, IS-IS does not require database synchronization over a circuit before the circuit is made available for data traffic. Also, because LSPs are not explicitly acknowledged on LANs, synchronization problems are somewhat more difficult to detect in IS-IS, and the LSP purge operation is not absolutely reliable.

The area routing scheme in IS-IS is subtly different from OSPF's area routing. IS-IS requires a single physically connected *Level 2 subdomain*, with areas (*Level 1 subdomains*) directly connected to it. Partitions of areas are automatically repaired by tunneling (Section 1.2.3) through the Level 2 subdomain. On the other hand, OSPF's central subdomain, called the OSPF backbone area, is not required to be physically connected, and OSPF has no provision to repair area partitions (see Chapter 6). IS-IS forces strict hierarchical routing between areas: Inter-area data traffic originating in one area follows a default route to the Level 2 subdomain, where it is forwarded by Level 2 routing to the destination area. In comparison, OSPF allows data traffic to bypass the backbone area through configuration of OSPF virtual links (Section 6.1.2).

IS-IS needed no modification to support CIDR addressing. The IS-IS protocol was developed at the same time that OSPF was designed. OSPF considered, but did not use, IS-IS as a starting point; see Section 3.2 for more information.

13.6 Historical Protocols

We have now discussed all the unicast routing protocols in use in the Internet today; multicast routing protocols are discussed in Chapter 14, Multicast Routing Protocols. However, additional unicast routing protocols have been deployed in or designed for the Internet in the past. They are mentioned briefly in this section for completeness; also included are further references for the interested reader.

The *Gateway-to-Gateway Protocol* (GGP) [101] was one of the Internet's first routing protocols, a Distance Vector IGP run by the ARPANET's routers when the ARPANET was the core of the Internet. GGP had a couple of unusual features for a Distance Vector protocol. To keep track of the state of a neighbor, a GGP router periodically sent GGP echo messages, expecting GGP echo replies in response. When j out of n (typically two out of four) replies were received, the neighbor was declared operational; if k out of n (typically three out of four) echoes failed to provoke responses, the neighbor was declared down. This procedure allowed the routing protocol to reject links having excessive error rates [146]. GGP also called for explicit acknowledgment of routing updates, allowing a GGP router to send changes only to a neighbor instead of continually rebroadcasting the entire routing table. GGP shared packet formats with another protocol that was being developed at the same time: EGP.

The *Exterior Gateway Protocol* (EGP) [162], [219] was the first instance of the class of Internet protocols called EGPs. Until replaced by BGP, EGP was the protocol used everywhere in the Internet for exchanging routing information between Autonomous Systems. EGP was a Distance Vector protocol that its designers felt did not have good enough convergence properties to be run over an arbitrary topology of ASs. For this reason, while running EGP, the Internet was forced into organizing its ASs into a strictly hierarchical tree structure. Since the AS topology was supposed to have no loops, EGP's routing metric could be ignored (a metric being something to compare two different paths but there being only a single possible path in strict tree), earning EGP the reputation of being a *reachability protocol* rather than a routing protocol. Experience with EGP was a driving force in the design of BGP, from the compactness of routing updates (indexed by metric and next hop) to the way network administrators configured EGP to accomplish rudimentary forms of policy-based routing ([206]).

The *Hello Protocol* [161] was a Distance Vector IGP. Hello was deployed within the original NSFNET network, which consisted of LSI-11 routers (Fuzzballs) interconnected by 56K links. Hello's distinguishing feature was its choice of routing metric: measured delay. As a result, Hello calculated least-delay paths for data traffic. When the NSFNET transitioned to IBM RT routers and T1 links, the Hello Protocol was replaced by a routing protocol (called the *NSFNET IGP* [207]) based on an early version of the IS-IS protocol specification.

Inter-Domain Policy Routing (IDPR) [236] is a link-state EGP. Designed as a replacement for the Internet's EGP protocol, IDPR competed against BGP for widescale deployment in the Internet and eventually lost. IDPR is capable of expressing very sophisticated routing policies. For example, using IDPR, an AS could specify that it only allows commercial traffic during the hours from midnight until 5A.M. IDPR also has superior security provisions, allowing digital signatures on routing information along the lines of [190]. IDPR is considerably more complicated than other Internet routing protocols, and its abandonment of the Internet's hop-by-hop routing paradigm probably sealed its doom. In the Internet, every router makes an independent decision on how to forward a packet, after consulting the router's routing table. In contrast, the first-hop IDPR router calculates the entire path of a datagram and then explicitly installs the path in all the IDPR routers on the way to the destination, a procedure sometimes called *flow setup*.

13.7   Interaction among Routing Protocols

As we have shown in this chapter, TCP/IP has many routing protocols. As originally designed, routers within an AS were to run a common routing protocol (IGP) among themselves, whereas a different routing protocol (EGP) was used to exchange routing information with other ASs. But in practice, routing in the Internet is a little more chaotic than originally designed, and it is not at all unusual for a router to be running three or four different routing protocols simultaneously.

When a router runs multiple routing protocols, it must arbitrate among them, performing the following tests on each learned route.

1. When a route is learned from a routing protocol, should it be accepted and installed in the routing table, to be used when forwarding data traffic?

2. When two or more routing protocols learn routes to the same destination, and all are acceptable, which route should be preferred?

3. When should destinations learned by one routing protocol be readvertised by another? If readvertised, what costs and other advertised parameters should be used?

These three tests are by no means independent. Only when a route passes test 1, the *route filter*, will it be eligible to enter the preference contest in test 2. And only if the route wins the preference test and is installed in the forwarding table will it be eligible for possible readvertisement by other routing protocols in test 3: A router readvertising a route that it does not really use in forwarding may create routing loops or black holes.

Designing these tests is a difficult task. Route filters are essentially hop-by-hop policy statements and work fairly well with Distance Vector algorithms, such as RIP and BGP. In fact, automated tools exist to generate BGP routing filters from Internet routing policy databases, such as the RIPE database [215]. However, route filters in general cannot be used on routes learned by the shortest-path calculation of a link-state routing protocol such as OSPF.

Deciding which routing protocol's route to prefer is made difficult because of the different, incomparable routing metrics employed by the various protocols. OSPF assigns a 16-bit cost to each link, with no bound on path cost (Section 11.3.1). RIP uses hop count, with a maximum hop count of 16 (Section 13.1). BGP, like its precursor, EGP, really has no metric, making all of its routing decisions based on user-defined policies (Section 13.3). Integrated IS-IS assigns a cost of 1 to 32 to each link, with path cost capped at 1,024 (Section 13.5). And the list goes on.

These differing metrics also make it difficult to readvertise routes from one protocol to another. Should you try to translate the metric from one protocol into another or simply require the network administrator to configure the advertised costs? Either way, some information is lost when readvertising, which may lead to routing loops in some circumstances. This information loss during readvertisement is the reason why IBGP is used to transport BGP routing information across ASs rather than just importing the BGP information into the IGP at one side of the AS and the readvertising back into BGP at the other (although you can make an IGP carry full BGP information in some cases; see Sections 7.6 and 11.6.1). There are other issues besides differing metrics that make readvertisement difficult. For example, not all routing protocols can even express the same set of destinations—RIPv1, still in common use today, cannot express general CIDR prefixes but is instead limited to the traditional Class A, B, and C networks with fixed-sized subnets (see Section 1.2.2).

There are very few documents describing the interaction of multiple routing protocols. RFC 1812, *Requirements for IP Version 4 Routers* [12], has a few sections explaining general principles for arbitrating between multiple protocols and readvertising information from one protocol to another. Although at one point it looked as though the IETF was going to attempt to write documents defining the interaction between every pair of Internet routing protocols, the only document written to date is the one describing OSPF-BGP interaction (see Section 11.6.1).

Nonetheless all router vendors have been forced to design interactions between the various routing protocols they support, and by now, all vendors support a common core functionality. They all allow you to specify which destinations you are willing to accept from a given routing protocol, and, depending on protocol, you can filter on additional parameters. For example, using RIP, you can usually say that you will accept a route but only if it is received from a particular RIP neighbor. When using BGP, you can specify that the route have a given AS path or that it originated from a particular AS, and so on. To arbitrate among multiple protocols wishing to write the same routing table entry, they usually allow you to associate a preference value with each accepted route. And the vendor usually allows you to specify the exact list of networks to readvertise into a routing protocol, together with costs and other protocol-specific advertised attributes, such as the ability to modify advertised AS paths in BGP. To be sure, this leaves a lot of the responsibility for making things work with the network administrator who creates all this configuration, but such is the state of the art.

Let us use the GATED program [83] as an example. Suppose that our GATED box is talking BGP to neighboring AS 174, from which we are willing to accept the networks 18/8, 192.1/16, and 199.18.93/24 but no others. Suppose that our GATED box is also talking RIP to router 10.1.4.200, from which we are willing to accept only 199.18.93/24 and 200.2.67/24. Furthermore, if we receive 199.18.93/24 from both BGP and RIP, we want the RIP route to win. Finally, we want the RIP routes, but not the BGP routes, imported into OSPF as external Type 2 routes of cost 1. This leads to the configuration file depicted in Figure 13.9.

```
import proto bgp autonomoussystem 174 {
    18.0.0.0 exact;
    192.1.0.0 masklen 16 exact;
    199.18.93.0 exact preference 2;
}
import proto rip gateway 10.1.4.200 {
    199.18.93.0 exact preference 1;
    200.2.67.0 exact;
}
export proto ospfase type 2 metric 1 {
    proto rip gateway 10.1.4.200 {
        199.18.93.0 exact;
        200.2.67.0 exact;
    }
}
```

Figure 13.9 Interaction between routing protocols in GATED.

Further Reading

The book *Routing in Communications Networks* by Steenstrup [237] provides a good description of routing algorithms used in packet-switching networks, such as the Internet. The book also covers routing in circuit-switched networks; high-speed networks, such as optical networks; and mobile networks, such as cellular and packet-radio networks.

For information on how the Internet's BGP routing is configured and managed, see *Internet Routing Architectures* by Halabi [89].

14

Multicast Routing Protocols

In this chapter, we compare and contrast the multicast protocols that have been developed for the Internet: DVMRP, MOSPF, PIM Dense, PIM Sparse, and CBT. This chapter builds on the basic information presented on multicast routing in Chapter 9. In particular, throughout this chapter, we use the multicast network shown in Figure 9.1 and the corresponding source-based trees and shared trees in Figures 9.3 and 9.4 to illustrate the operation of each protocol.

As summarized in Table 14.1, these protocols can be split into two categories: those that produce source-based trees and those that construct a shared tree.

Table 14.1 Categorization of Internet Multicast Protocols. (Asterisks indicate that the protocol relies on unicast routing to locate multicast sources.)

	Source-Based Trees	
Shared Tree	Broadcast-and Prune	Domainwide Reports
PIM Sparse*	DVMRP	MOSPF
CBT*	PIM Dense*	

The categories that we used for unicast routing protocols in Chapter 13 also apply somewhat to multicast routing protocols. The Distance Vector versus link-state debate is also present in the multicast routing arena. A router running a source-based protocol needs to know where a multicast source is, in order to calculate the router's place on the datagram's path, if any. DVMRP advertises source information using a standard Distance Vector mechanism. MOSPF, on the other hand, advertises its sources by using OSPF's link-state routing mechanisms. But a third mechanism is possible for a source-based multicast routing protocol: You can simply get the source information from the unicast routing, employing reverse-path forwarding (also called reverse-path broadcasting; see Section 9.3) to construct the path of each multicast datagram. This is the strategy of the Protocol Independent Multicast, Dense Mode (PIM Dense) protocol. Both PIM Sparse and CBT also depend on unicast routing so that their routers can forward multicast packets to the shared tree's RP for further distribution down to the leaves. In fact, the "protocol independent" in PIM is a reminder that any unicast routing protocol can serve this function.

Relying on unicast routing has its advantages. Unicast routing is ubiquitous in the Internet, and protocols that do not advertise source (or RP) routing information do not have to worry about routing updates and convergence times. However, relying on unicast routing makes incremental deployment difficult. DVMRP and MOSPF can handle situations in which multicast and unicast paths diverge (that is, they can forward multicast datagrams around nonmulticast routers), whereas the other protocols in this chapter require that the unicast path to the multicast source (or RP) consist completely of multicast-capable routers.

In the multicast equivalent of the IGP-EGP split, there are *intradomain* and *interdomain* multicast routing protocols. MOSPF, since it is built on top of an OSPF routing domain, is clearly an intradomain protocol. DVMRP and PIM Dense are definitely also more suited to intradomain use, although DVMRP plays both the intradomain and interdomain role on the MBONE. Both PIM Sparse and CBT were originally conceived as interdomain routing protocols, designed within the IETF's Inter-Domain Multicast Routing (IDMR) Working Group. However, due to difficulties in incremental deployment and in automated RP (core) placement, it now looks as though both protocols will be initially deployed as intradomain protocols instead.

14.1   Broadcast-and-Prune Protocols

Source-based multicast protocols can be further divided into broadcast-and-prune protocols versus those protocols that broadcast their group membership information (these latter broadcasts are sometimes called *domainwide reports*). In a broadcast-and-prune protocol, the source-based tree is initially built to encompass all network segments, regardless of group membership. The first multicast datagram will be sent along this initial tree. A router at a leaf of this tree may receive the datagram and realize that it has no group members on its attached segments. If so, the router indicates that it does not need to receive these datagrams anymore, by sending *Prune messages* to its upstream neighbor. This neighbor may in turn send a Prune to its upstream neighbor, and so on, until the tree has been rolled back to reach only group members.

Figure 14.1 shows an example from our sample multicast network. A multicast datagram with source S1 and destination G1 is initially forwarded to two segments without group members: 128.4.1/24 and 128.4.2/24. This causes R8 and R9 to send Prunes to R7, R7 to R4, and so on, until the tree on the lower left of Figure 9.3 is attained.

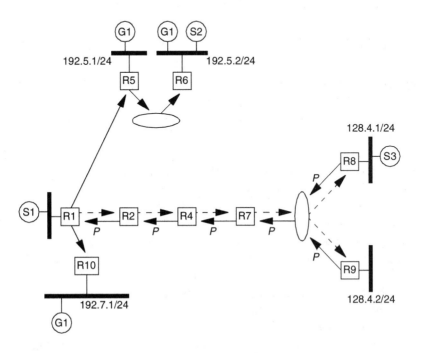

Figure 14.1 Operation of a broadcast-and-prune protocol.

Prune information is eventually deleted, to make the routing robust in the face of unexpected failures (implementation bugs and so on). This deletion causes the pruning process to periodically begin anew. If a new group member appears on a segment not currently on the tree, *Graft messages* are forwarded toward the source to extend the tree to the new group member. Graft messages need to be reliable, and so they are retransmitted until acknowledged. In Figure 14.1, if a host on 128.4.1/24 were to join G1, grafts would be sent from R8 to R7, R7 to R4, and so on, until the branch R1-R2-R4-R7-R8 is grafted onto the tree.

MOSPF, on the other hand, is an example of a protocol that broadcasts its group membership information throughout the routing domain. This allows MOSPF to restrict the initial tree to group members only, avoiding the broadcast-and-prune procedure entirely.

One other useful concept when discussing these protocols is data-driven versus control-driven actions. Data-driven actions occur in a router during the process of forwarding a multicast datagram. Examples include MOSPF routers building multicast cache entries, DVMRP routers sending Prunes, and PIM routers sending Assert messages. Control-driven actions occur because of the reception of routing protocol or IGMP messages, or external events, such as link failures. Examples of control-driven actions include the sending of Grafts in DVMRP, the broadcast of group information in MOSPF, and the creation of a branch of the shared tree in CBT.

14.2 DVMRP

The original design of the *Distance Vector Multicast Routing Protocol* (DVMRP) was documented in [255]. By the time that DVMRP was first implemented, by the UNIX **mrouted** program, the protocol had changed considerably. The **mrouted** code served as the DVMRP specification for several years, until the code was reverse engineered and an up-to-date DVMRP written specification was produced [202]. Even today, **mrouted** changes more quickly than the DVMRP specification can keep up. Almost all of the MBONE consists of multicast routers running DVMRP.

DVMRP is a broadcast-and-prune protocol that employs Distance Vector technology to advertise multicast sources. DVMRP uses IGMP's encapsulation. All DVMRP packets are encoded as IGMP Type 0x13, with the second byte of the IGMP header indicating the DVMRP packet type. There are separate DVMRP packet types for neighbor discovery (DVMRP Probes), distribution of multicast source information (DVMRP Route Reports), tree maintenance (DVMRP Prunes, Grafts, and Graft Acks), and for monitoring DVMRP routers (DVMRP Ask Neighbors 2 and Neighbors 2).

Each DVMRP router periodically broadcasts to its neighbors a list of sources and the distance from these sources to the router. In this way, a DVMRP router can calculate the previous hop on each multicast source's path, just as RIP calculates the next hop to the destinations it advertises: The previous hop on a source's tree is the DVMRP router that is advertising the shortest distance *from the source*. This calculation has all the convergence problems normally associated with a Distance Vector protocol (see Section 13.1), although DVMRP attempts to improve convergence by employing the techniques of split horizon with poison reverse and hold down.

In order to start the prune process, each router in a broadcast-and-prune protocol needs to know whether it is the leaf of a particular source's broadcast tree. In DVMRP, this is accomplished via reception of Route Reports. For example, in Figure 14.1, router R7 knows that it is not a leaf for source S1, because both routers R8 and R9 indicate that they are downstream by setting the cost of S1 to infinity in Route Reports sent back to R7 (in DVMRP, R8 and R9 are said to be *subordinate* to R7). R7 then knows that it cannot send prunes upstream until prunes have first been received from both R8 and R9.

Route Reports are also used to get rid of equal-cost paths to group members. At the top of Figure 9.3, routers R10 and R11 would both be sending DVMRP Route Reports onto segment 192.7.1/24, advertising source S2 with the same cost. On receiving each other's Route Reports, the two routers would agree that the router having the smaller IP address (assumed to be R10 in this case) is responsible for forwarding multicasts from S2 onto the segment.

14.3 MOSPF

The Multicast Extensions to OSPF (MOSPF) [171] is a source-based multicast routing protocol. MOSPF, described in detail in Chapter 10, allows introduction of a multicast routing capability to an OSPF routing domain. MOSPF has seen considerable deployment in private internets, and limited deployment at the edges of the MBONE. MOSPF routers can interoperate with regular, nonmulticast OSPF routers, and MOSPF capability can be introduced piecemeal into an OSPF routing domain.

MOSPF introduces no new OSPF packet formats but does add a new LSA, the group-membership-LSA, and flags MOSPF-capable routers by setting an appropriate bit in their router-LSAs. Group membership is broadcast throughout the entire MOSPF routing domain by flooding group-membership-LSAs.

Creation of MOSPF multicast routing entries is data driven. The first time a MOSPF router sees a datagram with a given source and destination group, the router performs a Dijkstra SPF calculation rooted at the datagram source. Non-MOSPF routers are avoided by this calculation, and since the location of group members is known in advance, the resulting tree extends only to active group members. In MOSPF, tiebreakers are introduced to the Dijkstra calculation so that all MOSPF routers produce exactly the same tree.

When the state of the network changes—for example, a link goes inoperational, group membership changes, and so on—updated LSAs are flooded, describing the new network state. When a MOSPF router receives one of these updated LSAs, the router deletes all multicast routing table entries that might possibly change, knowing that they will be recreated by the next matching data packet.

Since MOSPF routers have a global view of the routing domain, supplied by the link-state database, the routers can perform a special forwarding optimization. By examining a multicast datagram's TTL, a MOSPF router can tell when a multicast datagram has no chance of reaching the nearest group member. In these cases, rather than waste network bandwidth by forwarding the datagram, a MOSPF router simply discards the datagram instead. This is advantageous when hosts are performing expanding ring searches (Section 10.1.1).

In order to deploy MOSPF in the MBONE, the interactions between MOSPF and DVMRP have been defined (Section 10.6). MOSPF has a hierarchical multicast capability, used between areas and when multicasting datagrams to members outside of the AS. When so doing, MOSPF has incomplete group membership information and so requires certain routers at the area borders/AS boundary to receive all multicast datagrams, regardless of destination. Unfortunately this means that some datagrams get forwarded into areas of the routing domain that have no group members, wasting network bandwidth in the process.

14.4   PIM Dense

Protocol Independent Multicast, Dense Mode (PIM Dense) [60] can be thought of as DVMRP without the routing updates. PIM Dense is a source-based, broadcast-and-prune protocol that uses unicast routing to build reverse-path forwarding trees. The "dense" refers to the PIM designers' belief that PIM Dense mechanisms are more appropriate when group members are densely populated throughout the routing domain. When group members are few and scattered, PIM Sparse (Section 14.5) is thought to be a better protocol.

   Both PIMs run directly over IP, using IP protocol 103. In PIM Dense, there are message types to detect neighboring PIM routers (PIM Hellos) and to perform maintenance of source-based trees (PIM Join/Prunes, Grafts, and Graft Acks).

   PIM Dense must supply mechanisms for two functions that are implemented by DVMRP Route Reports: leaf detection and removal of equal-cost paths. For leaf detection, a PIM router can tell whether any other PIM routers are on a network segment by whether it is receiving PIM Hellos. The PIM router then assumes that all neighbors are downstream for any given source; if a neighbor is not downstream for a given source, it will simply send a PIM Prune message.

   Removal of equal-cost paths is data driven. Again using the example at the top of Figure 9.3, if this network is running PIM Dense, the first datagram sent from S2 to G1 will be multicast twice onto segment 192.7.1/24, once by R10 and once by R11. On receiving these data packets from segment 192.7.1/24, which is different than the correct incoming interface for source S2, R10 and R11 both multicast PIM Assert messages onto 192.7.1/24. Asserts contain metrics; on receiving each other's Assert, the two routers will agree that only the router advertising the smaller metric will continue forwarding multicasts from S2 onto the segment.

   Cisco has implemented both PIMs (Sparse and Dense), together with a gateway function to DVMRP, allowing deployment of PIM in some places at the edge of the MBONE.

14.5   PIM Sparse

Protocol Independent Multicast, Sparse Mode (PIM Sparse) [70] is one of two shared-tree multicast routing protocols developed by the IETF's IDMR Working Group. PIM's unique feature is that the forwarding of multicasts matching a particular source and destination group can be shifted off the group's shared tree onto a source-based tree, presumably when the traffic levels warrant the more efficient paths produced by a source-based scheme (Section 9.3.1). PIM Sparse shares packet formats with PIM Dense, running directly over IP, using IP protocol 103. PIM Sparse contains message types to detect neighboring PIM routers (PIM Hellos), maintain the shared tree (PIM Join/Prunes and Asserts), switch from shared trees to source-based trees (PIM Register and Register-Stop messages), and select Rendezvous Points, or RPs (PIM Bootstrap and Candidate-RP-Advertisement messages).

PIM Sparse elects a Designated Router for each network segment. When one of the network segment's hosts joins a group G1, the Designated Router sends Join messages toward G1's RP to add a new branch to the shared tree. The state of the shared tree is periodically confirmed by resending Joins toward the RP.

Branches of the shared tree are torn down when hosts leave a group. In this case, Prune messages are forwarded toward the RP. Branches are also torn down when unicast routing indicates that the best path toward the RP has changed. A new branch will then be grafted at the next Join refresh.

14.6 CBT

Core Based Trees (CBT) [16] is the other shared-tree multicast routing protocol developed by the IETF's IDMR Working Group. CBT, which has not yet been deployed in the Internet, runs directly over IP, using IP protocol 7. Separate message types are used to elect a Designated Router on LANs (CBT Hellos) and to perform maintenance of the shared tree (CBT JOIN_REQUEST, JOIN_ACK, QUIT_NOTIFICATION, ECHO_REQUEST, ECHO_REPLY, and FLUSH_TREE messages).

When a host joins a multicast group, the host's Designated Router forwards JOIN_REQUESTs to the group's core, adding a branch to the group's shared tree. Construction of the branch is confirmed by forwarding JOIN_ACKs in the reverse direction.

The state of the shared tree is periodically verified by sending ECHO_REQUESTs and ECHO_REPLYs between neighboring CBT routers on the shared tree. If a CBT router's upstream neighbor (the CBT router one hop nearer the core) is determined to be inoperational, the downstream branches of the tree are removed, using the FLUSH_TREE messages, and then these branches are reconstructed from the leaves, using the JOIN_REQUEST mechanism. When the host leaves a group, the host's branch is removed by sending QUIT_NOTIFICATIONs toward the core.

14.7 Interaction among Multicast Routing Protocols

The interaction among multicast routing protocols is not nearly as well developed as that among unicast routing protocols. Multicast routing interactions are more difficult than unicast interactions. Multicast protocols must agree on a single, strict tree for each multicast datagram, and not all multicast protocols even agree on the number of trees that should be constructed—the source-based protocols construct a tree for each source and destination group combination, whereas the shared-tree protocols construct a single tree for each group.

However, progress has been made in connecting specific multicast protocols (Section 10.6), and routers have been developed that attach MOSPF and PIM domains to the MBONE's DVMRP. Proposals have also started coming out of the IDMR Working Group for the way that interactions among various multicast routing protocols should be structured [15], [244], [245].

Bibliography

1. Address Lifetime Expectations (ALE) Working Group.
    `<http://www.ietf.org/proceedings/94dec/ipng/ale.html>`.

2. Alaettinoglu, C., T. Bates, E. Gerich, D. Karrenberg, D. Meyer, M. Terpstra, and
    C. Villamizer. *Routing Policy Specification Language (RPSL)*, April 1997.

3. Almquist, P. *Type of Service in the Internet Protocol Suite*. RFC 1349, July 1992.

4. Armitage, G. *Support for Multicast over UNI 3.0/3.1 based ATM Networks*. RFC 2022,
    November 1996.

5. Armstrong, S., A. Freier, and K. Marzullo. *Multicast Transport Protocol*. RFC 1301,
    February 1992.

6. ASExplorer. `<http://www.merit.edu/ipma/asexplorer>`.

7. ASN Numbers. `<ftp://rs.internic.net/netinfo/asn.txt>`.

8. ATM Forum Technical Committee. *LAN Emulation over ATM, Version 1.0*, January 1995.

9. ATM Forum Technical Committee. *Private Network-Network Interface, Specification Version 1.0 (PNNI 1.0)*, March 1996.

10. Baker, F. *IP Forwarding Table MIB*. RFC 1354, July 1992.

11. Baker, F. *IP Forwarding Table MIB*. RFC 2096, January 1997.

12. Baker, F. *Requirements for IP Version 4 Routers*. RFC 1812, June 1995.

13. Baker, F., and R. Atkinson. *RIP-2 MD5 Authentication*. RFC 2082, January 1997.

14. Baker, F., and R. Coltun. *OSPF Version 2 Management Information Base*. RFC 1850, November 1995.

15. Ballardie, T. *Core Based Trees (CBT version 2) Multicast Border Router Specification for Connecting a CBT Stub Region to a DVMRP Backbone*. Work in progress.

16. Ballardie, T. *Core Based Trees (CBT version 2) Multicast Routing Protocol Specification*. RFC 2189, September 1997.

17. Bates, T., and R. Chandra. *BGP Route Reflection, An Alternative to Full Mesh IBGP*. RFC 1966, June 1996.

18. Bellman, R. *Dynamic Programming*. Princeton University Press, 1957.

19. Berkowitz, H. *Router Renumbering Guide*. RFC 2072, January 1997.

20. Bertsekas, D., and R. Gallagher. *Data Networks, 2nd ed.* Prentice Hall, 1992.

21. Braden, R. *Requirements for Internet Hosts—Application and Support*. RFC 1123, October 1989.

22. Braden, R. *Requirements for Internet Hosts—Communication Layers*. RFC 1122, October 1989.

23. Braden, R., and J. Postel. *Requirements for Internet Gateways*. RFC 1009, June 1987.

24. Braden, R., J. Postel, and Y. Rekhter. *Internet Architecture Extensions for Shared Media*. RFC 1620, May 1994.

25. Bradley, T., and C. Brown. *Inverse Address Resolution Protocol*. RFC 1293, January 1992.

26. Bradner, S., and A. Mankin. *IPng: Internet Protocol Next Generation*. Addison-Wesley, 1996.

27. Brodnik, A., S. Carlsson, M. Degermark, and S. Pink. *Small Forwarding Tables for Fast Routing Lookups*. ACM SIGCOMM '97, September 1997.

28. Cain, B., S. Deering, and A. Thyagarajan. *Internet Group Management Protocol, Version 3*. Work in progress.

29. Callaghan, B., B. Pawlowski, and P. Staubach. *NFS Version 3 Protocol Specification*. RFC 1813, June 1995.

30. Callon, R. *Use of OSI IS-IS for Routing in TCP/IP and Dual Environments*. RFC 1195, December 1990.

31. Carnegie-Mellon University. *CMU SNMP archives*.
    `<ftp://lancaster.andrew.cmu.edu/pub/snmp-dist>`.

32. Case, J., K. McCloghrie, M. Rose, and S. Waldbusser. *Introduction to Version 2 of the Internet-Standard Network Management Framework.* RFC 1441, May 1993.

33. Case, J., K. McCloghrie, M. Rose, and S. Waldbusser. *Protocol Operations for Version 2 of the Simple Network Management Protocol (SNMPv2).* RFC 1905, January 1996.

34. Case, J., K. McCloghrie, M. Rose, and S. Waldbusser. *Structure of Management Information for Version 2 of the Simple Network Management Protocol (SNMPv2).* RFC 1902, January 1996.

35. Case, J., K. McCloghrie, M. Rose, and S. Waldbusser. *Textual Conventions for Version 2 of the Simple Network Management Protocol (SNMPv2).* RFC 1903, January 1996.

36. Casner, S. *Frequently Asked Questions (FAQ) on the Multicast Backbone (MBONE).* `<ftp://ftp.isi.edu/mbone/faq.txt>`, 1993.

37. Casner, S. `mtrace` *UNIX manual page.* mtrace(8).

38. Castineyra, I., J. Chiappa, and M. Steenstrup. *The Nimrod Routing Architecture.* RFC 1992, August 1996.

39. Chandra, R., and P. Traina. *BGP Communities Attribute.* RFC 1997, August 1996.

40. Chen, E., and T. Bates. *Destination Preference Attribute for BGP.* Work in progress.

41. Cheswick, W., and S. Bellovin. *Firewalls and Internet Security: Repelling the Wily Hacker.* Addison-Wesley, 1994.

42. Cisco Systems. *Cisco IOS Software Configuration.* `<http://cio.cisco.com/univercd/data/doc/software.htm>`.

43. Cisco Systems. *Introduction to Enhanced IGRP.* Cisco Technical Report #3.

44. Clark, D. "The Design Philosophy of the DARPA Internet Protocols." Proceedings, ACM SIGCOMM '88. *Computer Communication Review* 18, no. 4, August 1988.

45. Clark, D., and J. Wroclawski. *An Approach to Service Allocation in the Internet.* Work in progress.

46. Coltun, R., D. Ferguson, and J. Moy. *OSPF for IPv6.* Work in progress.

47. Coltun, R., and V. Fuller. *The OSPF NSSA Option.* RFC 1587, March 1994.

48. Comer, D. *Internetworking with TCP/IP, Vol. 1: Principles, Protocols, and Architecture.* Prentice Hall, 1995.

49. Conta, A., and S. Deering. *Internet Control Message Protocol (ICMPv6) for the Internet Protocol Version 6 (IPv6).* RFC 1885, December 1995.

50. Cornell GateDaemon project. `ospf_monitor` *UNIX manual page.* ospf_monitor(8).

51. Cornell GateDaemon project. `ripquery` *UNIX manual page.* ripquery(8).

52. Crawford, M. *A Method for the Transmission of IPv6 Packets over Ethernet Networks.* RFC 1972, August 1996.

53. Croft, W., and J. Gilmore. *Bootstrap Protocol.* RFC 951, September 1985.

54. Dalal, Y., and R. Metcalfe. "Reverse Path Forwarding of Broadcast Packets." *Communications of the ACM* 21, no. 12, December 1978.

55. Dang, W. **imm** *distribution.* **<ftp://ftp.hawaii.edu/paccom/imm>**.

56. Deering, S. *Host Extensions for IP Multicasting.* RFC 1112, May 1988.

57. Deering, S. *ICMP Router Discovery Messages.* RFC 1256, September 1991.

58. Deering, S. *Multicast Routing in a Datagram Internetwork.* Stanford Technical Report STAN-CS-92-1415. Department of Computer Science, Stanford University. **<ftp://gregorio.stanford.edu/vmtp/sd-thesis.ps>**, December 1991.

59. Deering, S. "Multicast Routing in Internetworks and Extended LANs." ACM SIGCOMM Summer 1988 Proceedings, August 1988.

60. Deering, S., D. Estrin, D. Farinacci, V. Jacobson, A. Helmy, D. Meyer, and L. Wei. *Protocol Independent Multicast Version 2 Dense Mode Specification.* Work in progress.

61. Deering, S., and R. Hinden. *Internet Protocol, Version 6 (IPv6) Specification.* RFC 1883, December 1995.

62. Deering, S., A. Thyagarajan, and W. Fenner. **mrouted** *UNIX manual page.* mrouted(8).

63. Delgrossi, L., and L. Berger. *Internet Stream Protocol Version 2 (ST2) Protocol Specification—Version ST2+.* RFC 1819, August 1995.

64. Demers, A., S. Keshav, and S. Shenker. "Analysis and Simulation of a Fair Queueing Algorithm." *Journal of Internetworking: Research and Experience* 1, 1990.

65. deSouza, O., and M. Rodrigues. *Guidelines for Running OSPF over Frame Relay Networks.* RFC 1586, March 1994.

66. Diffie, W., and M. Hellman. "New Directions in Cryptography." *IEEE Transactions on Information Theory.* IT-22, no. 6, November 1976.

67. Droms, R. *Dynamic Host Configuration Protocol.* RFC 1541, October 1993.

68. Enger, R., and J. Reynolds. *FYI on a Network Management Tool Catalog: Tools for Monitoring and Debugging TCP/IP Internets and Interconnected Devices.* RFC 1470, June 1993.

69. Eriksson, H. "MBONE: The Multicast Backbone." *Communications of the ACM* 37, no. 8, August 1994.

70. Estrin, D., D. Farinacci, A. Helmy, D. Thaler, S. Deering, M. Handley, V. Jacobson, C. Liu, P. Sharma, and L. Wei. *Protocol Independent Multicast—Sparse Mode (PIM-SM): Protocol Specification.* RFC 2117, June 1997.

71. Fenner, W. *Internet Group Management Protocol, Version 2.* October 1996.

72. Fenner, W., and S. Casner. *A "traceroute" Facility for IP Multicast.* Work in progress.

73. Ferguson, D. *The OSPF External Attributes LSA.* Work in progress.

74. Ferguson, P., and H. Berkowitz. *Network Renumbering Overview: Why Would I Want It and What Is It Anyway?* RFC 2071, January 1997.

75. Floyd, S. "TCP and Explicit Congestion Notification." ACM SIGCOMM. *Computer Communications Review* 24, no. 5, October 1994.

76. Floyd, S., and V. Jacobson. "Link-Sharing and Resource Management Models for Packet Networks." *IEEE/ACM Transactions on Networking* 3, no. 4, August 1995.

77. Floyd, S., and V. Jacobson. "Random Early Detection Gateways for Congestion Avoidance." *IEEE/ACM Transactions on Networking* 1, no. 4, August 1993.

78. Floyd, S., and V. Jacobson. "The Synchronization of Periodic Routing Messages." ACM SIGCOMM '93 Conference Proceedings, September 1993.

79. Francis, P., and K. Egevang. *The IP Network Address Translator (NAT).* RFC 1631, May 1994.

80. Frederick, R. **nv** *distribution.* **<ftp://parcftp.xerox.com/pub/net-research/nv-3.3beta>**.

81. Fuller, V., T. Li, J. Yu, and K. Varadhan. *Classless Inter-Domain Routing (CIDR): An Address Assignment and Aggregation Strategy.* RFC 1519, September 1993.

82. Garcia-Luna-Aceves, J. "Loop-Free Routing Using Diffusing Computations." *IEEE/ACM Transactions on Networking* 1, no. 1, February 1993.

83. GATED project Web pages. **<http://www.gated.org>**.

84. Green, P., R. Chappuis, J. Fisher, P. Frosch, and C. Wood. "A Perspective on Advanced Peer to Peer Networking." *IBM Systems Journal* 26, no. 4, 1987.

85. Gross, P. *Choosing a Common IGP for the IP Internet (The IESG's Recommendation to the IAB).* RFC 1371, October 1992.

86. Guerin, R., S. Kamat, A. Orda, T. Przygienda, and D. Williams. *QoS Routing Mechanisms and OSPF Extensions.* Work in progress.

87. Hafner, K., and J. Markoff. *Cyberpunk: Outlaws and Hackers on the Computer Frontier.* Simon and Schuster, 1991.

88. Hagouel. "Issues in Routing for Large and Dynamic Networks." Ph.D. thesis. Columbia University, 1983.

89. Halabi, B. *Internet Routing Architectures.* Cisco Press. New Riders Publishing, 1997.

90. Haller, N. "The S/KEY One-Time Password System." Proceedings of the ISOC Symposium on Network and Distributed System Security. San Diego, February 1994.

91. Handley, M., and V. Jacobson. *SDP: Session Description Protocol.* Work in progress.

92. Harrenstien, K., M. Stahl, and E. Feinler. *NICNAME/WHOIS.* RFC 954, October 1985.

93. Harris, S., and E. Gerich. "Retiring the NSFNET Backbone Service: Chronicling the End of an Era." *ConneXions* 10, no. 4, April 1996.

94. Haskin, D. *A BGP/IDRP Route Server Alternative to a Full Mesh Routing.* RFC 1863, October 1995.

95. Hedrick, C. *Routing Information Protocol.* RFC 1058, June 1988.

96. Hedrick, C., and L. Bosack. *An Introduction to IGRP.* Rutgers University, July 1989.

97. Heisenberg, W. *Physics and Beyond, Encounters and Conversations.* Harper and Row, 1971.

98. Hinden, R. *Internet Routing Protocol Standardization Criteria.* RFC 1264, October 1991.

99. Hinden, R., and S. Deering. *IP Version 6 Addressing Architecture.* RFC 1884, December 1995.

100. Hinden, R., S. Knight, D. Whipple, and D. Weaver. *Virtual Router Redundancy Protocol.* Work in progress.

101. Hinden, R., and A. Sheltzer. *The DARPA Internet Gateway.* RFC 823, September 1982.

102. Hubbard, K., M. Kosters, D. Conrad, D. Karrenberg, and J. Postel. *Internet Registry Allocation Guidelines.* RFC 2050, November 1996.

103. Huitema, C. *IPv6: The New Internet Protocol.* Prentice Hall, 1997.

104. Huitema, C. *Routing in the Internet.* Prentice Hall, 1996.

105. Iannucci, D., and J. Lekashman. *The Research Internet Gateways.* NAS Technical Report RND-94-008. `<http://science.nas.nasa.gov/Pubs/TechReports/RNDreports/RND-94-008/94-008.html>`, August 1994.

106. IEEE. *IEEE Standard for Information Technology—Protocols for Distributed Interactive Simulation Applications.* IEEE Std. 1278-1993.

107. IEEE. *IEEE Standard for Local and Metropolitan Area Networks: Media Access Control (MAC) Bridges.* IEEE Std. 802.1D-1990.

108. IETF Secretariat and G. Malkin. *The Tao of the IETF—A Guide for New Attendees of the IETF.* RFC 1718, November 1994.

109. Internet Architecture Board. *Applicability Statement for OSPF.* RFC 1370, October 1992.

110. Internet Architecture Board, J. Postel, ed. *Internet Official Protocol Standards.* RFC 2200, June 1997.

111. Internet Architecture Board, R. Braden, D. Clark, S. Crocker, and C. Huitema. *Report on IAB Workshop on Security in the Internet Architecture—February 8–10, 1994.* RFC 1636, June 1994.

112. ISO. *10589: Information Processing Systems—Data Communications—Intermediate System to Intermediate System Intra-Domain Routing Protocol.* 1992.

113. ISO. *Information Processing Systems—Open Systems Interconnection—Specification of Abstract Syntax Notation One (ASN.1).* International Standard 8824, December 1987.

114. ISO. *Information Processing Systems—Open Systems Interconnection—Specification of Basic Encoding Rules for Abstract Notation One (ASN.1).* International Standard 8825, December 1987.

115. Jacobson, V. "Congestion Avoidance and Control." *Computer Communication Review* 18, no. 4, August 1988.

116. Jacobson, V. **mrinfo** *UNIX manual page.* mrinfo(8).

117. Jacobson, V. "Pathchar—A Tool to Infer Characteristics of Internet Paths." MSRI talk. **<ftp://ftp.ee.lbl.gov/pathchar/msri-talk.ps.gz>**, April 1997.

118. Jacobson, V. **pathchar** *distribution.* **<ftp://ftp.ee.lbl.gov/pathchar>**.

119. Jaffe, J., and F. Moss. "A Responsive Distributed Routing Algorithm for Computer Networks." *IEEE Transaction on Communications* COM-30, no. 7, July 1982.

120. Johnson, M. "Analysis of Routing Table Update Activity After Resource Failure in a Distributed Computer Network." ACM SIGCOMM '83 Symposium, March 1983.

121. Kaliski, B., and M. Robshaw. "Message Authentication with MD5." *CryptoBytes* (RSA Labs Technical Newsletter) 1, no. 1. **<http://www.rsa.com/PUBS/crypto1.pdf>**, Spring 1995.

122. Katz, D. *Transmission of IP and ARP over FDDI Networks.* RFC 1390, January 1993.

123. Katz, D., D. Piscitello, B. Cole, and J. Luciani. *NBMA Next Hop Resolution Protocol (NHRP).* Work in progress.

124. Katz, D., Y. Rekhter, T. Bates, and R. Chandra. *Multi-Protocol Extensions for BGP-4.* Work in progress.

125. Kent, C., and J. Mogul. "Fragmentation Considered Harmful." Proceedings, *ACM SIGCOMM '87* 17, no. 5, October 1987.

126. Kessler, G., and S. Shepard. *A Primer on Internet and TCP/IP Tools and Utilities.* RFC 2151, June 1997.

127. Khanna, A., and J. Zinky. "The Revised ARPANET Routing Metric." Proceedings, *ACM SIGCOMM 1989*, Austin. September 1989.

128. Kleinrock, L., and F. Kamoun. "Hierarchical Routing for Large Networks: Performance Evaluation and Optimization." *Computer Networks* 1. 1977.

129. Knuth, D. *The Art of Computer Programming, Vol. 3. Sorting and Searching.* Addison-Wesley, 1973.

130. Krawczyk, H., M. Bellare, and R. Canetti. *HMAC: Keyed-Hashing for Message Authentication.* RFC 2104, February 1997.

131. Kumar, V. *MBONE: Multicast Multimedia for the Internet.* New Riders Publishing, 1997.

132. Labovitz, C., G. Malan, and F. Jahanian. *Internet Routing Instability.* CSE-TR-332-97, University of Michigan and Merit Network.

133. Laubach, M. *Classical IP and ARP over ATM.* RFC 1577, January 1994.

134. Lawrence, J., and D. Piscitello. *The Transmission of IP Datagrams over the SMDS Service.* RFC 1209, March 1991.

135. Leiner, B., V. Cerf, D. Clark, R. Kahn, L. Kleinrock, D. Lynch, J. Postel, L. Roberts, and S. Wolff. *A Brief History of the Internet.* **<http://www.isoc.org/internet-history/>**, 1997.

136. Li, T., B. Cole, P. Morton, and D. Li. *Hot Standby Router Protocol (HSRP).* Work in progress.

137. Lougheed, K., and Y. Rekhter. *Border Gateway Protocol (BGP).* RFC 1105, June 1989.

138. McCanne, S., and V. Jacobson. **sd** *distribution.* **<ftp://ftp.ee.lbl.gov/conferencing/sd>**.

139. McCanne, S., and V. Jacobson. **vat** *distribution.* **<ftp://ftp.ee.lbl.gov/conferencing/vat>**.

140. McCanne, S., and V. Jacobson. **wb** *distribution.* **<ftp://ftp.ee.lbl.gov/conferencing/wb>**.

141. McCloghrie, K., D. Farinacci, and D. Thaler. *Internet Group Management Protocol MIB.* Work in progress.

142. McCloghrie, K., D. Farinacci, and D. Thaler. *IP Multicast Routing MIB.* Work in progress.

143. McCloghrie, K., and M. Rose. *Management Information Base for Network Management of TCP/IP-Based Internets: MIB-II.* RFC 1213, March 1991.

144. McCloghrie, K., and M. Rose. *Structure and Identification of Management Information for TCP/IP-Based Internets.* RFC 1155, May 1990.

145. McKenzie, A. *ISO Transport Protocol Specification. ISO DP 8073.* RFC 905, April 1984.

146. McQuillan, J., I. Richer, and E. Rosen. *ARPANET Routing Algorithm Improvements.* BBN Report 3803. Bolt Beranek and Newman, April 1978.

147. McQuillan, J., I. Richer, and E. Rosen. "The New Routing Algorithm for the ARPANET." *IEEE Transactions on Communications* COM-28, no. 5, May 1980.

148. MAE East. **<http://www.mfsdatanet.com/MAE/east.html>**.

149. Malkin, G. *RIP Version 2 Carrying Additional Information.* RFC 1723, November 1994.

150. Malkin, G., and F. Baker. *RIP Version 2 MIB Extension.* RFC 1724, November 1994.

151. Malkin, G., and R. Minnear. *RIPng for IPv6.* RFC 2080, January 1997.

152. Mallory, T. "SPF Routing in the Butterfly Gateway." Slides given to X3.S3 Standards Committee, April 1987.

153. Manning, B. *Registering New BGP Attribute Types.* RFC 2042, January 1997.

154. Maufer, T., and C. Semeria. *Introduction to IP Multicast Routing.* Work in progress.

155. Maughan, D., M. Schertler, M. Schneider, and J. Turner. *Internet Security Association and Key Management Protocol (ISAKMP).* Work in progress.

156. Medin, M. "The Great IGP Debate—Part Two: The Open Shortest Path First (OSPF) Routing Protocol." *ConneXions* 5, no. 10, October 1991.

157. Merlin, P., and A. Segall. "A Failsafe Distributed Routing Protocol." *IEEE Transactions on Communications* COM-27, no. 9, September 1979.

158. Meyer, D. *Administratively Scoped IP Multicast.* Work in progress.

159. Meyer, G. *Extensions to RIP to Support Demand Circuits.* RFC 1582, February 1994.

160. Meyer, G., and S. Sherry. *Triggered Extensions to RIP to Support Demand Circuits.* RFC 2091, January 1997.

161. Mills, D. *DCM Local-Network Protocols.* RFC 891, December 1983.

162. Mills, D. *Exterior Gateway Protocol Formal Specification.* RFC 904, April 1984.

163. Mockapetris, P. *Domain Names—Implementation and Specification.* RFC 1035, November 1987.

164. Mogul, J. *Broadcasting Internet Datagrams in the Presence of Subnets.* RFC 922, October 1984.

165. Mogul, J., and S. Deering. *Path MTU Discovery.* RFC 1191, April 1990.

166. Mogul, J., and J. Postel. *Internet Standard Subnetting Procedure.* RFC 950, August 1985.

167. Morris, R. *Bulk Multicast Transport Protocol.* INFOCOM 97.

168. Moy, J. *Experience with OSPF.* RFC 1246, July 1991.

169. Moy, J. *Extending OSPF to Support Demand Circuits.* RFC 1793, April 1995.

170. Moy, J. *MOSPF: Analysis and Experience.* RFC 1585, March 1994.

171. Moy, J. *Multicast Extensions to OSPF.* RFC 1584, March 1994.

172. Moy, J. *OSPF Database Overflow.* RFC 1765, March 1995.

173. Moy, J. *OSPF Protocol Analysis.* RFC 1245, July 1991.

174. Moy, J. *OSPF Specification.* RFC 1131 (obsoleted by RFC 1247), October 1989.

175. Moy, J. *OSPF Standardization Report.* Work in progress.

176. Moy, J. *OSPF Version 2.* RFC 1247 (obsoleted by RFC 1583), August 1991.

177. Moy, J. *OSPF Version 2.* RFC 1583 (obsoleted by RFC 2178), March 1994.

178. Moy, J. *OSPF Version 2.* RFC 2178, July 1997.

179. Murphy, S., M. Badger, and B. Wellington. *OSPF with Digital Signatures.* RFC 2154, June 1997.

180. Nagle, J. *Congestion Control in IP/TCP Internetworks.* RFC 896, January 1984.

181. Narten, T., E. Nordmark, and W. Simpson. *Neighbor Discovery for IP Version 6 (IPv6).* RFC 1970, August 1996.

182. National Institute of Standards and Technology. *Secure Hash Standard.* NIST FIPS PUB 180. U.S. Department of Commerce, January 1992.

183. North American Network Operators Group (NANOG). **<http://www.nanog.org>**.

184. Novell. *NetWare Link Services Protocol (NLSP) Specification.* 1993.

185. Oehler, M., and R. Glenn. *HMAC-MD5 IP Authentication with Replay Prevention.* RFC 2085, February 1997.

186. Oran, D. *OSI IS-IS Intra-domain Routing Protocol.* RFC 1142, December 1991.

187. Ousterhout, J. *Tcl and the Tk Toolkit.* Addison-Wesley, 1994.

188. Perkins, C. *IP Encapsulation within IP.* RFC 2003, October 1996.

189. Perlman, R. "Fault Tolerant Broadcast of Routing Information." *Computer Networks*, December 1983.

190. Perlman, R. "Network Layer Protocols with Byzantine Robustness." Ph.D. thesis. Department of Electrical Engineering and Computer Science, MIT. August 1988.

191. Perlman, R., and R. Callon. "The Great IGP Debate—Part One: IS-IS and Integrated Routing." *ConneXions* 5, no. 10, October 1991.

192. Plummer, D. *Ethernet Address Resolution Protocol: Or Converting Network Protocol Addresses to 48-bit Ethernet Addresses for Transmission on Ethernet Hardware.* RFC 826, November 1982.

193. Postel, J. *Instructions to RFC Authors.* RFC 1543, October 1993.

194. Postel, J. *Internet Control Message Protocol.* RFC 792, September 1981.

195. Postel, J. *Internet Protocol.* RFC 791, September 1981.

196. Postel, J. *Simple Mail Transfer Protocol.* RFC 821, August 1982.

197. Postel, J. *Transmission Control Protocol.* RFC 793, September 1981.

198. Postel, J. *User Datagram Protocol.* RFC 768, August 1980.

199. Postel, J., and J. Reynolds. *File Transfer Protocol.* RFC 959, October 1985.

200. Postel, J., and J. Reynolds. *Telnet Protocol Specification.* RFC 854, May 1983.

201. Pummill, T., and B. Manning. *Variable Length Subnet Table for IPv4.* RFC 1878, December 1995.

202. Pusateri, T. *Distance Vector Multicast Routing Protocol.* Work in progress.

203. Pusateri, T. *IP Multicast over Token-Ring Local Area Networks.* RFC 1469, June 1993.

204. Pusateri, T. **ospfquery** *UNIX manual page.*
     <http://www.jnx.com/~pusateri/ospfquery.html>.

205. RAToolSet. **<http://www.isi.edu/ra/RAToolSet>**.

206. Rekhter, Y. *EGP and Policy Based Routing in the New NSFNET Backbone.* RFC 1092, February 1989.

207. Rekhter, Y. *NSFNET Backbone SPF Based Interior Gateway Protocol.* RFC 1074, October 1988.

208. Rekhter, Y., and T. Li. *A Border Gateway Protocol (BGP-4).* RFC 1771, March 1995.

209. Rekhter, Y., and T. Li. *Implications of Various Address Allocation Policies for Internet Routing.* RFC 2008, October 1996.

210. Rekhter, Y., R. Moskowitz, D. Karrenberg, G. de Groot, and E. Lear. *Address Allocation for Private Internets.* RFC 1918, February 1996.

211. Reynolds, J. *Helminthiasis of the Internet.* RFC 1135, December 1989.

212. Reynolds, J., and J. Postel. *Assigned Numbers.* RFC 1700, October 1994.

213. RFC Index. `<ftp://ds.internic.net/rfc/rfc-index.txt>`.

214. Rigney, C., A. Rubens, W. Simpson, and S. Willens. *Remote Authentication Dial-In User Service (RADIUS).* RFC 2138, April 1997.

215. RIPE database. `<http://www.ripe.net>`.

216. Rivest, R. *The MD5 Message-Digest Algorithm.* RFC 1321, April 1992.

217. Rose, M., ed. *A Convention for Defining Traps for Use with the SNMP.* RFC 1215, March 1991.

218. Rose, M. *The Simple Book, An Introduction to Management of TCP/IP-Based Internets.* Prentice Hall, 1991.

219. Rosen, E. *Exterior Gateway Protocol EGP.* RFC 827, October 1982.

220. Rosen, E. "The Updating Protocol of ARPANET's New Routing Algorithm." *Computer Networks* 4, 1980.

221. Rosen, E. "Vulnerabilities of Network Control Protocols: An Example." *Computer Communication Review*, July 1981.

222. `routed` *UNIX manual page.* routed(8).

223. Routing Arbiter Web pages. `<http://www.ra.net>`.

224. RSA Data Security. *PKCS #1: RSA Encryption Standard, Version 1.4.* 3 June 1991.

225. Schneier, B. *Applied Cryptography.* Wiley, 1994.

226. Schoffstall, M., M. Fedor, J. Davin, and J. Case. *A Simple Network Management Protocol (SNMP).* RFC 1157, May 1990.

227. Schooler, E. `mmcc` *distribution.* `<ftp://ftp.isi.edu/confctrl/mmcc>`.

228. Schulzrinne, H. `nevot` *distribution.* `<ftp://gaia.cs.umass.edu/pub/hschulz/nevot>`.

229. Schulzrinne, H., S. Casner, R. Frederick, and V. Jacobson. *RTP: A Transport Protocol for Real-Time Applications.* RFC 1889, January 1996.

230. Sedgewick, R. *Algorithms.* Addison-Wesley, 1984.

231. Seeger, J., and A. Khanna. "Reducing Routing Overhead in a Growing DDN." MILCOMM 86, 1986.

232. Simpson, W. *The Point-to-Point Protocol (PPP)*. RFC 1548, December 1993.

233. Sollins, K. *The TFTP Protocol (Revision 2)*. RFC 1350, July 1992.

234. Srinivasan, R. *RPC: Remote Procedure Call Protocol Specification Version 2*. RFC 1831, August 1995.

235. Srinivasan, R. *XDR: External Data Representation Standard*. RFC 1832, August 1995.

236. Steenstrup, M. *Inter-Domain Policy Routing Protocol Specification: Version 1*. RFC 1479, July 1993.

237. Steenstrup, M. *Routing in Communications Networks*. Prentice Hall, 1995.

238. Steiner. J., B. Neuman, and J. Schiller. *Kerberos: An Authentication Service for Open Network Systems*. Usenix Conference Proceedings, February 1988.

239. Stevens, W. *TCP Slow Start, Congestion Avoidance, Fast Retransmit and Fast Recovery Algorithms*. RFC 2001, January 1997.

240. Stevens, W. *TCP/IP Illustrated, Volume 1: The Protocols*. Addison-Wesley, 1994.

241. Tajibnapis, W. "A Correctness Proof of a Topology Maintenance Protocol for a Distributed Computer Network." *Communications of the ACM* 20, no. 7, July 1977.

242. Tanenbaum, A. *Computer Networks*. 3d edition. Prentice Hall, 1996.

243. Thaler, D. *Distance Vector Multicast Routing Protocol MIB*. Work in progress.

244. Thaler, D. *Interoperability Rules for Multicast Routing Protocols*. Work in progress.

245. Thaler, D., D. Estrin, and D. Meyer. *Grand Unified Multicast (GUM): Protocol Specification*. Work in progress.

246. Thurletti, T. `ivs` *distribution*. `<ftp://zenon.inria.fr/rodeo/ivs/version3.6>`.

247. `traceroute` UNIX manual page. `<http://ack.berkeley.edu/cgi-bin/traceroute.8>`.

248. Traina, P. *Autonomous System Confederations for BGP*. RFC 1965, June 1996.

249. Trusted Information Systems. *OSPF with Digital Signatures, Implementation Information*. `<http://www.tis.com/docs/research/network/ospf.html>`.

250. Tsuchiya, P. *On the Assignment of Subnet Numbers*. RFC 1219, April 1991.

251. UNH InterOperability Lab. `<http://www.iol.unh.edu>`.

252. Varadhan, K., S. Hares, and Y. Rekhter. *BGP4/IDRP for IP-OSPF Interaction*. RFC 1745, December 1991.

253. Vetter, B., F. Wang, and F. Wu. "An Experimental Study of Insider Attacks for the OSPF Routing Protocol."

`<http://shang.csc.ncsu.edu/papers/Wu-AESoIAftORP.ps.gz>`.
Submitted for publication, May 1997.

254. Villamizar, C. *Controlling BGP/IDRP Routing Traffic Overhead.* Work in progress.

255. Waitzman, D., C. Partridge, and S. Deering. *Distance Vector Multicast Routing Protocol.* RFC 1075, November 1988.

256. Waldbusser, S. *Remote Network Monitoring Management Information Base.* RFC 1757, February 1995.

257. Waldvogel, M., G. Varghese, J. Turner, and B. Plattner. *"Scalable High Speed IP Routing Lookups."* ACM SIGCOMM '97, September 1997.

258. Wall, D. *Mechanisms for Broadcast and Selective Broadcast.* Ph.D. thesis. Stanford University, June 1980.

259. Wall, D., and S. Owicki. "Center-Based Broadcasting." *Computer Systems Lab Technical Report TR189.* Stanford University, June 1980.

260. Wall, L., R. Schwartz, T. Christiansen, and S. Potter. *Programming Perl,* 2d edition. O'Reilly and Associates, October 1996.

261. Wang, F., B. Vetter, and F. Wu. "Secure Routing Protocols: Theory and Practice."
`<http://shang.csc.ncsu.edu/papers/CCR-SecureRP2.ps.gz>`.
Submitted for publication, May 1997.

262. Willis, S., J. Burruss, and J. Chu. *Definitions of Managed Objects for the Fourth Version of the Border Gateway Protocol (BGP-4) Using SMIv2.* RFC 1657, July 1994.

263. Wimer, W. *Clarifications and Extensions for the Bootstrap Protocol.* RFC 1542, October 1993.

264. Wright, G., and W. Stevens. *TCP/IP Illustrated, Volume 2: The Implementation.* Addison-Wesley, 1995.

265. Xerox Corporation. *Internet Transport Protocols, Xerox System Integration Standard XSIS 028112.* December 1981.

266. Zhang, L., S. Deering, D. Estrin, S. Shenker, and D. Zappala. "RSVP: A New Resource ReSerVation Protocol." *IEEE Network,* September 1993.

267. Zhang, Z. *Fixing Backbone Partition with Dynamic Virtual Links.* Work in progress.

Index